School of American Research
Advanced Seminar Series

DOUGLAS W. SCHWARTZ, GENERAL EDITOR

SCHOOL OF AMERICAN RESEARCH
ADVANCED SEMINAR SERIES

Chan Chan: Andean Desert City

ATLANTIC RICHFIELD CORPORATION
is gratefully acknowledged for its
support of the
School of American Research
Advanced Seminars.

CHAN CHAN: ANDEAN DESERT CITY

EDITED BY
MICHAEL E. MOSELEY
AND KENT C. DAY

A SCHOOL OF AMERICAN RESEARCH BOOK
UNIVERSITY OF NEW MEXICO PRESS • Albuquerque

Library of Congress Cataloging in Publication Data

Main entry under title:

Chan Chan, Andean desert city.

    (School of American Research advanced seminar
series)
      Bibliography: p.
      Includes index.
      1. Chan Chan (Peru)—Addresses, essays, lectures.
I. Moseley, Michael Edward.   I. Day, Kent C.,
1932–   II. Series.
F3429.1.C46C47   985′.16   80-54567
ISBN 0-8263-0575-X   AACR2

Acknowledgments

We wish to acknowledge the generosity and hospitality of Douglas W. Schwartz and his staff at the School of American Research for the opportunity to exchange information, ideas, and reminiscences in exceptionally pleasant surroundings. We owe special thanks to the late Wanda Driskell for her editorial assistance and advice during the preparation of this book. Our appreciation is also due David Noble and Phillip Brittenham for following this work through to completion.

Major financial support for the Chan Chan–Moche Valley Project consisted of grants from the National Geographic Society, the National Science Foundation, and Harvard University. Funds for additional research were provided by the Committee on Latin American Studies, Harvard University, the University of Texas Institute of Latin American Studies Archaeological Fund, the Canada Council, Columbia University Institute of Latin American Studies, the Institutional Scientific Research Pool of the Department of Anthropology, Columbia University, the Royal Ontario Museum, and the L. S. B. Leakey Foundation.

Permission to survey and excavate in Peru was authorized by the Instituto Nacional de Cultura del Perú in Lima and its local affiliates in Trujillo, Chiclayo, and Guadalupe (Provincia de Pacasmayo). When work began at Chan Chan we received valuable aid and advice from Guillermo Ganoza Vargas and Francisco Iriarte Brenner of the Comité Pro Restauración de Chan Chan.

Kent C. Day

Foreword

Chan Chan is one of the most extraordinary archaeological sites in the Western Hemisphere, rich in architectural and artistic splendor. Once possessing a social and political system of great complexity and a highly efficient economic organization, this great urban administrative center was the source of ideas that were crucial in shaping the succeeding Inca empire. Chan Chan's location on the sandy periphery of the Moche Valley on Peru's North Coast is a part of the Andean world with a long history of distinctive cultures and their superlative achievements.

The ruins of Chan Chan cover six square kilometers and are dominated by ten huge compounds, each of which was surrounded by thirty-foot-high adobe walls that protected and isolated the people within. Access to each compound was gained only through a single, well-guarded entrance that led by way of a narrow passage to a gigantic audience chamber, a series of courts, a reservoir, and a vast array of storerooms. In addition, each complex was the royal living quarters and contained a royal burial chamber, since these compounds were the administrative centers and final resting places for the priest-kings of the Chimú empire prior to its conquest by the Incas about A.D. 1465.

The Chimú empire was the culmination of 4,000 years of cultural development on the bountiful North Coast of Peru, where the sea provided the largest marine biomass in the Western Hemisphere as a strong underpinning for sedentary life. By 2000 B.C., communities of coastal fishermen had already grown large enough and could produce

enough surplus to allow the mobilization of workers from widely separated villages who constructed the region's first monumental architecture. This ability to mobilize large work forces became the foundation
of Andean civilization.

Around 1800 B.C., many of the shoreline communities were abandoned, and the population and administrative centers moved inland to
the Moche River Valley. There, a radical shift to agriculture supported an expanding population. A massive labor investment was also
begun on a sophisticated engineering venture that eventually produced
one of the most intensive irrigation systems in the New World, carrying water throughout the valley and into the adjacent desert.

The first indication that political power was becoming centralized
on the North Coast is found at the site of Caballo Muerto. About
1500 B.C., this town became the headquarters of a politically stable,
hereditary chiefdom that lasted nearly a thousand years. By the year
A.D. 1, the Moche Valley had experienced almost two millennia of
sedentary occupation, cultural stability, experience with impressive
construction projects, and a productive agricultural economy, all directed by a ranked political organization.

Out of this background emerged one of the major precursors of the
Chimú empire, the Moche culture, its political power symbolized by
the largest adobe pyramids in the New World. One pyramid, Huaca
del Sol, was built from more than 140 million adobe bricks by work
parties enlisted from throughout the region. Moche culture was a
complex organization of administrative, religious, craft, and agricultural specialists who were part of a centralized, militaristic, expansionist state that unified portions of the North Coast beyond the Moche
Valley. The central authority in this political system, as shown icon-
ographically, was one preeminent person who remained segregated
from the rest of society and who was seen by the public only on
formal occasions.

Just before the emergence of the Chimú empire at about A.D. 700,
there apparently developed at the site of Galindo in the Moche Valley
a social system with a new secular class headed by a paramount ruler
who was supported by traditional religious beliefs. The secular elite
controlled the wealth of the empire and lived in an exclusive residential area, while the lower classes lived on crowded hillsides separated
from the centers of public activity by a high adobe wall.

When the legendary founder of the Chimú empire sailed south on his balsa raft to a place near the present-day town of Trujillo in the Moche Valley, he initiated a kingdom of divine despots that incorporated all the main elements of the previous North Coast cultures. But perhaps the key to understanding the new cultural configuration is the system of inheritance in the royal line, which dictated that on the death of a king, his compound and any territory he had captured were to be retained in his name and administered in perpetuity by a separate bureaucracy. The new ruler had to build his own compound and conquer new territory, which was then taxed, organized, and administered in the name of the new king by a powerful elite that exercised absolute control over land, water, storage, and redistribution of goods. With each new king, the number of compounds increased, and each living king shared Chan Chan with the remains and bureaucracy of his predecessors. Out of this political and economic structure grew an empire that ultimately controlled nearly a thousand miles of the Andean coast and became one of the richest political entities in the Western Hemisphere.

The participants of the Chan Chan–Moche Valley research project gathered at the School of American Research in 1976 for a detailed examination and synthesis of their work on Chan Chan, its ecological foundations, its four thousand years of cultural antecedents, and its legacy to the Incas. The results, previewed in broad outline here, illuminate one of the outstanding cultures in New World prehistory, that of the Andean North Coast. Clearly, the work of this seminar group is a distinguished example of high-quality regional archaeology pursued in a productive, creative fashion.

Douglas W. Schwartz

School of American Research

Preface

This book is the result of an Advanced Seminar in archaeology held at the School of American Research in April 1976. The seminar participants had all been members of the Chan Chan–Moche Project of 1969–74. In the field, the archaeologists had gathered and analyzed data from a particular perspective; for instance, G. Conrad studied burial platforms in Chan Chan proper while R. Keatinge concentrated on the outlying areas. The School of American Research offered the expedition members the opportunity to develop a broader perspective and to work on a model of social process at Chan Chan and in the Moche Valley. The chapters in this book present the model developed at the Advanced Seminar along with different aspects of the research that give credence to the model. While the subject matter in the chapters may appear diverse at first, it is unified by a common goal: analysis of the architecture and patterns of environmental exploitation for the purpose of reconstructing the development of social, economic, and political organization on the North Coast of Peru.

THE SITE

Chan Chan is located at lat. 7°5' S, long. 78° W on the desert coastal plain about 550 kilometers north of Lima, Peru. The ruins of the site stand on a low rise northwest of the flood plain of the Moche Valley.

Much of Chan Chan blends into the desert plain on which the site stands. The massive adobe walls of the enclosures and the ruined heaps of huacas stand out clearly. Yet everything at Chan Chan is the same pale ochre color of handpacked, barren earth. A few breaks in the monotonous color and texture are provided by shrubbery growing in the relatively damp recesses of ancient wells. No one lives at Chan Chan, but the site is covered with a network of footpaths, frequently along the undulating tops of collapsed adobe walls. The quiet desolation of Chan Chan is enhanced by nearly constant onshore winds from the Pacific Ocean. Despite the winds, the sky remains overcast along the coast most of the year, and the diffused, weak daylight makes it difficult to distinguish the earth from the sky at the horizon. In contrast, on those rare occasions when the sky clears during the summer months, reflected light is blinding, shadows are deep, and heat is intense among the ruins.

Natural and human forces are responsible for the desolate signature of Chan Chan on the landscape. Presently earthquakes do little damage to the site, but it is likely that many of the thinner, tall adobe walls at Chan Chan collapsed during earthquakes soon after the site was abandoned. The greatest natural damage at the site, however, is due to moisture, either from infrequent torrential rains or the very damp air characteristic of the coast. Of course, the rains melted the earthworks at the site in dramatic fashion, but high humidity has been more constant and insidious. The dampness, for instance, causes the surface of exposed walls to flake away gradually or is absorbed by salts in many of the adobes, and the adobes crumble to dust. In addition, dampness and sunlight effectively destroy any organic materials left exposed.

The only insects that did much damage at Chan Chan were the termites that consumed some of the wood and canes used as posts or roof beams in structures. Other animals at the site take advantage of holes for burrows or wall tops for roosts but do little damage.

Human activities at Chan Chan changed the site more than the natural forces. As soon as the great enclosures were abandoned about A.D. 1470, Chimú squatters (Day 1973) moved in and built flimsy houses in courtyards. These last residents ripped wooden posts out of walls and chopped down wooden colonnades, presumably for firewood. They also cut holes through large walls to admit irrigation water to fields planted in open level areas (T. Topic 1971). These squatters' fields are the oft-referred-to "gardens" in Chan Chan.

Precolumbian damage to Chan Chan was relatively minor compared to what happened at the site during the Spanish Colonial Period (A.D. 1532–1821). Soon after the Moche Valley was settled by the Spaniards in about 1535, they began mining locally for silver and gold.

In a letter written to Charles V on March 19, 1541, Hernando Pizarro states that "at the edge of the town called Trujillo four or five silver mines were discovered" (Porras Barrenechea 1959:216). Since there are no significant natural deposits of precious metals in the Moche Valley, it is revealing that another sixteenth-century report states that near Trujillo "there are no mines but [there are] huacas that are interments of Indians from which quantities of gold and silver were removed" (Jiménez de la Espada 1965, 183:125). Mining for gold and silver at archaeological sites in the Moche Valley continued for 200 years (Holstein 1927), and Chan Chan undoubtedly was one of the targets. Apparently the burial platforms and forecourts were systematically looted at that time, perhaps along with the sacking of graves in ramps and other structures at Chan Chan. These activities left the burial platforms, in particular, with open pits and tunnels that over subsequent years eroded and collapsed. Soon after treasure hunting ended—as rich tombs were exhausted—another surge of looting began at Chan Chan under the inspiration of antiquities collectors. Destruction of the large cemetery south of Chan Chan probably began in the nineteenth century and continues today to satisfy the demand for ceramic vessels.

Presently agricultural activities are rapidly encroaching upon Chan Chan as irrigation canals are built to bring water to fields near the site. Settlers are moving into the ruins in response to local population increase and lack of available housing in nearby towns. Part of Chan Chan is an illegal garbage dump, and a paved highway cuts across the northern part of the site's center. One great wall at Chan Chan is a memorial marked by annual floral offerings to a group of political protestors who were executed against it in 1932.

Chan Chan will continue to suffer damage and will probably disappear in large part as industrial development and population growth put greater demands on the limited land available in the Moche Valley. We consider ourselves lucky to have worked at Chan Chan during the last phase of its existence.

THE CHAN CHAN–MOCHE VALLEY PROJECT, 1969–1974

Research conducted by members of the Chan Chan–Moche Valley project changed in emphasis over the five-year life of the project. Due to the lack of reliable information on the architectural composition of Chan Chan, the initial goal of the project was to map the site through aerial photography and ground survey (Moseley and Mackey 1974). In addition to mapping, excavation was conducted at Chan Chan and in the lower Moche Valley to provide a basic understanding of the history and functioning of a major Andean city in the context of its rural sustaining communities (Moseley 1969b).

As the work at Chan Chan proceeded, architectural patterns came to be recognized and formed the basis for a broad classification of the ruins. The large rectangular enclosures called ciudadelas were an obvious architectural category, as was the tract of small irregularly agglutinated rooms (SIAR) along the west side of the site. Various enclosures less elaborate than the ciudadelas but more formal in layout than the SIAR were classified as elite compounds. Once these major architectural complexes were located, they were reduced to component architectural groups for detailed mapping and/or excavation. In addition, entrances and access patterns between and among structures or, on occasion, larger groups were explored or partially cleared.

A grid system based on the British Ordinance system was used from the beginning of the project to pinpoint any spot within the Moche Valley. Coordinates of this grid were used to designate sites or assign letter and number titles to areas within large sites if necessary. Although the grid system could provide quadrilateral figures of practically any dimension for random sampling of architectural sites, it was not used for this purpose. Instead, structures or groups of structures were the sampling units for observation and comparison (Morris 1975: 201) at architectural sites, including Chan Chan. Throughout the life of the project the research strategy remained one of purposive selective sampling (Cowgill 1975:260), but no one was denied the opportunity for random sampling.

Excavation strategy differed at deeply buried sites, middens, and surface lithic sites. In one instance a bulldozer opened deep trenches, which were cleaned and slightly expanded by hand labor in order to gain control over materials contained in natural stratigraphic deposits. Exploratory trenches or pits on middens were excavated by arbitrary levels until a stratigraphic profile or block was isolated. This was followed by careful stratigraphic excavation of natural layers exposed in the profile or block. One of the lithic sites was covered with a grid, and all the surface artifacts were numbered and plotted on the grid as they were collected. Various statistical procedures were used in the analysis of materials from the stratified deposits and surface collections.

It was necessary to establish chronological control over rural sites in the Moche Valley and over the architectural components of Chan Chan in order to understand intersite and intrasite historical and functional relationships. Previous ceramic studies provided a general chronological framework of periods, but these seriations were not always refined enough for the purposes of the project. Since small sites were presumably occupied for a short time, it was assumed that ceramics from these sites would provide discrete assemblages for seriation. This seriation was to be supplemented by stratigraphic ceramic samples from deep deposits at large sites in order to establish relatively precise chronological control over several sites. This method (Moseley and Mackey 1972) proved successful at some sites in the Moche Valley but was not appropriate to Chan Chan. There, deep deposits were invariably mixed, probably due to frequent prehistoric clearing, cleaning, and construction activities throughout the occupation of the site.

Although ceramics from Chan Chan were sufficient to establish its contemporaneity with certain rural sites and to distinguish it from sites of other periods, another approach was adopted to pinpoint the sequence of construction of monumental enclosures within Chan Chan. Since ciudadelas were not superimposed upon one another, radiocarbon determinations were equivocal, and ceramics were often unreliable for fine chronological control, a method of seriating mass-produced adobes was devised (Kolata, Chapter 4). This adobe seriation, when checked against variations in U-shaped structures at Chan Chan, yielded a sequence for the construction of ciudadelas. The adobe seriation should be applicable to sites outside Chan Chan if the sites contain structures built of mass-produced adobes.

Functional interpretations of architectural phenomena began as progress was made toward solving historic problems even though these two efforts did not always follow one another in order. The function of certain structures—for instance, storerooms—was established on the basis of comparison of their form and layout with Inca storage facilities. Other structures, such as kitchens or workshops, were identified by their contents. Still other structures were identified by their relationship to other known structures or by their strategic location on access routes or by their proximity to entrances. In the case of royal burial platforms, the clues that first led to their identification were their relative isolation, the heavy looting of interior chambers, and the content of debris in looters' backdirt piles. Very few of the structure identifications were anticipated, and none was evident in the literature before the project began.

As time went by control over chronological issues improved, and new interpretations supplemented earlier ones. Furthermore, once trustworthy generalities were derived from the research, the larger questions of prehistoric Andean socioeconomic and political organizations were addressed. The results of these inquiries are presented here.

Moseley presents a model of Chan Chan political, economic, and social organization in Chapter 1. He begins with a review of the geographic and ecological conditions of coastal Peru with particular emphasis upon the large tracts of arable land on the North Coast plain between the Moche Valley and the Sechura Desert. In this area there were two prehistoric multivalley irrigation complexes, a smaller one in the Moche-Chicama basins and a much larger one connecting the valleys from Jequetepeque to Motupe. In his discussion of the repeated economic and political unification of the Moche-Chicama area, Moseley proposes that such organization was predicated upon available river water, land, cultigens, and an ancient pattern of structured exploitation of human labor.

Moseley and Deeds describe the irrigation systems in the Moche Valley in Chapter 2. Alterations in the Moche Valley irrigation network over an extended period of time are discussed along with some observations on the engineering problems faced by the ancient builders. Evidence is also presented for a great flood during the Chimú occupation of the valley.

Day (Chapter 3) offers a synopsis of the investigation of the monumental rectangular enclosures called ciudadelas that dominate Chan Chan. Then Kolata (Chapter 4) provides a chronological framework for the growth of Chan Chan based on the proportions and distribution of sun-dried bricks, or adobes, the most common man-made object at the site.

In Chapter 5 Conrad interprets the royal burial platforms in and associated with ciudadelas as structures which reflect the practice of "split inheritance." This death cult activity, previously known only among the Inca, meant that the principal heir of a dead king received power and status, but a second heir received the estate of the dead king.

A broad category of ruins at Chan Chan, less imposing than the monumental ciudadelas but more formal and spacious than the small irregularly agglutinated rooms, are elite compounds. Klymyshyn uses ethnohistoric sources in Chapter 6 to suggest that Chimú nobility— albeit a "lesser nobility" of court functionaries and bureaucrats— occupied these structures.

There are large areas of small irregularly agglutinated rooms (SIAR) at Chan Chan that had never been studied until the project began. J. Topic, in Chapter 7, describes and interprets them as lower-class residential areas where most of the craft production and manufacturing took place.

In Chapter 8, S. Pozorski reports subsistence information from ten sites in the Moche Valley that span the time from the Cotton Preceramic to the Late Horizon (see Table 1.1 in Chapter 1 for a time chart). She traces the steady development of reliance upon organized distribution of foodstuffs and concludes that food was largely redistributed by the state in Chimú times. Furthermore, the staples provided by the state varied according to the available resources at particular localities within the Moche Valley.

In the following chapter (9), Keatinge discusses the distribution of U-shaped structures at administrative centers in the Moche Valley during the Chimú hegemony. He then compares them to similar structures on top of platforms and mounds at the earlier site of Pacatnamú in the Jequetepeque Valley. He suggests that Pacatnamú was the site of a major oracle and the U-shaped structures there had a more sacred function than the later, secular administrative structures at Chimú sites.

In Chapter 10, T. Pozorski describes Caballo Muerto, a site which predated Chan Chan. The concentration of subsistence remains at the site indicates that it was the most economically important site in the Moche Valley. Indeed, Pozorski feels that the formal architecture and elaborate friezes are evidence that Caballo Muerto was the seat of a chiefdom. The site, therefore, provides an example of single-site dominance in the valley and represents the early part of a trend that later culminated in Chan Chan.

T. Topic summarizes in Chapter 11 excavations at Huaca del Sol and Huaca de la Luna at the site of Moche, where deep test trenches revealed the full stratigraphic record of occupation. Elsewhere, areas of high quality domestic architecture were partially cleared. She concludes that even during the Early Intermediate Period a well-defined class structure existed, and the Moche Valley was the center of an expansionist state supported by a bureaucratic administration. However, the lack of storage facilities at the site of Moche suggests that state-held redistributive powers later exemplified at Chan Chan were not yet in force during the Early Intermediate Period.

A comparison of the architecture at Galindo with that of Chan

Chan, Huaca del Sol, and Huaca de la Luna is made in Chapter 12. Here, Bawden suggests that enclosures at Galindo herald the formal architecture at Chan Chan and that the daislike platforms at Galindo are miniature versions of Moche Phase huacas (flat-topped pyramids). In addition, the existence of and control over storage facilities evidenced by the strategic location of large enclosures point to Galindo as a transitional site in the trend toward economic control by an elite.

In Chapter 13, Mackey reviews the evidence for Huari influence in the Moche Valley at the end of the Early Intermediate Period, evidence she finds insufficient to justify the idea that direct Huari influence was the major factor for the development of urbanism on the North Coast. As an alternative, Mackey suggests that urban precedents probably occurred farther north on the coast between the time of Moche's abandonment and Chan Chan's founding.

Continuities in socioeconomic organization from the Early Intermediate Period through the Late Intermediate Period to the Late Horizon are stressed in Chapter 14 (Day). Evidence of labor task units and storage among the late Moche, Chimú, and Inca is the basis for a model of ancient socioeconomic organization that was probably shared throughout much of the Andean area.

In addition to contributing specific information on Chan Chan and other sites, several of the chapters in this book make the point that the social, economic, and political patterns for which the Inca are famous and heretofore largely credited with inventing are present at Chan Chan. It is evident, too, that the patterns at Chan Chan were predicated in large measure upon earlier cultures in the Moche Valley rather than the result of trait diffusion from the south. Although traditional patterns are strongly evident in the Moche Valley and, by extension, much of the North Coast, there are differences in cultural content at various time periods. However, the identification of common precepts of social distinctions, economic management, and centralized control during much of the prehistoric occupation of the North Coast is an indigenous cultural development that was probably shared throughout the central Andes.

Kent C. Day

Contents

1
Introduction: Human Exploitation and Organization on the North Andean Coast

MICHAEL E. MOSELEY

Field Museum of Natural History

Man's occupation of the North Coast of Peru has been long, complex, and fundamentally important to the evolution of Andean society. Traditionally, archaeologists have interpreted northern prehistory in an analytical framework based upon Peruvian research performed further to the south. Drawing on results of the Chan Chan–Moche Valley Project and other recent investigations, this introductory chapter offers a new analysis from an alternative perspective. The northern desert is viewed as the major focus of coastal Andean civilization and a center of cultural evolution that can only be interpreted in its own terms.

This chapter is an attempt to outline a model of indigenous economic and political organization that makes North Coast archaeology intelligible as a network of systemically interrelated facts about past cultural development. Attention is concentrated on institutions of governance and centralized administration. This focus is necessary for understanding large settlements that were major power centers; such centers are the dominant topic of the individual seminar papers that

1

make up this volume. Finally, the essay is speculative, and while striving to present a consensus viewpoint, it does not represent a unanimity of opinion on all interpretive points by all seminar participants.

GEOGRAPHIC PERSPECTIVE

Human occupation of the North Coast must be seen within the potentials of the physical environment. The central Andean region may be divided into broad geographic quadrants. These four spheres differ both altitudinally in terms of the desert coast versus the upland sierra, and longitudinally in terms of the northern coast and sierra versus the southern desert and uplands. Diagrammatically these two axes quarter the central Andes:

```
                    Sierra Upland
    North  ——————————————+—————————————— South
                    Desert Coast
```

Distinctive conditions in each area produced diverging cultural adaptations that affected the manner in which North Coast populations articulated with other spheres of indigenous civilization.

Coast And Sierra

Life on the Pacific desert is influenced by the distribution of fresh water and arable land, which is, in turn, strongly influenced by the configuration of the Andean uplands. The southern mountain massif is high, wide, relatively flat, and receives little precipitation. To the north the average elevation decreases as the ranges become narrower, more bisected, and better watered. The Titicaca Basin is the largest expanse of flat, arable land in all the highlands; with an elevation of 3,700 meters and higher, it receives about 50 centimeters of rain per year. This contrasts with smaller, lower basins to the north. For example, near the Río Moche headwaters, the basin of Cajamarca lies more than 1,000 meters below the Titicaca plains and has 25 centimeters more rain annually.

Since the dispersal of highland rainfall determines the distribution and quantity of runoff crossing the desert coast, the northern rivers tend to discharge substantially more water than their southern coun-

terparts. Similarly, the distribution of flat, arable coast land is determined by the proximity of the mountains to the Pacific. Rugged foothills
push out into the ocean between the Moche and Cañete valleys,
creating a scarcity of arable terrain that curtails agricultural potential
even where fresh water is abundant, as at the Río Santa. South of the
Río Cañete the mountains pull back from the ocean, creating a coastal
plain, but a majority of the southern rivers carry little discharge, and
the larger water courses are deeply entrenched, allowing little water to
be diverted onto the available land. These factors greatly limit agricul-
.tural productivity along the South Coast.

Conditions are different in the northern coastal quadrant. Here the
mountains end well back from the Pacific, creating a very wide coastal
plain that is crossed by large rivers. For indigenous populations, the
combination of abundant land and water in the region from the Moche
Valley north to the Sechura Desert held the greatest agrarian potential
to be found along the Pacific desert. The long-term consequences of
the different conditions and adaptations in the four Andean quadrants
remains little explored.

The Titicaca Basin constituted the economic and demographic center of the sierra (Robinson 1964; Murra and Morris 1976), and it is
clear that the small population on the South Coast was closely tied to
and often subjugated by this highland center and nearby mountain
societies. In contrast, the North Coast populace was a far larger force
in Andean civilization, equal to, if not dominating, the north highland peoples. Ultimately, political development in the Andes may
prove to have been a push-pull fluctuation between the two principal
geographic quadrants: the northern focus on the coast with the Chimú
empire and antecedent Moche state, and the southern focus in the
sierra with final Inca preeminence growing out of earlier Tiahuanaco/
Huari polities.

The Northern Periphery

The north Andean coast consists of a central core, or nuclear region, flanked by two peripheral areas. The great Sechura Desert is the
largest physiographic break in the landscape. This wide, barren plain,
not crossed by rivers for 125 kilometers, formed a natural boundary
separating distinctive cultural developments.

Until approximately 3,000 B.C. the littoral zone north of the Sechura

Desert supported mangrove swamps and relatively moist conditions. Early populations relied on mangrove mollusks, other invertebrates, and wild plant foods (Richardson 1973). As yet, there is no evidence for the pursuit of megafauna or for the production of stone projectile points.

The advent of agriculture did not alter the peripheral status of the region. Its rivers, although often large, lie entrenched below the arable plain, and local societies did not develop the population levels, technology, and organizational principles to mobilize large reclamation projects. Some sharing of ideas about art and iconography occurred with people to the south, as attested by stylistic similarities between Vicús, Gallinazo, and Moche ceramics. However, it was not until the heavy influx of Chimú influence that monumental construction and other evidence of complex sociopolitical organization appears in the northern periphery. At that time, the area was wrested away from long-standing ties to the Ecuadorian sphere of influence and brought within the confines of central Andean civilization. This transformation was executed either by people from the Lambayeque area, or, slightly later, by imperial armies directed from Chan Chan.

The Nuclear North

The nuclear section of the North Coast is a wedge-shaped plain stretching from the Río Moche to the Sechura Desert. It is separated from the southern periphery by the pull-back of the mountains from the sea and the emergence of a true coastal plain, which first arises at the mouth of the Moche River and stretches northward becoming progressively wider (Robinson 1964). The plain endows the nuclear North Coast with far more arable land than exists to the south.

When man first entered the coastal plain, savannalike conditions apparently existed along the transecting rivers and their fringes. These valleys were the preferred habitat of megafauna, including horse and mastodon. The fauna moved up and down the plain from one valley to another and did not penetrate the moist northern periphery or the rocky southern periphery in large numbers. Man adjusted his activities to exploiting this faunal enclave, and the cultural hallmark of this adaptation is the Paiján or Long-Stemmed Projectile Point (Ossa and Moseley 1971; Ossa 1973). With time, hunting gave way to reliance upon marine resources, and around 3,000 B.C. people began looking

4

to the sea as a primary source of subsistence. Within one millennium permanent communities, such as Huaca Prieta (Bird 1948), arose along the coast. Although some settlements were of substantial size, none rivaled the far larger maritime communities found south of the Río Moche.

Agriculture ultimately brought the nuclear north to cultural pre-eminence, and the economic landscape can be summarized in terms of Prehispanic irrigation systems. Reclamation projects pushed into desert areas beyond the confines of modern cultivation by the time of Christ (Kosok 1965; Willey 1953). A distinguishing feature of the nuclear north was the presence of very large canals linking two or more valleys into a single massive irrigation system. La Cumbre canal, running from the Chicama to the Moche Valley, was built by the Chan Chan dynasty (Kus 1972); other intervalley linkups lack precise dating but are probably of comparable or greater antiquity.

During its stage of maximum agrarian development, the nuclear north consisted of two central multivalley complexes flanked by small single-valley irrigation systems (Figure 1.1). One multivalley unit was the Moche and Chicama Basins (Figure 1.2). To the south lay the small Río Virú, and then the tiny Chao drainage, each forming an independent irrigation system. For millennia the four valleys from Chao to Chicama constituted a tightly integrated cultural area that was often politically consolidated.

North of the Río Chicama, the wide plain of Quebrada Cupisnique formed a physiographic and cultural break splitting the nuclear north. Above the split lay the greatest irrigation system of the entire Pacific coast, the Lambayeque megasystem connecting five rivers from the Jequetepeque to the Motupe. The Ríos Jequetepeque and Chancay-Lambayeque were the principal affluents feeding the vast complex, which probably accounted for one-third of all land reclaimed along the Andean desert (Kosok 1965). North of the megasystem lies the tiny Olmos Valley, and beyond this marginal agrarian enclave spreads the Sechura Desert.

In spite of its disproportional importance, the Lambayeque mega-system is little explored. While it may well have shared early political ties with the Moche-Chicama region, pronounced stylistic bonds are not evident until the Middle Horizon and Phase V of the Moche art sequence (see Table 1.1). A Moche V presence in the Lambayeque region is reflected in murals at Huaca Facho (Donnan 1972) and in

5

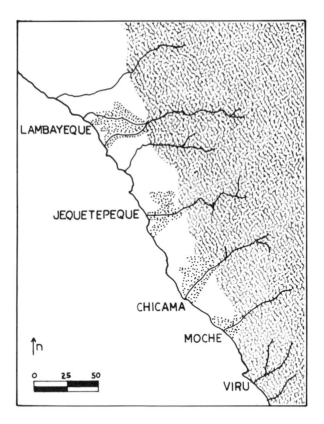

FIGURE 1.1. The North Coast of Peru.

excavations at Pampa Grande (Day 1976). The latter vast settlement is generally contemporary with the somewhat smaller site of Galindo, some 150 kilometers to the south. Although there are differences between the two sites, ceramics and other artifacts reveal an integrated, shared style and iconography implying some form of political unification of the Lambayeque and Moche-Chicama regions. While there was a subsequent lapse in political bonds before the Chan Chan dynasty exerted its hegemony, the nuclear north retained a long tradition of cultural ties and interrelationships.

The Southern Periphery

The nuclear north differs from its southern periphery in two ways. First, the south lacks a flat coastal plain, and second, because of a complex of ocean currents flowing along the coast, its marine resources are distinct. Stretching from Chile north to the mouth of the Río Santa

6

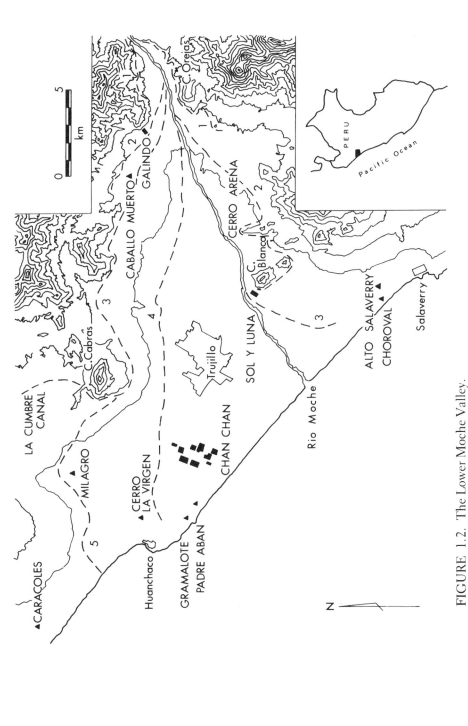

FIGURE 1.2. The Lower Moche Valley.

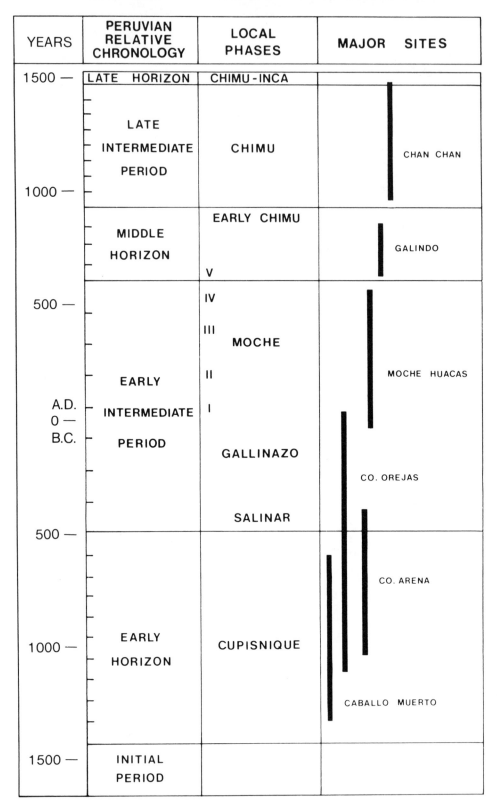

YEARS	PERUVIAN RELATIVE CHRONOLOGY	LOCAL PHASES	MAJOR SITES
1500 —	LATE HORIZON	CHIMU-INCA	
	LATE INTERMEDIATE PERIOD	CHIMU	CHAN CHAN
1000 —			
	MIDDLE HORIZON	EARLY CHIMU	GALINDO
		V	
500 —		IV	
		III MOCHE	
	EARLY	II	MOCHE HUACAS
A.D. 0 — B.C.	INTERMEDIATE	I	
	PERIOD	GALLINAZO	CO. OREJAS
		SALINAR	
500 —			
			CO. ARENA
1000 —	EARLY HORIZON	CUPISNIQUE	
			CABALLO MUERTO
1500 —	INITIAL PERIOD		

TABLE 1.1. Chronological ordering of Moche Valley sites.

is a near-shore phenomenon known as upwelling which involves the rise and surfacing of cold, nutrient-rich waters from the ocean floor. Upwelling promotes a prodigious food chain that supports the largest marine biomass in the western hemisphere. Thus, the sea south of the Río Santa is far richer than it is to the north of the Río Moche. How far below the Santa/Moche boundary the southern periphery of the North Coast extends is somewhat arbitrary. Traditionally, the line is drawn between the small Huarmey Valley and the trivalley irrigation complex of the Ríos Fortaleza, Pativilca, and Supe.

Differences in marine and terrestrial resources between the nuclear north and its southern periphery resulted in different patterns of adjustment. Southern hunting-gathering was oriented toward the exploitation of seasonally available lomas (hillock) plants and animals (Engel 1970), paralleling the early lomas utilization on the Central Coast of Peru (Lanning 1967), and probably reflecting little southward penetration of megafauna into the mountainous coast.

Later, when people turned to intensive exploitation of the sea, littoral resources from the Río Santa southward supported maritime communities of exceptional size. During this preceramic stage, the lower periphery of the North Coast again developed in parallel with the central Andean coast, where people lived in vast settlements, built large monuments, and developed complex forms of sociopolitical organization.

Intensive agriculture took hold along the southern periphery at about the same time as it did further north. Below the Río Santa the earlier maritime adaptation supported both the growth in population and the rise of organizational principles that allowed mobilization of large work forces for construction purposes. These developments, in theory, also allowed southern populations to initiate reclamation projects faster and on a larger scale than northern societies. By about 1000 B.C. irrigation was firmly established in the southern periphery, and some moderate-sized valleys, such as the Casma, may have approached their agricultural potential at this time. Yet by the beginning of the Christian era, Moche political and cultural sovereignty had pushed down to the Nepēna Valley. Cultural domination stopped at the Casma Valley, which had been the seat of an earlier powerful polity, but Moche political influence very likely extended farther south. After this period of unification, the southern periphery was either controlled or strongly influenced by the nuclear north. The rise of northern domi-

9

nance reflected availability of both land and water to support continued economic growth, whereas the scarcity of arable land inhibited continued agricultural expansion in the south.

CULTURAL PERSPECTIVE

The North Coast has exceptional economic potential—specifically agricultural potential in the nuclear area. This potential can be realized by people who have the option of acting either independently in an entrepreneurial manner or collectively in a corporate manner. The first option is most prevalent in those areas where resources are not exceptionally rich, or where utilization is insecure and entails high risks. These settings often occur in small valleys, such as the Chao and Olmos. Sometimes they are present in areas of larger drainages that lie beyond the confines of prime lands where scant water supply, poor soil conditions, or salinity create problems for agriculture.

Today, as in the past, the vast majority of northern agriculturalists work collectively in exploiting the most auspicious economic settings, which are the larger valleys and the prime lands of the smaller drainages. There is nothing to suggest that these areas were ever seats of entrepreneurial activity. Rather, the archaeological record underscores a long tradition of collective organization and exploitation. Indeed, corporate organization constituted the backbone of North Coast civilization.

The following discussion attempts to outline the major components of northern corporate organization. While diachronic considerations are relevant, the principal concern is more synchronic and directed at the structure of statecraft.

Taxation

The extraction of taxes in the form of labor constituted the cornerstone of Andean statecraft and corporate organization. The institution generated a "labor intensive" economy, and political manipulation of the tax structure was largely synonymous with manipulation of the economic structure.

The Inca extracted labor by means of the mit'a tax levied upon subject communities. This tax required males to devote periods of service to the state while females produced quantities of fabrics for the

10

administrative hierarchy (Murra 1956, 1962). The state, in turn, was thought to have certain obligations to its taxpayers. These obligations included reciprocating with symbolic goods and ceremonies, as well as redistributing products and produce among the masses.

Archaeological expressions of mit'a-like principles on the North Coast have several forms. Certain Chimú and earlier sites can be identified as formal, state-built architectural complexes that served as administrative foci for directing large work forces mobilized by taxation for purposes of building and running corporate agricultural undertakings (Keatinge 1974). In this context the tax structure makes the strategy of economic investment intelligible. Economic growth was not a simple matter of raising additional taxes. Rather, real growth rested upon the acquisition of additional productive resources—specifically arable land. The tax structure allowed this growth to develop in two ways: by investing labor in reclamation or in conquest. The massive irrigation programs of the Chimú and Moche polities, as well as the great terracing projects of the Inca, are products of the first strategy.

The subdivision of large construction projects into repetitive segments is another expression of mit'a-like organization: canals were dug in isolated segments subsequently linked to one another, adobes in the great Huaca del Sol and Huaca de la Luna were laid up in columnar sections, and the walls of Chan Chan were built in independent sections with a cane pole marking the end of each section. The segments of a construction project can be identified as work task units (Day 1973), and there is evidence that each unit was a tax measure built by a different team of laborers fulfilling a mit'a-like levy for their group (Moseley 1975c).

The tax structure provides a basis for understanding the size and social composition of political centers such as Chan Chan and Cuzco. Both historically documented centers of empire are vast monuments disproportionate in size and scope of labor investment to contemporaneous sites of their respective realms. Yet the amount of labor devoted to construction reflects neither large numbers of inhabitants nor massive proletariat populations (Rowe 1967; Moseley 1975a). Rather, both capitals were built by nonresident work forces and were products of a corvée system.

Within the context of mit'a-like organizations, Chan Chan and Cuzco indicate that earlier sites with disproportionately large labor expenditures, compared to contemporaneous settlements, reflect

11

analogous political abilities to mobilize labor. On the North Coast there is a temporal succession of four large sites. For its particular time period, each architectural complex represents the largest labor investment made in monumental construction on the entire Pacific coast, and occasionally in the entire Andean region. These vast monuments are Chan Chan (Chimú, largely Late Intermediate Period); Pampa Grande (Moche Phase V, Middle Horizon, in part); Huaca del Sol and Huaca de la Luna (Moche Phases I–IV, largely Early Intermediate Period); and Sechín Alto (Sechín-Casma, Early Horizon, in part).

The taxation structure allows archaeologists to treat different foci of labor expenditure as more than random historical phenomena. For example, the mass of monumental construction at Pampa Grande far exceeds the volume of similar architecture at Galindo or any other Moche Phase V settlement. The implication is that Pampa Grande was the center of a polity to which Galindo and its sister settlement rendered corvée levies. This type of perspective is also useful in assessing even earlier cultural relationships. For example , the highland site of Chavín de Huántar is often viewed as the major center of early influence and development in the Andes. Yet, the main monumental mound at Sechín Alto in the Casina Valley on the Central Coast is some fifteen times the size of its Chavín counterpart (Tello 1956). This implies that the North Coast was more than a cultural backwater area during the formation of Andean civilization.

Reciprocity

Andean polities provided taxpayers with certain ceremonies and goods of symbolic or prestige value. These goods were manufactured commodities, and the level of demand was such that the institution of reciprocity placed many arts and crafts in the service of the state. This relationship is evident in the Inca's forced resettlement of artisans in communities adjacent to Cuzco, including metalsmiths taken from Chan Chan. At Chan Chan the evidence of craft production and metal working is massive and pervasive among the quarters of the lower class (J. Topic, Chapter 7). No other Chimú settlements exhibit a comparable level of manufacturing. The scale of production was apparently large enough to extend beyond the consumption of the resident nobility and include the goods required for reciprocity among

12

the elite class on a national scale. At Huaca del Sol and Huaca de la Luna, lower-class architecture is poorly preserved and little explored. However, craft production is in evidence at the site (T. Topic, Chapter 11) and may have served more than a local market.

Methodologically, the consequences of reciprocity placing certain arts and crafts in the service of the state is important. At one level this resulted in "corporate styles" composed of objects of relatively standardized form, decoration, and iconography, the production of which was state-sanctioned for state ends. "Cuzco polychrome" pottery is an Inca manifestation of this phenomenon. However, the most tightly integrated ceramic corporate style comprises the stirrup-spout vessels of Moche Phases III–V. Of course not every polity emphasized the same media in contending with reciprocity. The Chimú did not share the degree of concern with ceramics that the Moche polity had; rather, the emphasis was on metalworking.

Obviously, not every integrated style of elaborate artifacts appearing on the North Coast was spread by reciprocity. However, many certainly were, and their distribution in time and space is a direct reflection of the taxation system and the political climate.

Redistribution

In the North Coast archaeology, a series of fundamental questions centers upon the extent to which the state actually managed economic production and engaged in moving produce between large masses of consumers and producers. Tentative explorations of the issues exist in studies of past agricultural and storage practices.

In the Moche Valley, investigation of preserved fields and canals indicates that most, if not all, canal reclamation projects were state-instituted and state-run. If food crops were grown, rather than industrial cultigens such as cotton, and if the Moche Valley typified other valleys, then the state was most likely involved in large-scale redistribution of subsistence goods.

A variety of storage facilities was employed in the past, some serving private or domestic purposes, and others corporate ends. At Galindo, an isolated area of approximately one square kilometer is occupied by single and multiroom storage structures lacking formal architectural patterning (see Bawden, Chapter 12). The rooms contain sherds from large-volume vessels presumably related to food storage, and the situation suggests centralized administration of subsistence goods at the settlement. However, this site was not the center of a polity. At Pampa Grande and particularly at Chan Chan, there are formal, state-built storage facilities consisting of rows of three or more similar-sized rooms, each entered by a single raised doorway. Excavation indicates careful systematic removal of the rooms' contents at the time of abandonment. These facilities seem far more compatible with the storage of valued commodities relevant to reciprocity than with the storage of bulk produce involved in the redistribution of subsistence goods. However, the situation is far from clear.

Dynastic Succession

In the two historically documented cases of Andean empires, the apex of political power was held by a dynasty of potentates. Drawing upon the Chimú and Inca, an argument can be made for the association of the following phenomena: (1) empire, (2) labor taxation, (3) reciprocity-related corporate styles, (4) a capital of disproportionate size, and (5) dynastic rule.

Historical sources document the existence of a major dynasty in the Lambayeque region, but do not specify its physical setting (Rostworowski 1961; Kosok 1965). The dynasty began at an earlier date than either the Chan Chan or Cuzco successions. However, after its founding the Lambayeque dynasty remained unilinear—and presumably politically unified—for only several generations. Five or more heirs then established their own separate dynasties and, by implication, their own polities within the formerly unified realm. Kosok (1965) dates the breakdown of unilinear rule to a period of some five generations before the rise of the Chan Chan dynasty. This generates the hypothesis that the short-lived period of dynastic and political unity in Lambayeque dates to Moche Phase V times and that Pampa Grande is the central manifestation of this polity.

This scenario is comparable with the position of Huaca del Sol and Huaca de la Luna as the center of an earlier polity. The capital of this state was abandoned at the end of Moche Phase IV, and the northward transferral of political power correlated with the reorganization in corporate style that dramatically distinguished Phase V from Phase IV in the Moche art sequence. This correlation of political and stylistic change raises questions about the significance of earlier shifts between

14

phases of the Moche art sequence. Whatever their cause, they seem to mark less consequential events than does the shift to Phase V art.

At an earlier horizon the vast Sechín Alto complex reflects the center of a major multivalley polity. Yet, other than Tello's (1956) notation of its exceptional magnitude and test excavations suggesting great antiquity (Collier 1962; Thompson 1961), the far-reaching implications of this great monument remain unfathomed. The site shares at least one important physical attribute with the later centers of Huaca del Sol and Huaca de la Luna, and Pampa Grande: while these sites each have a number of platform mounds, one is disproportionately large and has three to five or more times the volume of the next largest structure. Architecturally, this gives the impression of a rather singular focus of political power at each center.

Although dynastic rule undoubtedly had many configurations, Conrad (Chapter 5) makes a case for the Chimú following a form of succession characterized by "split inheritance" among the royalty. Here each succeeding potentate receives the reins of state, but does not inherit his predecessors' estates. These estates and their revenues pass to junior heirs who form a corporation or lineage charged with venerating the dead king.

The inheritance system may relate to the Chimú concern with the acquisition of arable land. If a king inherited the rule of state, but not lands or their revenue, then his principal means of economic betterment was to invest corvée labor in securing new land by reclamation or conquest.

The hallmark of split inheritance is the "one king/one palace/one burial platform" syndrome of the later ciudadelas at Chan Chan. The four earliest royal compounds seem to be variations on this theme, with some palaces serving more than one potentate, and some lacking a platform (Kolata, Chapter 4). Although Galindo was not a major capital, the palace-platform syndrome is sharply defined at the site, suggesting the institution has even earlier origins.

At Chan Chan successive rulers built their ciudadelas in different parts of the site. This spatial separation underlies the proposition that if each king had to construct his own quarters and mausoleum, he was obviously not inheriting the material goods of his predecessor. A succession of vertically stacked palaces would be compatible with the spatial segregation called for by split inheritance, but the architectural end product would be very different in configuration from Chan Chan.

Speaking impressionistically, I think Huaca del Sol constitutes a vertical succession of separate administrative quarters each associated with a different ruler. Huaca del Sol is structurally and functionally distinct from Huaca de la Luna. The latter is a complex of three independent platforms. Floors in the Huaca de la Luna complex are clean and not associated with activities leading to refuse accumulation, while interior walls were frequently ornamented with elaborate anthropomorphic and zoomorphic murals. On the other hand, Huaca del Sol is a single vast platform. Episodes of massive looting, which included hydraulic mining, were directed at the highest section of the mound, and ultimately carried away at least two-thirds of the entire monument. The incorporation of high-status graves in the preserved remnant of the mound supports the proposition that the great episodes of looting were directed toward finding tombs of great wealth situated in the highest section of Huaca del Sol.

The interior profile left by looting reveals at least eight separate stages of construction, each separated from the next by a period of use when courts, corridors, and rooms on the flat summit served as activity areas. In many cases activities on the summit led to refuse accumulation, garbage buildup, and deposits of animal dung (S. Pozorski, Chapter 8). In no case, however, were the interior walls decorated with ornate murals or art work.

Thus, Huaca del Sol can be seen as (1) being the largest and most important structure in the Moche III–IV polity; (2) supporting summit architecture compatible with bureaucratic functions; (3) housing secular behavior and residential activity; and (4) incorporating rich tombs within its different stages of construction. All these features are compatible with Huaca del Sol constituting a vertical succession of separate administrative facilities of a dynasty bound by principles of split inheritance.

Prehistoric platforms clearly served many purposes, and a majority of mounds were built and used in two or more stages. However, the largest of all platforms—Pampa Grande, Huaca del Sol, and Sechín Alto—clearly carried bureaucratic and political connotations, and these connotations very likely included dynastic rule and split inheritance.

Administration

Split inheritance produced "junior" lineages of nobles, and these nobles were presumably concerned with administering the legacies of the past monarchs. Likewise, the presumption is that the top echelon of a living king's bureaucracy was staffed by relatives and members of the royal class. At Chan Chan the elite compounds can be argued to have housed the upper echelon of the Chimú bureaucracy (Klymyshyn, Chapter 6). By extension, many of the elite complexes at the capitals of earlier polities probably served analogous purposes.

The nature of administration outside these major sites and valleys is not entirely clear. In Chapter 2, Deeds and I argue that irrigation in valleys such as Virú and Chicama comprised complexes of potentially autonomous economic entities capable, in theory, of supporting independent political bodies. In this sense, the North Coast hacienda/plantation system at the turn of the present century seems to represent a not entirely unique adaptation to the economic landscape. The impression is that in the past, much rural administration was carried out by local nobility, perhaps analogous to the class of hacienda owners at the turn of the century.

During periods of political incorporation there is good evidence from some valleys that the foreign bureaucracy implemented its policies from large administrative centers founded and built by the state. The phenomenon is well defined between Virú and Nepeña for the Huaca del Sol and Huaca de la Luna polity (T. Topic, Chapter 11) and is clearly documented in a Chimú context at Farfán in Jequetepeque (Keatinge, Chapter 9). Thus, while greatly elaborated by the Inca at state-built centers such as Huanaco Pampa, the practice had considerable antiquity.

Chimú state-built sites serving administrative purposes were constructed according to the architectural canons of Chan Chan, giving them a distinctive physical appearance and linking them with the ruling bureaucracy. In addition, the bureaucracy also concerned itself with another form of settlement that can be termed "state-founded" as opposed to "state-built." State-founded sites are residential settlements built and inhabited by members of the agricultural class at specific locations selected by the ruling administration (Keatinge 1975b). This practice rests on principles similar to those underlying the later elaborate mitama colonization programs of the Inca.

Formal policies dictating where agriculturalists can and cannot live are a logical derivative of the centralized administration of both irrigation agriculture and large-scale reclamation. Such manipulation of the location of agrarian settlements very likely has considerable antiquity on the coast, yet the practice is difficult to document until formalized to the point where a rural site is situated in a telling location, or is endowed with unusual architectural or other properties.

Sacred and Secular

Isolating the sacred or religious aspects of administration from the secular concerns of North Coast governance poses many problems. In the case of the Chan Chan dynasty, kings were apparently held to be divine or semidivine beings, and if split inheritance did not promote ancestor worship, it certainly perpetuated the reverence of former monarchs. Insofar as secular and sacred merged at the apex of the body politic, there is little reason to suppose sharp distinctions prevailed at lower levels.

Traditionally, archaeologists have relied upon art and iconography to make statements about sacred versus secular affairs. However, the institution of reciprocity placed certain arts and crafts in the service of the state. Therefore, while the iconography of elaborate textiles or fancy ceramics might have religious connotations, the distribution of these goods in space and time may often relate to secular aspects of governance such as payment for mit'a or other services. Extrapolating from the Inca, it may be supposed that each major Andean polity had its own "official" creed or theology. These, presumably, charged the iconography of the arts and crafts associated with the supporting administration. However, where in this network the secular leaves off and the sacred begins becomes a moot point.

Phrased in modern parlance, I doubt there ever was a North Coast "state" of consequence without a concomitant "church." However, the case for a major "church" existing without a concomitant "state" is cogently argued by Keatinge (Chapter 9). This phenomenon is of singular significance because it provided an alternative to statecraft and a different mechanism for coordinating the activities of large numbers of people.

The focus of this organizational alternative was Pacatnamú, which Keatinge identifies as the great North Coast pilgrimage center that ethnohistorical sources describe for the Jequetepeque Valley. The sanctity of the site drew devotees from a radius of hundreds of kilometers, crosscutting political frontiers. By means as yet unclear, Pacatnamú commanded the labor resources to make it an imposing architectural

18

center and an unusual concatenation of mounds and platforms. Although in part contemporary with Chan Chan and its Farfán administrative satellite, Pacatnamú is different in structure and layout—no doubt reflecting its special function.

Future research must establish the means by which Pacatnamú secured and maintained its power base, and then compare this system with that at the pilgrim nexus of Pachacamac on the Central Coast. If both share similar organizational principles, then the phenomenon of sacred centers may have constituted a fairly pervasive alternative to more secular forms of statecraft.

Finally, consideration of sacred phenomena on the North Coast cannot bypass one event with very profound overtones. This is the transformation of burial patterns in which corpse positioning changes from an extended supine to a flexed seated posture. The former carries through Moche Phase IV and apparently Phase V as well, whereas the latter pattern prevails during the Chimú dynasty. The transformation registers in the burials of both upper and lower classes and must have permeated all strata of society. It must reflect a profound alteration in belief systems concerned with how people are to enter afterlife, if not more broadly with the nature of afterlife itself.

Chronological vagueness and inadequate burial samples from the time of transition mask the mechanisms by which the change spread and took hold. This is unfortunate because the change very likely relates to a new era of organization arising on the North Coast after the collapse of Pampa Grande and Moche Phase V.

DEVELOPMENTAL PERSPECTIVE

The North Coast of Peru is one of the more auspicious human habitats in the western world. For millennia it supported large numbers of people engaged in the complex activities that make up civilization. As archaeologists probe the nuclear north, its long occupation reflects new and larger intricacies that defy easy synthesis. Thus, summarizing the course of cultural development must be done in tentative, outline form. Two overlapping perspectives capture certain significant trends in the occupation of the desert plain: man's manipulation of nature, and man's manipulation of man.

19

Man and Nature

Coastal civilization depended upon man's economic abilities to support large, dense populations. The economic history of the nuclear north falls into three phases of development, the last of which meets the demographic prerequisites for civilization.

The earliest occupation of the region is associated with a hunting-gathering adaptation. The archaeological hallmark is the so-called Paiján point, or long-stemmed projectile point. Although of great antiquity, associated with radiocarbon dates falling around 10,000 B.C., the known spatial distribution of this artifact type is restricted. It does not occur north of the Sechura Desert or to the east in the Andean uplands, and it appears only sporadically south of the Río Moche in areas of mountainous coast. Thus, the Paiján point distribution correlates with the topography of the flat coastal plain. This presumably reflects a hunting adaptation geared to small game and megafauna moving longitudinally up and down the Pacific plain. In theory, this fauna did not enter the more forested areas above the Sechura Desert or the rugged sierra uplands. Although it penetrated the southern hilly coast in small numbers, there people pursued a different adaptation geared to the exploitation of seasonal lomas resources. It is unclear whether the Paiján phenomenon represents a horizon or tradition in archaeological parlance. Whether short- or long-lived, the known sites and settlements bespeak neither large nor sedentary populations. They do, however, underscore the distinct character of human residence on the North Coast from its inception.

The succeeding economic adjustment focused upon utilization of littoral resources, and was first defined by Bird's (1948) excavations at Huaca Prieta. The recent research of S. Pozorski (Chapter 8) shows both the developmnt of this subsistence pattern through time and its adjustments to local shoreline conditions of rocky and sandy beach. There is ample evidence of small and moderate-sized communities of sedentary fishermen, and some sites contain nonresidential architecture built by group labor for public or esoteric ends.

However, the preceramic maritime adaptation had its greatest social consequences south of the Río Moche in the area stretching into the Central Coast, where fishing communities of great size arose. At many, the residents were mobilized to erect platform mounds and other monumental architecture. More important, though, is the evidence that labor forces were mustered from widely separated communities to

20

build monuments that conferred no apparent economic benefits upon either the individual laborer or his settlement. Elsewhere I have argued that the ability to mobilize and coordinate labor which arose in a maritime context established the foundations of Andean civilization (Moseley 1975b).

It is not by chance that the nuclear North Coast was largely peripheral to these preceramic developments, nor is it fortuitous that the maritime communities above the Río Moche seem less elaborate than their southern counterparts. Marine upwelling of nutrient-charged waters makes Peru's coastline the richest in all the western world. Upwelling ends near the Río Santa, somewhat below the northern plain, and there is a marked change in ocean biomass above and below this zone, which endowed the southern maritime economy with far greater potential than existed in the north.

The consequences of this situation were major, with reverberations lasting more than a millennium. This was because the southern maritime societies developed a degree of preadaptation to irrigation that the north did not, and the south was able to engage in reclamation on a larger scale at an earlier date than the north.

Coastal agriculture is predicated upon river water, land, cultigens, and human labor. Two categories of land are available for cultivation. The first and largest is the desert, the use of which requires large, coordinated labor investments for building and maintaining irrigation canals. The second and far smaller category comprises the river flood plains. These are essentially self-watering due to seasonal inundation of the land; cultivation can be accomplished by means of flood-water farming that requires little labor. The earliest coastal agriculture occurred in the context of these self-watering lands. Use of industrial cultigens (cotton for nets and fabrics, and gourd for net floats and containers) became ubiquitous among the preceramic maritime communities. Food plants are also present in minor quantities at many sites. However, their early occurrence has the following general characteristics: (1) they are not as common as marine foods, and only rarely as abundant as industrial cultigens; (2) they are generally composed of fruits, condiments, and crops that do not constitute agricultural staples; (3) they vary substantially in type and frequency among contemporary settlements; and (4) staples, when present (maize in particular), are extremely rare. These characteristics reflect at least two features affecting the course of early agriculture. First, the sea could amply supply people's dietary wants but not their industrial needs, and plant cultivation took its emphasis accordingly. Second, self-watering land suitable for flood-water farming is a very limited commodity, and the circumscribed availability of this land set well-defined strictures both on the types of crops grown and on the overall level of agricultural output.

Reclamation of the desert broke these strictures. It opened to cultivation great quantities of land suitable for many different crops, and combined with water management to mitigate the seasonality of agricultural production. However, the pace and scope by which reclamation can be initiated is proportional to the size of the labor forces that can be organized for purposes of canal construction and farming. Herein lay the preadaptation to irrigation agriculture of the coastal societies below the Río Santa. Their maritime economy supported the rise of large populations and potential labor forces. Within this economic context developed the organizational principles needed to mobilize and coordinate labor for purposes of large-scale construction.

The factors triggering the shift from marine exploitation to intensive agriculture are not clear. While they seem to have taken hold at the same general time, the south moved into the new economic adaptation on a larger scale and at a faster rate than did the nuclear north. The north was presumably bound to a more gradual development entailing feedback between increasing agricultural production, raising population levels , and redirecting greater labor back into reclamation.

Intensive agriculture occasioned wide changes in settlement patterns, with people moving away from the shoreline and into valley interiors with arable land (S. Pozorski, Chapter 8). This shift is intelligible in terms of a model postulating that reclamation began away from the coast in so-called valley neck areas. Although expanses of flat arable land are not wide, these settings have two favorable attributes. First, gradients are steep and large labor investments in long lead-off canals are not required to divert river water onto arable land. Second, drainage and salinization are not significant problems. The model then posits that through time irrigation moved downstream into flatter, wider stretches of land where greater labor investments were needed for lead-off canals and for drainage systems to combat salinization. Of course, local topographic and water table conditions vary greatly from one drainage to another, and idiosyncratic development is expected. Yet in a majority of cases valley neck settings seem to be the first focus

22

of inland activity, which is then followed by progressive growth into lower-lying localities. In the Moche Valley the down-valley shift from Caballo Muerto to Huaca del Sol and Huaca de la Luna can be read as reflecting these principles.

One tenet of this model is that reclamation requires less labor investment in settings of steep gradients with less arable land than it does in areas with more land with shallower gradients. From this follows the assumption that the former settings will develop faster and achieve their agricultural potential earlier than the latter. This conclusion is of some significance if the great sites of the North Coast are read as economic as well as political barometers. Sechín Alto is situated in the Casma Valley of the mountainous coast with steep gradients but circumscribed agricultural potential that could rapidly be achieved because of preadaptation to irrigation. In time it was superceded by Huaca del Sol and Huaca de la Luna in a flatter valley with greater agricultural potential. In turn, power shifted to Pampa Grande in the largest and widest of the northern valleys, but also the most difficult to reclaim. From this perspective, political development simply followed the realities of agricultural potential and its labor and organizational prerequisites. The course of development endured several millennia and broke with the rise of the Chan Chan dynasty, when man's control over man assumed dominance over man's manipulation of nature.

Man and Man

Economic development underwrote the demographic prerequisites for complex society; the origins of North Coast civilization, however, rested upon the formation of organizational principles that channeled and directed the actions of large populations. Many different principles affecting all aspects of life were involved . In Chapter 2 Deeds and I discuss the possible configuration of certain higher-order institutions and attempt to fit these into a functionally coherent model of governance at the apex of Chimú political structure. The Chan Chan dynasty, however, only encapsulates the end products of millennia of organizational evolution, thus leaving the processes of development to be sought in earlier times.

There is sufficient evidence on hand to argue that the basic principles of Chimú statecraft were fully formulated during the reign of the polity based at Huaca del Sol and Huaca de la Luna. Differences in the systems of governance are largely a matter of degrees of institutional elaboration, rather than of the operation of distinct types of principles. Further, from the Río Chicama to the Río Nepeña, the Moche Phase III and Phase IV occupation is tightly integrated to the verge of being culturally homogeneous. This integration reflects well-formulated principles of organization rather than a nascent stage of development. Thus, the institutional components of coastal civilization have far earlier origins.

These origins no doubt extend back in time at least to the creation of the Caballo Muerto Complex, if not to earlier periods that remain little explored. In part they must also lie somewhat below the nuclear North Coast. The vast center of Sechín Alto looms up in the Casma Valley as the largest early monument on the Pacific coast, if not the entire Andean area. Here the labor investment in construction ranks with that at Huaca del Sol and subsequent political centers. The conclusion must be that Sechín Alto was based upon organizational principles of broadly comparable potency. It is not clear whether these were necessarily similar in kind to later institutions of statecraft, nor whether they were undergoing initial formation at Sechín Alto or had even earlier antecedents. It is evident, however, that large-scale organization has very great antiquity on the coast.

2

The Land in Front of Chan Chan: Agrarian Expansion, Reform, and Collapse in the Moche Valley

MICHAEL E. MOSELEY
Field Museum of Natural History

ERIC E. DEEDS
University of California, Berkeley

INTRODUCTION

The Moche Valley has been the seat of a disproportionate amount of political power for the past two millennia. This power is expressed physically in large-scale construction at three sites, Huaca del Sol and Huaca de la Luna, Chan Chan, and colonial Trujillo. In terms of labor expenditure these sites were the biggest corporate undertakings in northern Peru for the time period in which each was built. The correlation of construction size with political power is straightforward. Trujillo was the major Spanish administrative center north of Lima. Chan Chan was the capital of the second largest native polity to arise in South America: at its height it exercised control over at least 66 percent of the irrigated coast lands. Huaca del Sol and Huaca de la Luna, because of their unrivaled size , can be inferred to have been the center of an earlier polity.

It is significant that Moche is a modest-sized valley that, when it was a political center, always exercised hegemony over the larger adjacent Chicama Valley. The larger valley seems to have governed the smaller only when both were under rule imposed by the Incas. Chicama has twice as much cultivated land as Moche and thus the resources to support a population twice the size of its political regent. This fact raises the issue of how a small demographic center in coastal Peru achieved sovereignty over a far larger area.

It is also significant that the three Moche power centers do not constitute an uninterrupted political continuum. Spanish Trujillo is separated from imperial Chan Chan by the Inca conquest. In turn, Chan Chan is separated from Huaca del Sol and Huaca de la Luna. During this time the major settlement in the Moche Valley was Galindo, a relatively minor center that was overshadowed by Pampa Grande, in the Lambayeque Valley, which was probably the seat of the dominant North Coast polity during the Moche Phase V times.

The phenomenon of repeated political ascendancy coupled with the subjugation of a larger demographic center can either be viewed as historical accident or treated as a significant nonrandom pattern distinguishing the Moche Valley from other coastal areas. Our purpose in this presentation is four-fold and includes (1) formulating a model of canal expansion in the Moche Valley; (2) reviewing the local development of irrigation; (3) contrasting this water management system with irrigation in adjacent valleys; and (4) arguing that the Moche system provided economic conditions favorable for repeated political ascendancy of the local population.

GENERAL CONSIDERATIONS

The most arid region in the Western Hemisphere stretches for 3,000 kilometers along the Pacific Coast of South America from northern Peru into northern Chile. Showers of consequence—which fall only about once per decade—are generally associated with a phenomenon known as El Niño which is a short-term shift in meteorological patterns and a temporary change in ocean currents. The barren desert is made habitable for a dense population only by means of irrigation agriculture that feeds off streams with headwaters in the Andean uplands, where annual rains fall at elevations above 1,500 meters.

Kosok (1940, 1958, 1965), the first scholar to conduct a broad survey of ancient and modern canal systems on the coast, made a number of important observations. The basic unit of irrigation is the single coastal valley bounded by desert and fed by a river or stream carrying Andean runoff. There are roughly 57 such valley units, or drainages, along the Peruvian coast. In the north, the Andes pull inland from the ocean, creating a flat coastal plain and providing the region with more potential arable land than exists in the south. Some Prehispanic polities constructed canals linking the irrigation systems of separate valleys. The largest such supersystem was in the Lambayeque region where 5 valleys were interconnected by canals. This multivalley complex represented one-third of all the land reclaimed on the coast and, by inference, housed one-third of the desert population. Yet, as Kosok (1958, 1965) notes, the area was dominated by the 2-valley Moche-Chicama supersystem immediately to the south. Below the Moche Valley there are 9 single-valley irrigation systems before intervalley systems sporadically reappear on the Central and South coasts.

Water and Land

The temperature along the Peruvian seaboard is remarkably uniform. Differences in mean temperatures between the warmest and coolest months average only about 10°F. The climate allows cultivation to go on throughout the year. As a result, topography, land, and water are the principal natural features affecting agricultural output. The 57 drainages crossing the desert plain are dependent upon seasonal precipitation in the mountains. The rivers carry a maximum discharge between January and March, but during July and August, the highland dry season, many smaller drainages cease flowing.

The coastal drainages are relatively short, have steep gradients, and flow through the mountains in narrow gorges in a westerly direction roughly perpendicular to the coast. Around 500 meters in elevation, nearing the coast, the drainages begin to broaden their flood plain. With decreasing altitude, flood plains funnel outward into broad alluvial triangles behind the shoreline. These are the areas of intensive cultivation.

The higher alluvial terraces situated somewhat inland and along valley sides tend to have light, well-drained soils. These are the most favorable farmlands. Today the majority of large agrarian cooperatives engaged in intensive, mechanized agriculture work these lands.

As rivers cross the desert and approach sea level, terrain adjacent to a water course and low-lying land tends to have an increasingly higher water table, and these poorly drained soils are susceptible to salinization when irrigated. Approaching a river mouth there is also progressive decrease in ground slope and gradient. As a result, progressively longer lead-off canals must be built to transport water away from a river channel and onto reclaimed land.

Early Water Management

Current knowledge about coastal water management is two-fold. First, the earliest canals and fields have not survived, and understanding of these systems is inferential, relying upon indirect evidence (Moseley 1974). Second, the later systems have physical survivals, and knowledge can be acquired through direct as well as indirect evidence.

Where studied, the first canals surviving in the archaeological record are about two thousand years old. They are remnants of large hydraulic systems, products of massive labor investment and sophisticated engineering, and can be identified as corporate undertakings. These remnants of later Prehispanic irrigation systems survive because they were larger and embraced more reclaimed land than their modern counterparts. Thus they have not been destroyed by recent farming.

Turning to their antecedent systems, it is clear that large-scale irrigation developed relatively early. About 1800 B.C., the coastal population was relying on a maritime economy. Plant foods were of secondary importance and cultivation presumably went on in seasonally inundated areas along the rivers by means of flood-water farming.

There is a temporal correlation of three events occurring roughly between 1800 and 1500 B.C.: the abandonment of many of the early littoral communities; the shift inland of monumental construction (and by inference the centers of political administration); and the increased consumption of cultivated plant foods combined with the gradual spread of agricultural staples. Large numbers of people cannot live away from the coast, erect vast monuments, and consume substantial quantities of agricultural foods without cultivating the desert. The inference is that irrigation agriculture developed and expanded about 1800 B.C. Valley necks and inland locales were probably the initial setting of the new economy (Moseley 1975c), perhaps because the inland settings required shorter lead-off canals and therefore less labor investment. Furthermore, these areas provided more immediate access to light, well-drained soils, and steeper gradients would make water control and distribution easier. In the following millennium, larger and longer canals were pushed out laterally and extended downvalley.

THE MOCHE VALLEY: THE PHYSICAL SETTING

Irrigation in the Moche Valley has been affected by two important physical variables: land and water. The water source, the Río Moche, is not unusual in its characteristics. The land, however, is. There are but two regions of Peru with a developed coastal plain where wide, flat lands separate the mountains from the sea. The smaller plain is on the South Coast. The larger plain emerges at the mouth of the Río Moche and stretches northward, becoming progressively wider through the Lambayeque area. Thus, the Moche Valley has no plain south of the river. Yet one is present to the north and includes the land tracts of the Pampas Esperanza, Río Seco, and Huanchaco. This unusual topographic situation strongly influenced local irrigation practices.

Río Moche

The Moche River forms a medium-sized basin of about 1,560 square kilometers. Its tributaries reach the Continental Divide and the zone of regular annual rains. The river rapidly descends the western slope of the Andes and is entrenched in narrow canyons for most of its 110-kilometer course. At about 600 meters the flood plain broadens to around 0.75 kilometers. Descending another 400 meters, the flood plain gradually broadens to 1.25 kilometers. Below the 200-meter contour, the river enters the coastal flatlands and fans outward in a broad alluvial triangle about 25 kilometers wide at the coast (Figure 2.1).

The Río Moche is a perennial stream with marked seasonal variation in flow. Discharge peaks between January and May when the average monthly runoff ranges from 10 to 34 cubic meters per second. During the remainder of the year flow diminishes and discharge drops to less than 4 cubic meters per second. Because the Andes are not well forested, the annual rains cause substantial erosion. Consequently the Río Moche carries vast amounts of alluvium during periods of high water. This results in great quantities of suspended silt and sediment being injected into irrigation systems. On the positive side, the allu-

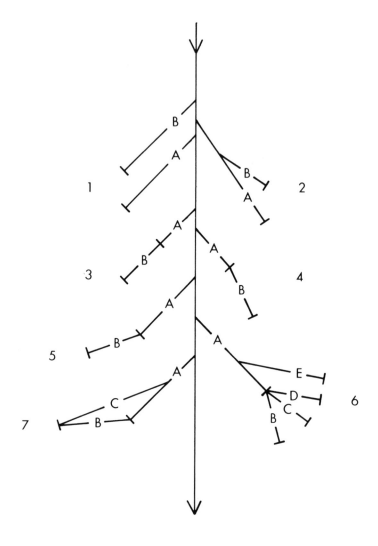

FIGURE 2.1: A structural model of irrigation systems in the Moche Valley.

vium replenishes nutrients in the cultivated fields and contributes to rapid soil formation on reclaimed desert lands. On the negative side, principal canals must have sufficient gradients to keep water moving, thereby inhibiting deposition until the fields are reached. Exceptional years of high discharge with heavy alluvium can produce silting-in of canals and thus choke off the irrigation system.

30

Topography

During the latter part of the Cenozoic Era, the river course gradually eroded southward. Alluvium was deposited on the north side of the drainage while the south side was cut into and worn away. Thus, although the lower valley is **V**-shaped in profile, the sides are asymmetrical. The north is relatively flat, with a gentle slope down to the river course. The south side is irregular and hilly, with sharp slopes. There are three prominent hills of bedrock adjacent to the south side of the river: Cerro Orejas, at the valley neck; Cerro Arena, at midvalley; and Cerro Blanco, near the valley mouth. There is only one such major eminence in the north, Cerro Cabras, situated about ten kilometers northwest of the river.

The effects of local topography upon irrigation are as follows: The south side of the valley has less potentially arable land due to its steep rise away from the river. However, the land available for irrigation can be reclaimed with relatively short lead-off canals. The north side has far more arable land, and Cerro Cabras is the only major obstacle to lateral canal expansion. However, shallow gradients require very long lead-off canals to reclaim the available land.

The distribution of lowlands with drainage problems is also affected by the asymmetrical configuration of the valley. South of the river such lands extend inward only to the vicinity of the pueblo of Moche. North of the river, lowlands are far more extensive. They stretch to the eastern margin of Chan Chan and project upvalley to the area of colonial Trujillo. Traditionally these lowlands were farmed by means of sunken gardens that tapped the high water table, rather than by canal irrigation.

Irrigation System

Arid land in the lower Moche Valley has been reclaimed by two sets of canals, one on the north and one on the south side of the river (Figure 1.2). Both draw from, and are united by, the river. The two canal sets may be conceptualized as two subsystems within a single valley-wide irrigation system (T. Topic 1971; Rodríguez Suy Suy 1973; Farrington 1974). In idealized overview, the system has the appearance of a series of nested **V**'s (**V̇**). These open toward the valley mouth, with their axis on the river.

Viewed synchronically there are, or have been, three principal ca-

31

nals in each subsystem in the study area. These are generally "Maximum Elevation Canals" (MEC), or channels having the highest elevation in some section of the valley. MECs represent the maximum limits of reclamation. Collapse of the indigenous system has resulted in the partial breakdown of all but one of these principal canals.

Areas adjacent to Chan Chan also received water from the northerly Chicama Valley by means of an intervalley canal some 80 kilometers long known as the Chicama-Moche or La Cumbre canal (Kus 1972). Upon leaving the Chicama basin, the canal transported but did not distribute water until it united with the Vinchansao MEC above Chan Chan. The combined La Cumbre–Vinchansao waters were then distributed by an extension of the latter channel that formed the MEC for the Pampas Esperanza, Río Seco, and Huanchaco.

The following summary lists the principal Moche Valley canals from east to west and gives them a letter-number designation for ease of reference. The modern counterpart canals are shown in parentheses.

Designation	*Description*
Southern subsystem:	
S1	Cerro Orejas MEC (modern Orejas)
S2	Cerro Arena–Cerro Blanco MEC (Santo Domingo)
S3	General de Moche (modern General)
Northern subsystem:	
N1	Puento Serrano MEC (modern Serrano)
N2	Moro Viejo MEC (modern Moro)
N3	Vinchansao MEC (modern Vinchansao)
N4	Mochica (modern Mochica–Valdivia)
N5	La Cumbre–Vinchansao extension, or Río Seco MEC (no modern counterpart)

Only the S3 (General) MEC remains in full use. All other canals have atrophied to varying degrees, and the intervalley N5 complex is not operational. Table 2.1 summarizes the amount of land reclaimed by the Prehispanic irrigation system and the amount of land under cultivation in recent years, as calculated from 1942 aerial photographs. The 1942 base line calculation is somewhat conservative due to the recent introduction of well pumps. This does not, however, alter the fact that the amount of land farmed in recent decades is about 30 to 40 percent less than the 211 square kilometers embraced by ancient irrigation.

The disparity between ancient and modern irrigation in the valley is mitigated by a number of factors. First, not all areas into which prehistoric reclamation channels pushed were effectively farmed. Second, not all ancient canals were equally extensive at the same time. Third, the table includes areas formerly farmed by means of sunken gardens that are now leveled and cultivated by irrigation-drainage techniques. Fourth and finally, ancient and modern agriculture entailed different crops with somewhat different land-water requirements. Table 2.1 contrasts two synchronic agricultural maximums—the 1942 historic against the total prehistoric system.

THE MODEL

A model expressing the structural principles of canal conduct as it relates to agricultural expansion, reform, and collapse is a useful heuristic device for summarizing the history of local water management. The following model is germane only to elevated terrain within the Moche Valley. It does not pertain to areas with a high water table where sunken gardens or drainage systems were critical to reclamation, nor necessarily to other valleys.

Structural Principles

In an indigenous coastal irrigation system, such as that fed by the Río Moche, agrarian expansion is dependent upon reclaiming new terrain through the construction of new water channels. Expansion can be achieved by two fundamental means. First, a new channel can be cut at an elevation above an extant canal. This is expansion by "elevational increase." The increase is obtained either by building a new canal farther upstream (Figure 2.1, No. 1) or by cutting a new channel with low gradients off an extant canal with steeper gradients (Figure 2.1, No. 2). Second, a new channel can be cut at the end of an extant canal, thereby lengthening the canal. This is expansion by "extension." The extension may have the same gradient as the parent canal (Figure 2.1, No. 3) or the gradient may differ (Figure 2.1, No. 4).

Application of the Principles

The operation of these two principles is governed by strategic considerations of topography, surface geology, water sources and quantity, engineering skills, labor investment, and the location and nature of the lands destined for reclamation.

In a small valley such as that of the Río Virú, water is limited, and a single large canal or set of canals could monopolize the water, leading to a single polity in the valley (see pp. 49–50), if it were not for features of the groundwater flow, which allow subsurface water to be tapped at several points along the river's course. Each point generates an essentially independent canal network.

The Chicama Valley, on the other hand, has a large river; therefore water is not the limiting factor. There is sufficient water and land to allow for multiple independent canal networks down the length of the river; each canal network is potentially an independent polity.

The Moche Valley presents a balance of features in which water limitations prevent the development of independent canal systems, while groundwater seeps, such as in Virú, are rare. These features tend to favor the development of a single valley-wide political structure.

The two principles are used together in varying combinations. The simplest is where a new channel is cut at the end of an extant canal, but at a lesser gradient (Figure 2.1 , No. 5). Here extension is directly combined with elevational increase in a single step. Often, however, increase follows extension, and added elevation is attained in a steplike manner by a series of new canals, each with a lesser gradient than its predecessor (Figure 2.1, No. 6). Elevational increase is also the primary means of "straightening" and shortening a water course (Figure 2.1, No. 7).

Agrarian collapse proceeds along the same two lines, but in opposite directions. Loss of arable land occurs with elevational decrease and contraction of canal courses.

AN ARCHAEOLOGICAL OVERVIEW

A brief overview of the development of irrigation in the lower valley provides background for a more detailed consideration of the lands adjacent to Chan Chan.

Lowlands

A strict reading of the elevational increase principle would argue that canal building began near the river mouth and then advanced progressively upstream. This, however, is an improper application of the model to low terrain with a high water table where flood-water farming and sunken gardens are more apropos. At Chan Chan, early monuments such as Chayhuac and Huaca Higo are built in part upon fill apparently derived from sunken field construction. This implies that nonirrigation reclamation of the lowlands was under way by or before the beginning of the Chimú dynasty.

Inception of Irrigation

Canal construction can be argued to have started during the second millennium B.C. in inland settings with well-drained soils and steep gradients. Upstream from Cerro Orejas and Cerro Galindo, which form the valley neck, there are three large early platform mounts spaced 5 to 10 kilometers apart. The location of these sites suggests that both the S1 (Orejas) and N1 (Serrano) canals had their intakes and initial channel sections established when the platforms were built in Salinar and earlier times.

The Caballo Muerto complex is situated about two and one-half kilometers below the valley neck and about two kilometers north of the river, and has radiocarbon assays ranging from about 1400 to 800 B.C. The location of the complex is evidently tied to the intake and initial section of the N3 MEC (Vinchansao). Seven of the eight principal platforms in the complex are situated above or upslope from the N3 canal. Huaca de los Reyes is farthest upslope and lies about one kilometer above the canal. It was built atop gravel alluvium that lacks fine silt deposits characteristic of reclaimed land that has been irrigated. This lack of silt indicates that the N2 (Moro) canal had yet to be extended to its ultimate MEC position above the complex. One large platform in the complex is situated about two hundred meters below the N3 canal. It could be either a very early structure trapped in irrigated land by subsequent elevational increase of the canal, or an important structure built within lands reclaimed at the time.

That the complex is associated with the N3 canal is confirmed by the copious amount of adobe used in construction, which implies a nearby source for both water and silt. The Caballo Muerto complex is the largest site with monumental construction in the valley for its time period. Its size and location are not fortuitous. The N3 canal had the greatest agricultural potential of any component in the Moche Valley irrigation system. The complex no doubt had a disproportionately large agricultural resource base to draw upon, even before the N3 canal was pushed to its present elevation.

The N4 (Mochica) canal might have been operational at an early date, as perhaps indicated by Caña Huaca, a midvalley platform about three kilometers north of the river. Caña Huaca dates to the latter part of the Initial Period, or to the Early Horizon (see Table 1.1). Two types of material were used in its construction, conical adobes made of fine silt, and clean fill of granular particles of granite. The structure also seems to have been built atop a sheet wash of granular granitic particles. The fill and basal sheet wash lack silt. Thus, the area was not irrigated at the time the platform was built. The adobes, however, point to the proximity of both water and irrigation-laid silt. The adobes are characterized by fissures between their hand-packed layers of mud, and some bricks are about one meter high. The weight of the bricks and the prevalence of fissures make it clear that the adobes could not have been transported very far without breaking. Evidence suggests that nearby farming went on at the time of construction of Caña Huaca, but a tie to the N4 canal is speculative.

The S1 (Orejas) canal probably supplied the water and silt to build the adobe platform of Huaca Huatape at the foot of Cerro Orejas. This moderate-size platform is probably a Salinar construction. It is clear that the S1 canal had not achieved its surviving maximum elevation at the time of construction, but it is not clear whether the channel passed above or below the huaca. There are low-density scatters of Salinar sherds on either side of the surviving maximum-elevation canal two to three kilometers downchannel from the platform. They indicate a similar linear extent for the channel but not a high elevation.

The S2 (Arena) canal is not securely dated at present. There is a terminal Gallinazo Phase occupation at the settlement of Huaca del Sol and Huaca de la Luna. Water requirements could have been met either by an early version of the S3 (General) canal or by the S2, which at some time underwent extension and was brought around the south side of Cerro Blanco to the foot of Huaca de la Luna. The huacas were abandoned at the end of Moche Phase IV but later were reoccupied early in Chimú times, and the S2 canal could relate to either occupation.

Moche Phase Reclamation

During the Moche Phase, all canals except the S3 (General) and perhaps the S2 (Arena) were extended and elevated to beyond the limits of modern cultivation. On the north side of the river, the N1 (Serrano) and N2 (Moro) achieved their preserved MEC status by Moche Phase IV times. Between the Caballo Muerto complex and the dissected flanks of Cerro Cabras there is a large flat tract of arable land known as the Pampa Arenal. This was reclaimed by the N3 (Vinchansao). The preserved MEC channel clipped a Moche Phase III cemetery, while Phase IV cemeteries and sherd scatters are strung out along and behind the upper canal bank. At one time, the terminal end of N3 flowed back into the lower N4 (Mochica) channel. Later, however, the N3 was elevated and extended around the flank of Cerro Cabras. Thus, Pampa Esperanza and the land above Chan Chan were re-claimed during the Moche occupation. This expansion correlates in time with the valley's first assumption of regional political hegemony over a large section of the North Coast.

Dune Formation

Today much of the south side of the valley is buried by deep deposits of unconsolidated aeolian sand. Saltating sand originates behind the beach in the vicinity of Puerto Salaverry and moves inland as crescent-shaped dunes which cross Cerro Arena, then lose momentum and blanket the valley side up to the foothills of Cerro Orejas. The dunes now cover arable land at the lower end of the S1 (Orejas) MEC, the middle section of the S2 (Arena) MEC along with the adjacent arable land, and many Salinar structures within the Cerro Arena settlement area. The settlement could not have been occupied if the sands were present, and it can be argued that formation of active dunes was a relatively late phenomenon. Adjacent to the river at the foot of Cerro Arena, there are dunes with only surface Chimú occupations, some sites of which produce Red, white, black ceramics.

At Huaca del Sol and Huaca de la Luna there are two lines of evidence for the presence of saltating sands during the Moche occupation. The first relates to burial by sand of architecture in the plain between the two huacas. To the south and east of Huaca del Sol is residential construction completely filled with clean aeolian sand. The structures are no earlier than Phase III of the Moche ceramic sequence, and intruded into the sand burying one building was a Phase IV burial. In the center of the plain between the huacas there is a cemetery with Moche and Chimú interments in the top of a low adobe platform of undetermined dimensions. The cemetery is level with the surrounding plain because the sides of the platform and areas between it and other structures are filled in by aeolian sand. The second line of evidence is stratigraphic. A deep trench in the center of the plain encountered a continuous stratum, about 75 centimeters thick, of clean aeolian sand. A comparable stratum, or the same deposit, was found in at least two test pits in the vicinity. If the sand deposits at the site are related to the dunes on the south side of the valley, as is highly probable, then dune formation began by or during Moche Phase IV times.

The impact of saltating sands on the occupation of the site is not clear. Other than intrusive burials, the sand-covered architecture shows no reuse. The structures are very well preserved and exhibit little weathering, indicating they were buried very shortly after they ceased to be used. The incursion of sand could have caused abandonment of the structures, but this cannot be proven. The profiles of the strata trench and test pits in the center of the plain are more difficult to interpret. The aeolian sand deposits are capped by one to two meters of consolidated silt mixed with occupation debris. This cap apparently represents a water-laid deposit of melted adobe with secondarily derived cultural debris.

After the site was abandoned and sand filled in and around structures, bringing the plain to a somewhat uniform level, the entire area was inundated by water. This flooding is evident from the cemetery in the adobe platform in the center of the plain. The bricks in the structure have all partially melted and reconsolidated into a compact mass. The Moche Phase interments are encased in and covered by this consolidated matrix. The later Chimú interments, some with Red, white, black ceramics in the same cemetery, are intruded into the matrix. These grave pits are distinct and filled with unconsolidated, soft sediments (Donnan and Mackey 1978), indicating that the incursion of water came after Moche Phase IV, but before the use of Red, white, black ceramics. The thorough soaking of the cemetery platform suggests that water action also accounts for the silt deposits capping the aeolian sands in the strata and test pits.

In summary, it is evident that saltating sands had encroached upon the Huaca del Sol settlement by or during Moche Phase IV but need not have been a direct cause of site abandonment. However, some south-side agricultural collapse was caused by the incursion of sand. Thus, dune formation and localized agrarian collapse on the south side of the valley were no doubt significant factors in the Moche Phase V settlement of Galindo being founded on the north side of the valley.

THE NORTH SIDE OF THE VALLEY

The following consideration of the north side of the Moche Valley focuses upon the coastal plain as defined by geomorphological criteria, and summarizes canal construction on the Pampa Esperanza , Pampa Río Seco, and Pampa Huanchaco so far as it is evident from archaeological survey.

Pampa Esperanza

The Pampa Esperanza irrigation system is illustrated in Figures 2.2 and 2.3. In these maps, contour lines are deleted; elevation decreases from top to bottom and from right to left. Canals are designated by uppercase letters, as is one major wall. Figure 2.2 is an overview of the principal canals entering and crossing the pampa . The N3 (Vinchansao) MEC enters at the top right and is seen as channels C and D on the plan. The N3 MEC unites with the intervalley La Cumbre and flows west in channel E, which is the beginning of the N5 (Seco) MEC. The N4 (Mochica) canal enters at the center right, at several stages of elevation, and is seen as channels A, B, H, I, and K. K is the modern terminus called the Valdivia canal. Shown also in Figures 2.2 and 2.3 is the Great North Wall of Chan Chan, designated G.

In general, the two maps show a sequence of principal canals built at progressively higher elevations, culminating in the Vinchansao MEC (D) linkup with the La Cumbre intervalley canal, with the N5 or Seco channel (E) carrying their combined flow.

The earliest major canal, A, is the lowest deserted channel. It was built and abandoned during the Moche Phase occupation. Subsequently channel A was partially filled in, leveled, and farmed over. Abandonment of this canal was, presumably, the product of cutting a new

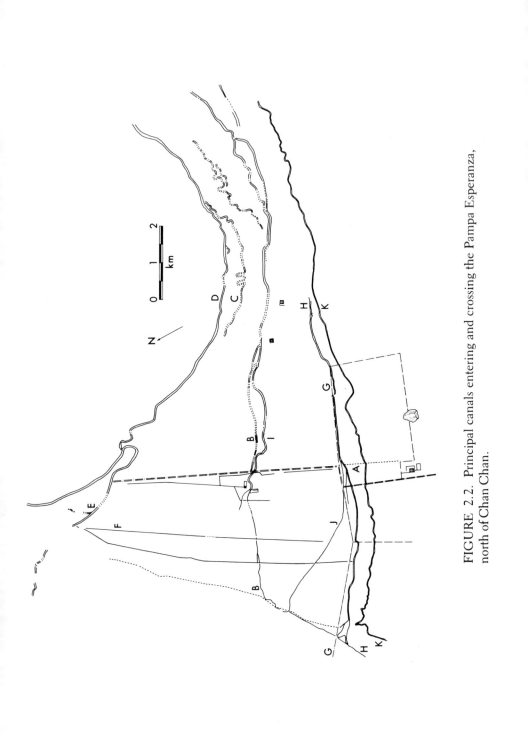

FIGURE 2.2. Principal canals entering and crossing the Pampa Esperanza, north of Chan Chan.

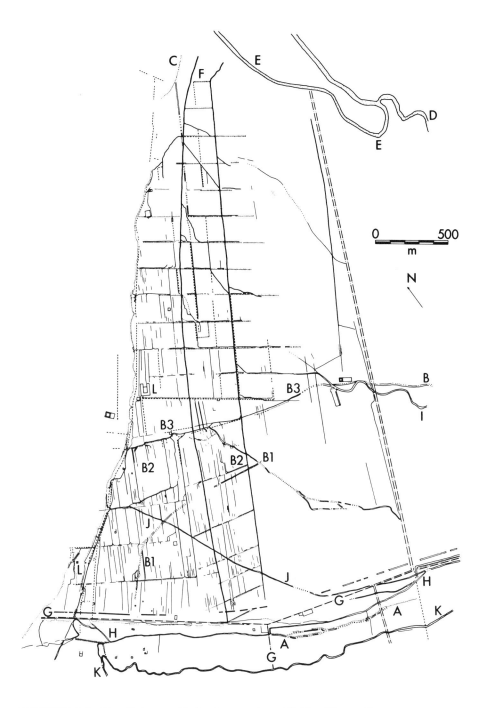

FIGURE 2.3. Detailed map of irrigation canals and fields of Pampa Esperanza, north of Chan Chan.

canal, B, the N4 (Mochica), at a higher elevation on the plain. The western end of the Mochica underwent several stages of elevational increase through time (B1, B2, B3). During its early stage, the angular end of the channel (B2) imparted an angular arrangement to certain fields in the newly reclaimed land. With the elevation and "straightening" of the watercourse, additional new fields were laid out in a rectilinear pattern that was also partially extended to the older area of cultivation. The western 5 to 10 kilometers of the N4 (Mochica) canal were presumably abandoned during the Moche Phase in response to the opening of the Vinchansao MEC.

Today the N4 transports water along the southwestern edge of Pampa Esperanza to within two kilometers of the mouth of the Río Seco and the settlement of Huanchaco. Huanchaco has a Prehispanic occupation going back in time at least to the Salinar Phase, and the settlement no doubt received water from the N4 by Moche times if not earlier. When the early A channel was cut, it had greater elevation and potential reach than it does today and could easily have extended to the south side of the mouth of the Río Seco.

During the fourth phase of the Moche occupation, the Vinchansao was extended up to the northwest corner of Pampa Esperanza. The early course of the canal is not entirely preserved. Its initial channel is C, and its distal end may be channel E. A series of secondary canals fed by the MEC ran parallel to each other and descended the pampa perpendicularly. Fields on the new land were laid out in a regimented rectilinear manner.

Early in the Chimú dynasty, construction of the intervalley canal was completed. Tying it into the valley system required elevating the distal end of the Vinchansao (D) and cutting a major channel, E, to carry the combined waters west. The old Moche Phase end of the Vinchansao may or may not have formerly occupied channel E. In either case, the linkup of the intervalley canal required substantial reworking of the principal canals at the northwest end of the pampa. In the process, the old secondary canals feeding the Esperanza fields were blocked and cut off, necessitating the Chimú construction of new distribution channels. Two (F) were opened on the western side of the pampa and one in the center of the region.

There are two rural administrative centers on the western edge of the pampa (Figure 2.3, L) of the general type defined by Keatinge (1974) and by Keatinge and Day (1974). C-shaped audiencia variants (Andrews 1974) are associated with the Esperanza centers, which may have been built to administer agrarian reform accompanying the new (F) distribution channels. Whatever the case, the centers went out of use at an early date, and feeder canals and fields supplied by the F channels were cut into and around the buildings.

Midway into the Chimú dynasty, when Ciudadela Gran Chimú was in use and its open annexes were being constructed, the Great North Wall of Chan Chan, G, was extended westward some four kilometers. The wall ran perpendicular to Pampa Esperanza and Pampa Río Seco and blocked the distribution canals there. Blocking the fields below the wall led to a water surfeit above the wall. To alleviate the situation, excavation of two new canals was begun. These were adjacent to the wall with one channel paralleling it on either side. The downslope canal was presumably intended to water the stranded fields by tapping into a still functional section of the N4 canal east of the pampa.

Before the two channels were completed, a vast quantity of water spread over Pampa Esperanza, eroding fields and furrows. A large deposit of fine alluvium, transported by sheet wash, filled in the two unfinished channels. The channels have a total length of about five kilometers, and alluviation and water damage are evident for their entire course, particularly in the Pampa Río Seco, where extensive sections of the Great North Wall were washed away and never repaired. A truly prodigious flow is therefore implied.

There is straightforward evidence that the water came essentially all at once and that the region never again experienced comparable water damage. First, principal canals in use at the time, including the N5 (Seco), N3 (Vinchansao), and La Cumbre were washed out at many points along their courses. In quebradas, water flowing from upslope, above a canal, removed large sections of channel, or if the canal was aqueducted, large sections of the support structure were washed away. Destroyed areas were subsequently repaired. Repaired canal sections either have never washed out or have been damaged substantially less than before the original reconstruction. Second, in some cases of extensive destruction the area of damaged channel was bypassed by a new section of canal built at a slightly higher elevation. These bypasses either have never washed out or have washed out with measurably less damage than the original damage to the abandoned channel. Third, canals abandoned prior to the epoch of extensive water damage are silted in or cut through, whereas canals cut afterward, that is, channels H, J, and I, show comparatively little erosion or alluvial filling. Fourth, and finally, in fields, washed-out furrows that were repaired have not been washed out again.

Repair of the principal canals did not alter the situation created by construction of the Great North Wall of Chan Chan, the Esperanza stretch of which was rebuilt after the wash-out. To feed the fields below the wall, a new channel, H, was cut. It was a rather irregular canal, and in the west it dropped into and followed the abandoned course of canal A. Canal H was fed by the N4 (Mochica) canal, which suffered elevational decrease and was essentially in its modern course, K. This loss of elevation derives from the original abandonment of the western section of the N4 canal after replacement by the higher N3–N5 MEC. The latter could supply the fields above the Great North Wall, and when the N4 was reactivated, it was cut at a lower elevation, since its purpose was to supply fields below the wall.

Agrarian collapse on Pampa Esperanza took place rather rapidly. The N5 MEC and intervalley linkup were abandoned as were all lands north of B, the N4 maximum-elevation channel. An attempt was made to revitalize canal B by cutting a new channel, I, in and below the old filled-in course. This attempt bisected the large walled road leading out of Chan Chan, and the road was presumably no longer in use. It is unclear whether I was successful; it seems not to have been.

Another revitalization attempt was made by cutting a new channel, J, off of canal H. But the gradient was incorrectly calculated and J channel never carried water. Finally, canal H dropped from use. Collapse eventually stabilized and stopped with the opening of canal K, the modern maximum-elevation channel.

Pampa Río Seco and Pampa Huanchaco

Pampa Río Seco and Pampa Huanchaco are northward extensions of the coastal plain. Pampa Río Seco is the cobble- and gravel-strewn flood plain, about five kilometers wide, of a small drainage basin that last discharged water into the Pacific during the 1925 niño. This rocky plain has less agricultural potential than the level alluvial lands of the flanking pampas. The Moche Phase N3 and N4 canals conformed to this structural division of the coastal plain by reclaiming the entirety of Pampa Esperanza and avoiding the Río Seco.

Reclamation of the two western pampas was a Chimú undertaking.

Two canals were involved, and their relationship is shown in Figure 2.4, a plan map of the El Milagro plain, which is in the center of Pampa Río Seco. Channel A is the earlier and lower water course, while Channel B is the later N5 (Seco) MEC. East of the Milagro plain, channel A was not preserved. Its water source was, apparently, the N3 (Vinchansao) before the N3 was elevated and linked up with La Cumbre. The A channel crosses the Milagro plain and Pampa Río Seco and then extends up to and along the eastern edge of Pampa Huanchaco. It is the first and earliest preserved channel in both pampas. In the center of the Milagro plain the channel is associated with a small administrative center, C, that contains a poorly preserved elongated U-shaped audiencia variant. At some time after channel B, the N5 MEC, was built, both the A and B canals were washed out at many points. Only the eastern kilometer or so of the A channel was repaired, and this repaired section was fed by a small canal dropping down the eastern edge of the Milagro plain from the B channel.

Construction of the B channel was a complex matter that entailed a number of surveying errors and the cutting of abortive channels. Before B was cut, half a kilometer across the Milagro plain a rural administrative center, D, was built near its projected course. The center has a trocadero audiencia variant (see Kolata, Chapter 4), and it presumably served to supervise construction of the canal. The canal course was originally miscalculated, and the revised course clipped one of the wings of the structure.

At the western edge of the plain, channel A passes above El Milagro de San José, E, the largest and most elaborate of the known administrative centers. If this site was functionally related to channel B or to the lands it watered, then it was the last administrative center built in conjunction with the valley irrigation system. The complex contains a number of different types of audiencia variants, including C-and elongated U-shaped forms. The only Chan Chan compound that has analogues for almost all the Milagro audiencia variants is Uhle, one of the earliest monumental enclosures.

On Pampa Huanchaco the constructional history of the N5 MEC, or B channel, is extremely complex. For the sake of simplicity this history can be reduced to three stages. The first entailed extending the N5 canal out of the Río Seco flood plain and onto Pampa Huanchaco. This stage brought water to a somewhat higher elevation than was attained by the earlier Milagro A channel. However, the N5 canal was

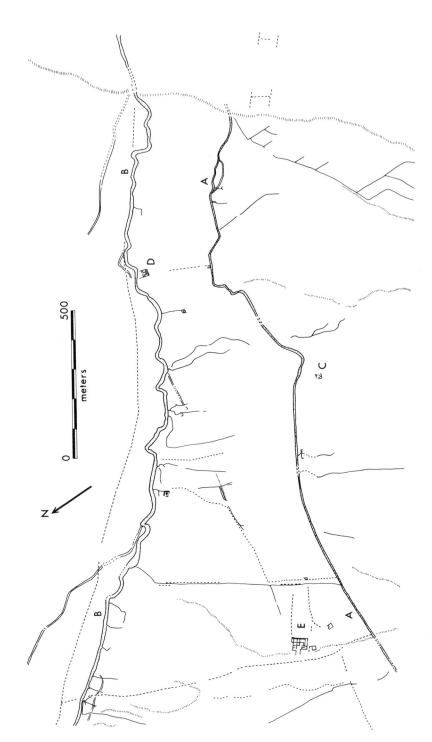

FIGURE 2.4. Two Chimú canals on the Pampa Río Seco. The lower canal (A) is earlier than the upper canal (B).

simply turned downslope and worked into the earlier field system. The second stage was a truly massive reclamation project. The N5 canal was elevated to its preserved MEC status and extended many kilometers to the ocean bluff, encompassing virtually all flat land on the pampa. One part of the project entailed constructing a large walled road that crossed the pampa and the irrigation system. Feeder canals passed under the road through culverts (T. Topic 1971). The road dropped into the Río Seco and subsequently led to Chan Chan. In the Río Seco a state-instigated settlement known as Cerro Virgen was built on both sides of the road (Keatinge 1975b). Before this massive reclamation project was fully completed and the elevated N5 MEC was operational, vast quantities of water washed over the pampa obliterating extensive sections of the MEC, silting in feeder channels, and eroding the fields fed by the early A canal. In the third and final stage, the N5 MEC was repaired along all but the last few kilometers of its course. However, it never carried water the complete length of the repaired course. Instead, as in the first stage, the canal was turned downslope and worked into the earlier Milagro A channel field system. The A canal had also been washed out by flooding, but was never repaired because of replacement by the N5 MEC.

Agrarian collapse on the Pampa Río Seco and Pampa Huanchaco was swift and complete. The N5 MEC dropped from use, and there is no evidence of any later revitalization attempts.

AGRARIAN COLLAPSE

In the Moche Valley there is no evidence of agrarian collapse due to endogenous causes such as salinization or bureaucratic mismanagement of irrigation. There are, however, two cases of collapse due to exogenous causes.

The first collapse was due to dune formation on the south side of the valley. The process was under way during Moche Phase IV times, and involved a permanent loss of arable land.

The second collapse of the irrigation systems also had its origin in nature but was caused by massive destruction by flooding. The same event is implicated in the flooding of the plain between the Huaca del Sol and Huaca de la Luna but not in the triggering of the active dune formation that swamped the south side of the valley at a substantially earlier date.

Flooding was not due simply to a rise in the Río Moche. High elevation canals well above the river flood plain and canals crossing the Río Seco were washed out by waters descending from above the channels. Torrential rains are, thus, clearly a factor.

On the desert coast of Peru torrential rains are never localized events descending solely on one valley or region. Rains of consequence, such as those of 1925, are always associated with niño meteorological and current reversals. Niños affect vast areas of the coast, but are more intense in the north of Peru than the south. Thus, the massive wash-out of the Moche Valley irrigation system can be attributed to niño-induced flooding.

The irrigation system never experienced subsequent water damage of comparable magnitude. Even after abandonment of the northern pampas the combined erosional effects of the 1925 rains and all prior niños have been substantially and measurably less than the devastation that washed out the Chimú irrigation system. Thus, a niño of truly catastrophic scope—far larger than any after the Spanish Conquest—is implied.

The impact of this phenomenon upon coastal civilization was staggering. All means and modes of agricultural production were no doubt destroyed, and the damage must have required years to repair. Foodstuff stored in adobe structures, floor pits, or sunken vessels must have been wiped out. It is no coincidence that the Ñaymlap account of Prehispanic rulers in the Lambayeque area mentions not only a cataclysmic flood of "30 days" duration, but an ensuing "interregnum" period of famine and pestilence (Kosok 1965). Nor does it seem coincidental that the Chimú conquest of Lambayeque followed upon the interregnum. The Chimú had only to reconstruct one major canal—the N3—to regain their economic footing, whereas reconstruction of the Lambayeque irrigation complex entailed repairing a multitude of channels.

Be that as it may, the Chan Chan dynasty recovered from the niño cataclysm and reconstructed the irrigation system with some obvious losses. Although rebuilt, the Pampa Huanchaco system never carried water again, which implies that the N5 canal was also inoperative. Pampa Río Seco dropped from use, in turn suggesting that there may have been substantial problems with reconstructing La Cumbre canal. The N3 was rebuilt, and assuming that it worked, the irrigation system returned to the approximate size it had been at the end of Moche Phase reclamation.

48

Abandonment of Pampa Esperanza and the land in front of Chan Chan was probably closely linked to the abandonment of the city. There are no indications that the pampa was cultivated during either the Inca or the Spanish occupations. Spanish chronicles do not mention Chan Chan as being occupied at the time of European contact. Survey and excavation at Chan Chan have not revealed Inca artifacts in a context associated with the primary occupation of the ciudadelas or monumental architecture. Yet it is fully evident that under Inca aegis a monumental compound based on Chan Chan prototypes was built at Chiquitoy in the Chicama Valley (Conrad 1974).

Given this situation, one could argue for the following scenario: After the conquest of Chimor, the Inca deliberately undermined the economic power and prestige of the Chimú, their largest and only effective rivals for Andean hegemony. In the Moche Valley this entailed cutting—literally or figuratively—the N3 MEC, thereby undercutting the valley's agrarian base. The administrative functions formerly performed by Chan Chan were reduced and shifted to Chiquitoy. Finally, the Chimú nobility was either forcibly relocated within the Moche Valley or relocated when the land in front of Chan Chan and the city itself reverted to desert.

COMPARISONS

The following discussion assumes a general, but not universal, correlation between economic and political unity. It assumes that areas economically integrated are likely to have a higher incidence of political integration than regions lacking economic unity.

In coastal Peru any canal taking water directly from a river constitutes a unit of agricultural production that is structurally independent. Economic fortunes relate principally to the amount of water that can be diverted to fields and the area of land that can be irrigated. Economic production is not related to other canals feeding off the same river so long as there is equal access to river water, and so long as one canal is not dependent upon or affected by drainage or runoff from another canal. If there is equal water access, and if the independent canals feeding off a river irrigate about the same amount of land and have roughly comparable levels of economic output, then there is a pattern of comparable but autonomous units of agricultural production. Following from the assumed correlation between economic and political unity, there will also be a matching pattern of comparable but autonomous polities.

This, of course, is an idealized model, but it is found in both the Virú and Chicama valleys. Each valley has a multitude of independent canals, and these are associated with a multitude of moderate- or large-sized sites that can be interpreted as sociopolitical foci. Both valleys lack sites of disproportionately large size such as Chan Chan that might be construed as a "central place" exercising hegemony over the entire valley or other valleys. In other words, it is possible to see these valleys as having been divided into multiple autonomous econo-political units.

The Moche Valley stands in contrast to its flanking valleys. Starting with the Caballo Muerto complex, there is only one large site in the lower valley with massive monumental architecture at any one time period. Local sites contemporary with a principal center have little monumental architecture, and when present it represents a tenth or less of the labor investment expressed at the principal center. This distinction seems to be a straightforward expression of political unity in the lower Moche Valley. It can be argued that this unity relates to the nature of the local irrigation system.

IRRIGATION AND POLITICAL ORGANIZATION

The interplay among society, political structure, and subsistence based upon artificial water distribution has been investigated by many scholars, most notably Wittfogel (1957). Some totally reject Wittfogel's formulations, while others argue for modifications or propose alternative hypotheses. Yet few deny the fundamental relationship among irrigation, social institutions, and political organization. There is also limited consensus that, once established, irrigation is associated with a tendency toward expansion of centralized authority (Downing and Gibson 1974:x).

Our position is that there is a definite correlation between the structure of coastal irrigation systems and the structure of the political systems they support. It would be naive to see such correlations as anything other than highly complex, and basically unexplored in the Andean area. In the case of the Virú and Chicama valleys, we have advanced a simplified model that ties multiple canals with multiple units of economic production that in turn correlate with the support of multiple independent polities. In the case of the Moche Valley we are advancing an antithetical model.

The argument is as follows: There were only two canals of consequence in the Moche Valley system, the N3 (Vinchansao) and the N4 (Mochica), and the latter ultimately replaced the former. There was never parity among the independent canals feeding off the Río Moche. The N3 always irrigated more land and had greater economic potential than other local canals. Control of the N3 canal meant initially nominal and ultimately real control of the lower valley. This control is first evident at Caballo Muerto; the valley was either politically unified at this time or was about to be. The polity based at Huaca del Sol and Huaca de la Luna developed out of this centralized political tradition and essentially completed the trend toward economic unity by extending the N3 to encompass all of Pampa Esperanza, with the consequent partial dropout of the N4 canal. At the same time, Moche Phase foreign conquest was essentially a matter of pitting a unified population against adjacent populations that were not unified. The rise of the Chimú dynasty was basically a replay of these Moche themes. It grew out of a centralized political tradition. The Chimú economic base was expanded first by pushing into Pampa Río Seco and Pampa Huanchaco via the Milagro A channel, and then by bringing Río Chicama water to the coastal plain, by which time the conquest of Chicama must have been completed. Collapse of the Chimú achievement still left the productive north side of the valley relatively integrated even with only the atrophied N3 and N4 canals. These had never supported independent rival polities. Thus, colonial Trujillo was founded in the setting of a prior centralized bureaucracy and a still relatively uniform economic system.

Granted, this is a rather ambitious scenario. It does, however, address the pattern of repeated political ascendency of the Moche Valley as well as the extension of hegemony over larger populations, and avoids the dismissal of these events as historical accidents.

TABLE 2.1
AREAS OF RECLAIMED LAND

	Prehispanic and Modern				
	A	B	C	D	E
I. North Side					
A. Modern					
1. Moro	6.456	6.27	3.94	5.03	3.21
2. Vinchansao	15.183	14.74	9.27	11.83	7.54
3. Mochica-Valdivia	81.401	79.00	49.68	63.43	40.42
B. Prehispanic					
1. Puente Serrano MEC	0.646		0.39		0.15
2. Moro Viejo MEC	8.636		5.27		4.29
3. Vinchansao MEC	9.940		6.07		4.94
4. Mochica Principal Canal					
a. First raise	0.914		0.56		0.45
b. Second raise	7.608		4.64		3.78
5. Lower Valdivia Pampa	13.550		8.27		6.73
6. Pampa Rio Seco					
a. Upper	15.543		9.49		7.72
b. Lower	3.989		2.43		1.98
II. South Side					
A. Modern					
1. Cerro Oreja	1.393	5.51	3.71	1.09	0.69
2. Santo Domingo	7.385	29.20	19.68	5.75	3.67
3. General de Moche	16.514	65.29	44.01	12.87	8.20
B. Prehispanic					
1. Cerro Oreja MEC	1.694		4.51		0.84
2. Cerro Arena/ Cerro Blanco MEC	10.540		28.09		5.23

	F	G	H	I
III. Totals				
A. North Side				
1. Modern	103.040	62.88	80.29	51.16
2. Prehispanic	163.866	100.00		81.37
3. Prehispanic not now in cultivation	60.826	37.12		30.20
B. South Side				
1. Modern	25.292	67.40	19.71	12.56
2. Prehispanic	37.526	100.00		18.63

	A	B	C
3. Prehispanic not now in cultivation	12.234	32.60	6.07
C. Whole Valley			
1. Modern	128.332		63.72
2. Prehispanic	201.392		100.00

EXPLANATION:

A — Area in square kilometers.

B — Area irrigated by a given canal/total modern irrigated area on that side of the river (as %; modern canals only).

C — Area irrigated by a given canal/total Prehispanic irrigated area on that side of the river (as %).

D — Area irrigated by a given canal/total modern irrigated area in the valley (as %).

E — Area irrigated by a given canal/total Prehispanic irrigated area in the valley (as %).

F — Area in square kilometers.

G — Total modern irrigated area on a given side of the river/total Prehispanic irrigated area for that side (as %).

H — Total modern irrigated area on a given side of the river/total irrigated area in the valley (as %).

I — Total irrigated area on a given side of the river/total Prehispanic irrigated area in the valley (as %; except in III.C., where it is the total irrigated area in the valley/total Prehispanic irrigated area in the valley).

3

Ciudadelas: Their Form and Function

KENT C. DAY

Heritage Museum
Layton, Utah

Central, or nuclear, Chan Chan (Figure 3.1) covers an area of about six square kilometers. This area contains ten large rectangular enclosures, nine of which share many formal architectural characteristics in common. Theses particular enclosures are called ciudadelas, and they are named (clockwise from 12, Figure 3.1) Squier, Gran Chimú, Bandelier, Uhle, Chayhuac, Tschudi, Rivero, Laberinto, and Velarde. The exceptional enclosure is Tello, which is designated a compound. The nine ciudadelas are all rectangular in plan, oriented along an approximate north-south axis, and arranged in a rough rectangle around the center of the site. In area the ciudadelas range from 87,900 square meters (Ciudadela Rivero) to 221,000 square meters (Ciudadela Gran Chimú). The other ciudadelas have an average area of about 140,000 square meters.

Ciudadelas are surrounded by battered adobe walls up to nine meters high. The base of these walls is one and one-half to two meters thick, and they were built upon a layer of large boulders that is partially submerged in the earth. Adobes in these walls were laid up in blocklike sections about two meters square with well-defined horizontal and

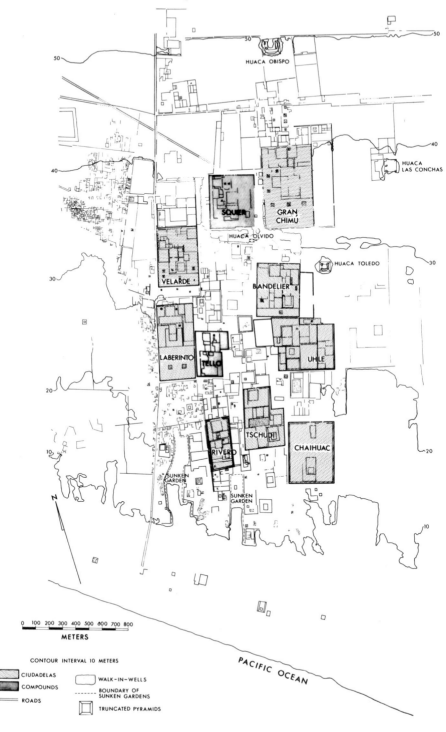

FIGURE 3.1. Plan map of central or nuclear Chan Chan.

vertical joints. Each block is surrounded with mortared, evenly laid, but unbonded adobes. This framework is filled with other adobes, frequently in a jumbled mass as if they were hurriedly dumped in place. Large canes that sometimes protrude above the walls or are exposed in collapsed walls are usually located at the line of vertical joints. These joints and canes were probably construction devices used to record the labor units expended in the building of the walls. Although tapia (rammed earth) was not used extensively at Chan Chan, the great tapia walls in Ciudadela Rivero and the tapia burial platforms in Ciudadelas Rivero and Bandelier all exhibit joints that indicate they were also constructed in sections. Clear impressions of plain-weave textiles on recently exposed vertical sides of tapia sections indicate the sections were made of a sticky mass of gravel and clay that was pounded into shape. Although it is possible that tapia structures were built in sections to allow drying and prevent collapse, it is more likely that the sections are records of labor units.

The interiors of ciudadelas are arranged in a common pattern even though there are individual differences that give each ciudadela a distinctive character. All ciudadelas have major internal divisions labeled north sector, central sector, canchón, or wing. These divisions vary in size but retain the same relative positions and contain fundamentally the same layout of similar structures in all of the ciudadelas. For present purposes, Ciudadela Rivero (Figure 3.2) is used as a standard model for the ciudadelas.

In each ciudadela there is a single entrance near the center of the north wall that allows access to the north sector and hence, the rest of the enclosure. Ciudadela Rivero is exceptional in that it also has an entrance through the west wall. However, this side entrance does not allow as direct access to the ciudadela as the standard north entrance. The north entrance to Ciudadela Rivero is about a meter and a half wide and five meters long. Jambs on the outer corners of the entrance were small, square wooden posts set flush in each corner of the wall. The sides of the entrance were decorated with carved wooden figures set in niches. A narrow path worn in the plaster floor indicated that the majority of pedestrians who entered and left the ciudadela walked in single file or one by one. The single north entrance to Ciudadela Tschudi appears to be the same size as the north entrance to Ciudadela Rivero but undecorated. Burned material on the floor of the entrance to Ciudadela Rivero and scorched adobes on each wall above the entrance indicate it had a wooden lintel surmounted by adobes.

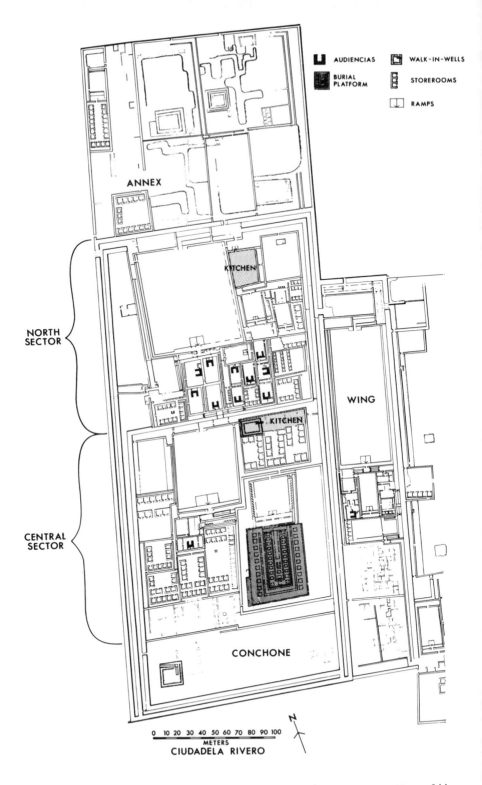

FIGURE 3.2. Plan of Ciudadela Rivero. Note the strategic position of U-shaped audiencias in relationship to storerooms in the north and central sectors (Day 1973).

North entrances give access to east-west corridors that lead to large entry courts in the north end of the north sectors. These courts have low benches along the east and west sides and a pilastered entrance in the north wall. There are usually openings near the north ends of the east and west walls that give access to other corridors. A high bench stands along the south wall of the entry court, and a central ramp rises from the court floor to this bench. In every case these ramps were looted. Occasional finds of human bone, scraps of textiles, and sherds in backdirt beside the ramps give evidence that the ramps contained dedicatory burials. There are mud friezes of animals and horizontal "clapboards" on the walls of the entry court in Ciudadela Tschudi. In the entry court walls of Ciudadela Laberinto there are wall niches and geometric mud friezes of birds. The "Hall of the Arabesques" in Ciudadela Gran Chimú (Squier 1877) is the south wall of an entry court. Entry courts also contain remains of at least one free-standing colonnade located near the north central part of the court. These colonnades were low rectangular platforms with wooden columns spaced about one and one-half meters apart.

Entrances in the south wall of the entry courts open to corridors that contained rows of wooden columns that supported cane, reed, and earth roofs. Auxiliary courts are located to the east and west of these corridors. A complex system of narrow corridors connects the auxiliary courts to groups of U-shaped structures that occur singly or in pairs within relatively small courtyards.

The most common U-shaped structures in this context within ciudadelas are called audiencias, which are square to slightly rectangular in plan and have floor areas of five to six square meters. Audiencias are open at one end, and their walls are about one meter thick. There is a pair of niches on the inside face of each wall about a meter above the audiencia floors. Large wooden posts occur in audiencia walls and a pair of post molds is usually located at both sides of the open end in front of audiencias. Debris on the floors indicates that audiencias had heavy roofs made of cane and reeds tied with twine and covered with a thick layer of earth. Although the form of the roofs is not known, it is possible that they were a single-shed or assymetrical gable arrangement as depicted in fine line drawings on Mochica pottery or modeled on Chimú vessels.

There are small rooms beside or behind audiencias. In some cases there is another small U-shaped structure in the same court as an audiencia. Some audiencias are undecorated, and others have elaborate mud friezes of birds or geometric designs on their walls.

Most audiencias were burned or looted soon after the site was abandoned. Wooden posts were torn from walls and pits dug in the floors. Backdirt from these pits frequently contained human bone, an indication, later confirmed by Andrews (1974), that burials were common within or in front of audiencias.

There are yet more narrow corridors beyond the audiencias that connect them to other courts containing storerooms. Storerooms are two to four meters square, have walls about one meter thick, and are arranged in contiguous rows. The rows are arranged in front of one another or in a U-shaped arrangement along three sides of a court. Every storeroom has a single entrance about a meter high, and the entrances always face the interior of the court. The well-preserved rows of storerooms in various ciudadelas have steeply sloped walls that undoubtedly supported a continuous gabled roof along each row.

Although nothing was found in the excavated storerooms in Ciudadela Rivero, the form, layout, and elevated entrances of the structures are analogous to Inca storerooms. In addition, there was nothing associated with the storerooms at Chan Chan to suggest the structures were used as residences or as workshops as formerly supposed (Squier 1877; Mason 1957). Furthermore, the barren interiors of storerooms indicate they were systematically emptied of whatever goods they contained. Incidentally, storerooms seldom, if ever, contain evidence of having been burned or looted.

The central sectors of ciudadelas have the same general layout as the north sectors. The two sectors are separated by a large wall that has an entrance similar to the principal entrance to ciudadelas. Central sectors have entry courts, corridors, audiencias, and storerooms in much the same relative positions as those structures in north sectors. Central sectors, however, consistently have fewer audiencias and more storerooms than north sectors. Central sectors are, by their very location, more isolated and difficult to enter than north sectors. Due to the greater isolation, it is clear that the larger numbers of storerooms in central sectors were more secure than those located elsewhere in ciudadelas.

With the exception of Ciudadela Laberinto, there is a burial platform in or adjacent to the southeast corner of central sectors of ciudadelas. Burial platforms (Conrad, Chapter 5) are the most heavily and thoroughly looted structures in ciudadelas. The burial platform in Ciudadela Rivero, for instance, is little more than a heap of tapia blocks riddled with holes, trenches, and tunnels. Huge piles of backdirt surround burial platforms except in Ciudadela Tschudi where the debris was recently removed by the Comité Pro Restauración de Chan Chan.

A wing is attached to the east side of Ciudadela Rivero or incorporated into the east side of central sectors of other ciudadelas. Like north and central sectors, wings contain entry courts, corridors, audiencias, and storerooms. The layout of these structures follows the same general pattern as elsewhere in the ciudadelas, but because wings are the smallest interior divisions of ciudadelas, they contain fewer structures than the other sectors.

The back or south ends of ciudadelas are called canchones, a term commonly used in Peru to designate large, relatively level rectangular areas. Canchones in ciudadelas lack formal architecture comparable to that in other interior divisions. Canchones contain walk-in wells, domestic debris, and remains of informal, compactly arranged rooms. Access to canchones is by means of corridors from north sectors that stretch the length of the west side of ciudadelas, thus avoiding passage through central sectors. Canchones apparently housed a resident population of low-status retainers (McGrath 1973), probably service and maintenance personnel.

OTHER FORMS OF ARCHITECTURE AT CHAN CHAN

Four other forms of architecture were found at Chan Chan. They are discussed briefly here in order that the ciudadelas may be understood in context. Only then is interpretation of the ciudadelas' function possible.

Elite compounds. Annexes are attached to the north ends of ciudadelas and form a substantial barrier in front of the north entrances. Annexes are highly variable in size and are not as formally planned as the divisions within the ciudadelas. Although the annex of Ciudadela Rivero is aligned with the rest of the enclosure and contains storerooms and wells, it, like other annexes, is classified as an elite compound and is not considered an integral part of the ciudadela.

Between and beside the ciudadelas there are extensive areas of elite compounds (Klymyshyn, Chapter 6). The architecture here is less grand than that of the compounds but has formally planned elements nonetheless.

SIAR. Tracts of small irregularly agglutinated rooms—presented under the acronym SIAR (J. Topic, Chapter 7), or nucleated habitations (West 1970)—are concentrated along the western side of the site and occur among some of the elite compounds. If SIAR existed on the east side of the site, they were destroyed by intensive modern cultivation of that area.

Huacas. There are four huacas on the outskirts of Chan Chan. The largest of these, Huaca Obispo, is located to the north. It was probably square in plan, but a huge trench was dug into it from the north, leaving a U-shaped mound of rubble with an apron of backdirt along the north side. This destruction apparently occurred during the sixteenth or seventeenth centuries because Huaca Obispo was already a ruin when Martínez de Compañon studied the site. Despite destruction, it is estimated that Huaca Obispo was about 100 meters square at its base and 20 meters high. When I briefly examined Huaca Obispo, I found that it was constructed of water-worn cobbles packed into 1½- to 2-meter square "frames" or blocks of carefully laid cobbles. These construction units are arranged side by side throughout the interior of the huaca. The outer shell of Huaca Obispo was a series of adobe and mud plaster terraces about 1½ meters wide separated by high, slightly battered adobe walls. There are free-standing adobe walls at least 1 meter high along the edges of the terraces, giving the impression that each terrace was like a corridor that went around the huaca. Nothing was found on the summit, nor was there any evidence of an access system to the summit and terraces.

Huaca Toledo is located on the east side of the site. It is smaller than Huaca Obispo (perhaps 75 meters square at its base and 15 meters high) and is little more than a heap of cobbles. The near total destruction of Huaca Toledo lends credence to persistent local stories of a large treasure's having been found there during the Colonial Period.

Huaca Las Conchas lies northeast of Huaca Toledo. The former was built of adobes and derives its name from the looters' discovery of mud plaster shells appliquéd to the walls of the huaca. There is a series of small rectangular enclosures adjacent to one another beside the huaca.

62

Huaca El Higo is located south of Huaca Las Conchas in the midst of a sugarcane field. Probably quite extensive at one time, this huaca presently consists of mounds of melted adobe and traces of walls.

Sunken Gardens and Cemetery. There are two important features on the bluff along the southern edge of Chan Chan . One of these is a series of large sunken gardens also called mahamaes, or wachaques (Parsons 1968; Rowe 1969; Moseley 1969a), dug into the edge of the bluff along the lower part of dry stream channels. Crops are now grown in these sunken gardens, and apparently they were used for this purpose in the past. The gardens, however, are relatively small in comparison with the size of Chan Chan and could not have supplied a particularly significant amount of food for the residents of the site. On the other hand, gravel and soil removed from the gardens were possibly used as building material (Rowe 1969).

The other feature along the bluff to the south of the site is a large cemetery. This area is a windblown strip of sand pockmarked with looted graves and pits dug into backdirt. Like most looted cemeteries on the Peruvian coast, there are scraps of textiles, moldering bones, pottery fragments, and pieces of wood scattered amid the desolation.

SIGNIFICANCE OF THE GREAT ENCLOSURES

There are ten great enclosures at Chan Chan and there were ten Chimú kings (Rowe 1948; Rostworowski 1961). Since there are no other structures at the site as monumental and elaborate as the large enclosures, it is assumed that each was a royal residence during the uninterrupted succession of the ten Chimú rulers. It follows, therefore, that the enclosures were built sequentially (Kolata, Chapter 4) and that older ones were maintained even as new ones were built. There is no superimposition of large enclosures to aid in the determination of the construction sequence. Furthermore, ceramics found within the enclosures have not been particularly useful in defining each generation represented by the construction of an enclosure. Everyone associated with the Chan Chan–Moche Valley Project agrees there is a construction sequence at Chan Chan, but opinions (Day 1973; Andrews 1972; J. Topic 1977; Conrad 1974) differ amiably from one another and from the sequence presented here by Kolata (Chapter 4).

The nine enclosures called ciudadelas are the most formally planned and uniform enclosures. Each has high surrounding walls, a single principal entrance, and a quadripartite interior layout. A repeated pattern of corridors, courts, more corridors, audiencias, yet more corridors, and storerooms occurs within three of the interior divisions of ciudadelas. The interrelationships of the structures coupled with the complex corridor system are the keys to understanding the function and importance of ciudadelas. Storerooms in ciudadelas housed many more goods than did storerooms elsewhere in the site. These storage facilities could only be reached by a system of corridors that passed by audiencias. It is the strategic position of these U-shaped structures rather than anything inherent in their form that indicates audiencias were administrative control points in ciudadelas. Furthermore, the concentration of audiencias and storerooms within ciudadelas demonstrates that these particular enclosures were major administrative centers and bureaucratic headquarters of the Chimú empire.

Administrative audiencias and storerooms were probably actively used during the occupation of a ciudadela. The products or other materials stored in ciudadelas were probably rotated continuously to provide social sustenance and panoply for royalty, to recompense the labor investment for construction and maintenance, and to absorb further production. Large quantities of goods were consumed at the death of a monarch to stock his burial platform. Perhaps these goods were provided for a happy afterlife of the deceased king, but as long as production remained high, it was necessary to dispose of goods in order to keep the system operating.

In a sense the ciudadelas were the headquarters of a consumer class in a bureaucratic hierarchical society. Moreover, Chan Chan was probably the seat of a nonmechanized industrial society where products were mass-produced by artisans and craftsmen in the SIAR (J. Topic, Chapter 7). Perhaps these products filtered through officials in elite compounds and accumulated in royal ciudadelas. Since no monetary system existed in Peru before the arrival of the Spaniards, the Chimú—like their Inca successors—probably exchanged labor, goods, services, and access to land on the basis of reciprocity and according to social standing.

Storage facilities in ciudadelas, of course, could only hold a finite volume of goods at one time. The inventory had to turn over in order to provide the opportunity for people to produce materials or supply labor as their contribution to the reciprocal network. Therefore, goods had to be dispensed or recycled as well as conspicuously consumed in ceremonies or in tomb offerings by ciudadela residents.

The royal administration at Chan Chan benefited materially in this system but was also obliged to do so in order to prevent unemployment for the workers. Such a condition would cause the system to collapse back to its roots in strictly local social and reciprocal relationships. Furthermore, the administrators were under constant pressure from the population to provide arable land either through military conquest or amplification of irrigation canals. In the latter case, the administration was vulnerable because an unpredictable natural disaster such as a torrential rain or severe earthquake could result in widespread suffering and regicide. An event like this apparently occurred at least once on the North Coast when Lord Fempellec was bound hand and foot and cast into the sea by his people after a thirty-day rain (Cabello Valboa 1951 [1586]:328–29).

The socioeconomic system elaborated by the Chimú was imperfect. The overwhelming concern with security expressed in the controlled access, high walls, and tortuous corridors of ciudadelas indicates a profound social and economic gulf between royalty and the rest of the populace (Klymyshyn, Chapter 6). Perhaps the Chimú royalty had manipulated labor, reciprocity, and redistribution into a burdensome bureaucracy that had become unstable through its very rigidity, and change was imminent. If the Chimú were already off balance internally, then the way was prepared for the rapid Inca conquest of the North Coast.

Several years ago Rowe (1948) pointed out the general similarities between Moche and Chimú ceramics and also suggested that the Inca adopted certain organizational principles from the Chimú. Larco Hoyle (1938–39), in his study of "Mochica" iconography, relied heavily upon Chimú and Inca ethnohistory for interpretation, thus emphasizing continuities among those cultures.

More recently it has become clear that corporate or mit'a labor organization was already in use in the Moche Valley before Chan Chan was founded (Moseley 1975b; Hastings and Moseley 1975) and existed on the coast as early as the Late Preceramic (see Table 1.1 for time chart; Feldman 1977). In addition, there is evidence that the storage of products in association with monumental architecture was also extant before Chimú storerooms were built at Chan Chan and certainly before Inca storerooms were constructed. These and other continuities discussed in the following chapters are a conscious effort to use ethnohistoric sources in the interpretation of archaeological data and to create a base line for comparison beyond the level of attribute analysis of selected artifacts. If a similar comparative base covering a substantial segment of time can be established, then regional and temporal variations can be studied. The reward will be a better understanding of human adaptability and culture change in the Andean area.

4

Chronology and Settlement Growth at Chan Chan

ALAN LOUIS KOLATA

Field Museum of Natural History

INTRODUCTION

It is the intent of this chapter to place in temporal sequence the major architectural structures of Chan Chan and to suggest some of the ramifications the evolution of their form held for Chimú economic and political organization. Normally temporal control of a site may be obtained by careful ceramic seriation. However, at Chan Chan this method suffers inherent limitations. First, it is extremely difficult to obtain undisturbed ceramic samples. The Chimú practiced systematic refuse disposal and used both artificial fill and ceramic-laden adobes to construct the city (Moseley and Mackey 1973). Second, even undisturbed ceramics collected from rooms within structures or directly from a structure's walls do not necessarily date the time of construction; they simply provide a *terminus ante quem*.

For these reasons, it has been necessary to search for an alternate method of building a chronology. In this regard, the procedure that has proven most effective derives from an examination of the architecture and its constituent parts. That is, the temporal sequence of Chan Chan's architecture is reflected in (1) architectural morphology, and

67

(2) attributes of the mud bricks. Unlike ceramics, these two datable elements have a direct relationship with the structures, and thus no ambiguous associations can mar the hypothesized construction sequence.

In the following discussion I first describe the chronology based on attributes of mud bricks and then that based on the evolution of certain architectural forms. I illustrate how these independently generated temporal sequences serve to clarify and reinforce each other.

THE CHRONOLOGY BASED ON ADOBES

During survey at Chan Chan in 1974, it became apparent that the mud bricks used in construction of the most significant architecture varied tremendously in dimensions. Variation in soil type was also recognized but was not significant for chronological purposes. Although all of the adobes are rectangular and mold-made, they vary significantly in terms of the height-to-width ratio. Three categories based on shape, or proportionate dimension, were recognized (Figure 4.1):

1. "tall" bricks, proportionately taller than they are wide;
2. "square-ended" bricks, proportionately as wide as they are tall; and
3. "flat" bricks, proportionately wider than they are tall.

It is essential to note that although there exists a gradation in size from large adobes at the base of walls to very small adobes at the wall summit, the relative proportion (height-to-width ratio) of the bricks is maintained throughout. Thus the absolute size of adobes does not affect these categories. It is simply a function of wall construction: a sturdy wall requires large adobes at the base and smaller, lighter bricks near the top. Measurements on over 10,000 adobes at Chan Chan verify that this property of proportion maintenance exists for all three brick types. Confusion between types is eliminated by the fact that the adobes possess mold marks clearly evident along the two longest sides. Thus it is possible to orient the bricks to their original position and avoid confusing a flat adobe flipped on end with a tall adobe.

A survey of the adobes in the ciudadelas of Chan Chan revealed that the three brick types are rigidly segregated. There is virtually no mixture of types within distinct structures. This consistent segregation of adobe types has an important implication: the bricks have chronological significance.

BRICK TYPE	DIMENSIONS (height : width)

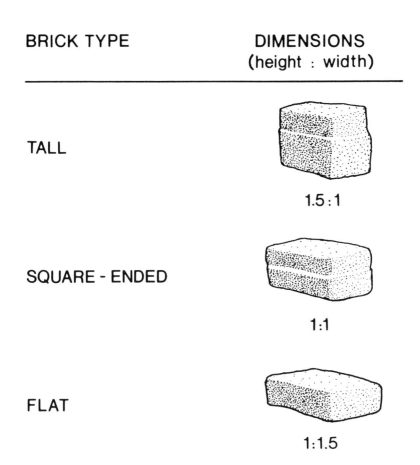

TALL   1.5 : 1

SQUARE - ENDED   1:1

FLAT   1:1.5

FIGURE 4.1. The three major brick types at Chan Chan.

The segregation of brick types is represented graphically in Figure 4.2. This figure is the computer-generated "master graph" for Chan Chan representing the range of variation in brick ratios (height to width) along the horizontal axis and the frequency of occurrence of a given ratio along the vertical axis.

In this graph, the actual ratio of height:width dimensions may be determined by multiplying the numbers along the horizontal axis by a factor of .008. Thus the total variation in height:width ratios of bricks is from .32 (1:3.1) to 3.28 (3.2:1). More important, it is obvious from this graph that there is significant clustering in certain brick dimen-

69

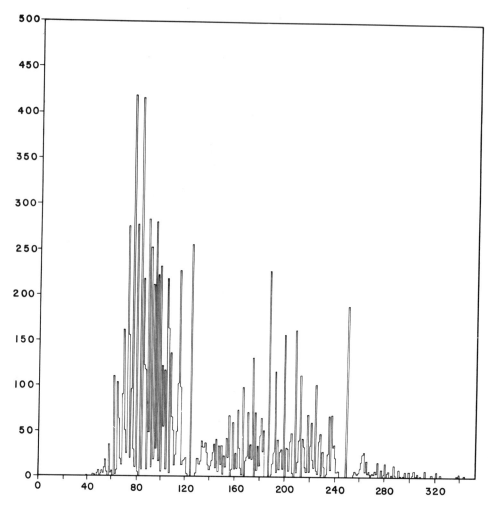

FIGURE 4.2. Master graph of brick ratios. The horizontal axis is the range of brick ratios and the vertical axis is the count of bricks.

sions (that is, certain ratios occur more often than others). These clusters correspond generally with the preliminary, nonquantitative analysis into three brick types: flat, square-ended, and tall.

Specifically, on the horizontal axis, the clustering between 40 and 110 represents the flat type of brick dimension (width greater than height). In this cluster, the peak, or most typical dimension, at 75 corresponds to a height:width ratio of 1:1.5. The other obvious cluster, between 140 and 230, represents the tall type of brick dimension (height greater than width). In this cluster, the peak, at 185, signifies a height:width ratio of 1.5:1.

70

Two modest clusters also occur in this graph. One, with a peak at 125, refers to the square-ended brick type with a height:width ratio of 1:1. The other, peaking at 250, appears to indicate the presence of a "hyper-tall" brick type with a height:width ratio of 2:1. For reasons outlined below, I regard the square-ended brick variety as a distinct, significant category. However, without further quantitative analysis, it is impossible to determine the significance of the peak in the "hyper-tall" range.

In brief, then, the master graph of brick ratios at Chan Chan verifies the existence of at least two discrete brick categories, the flat and the tall varieties. It suggests that two more, the square-ended and "hyper-tall" varieties, may also be "real" categories. Independent evidence from the field both supports these quantitative conclusions and provides a direction of evolutionary development for the brick types. That is, the variation in the various adobe types may be shown to be a form of stylistic evolution—a function of temporal change.

Several lines of evidence demonstrate that the direction of development was from the flat to the square-ended to the tall adobe type. The most significant evidence is stratigraphic. In several widely separated areas of Chan Chan, stratigraphic excavations revealed structures built with flat adobes beneath more extensive construction of square-ended or tall adobes. Likewise in these excavations square-ended adobes consistently underlay construction of tall brick. It is this clear stratigraphic position of the square-ended brick between the other two adobe types in a number of separate cuts that leads me to accept it as a significant, "real" category. Moreover it provides a logical stylistic link between the flat and tall adobe styles.

The phenomenon of brick reuse further supports the flat-to-tall sequence. In certain buildings there are clear indications of reused flat adobes in association with primary construction of "new" tall adobes. I have never encountered the reverse, i.e., reused tall adobes in association with the flat type.

A third verification of this brick sequence derives from the type of adobe in the large architectural complex of Galindo, a Moche V settlement in the upper Moche Valley. Galindo contains considerable stone architecture as well as an adobe compound with rudimentary similarities to the ciudadelas of Chan Chan (Bawden, Chapter 13). In this compound there are significant numbers of flat adobes equivalent to the flat brick type in Chan Chan. The equivalency in adobe types in the structures of late Moche and early Chimú times is strongly supported by computer analysis, which shows near coincidence in the respective curves of brick ratios. It is logical, then, that the brick sequence may be extended from the Moche V structures at Galindo to the earliest flat adobe constructions at Chan Chan.

In summary, there is substantial evidence, both quantitative and qualitative, supporting the existence of an adobe sequence at Chan Chan consisting of three, or possibly four brick types. This sequence provides the first unambiguous relative chronology for the city since the datable elements are from absolutely secure contexts. The association of these brick types with the major architecture at Chan Chan is shown in Table 4.1.

TABLE 4.1
BRICK TYPES AT CHAN CHAN

Brick Type	Units of Association
Tall	Rivero
	Tschudi
	Bandelier
	Velarde
	Squier
Square-ended	Squier (?)
	Gran Chimú and Annexes
	Laberinto (sections)
Flat	Laberinto
	Tello
	Uhle
	Chayhuac

THE CHRONOLOGY BASED ON CHANGING ARCHITECTURAL FORM

There is a series of **U**-shaped structures possessing a symmetrical arrangement of niches, bins, or troughs within the compounds at Chan Chan (Figure 4.3). These structures also occur in rural areas surrounding the city and in other valleys such as Chicama and Virú (Keatinge 1974; Collier 1955). Andrews (1974) and Moseley (1975a) believe that the structures served bureaucratic functions; perhaps they were used primarily for regulating the flow and storage of state-owned goods. These open-ended structures vary in architectural form (size, type of internal features) and context. I have found that, when ordered temporally, this variation corroborates and refines the construction sequence based on adobes.

Andrews (1974) originally proposed a seriation of the U-shaped structures at Chan Chan, termed generically "audiencias." The seriation began with the "standard audiencia," a structure with six interior niches (Figure 4.3:19,20), and progressed through the "audiencia variant" (Figure 4.3:12,17,18) and "trocadero variant" (Figure 4.3:13,14,15) to the "trocadero" (Figure 4.3:16), a U-shaped structure possessing interior troughs. In this scheme, the earliest audiencias at Chan Chan followed a standardized plan, but through time, they were subject to increasing variation in architectural form. This seriation suggests that the earliest enclosures at Chan Chan were constructed at the southern end of the site in ciudadelas Chayhuac, Tschudi, and Rivero (Figure 4.6) and were followed by the ciudadelas in the central section of the city—Velarde, Bandelier, Laberinto, Tello, and Uhle. The final construction phase is represented by ciudadelas Squier and Gran Chimú in the northern terminus of the site (Figure 4.6).

In developing this seriation, Andrews (1974:260) remarks that the "order presented here is based mostly on subjective interpretation of stylistic variations among the U-shaped structures" and "is not supported by other chronological markers." As in any seriation, stylistic variation may be ordered logically in several different ways, but the direction of the variation must be determined from data not contingent on the variation itself.

Using the brick chronology as just such an independent confirmation of the direction of stylistic evolution, I have been able to construct a new seriation of the U-shaped structures at Chan Chan. This seriation benefits not only from an external source of verification, but also from excavations completed in 1975 revealing additional types of audiencia structures unknown to Andrews. The revised audiencia seriation is illustrated in Figure 4.3 where 1 is the earliest and 20 the latest structure.

I propose that the first audiencias were constructed in the eastern sections of ciudadela Uhle (Figure 4.3:1–4). They are simple, elongated U-shaped structures containing two interior niches or bins. The western sections of Uhle contain related types of audiencias that elaborate on the earliest structures (Figure 4.3:5–9). These later structures display an unusual variety of features: niches, bins, or troughs; L-shaped niches or bins; external niches or bins; C-shaping of the entire

73

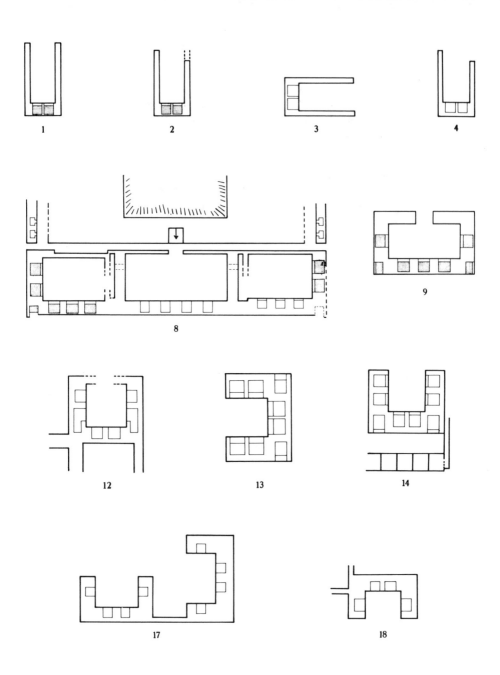

FIGURE 4.3. The audiencia seriation at Chan Chan.

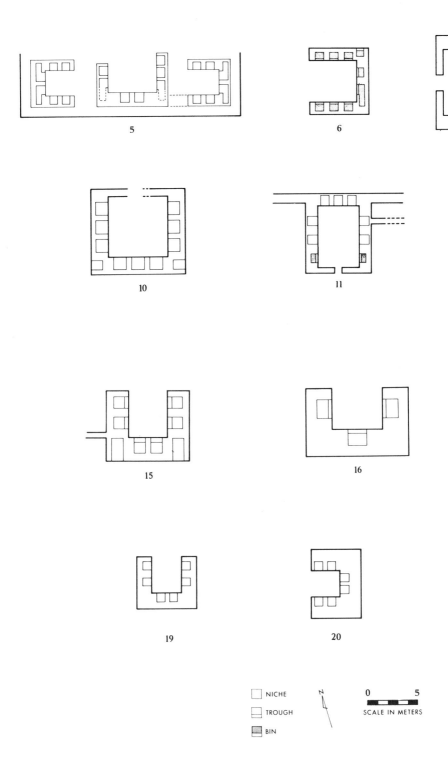

5

6

7

10

11

15

16

19

20

☐ NICHE

☐ TROUGH

▨ BIN

N

0   5

SCALE IN METERS

structure; and agglutination of different structural types in a single complex (Figure 4.3:8). In fact, diversity of form may be said to be the chief characteristic of the audiencias in Uhle. Of the 22 structures in this enclosure, only 3 are identical.

The audiencias in Uhle are demonstrably among the earliest because they form logical prototypes for the other U-shaped structures in the city, and, more important, they were constructed with the flat adobe, chronologically the earliest in the brick sequence. This information, of course, provides a secure anchor for the architectural seriation at its early end. Moreover it apprises us of the direction of stylistic evolution.

The next set of audiencias constructed was in Tello (Figure 4.3:10,11). These structures, like those in Uhle, were built with the early, flat adobe. However, I place them in a later period of construction because of a marked reduction in audiencia types (as indicated below, this reduction in types through time characterizes the entire seriation). The audiencias in Tello retain certain features found in Uhle: C-shaping and the presence of interior bins and exterior niches. However, both the elongated U form and the agglutinated complex have disappeared. In addition, the popularity of the interior bins has begun to wane.

Laberinto contains the third set of audiencias (Figure 4.3:12–15). This enclosure and the structures inside it were built predominantly with the flat adobe, but it is important to note that certain areas possess a significant admixture of the square-ended adobe— chronologically a middle phase in the brick sequence. This indicates that Laberinto follows both Uhle and Tello in the construction sequence at Chan Chan. The types of audiencias in Laberinto appear to confirm this position. C-shaped structures (Figure 4.3:12) and a tendency toward increase in overall dimensions (begun in Tello, Figure 4.3:10) link the audiencias in Laberinto with those in Tello. The interior bin feature prevalent in Uhle but on the wane in Tello disappears altogether in Laberinto. In its place, a troughed form (Figure 4.3:13–15) comes into vogue, represented among nearly half of the audiencia structures in that enclosure.

Large U-shaped structures with interior troughs become the standard in the succeeding ciudadela, Gran Chimú (Figure 4.3:16). In this compound, the largest in Chan Chan, the number of troughs in the audiencias is reduced to three or four, but the gross size of the structure reaches its maximum. This enclosure, and in fact the entire northern end of the city, was constructed with the square-ended style of adobe, confirming its position after Laberinto in the construction sequence.

76

The remaining four ciudadelas containing audiencias (Velarde, Bandelier, Tschudi, and Rivero) were all built with the tall adobe, the latest in the brick sequence. However, it is possible to differentiate among them chronologically on the basis of stylistic evolution in the audiencia seriation. The trends in formal development in this last set of structures unfolded logically and in temporal progression. These trends were (1) a transition from troughs to niches in the interior, (2) gradual reduction in the size of the structure, and (3) increased standardization in all structural aspects, that is, in overall dimensions, the number and size of the niches, and so forth.

Specifically, Velarde represents the first stage in the progression toward a standardized six-niched audiencia. Here the troughs have been replaced by niches, but in other respects, such as gross size and number of interior features, the audiencias replicate those in Gran Chimú (Figure 4.3:17,18). Bandelier reflects the continuation of this process. In the southern sector of this enclosure, the audiencias remain as large as those in Velarde but are now provided with six rather than four niches (Figure 4.3:20).

The process of this stylistic evolution culminates in the audiencias of Tschudi and Rivero (Figure 4.3:19). These structures are reduced in size from those preceding them and invariably contain six interior niches. Moreover they appear to be constructed according to more rigid specifications that allow for little variation in structural size or internal features. In short, these final structures have become "standard audiencias" in every respect.

The implications of this audiencia seriation, particularly for the constructional history of Chan Chan, are radically different from those derived from the original Andrews seriation. For instance, rather than an initial "standard audiencia" undergoing experimentation and transformation into a variety of forms, it is apparent that the stylistic evolution in audiencias was *away* from formal diversity and toward a single, standardized structure. The implied cultural correlates of this and other architectural patterns will be considered in the conclusion.

THE ORDER IN THE GROWTH OF CHAN CHAN

The two relative chronologies elaborated here (adobe and architectural form) provide the temporal control over the architecture at Chan Chan essential to understanding settlement structure and growth. When used in conjunction, these chronologies have enabled me to map in some detail the construction history of the city.

The original nucleus of the city was formed by a Chayhuac-Uhle axis in the southeast corner of the site (Figure 4.4). Uhle was built in at least two major stages, an eastern and a western sector. Later, large annexes were extended to the north and west. The city then grew laterally from Uhle toward the west with the construction of enclosures at Ciudadelas Tello and Laberinto. It is especially interesting to note that Laberinto was the first ciudadela constructed with a formal, tripartite ordering of the internal architecture. Thereafter every ciudadela conformed to this design (Figure 4.4).

A second major phase of construction within Chan Chan began with the erection of the largest enclosure, Gran Chimú, and nearly all the architecture to its north and west. This phase included the construction of the "great wall" defining the northern limits of Chan Chan (Figure 4.5). It is this period of construction that coincides with the use of the square-ended style of adobe in the city. Oddly enough, except for portions of Laberinto and some architecture surrounding it, this type of adobe (and the period it defines) is confined to the northern end of the settlement.

In the third and most extensive building phase, the remaining five ciudadelas were constructed within the boundaries defined by the original Chayhuac-Uhle axis on the east, Gran Chimú on the north, and Laberinto on the west. Essentially this late phase of construction involved a filling in of space in the south-central sectors of Chan Chan (Figure 4.6).

The specific sequence of construction of these ciudadelas was as follows: first Velarde was constructed along the western border of the city immediately north of Laberinto. A southern extension of this compound abuts the northern wall of the older Laberinto, virtually severing access to it. This pattern of infringing on annexes of older ciudadelas is replicated by the construction of Bandelier, the next compound in the sequence. In erecting Bandelier, the builders leveled most of Uhle's northern annex, thereby severely impeding access to the only entrance into Uhle, located in its northern wall (Figure 4.6).

This attempt to fit new construction projects into space defined by older enclosures, rather than expanding into entirely vacant areas, suggests that land around the city was at a premium. It seems likely that the needs of a growing population, reflected in the accelerated pace of construction at this time, demanded efficient, extensive utiliza-

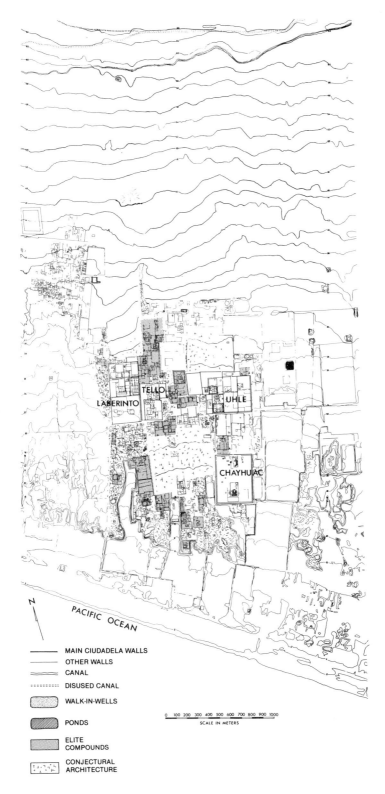

N

PACIFIC OCEAN

MAIN CIUDADELA WALLS
OTHER WALLS
CANAL
DISUSED CANAL
WALK-IN-WELLS
PONDS
ELITE COMPOUNDS
CONJECTURAL ARCHITECTURE

0 100 200 300 400 500 600 700 800 900 1000
SCALE IN METERS

TELLO
LABERINTO
UHLE
CHAYHUAC

FIGURE 4.4. The initial major phase of construction at Chan Chan: Ciuda-delas Chayhuac, Uhle, Tello, and Laberinto.

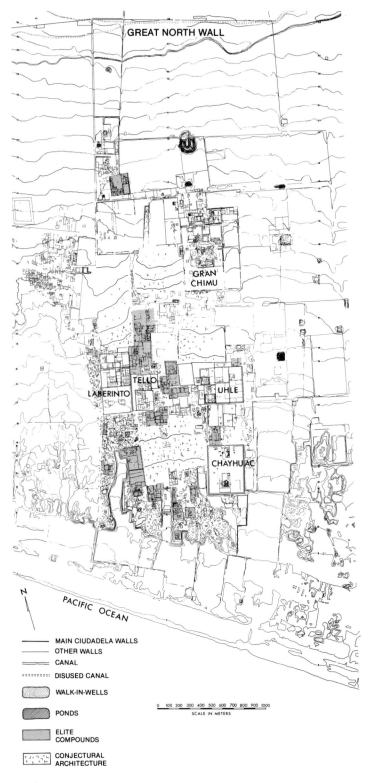

GREAT NORTH WALL

GRAN
CHIMU

TELLO

LABERINTO

UHLE

CHAYHUAC

N

PACIFIC OCEAN

——— MAIN CIUDADELA WALLS

——— OTHER WALLS

=== CANAL

:::::::::: DISUSED CANAL

WALK-IN-WELLS

PONDS

ELITE
COMPOUNDS

CONJECTURAL
ARCHITECTURE

0 100 200 300 400 500 600 700 800 900 1000
SCALE IN METERS

FIGURE 4.5. The second major phase of construction at Chan Chan: portions of Ciudadelas Laberinto, Gran Chimú, and the "Great North Wall."

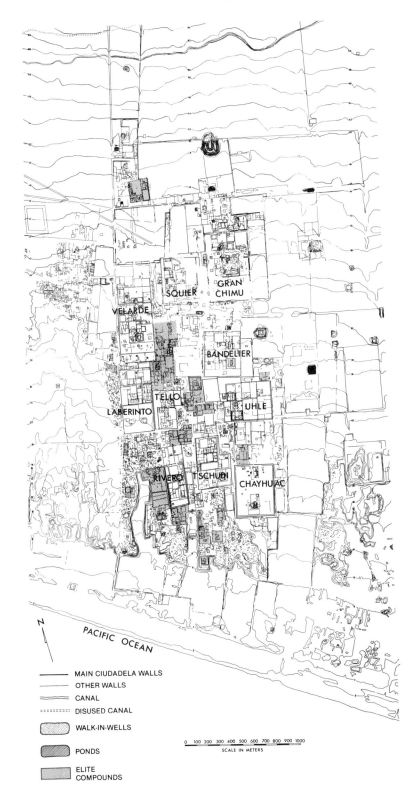

FIGURE 4.6. The final major phase of construction at Chan Chan: Ciudadelas Squier, Velarde, Bandelier, Tschudi, and Rivero.

tion of all arable land. In addition, the fact that these "new" ciudadelas were allowed to impinge upon annexes and cut access routes to already established compounds indicates significant change in the relative status or function of these older ciudadelas, perhaps both. The precise meaning of this change remains problematical, although the hypothesis advanced by Conrad (Chapter 5) that the ciudadelas, as palace compounds, were transformed into mausoleums on the death of the king offers a possible solution. (In this regard it is critical to note that the principle of infringing on older architecture does not extend to the ciudadela itself; it remains inviolate.)

The final ciudadelas built were Tschudi and Rivero in the southernmost section of the city (Figure 4.6). Architecture clearly related to Tschudi by context and brick type expanded into the area between the old Chayhuac-Uhle axis. This expansion involved massive earth removal in the construction of a large walk-in well and its supporting architecture and constitutes an ambitious kind of urban renewal. It also echoes the pattern of infringing upon older construction established previously. In a similar fashion, the northern annex of Rivero and its related structures encroach upon, and in some sections incorporate, the southern annex of Tello (Figure 4.6).

One ciudadela has been ignored in this constructional history. Evidence for the position of Squier (Figure 4.6) in this sequence is ambiguous. The brick type used in construction of this enclosure emphasizes this ambiguity. The curve of the brick ratios does not fit comfortably in either the square-ended or tall categories, but rather somewhere between the two. One poorly preserved audiencia remains in the southeast corner of the compound. This structure contains six niches and seems to be a version of the late "standard audiencia," although its poor construction imparts to it a somewhat unusual appearance. Because of these peculiar conditions, I would feel secure only in placing Squier after Gran Chimú in the construction sequence.

CONCLUSIONS: RAMIFICATIONS OF THE ORDER

The manner in which a settlement grew carries implied information about the cultural meaning of that growth. The chronology developed here has made it possible to subdivide Chan Chan into a series of syn-

chronic architectural complexes that contain implications very different from those of the site as a whole. Establishing such a series of
architectural complexes is critical for reconstructing changing patterns
of human occupation and activity within the settlement, that is, for
understanding the cultural conditions that structured the growth of
the city.

From the order of settlement growth that I have determined, it is
possible to document the birth, expansion, and ultimate contraction of
the Chimú state and the empire it controlled. The first construction
activity at Chan Chan occurred soon after the demise of Galindo, the
Moche V settlement in the upper Moche Valley. The brick ratio
curves for Galindo and Chayhuac, the first of the royal compounds at
Chan Chan, nearly coincide, arguing for close temporal position.
Even if one posits a brief hiatus after the abandonment of Galindo, the
complete shift in political power from the upper reaches of the Moche
Valley to the river mouth manifests a remarkable social change.

Chayhuac has the simplest internal organization of any ciudadela at
Chan Chan, consisting primarily of open space, plazas, some courts,
storerooms, and a burial platform (Conrad, Chapter 5). Uhle, the
second enclosure and part of the original nucleus of the city, shows
evidence of increasing complexity in the form of several major stages of
construction and the development of the audiencia structure. It is the
appearance of the audiencia that is of particular interest here. As I have
noted, these structures, which occur both in Chan Chan and its rural
hinterland, appear to be a tool of a state-controlled, centralized administration designed to regulate the flow and storage of agricultural produce
and other valued commodities. The several kinds of audiencias in
Uhle (Figure 4.3:1–9) suggest that at this time the Chimú were
beginning to experiment with this structure as an efficient administrative device. They had begun, in other words, a process of political and
economic consolidation that would culminate in the the highly stratified, centrally organized bureaucratic state portrayed in the ethnohistorical record (Rowe 1948).

The economic nature of this consolidation is reflected in the construction of audiencias in areas outside the city. These rural sites were
most probably designed to exploit the vast land and water resources
north of Chan Chan in order to maintain the city and its expanding
sphere of influence (Keatinge and Day 1973). The two rural administrative settlements within the vicinity of the Moche Valley, El Milagro
de San José and Quebrada del Oso (Keatinge 1974), may be linked by

their **C**-shaped audiencias to identical structures in Uhle (Figure 4.3:7,9). This correspondence in audiencia types suggests that even during this formative stage, the Chimú held dominion over the valley. In fact, the appearance of an audiencia site in the Virú Valley, V-124A (Collier 1955), containing a structure similar to one in Uhle (Figure 4.3:5), suggests that the Chimú had already begun a program of imperial conquest.

Through time, the increasingly rigid and bureaucratic organization of the Chimú state is even more clearly reflected in the architecture at Chan Chan. With the construction of Laberinto, the highly formal, tripartite structure of the ciudadela was instituted (Figures 4.4–4.6). This canon of architectural design became the governing principle in the construction of all other ciudadelas. Concurrent with the change to this formal internal structure of the ciudadelas was the reduction in the types of audiencias employed, seemingly indicating a parallel attempt to standardize important architecture. If state organization implies standardization (of procedures, regulations, architecture), the Chimú polity was no exception.

The political power of the Chimú empire expanded through the second major phase of building activity at Chan Chan, defined by the construction of Gran Chimú and its annexes. Since the political and economic power of the state was centered in the palace compounds, the sheer magnitude of this, the largest enclosure in Chan Chan, with its numerous banks of storerooms, elaborate annexes, and spacious plazas, attests to its prominence in the history of the Chimú conquest state.

In the third and final phase of development in the city, the scale of the ciudadela is diminished considerably and steadily until Rivero, one of the last and smallest compounds. In tandem with this reduction in the size of the ciudadela was a decline in total storage space. Areas tied up in storage had increased consistently from Chayhuac to Laberinto, reaching a peak in Gran Chimú. Thereafter the trend was that space devoted to storage was reduced with each ciudadela built. If gross storage space can be taken as a crude indicator of wealth and power, with the onset of this phase, the economic and perhaps political fortunes of Chan Chan had begun to wane. This period of apparent economic decline is decidedly not paralleled by a weakening of the state bureaucracy. It is at this time that many of the elite compounds that Klymyshyn (Chapter 6) has described as residences of minor no-

84

bles, the presumed administrators of the government, were constructed. Through time, it seems, the bureaucratic infrastructure of the Chimú state had continued to swell. Similarly, increased standardization in both the ciudadelas (Tschudi and Rivero are the most rigidly organized) and their administrative structures (only the "standard audiencia" was built now) suggests that the control of the central government over the Chimú people had deepened.

It is possible that the burden of maintaining this expanded bureaucracy during a period of economic recession placed intolerable internal strains on the empire of Chimor and rendered it less able to counter the external threat posed by Inca aggression.

The Burial Platforms of Chan Chan: Some Social and Political Implications

GEOFFREY W. CONRAD

Harvard University

INTRODUCTION

Variation in burial patterns is one of the major indications of Chan Chan's complex social and political organization. Mortuary practices in the city range from very simple to extremely elaborate. Included among the different funerary places and treatments are a vast cemetery on the bluff at the south end of the site; scattered smaller cemeteries; dedicatory burials in ramps, audiencias, and other constructions; and a variety of specialized mortuary structures inside the city and around its perimeter.

The most elaborate burial places in Chan Chan are a series of nine platform mounds associated with the ciudadelas and cuadros[1] of the civic center. There are ten major compounds in the city; with the exception of Tello, each great enclosure contains a truncated pyramidal mound that is its largest single structural component and, in a general sense, its dominant feature. The nine mounds share a number of distinctive architectural characteristics, and they have been classed together as burial platforms.

A burial platform is defined as an elevated structure specifically designed and built with one or more internal receptacles to hold deceased individuals and mortuary offerings. At Chan Chan burial platforms take the form of truncated pyramid mounds containing multiple prepared cells entered from above. Access to the top of the platforms, and thence to the cells, is via a ramp or system of ramps along one face of the mound(s). Adjacent to this face is a forecourt that controls entrance to the ramp system. Both the platforms and their forecourts are surrounded by an enclosure wall that separates the burial platform complex(es) from their surroundings.

The purposes of this chapter are to present the evidence underlying the burial platform definition, to identify the persons buried in the Chan Chan platforms, and to offer a functional interpretation of the compounds housing the platforms. Finally, I will develop and evaluate a hypothetical explanation based on ethnohistoric analogy for the organizational principles responsible for the construction of the great enclosures and their platforms.

BURIAL PLATFORM CHARACTERISTICS AND VARIATION

The burial platforms associated with the major compounds share a number of features beyond those inherent in their definition. Every platform is characterized by multiple internal cells. All platforms are oriented north-south, with their forecourts and access ramps on the north side, and all but the Squier platform possess structural additions built sometime after the original construction. Furthermore, each platform is the most heavily looted building in its compound: in fact, these mounds are the most thoroughly plundered components of the entire civic center.

Figure 5.1 depicts as an example Huaca Las Avispas, the Laberinto platform. (Two other burial platforms have individual names: the Tschudi platform is sometimes referred to as El Presidio and the Rivero platform as Huaca de la Misa. To simplify matters each platform will henceforth be labeled with the name of its compound.) The typical features are present: forecourt and ramp system on the north side; internal cells (25 in this platform); and a structural addition, in this case a U-shaped ring section filling in an old corridor on all but the north side of the platform.

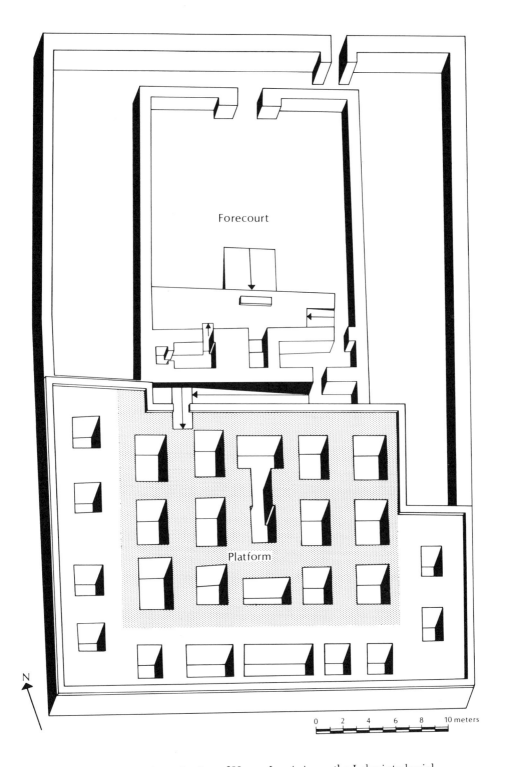

Forecourt

Platform

N

0　2　4　6　8　10 meters

FIGURE 5.1. Isometric projection of Huaca Las Avispas, the Laberinto burial platform. The stippled area is the original platform, which is surrounded on three sides by a structural addition containing further cells. Note the central T-shaped cell in the original platform. Arrows indicate direction of rise of ramps.

Beyond this basic similarity the platforms exhibit variation in a number of characteristics: size (Table 5.1), location, principal construction material, number and type of cells, design of the forecourt, and structural additions.

TABLE 5.1
DIMENSIONS OF CHAN CHAN BURIAL PLATFORM
COMPLEXES (IN METERS)

| Platform Complex | Enclosure | | Platform | | Height* |
	Length (N–S)	Width (E–W)	Length (N–S)	Width (E–W)	
Gran Chimú	190	90	150	80	12 +
Bandelier*	147	80	69 (f)	51 (f)	1 (f)
			41 (ss)	15.5 (ss)	3 (ss)
					4 (total)
Uhle	89	112.5	47.5	67.5	8
Chayhuac	128	75	48	55	10.5
Tschudi	114	78	57	42.5	5
Rivero	111	77	59	50	9.5
Laberinto	70.1	61.4	23.5	31.8	3.5
Velarde	128	81	69	68	11
Squier	52	34	27	27	3.5

*(f) = foundation; (ss) = superstructure

Location

Figure 5.2 shows the locations of the burial platforms. The Gran Chimú, Bandelier, and Velarde platforms lie entirely within the central sector of their ciudadelas. The Tschudi platform is confined to the rear sector, or canchón; the Rivero platform overlaps the central sector and canchón; and the Laberinto platform is situated in an exterior court opposite the northeast corner of the main structure. Of the platforms associated with cuadros, the platforms of Chayhuac and Uhle occur inside enclosed subdivisions in the south-central part of the compound, while the Squier platform is built along the exterior of the compound's west wall.

Principal Construction Material

The principal construction material was either tapia or adobe. The Chayhuac, Tschudi, and Rivero platforms were built primarily of tapia; all others were of adobe.

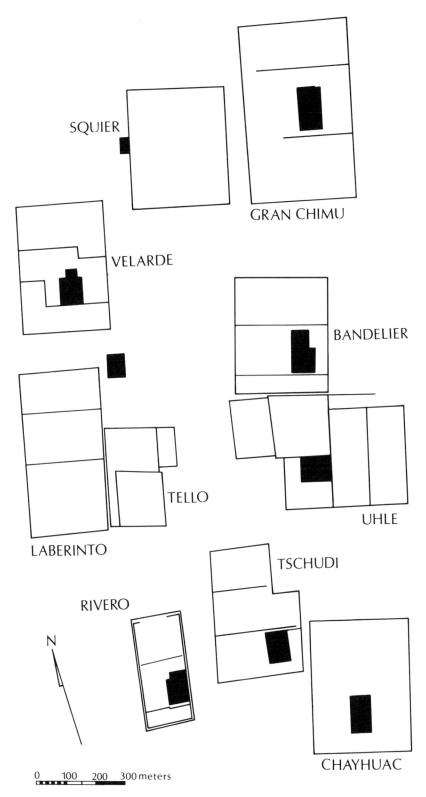

SQUIER

GRAN CHIMU

VELARDE

BANDELIER

TELLO

UHLE

LABERINTO

TSCHUDI

RIVERO

N

CHAYHUAC

0 100 200 300 meters

FIGURE 5.2. Simplified map of central Chan Chan showing the locations of the major compounds (outline) and their burial platforms (solid black).

As Kolata states in Chapter 4, three distinct types of bricks were used in Chan Chan: flat, square-ended, and tall. Each of the adobe platforms was built with one of these types. Flat adobes were the principal construction material in Uhle. The Gran Chimú platform was built with square-ended bricks. Tall adobes characterize the Bandelier, Laberinto, Velarde, and Squier platforms.

Finally, five platforms were constructed with both tapia and adobes, though in each case one material played a decidedly minor role. Of the tapia platforms (Chayhuac, Tschudi, Rivero), Chayhuac has a forecourt wall and structural addition of flat adobes. The Rivero platform has a structural addition of tall adobes, while surviving traces of brick masonry indicate that at least some of the cells in the Tschudi platform may have been sealed with tall adobes. Furthermore, the Tschudi and Rivero platform complexes are both enclosed by walls erected with tall bricks. The Bandelier and Velarde platforms, which were built primarily with tall adobes, have low tapia foundations.

Number and Type of Cells

At the most inclusive level of classification, all cells may be grouped together as rectilinear chambers. However, significant typological distinctions are possible: the most important is the difference between principal and secondary cells.

Three examples of principal cells survive—one apiece in the Bandelier, Tschudi, and Laberinto platforms. In all of these cases the principal cell is a chamber whose floor plan is shaped like a hollow letter **T** with the cross to the north. Each of the three visible cells of this type occupies the central position in its respective platform and is much larger and more elaborate than the surrounding chambers (Figure 5.1).

Secondary cells are smaller and simpler than principal chambers. These lesser cells are found in the noncentral parts of all of the platforms and are basically of two types: simple shaft and boot-shaped (Figure 5.3).

As its name implies, the simple shaft is a plain rectangular chamber. Sometimes the shaft has a narrow, roof-supporting ledge around its sides in the upper half of its height, giving it a stepped appearance. Less frequently one corner of the bottom of the shaft has been slightly extended, so that the cell has an **L**-shaped floor plan . The simple shaft

92

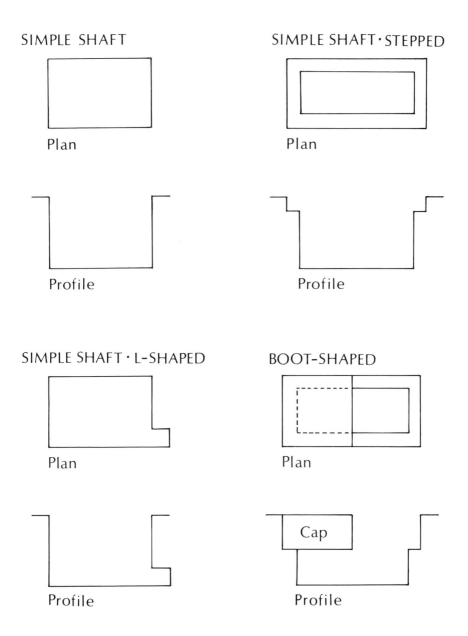

SIMPLE SHAFT

Plan

Profile

SIMPLE SHAFT·STEPPED

Plan

Profile

SIMPLE SHAFT · L-SHAPED

Plan

Profile

BOOT-SHAPED

Plan

Cap

Profile

FIGURE 5.3. Schematicized depictions of the different types of secondary cells found in the burial platforms.

and its subtypes are found in all of the platforms; the stepped variant occurs in the Gran Chimú, Rivero, Laberinto, and Velarde platforms, while the L-shaped floor plan seems to be limited to Rivero.

Boot-shaped cells are those in which the actual chamber is built with a sealed top and must be reached via a vertical shaft at its north end. In profile such a cell resembles a boot. Though treated here as a separate type, these cells may also be seen as stepped simple shaft cells in which half of the shaft was roofed during the original construction, before the chamber had been used. The type may have been employed only when the principal construction material of the platform was tapia, since it is known to occur only in Tschudi and Rivero.

I believe that the pattern seen in Bandelier, Tschudi, and Laberinto—a large central cell surrounded by smaller chambers—was in fact common to all of the burial platforms. It has been noted that the platforms are the most heavily pillaged structures in the civic center; it must be stressed here that in every case the distribution of damage within the platform is identical. In all of the platforms in which a central principal cell is not directly visible, the degree of looting is greatest exactly where one would expect that cell to have been. The surrounding zone, which consistently contains only secondary cells, is always better preserved. This uniform pattern of looting is undoubtedly based upon uniform organization of cells in the platforms.

I therefore contend that all of the platforms were characterized by a pattern of a single predominant chamber, presumably T-shaped, surrounded by a variable number of smaller cells.

The actual numbers of cells in the platforms are difficult to determine because of the damage done by looting, but estimates range from 15 in Squier to 100 or more in Gran Chimú. The exact total is known for only two platforms: that of Laberinto, which has 25, and that of Tschudi, which has 48. The foundation of the Bandelier platform has a regular pattern of shallow depressions marking locations for 49 cells; for some reason the superstructure was ultimately built on a smaller scale than the foundation and contains an unknown number of cells. The total was obviously less than 49.

Forecourt Design

Four different basic designs have been recognized and designated as Types A through D (Figure 5.4).

The Type A forecourt is a single enclosure with a bench along its

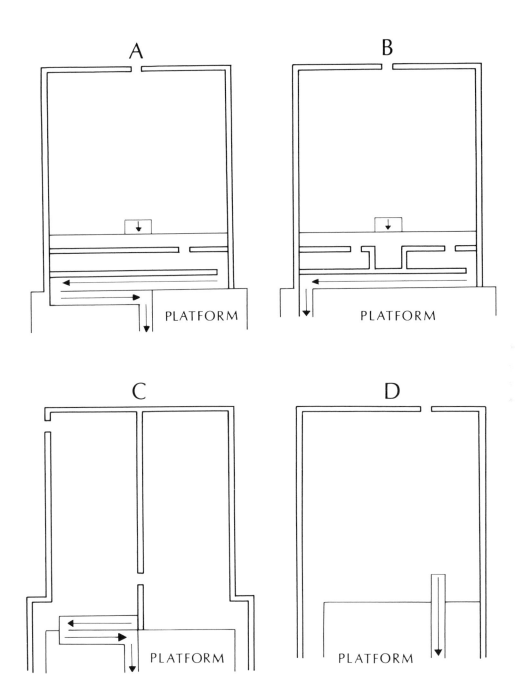

FIGURE 5.4. Schematicized depictions of the different forecourt designs found with the burial platforms. Arrows indicate direction of rise of ramps.

south end, against the north face of the platform. Spanning the bench from east to west is a single long room, behind which is the main ramp system. This series of ramps is also set against the north face of the platform and is of a "switchback" type. That is, it consists of three ramps. The first runs laterally along the face of the platform, rising from east to west. Directly behind this incline, and connected to it by a small landing, is a second lateral ramp rising in the opposite direction, from west to east. The third ramp has its foot at the head of the second and rises to the south, terminating at the top of the platform. Forecourt layouts of this type are found in Rivero and Tschudi.

Type B is also a single forecourt with a bench at the south end. However, the single long room atop the bench is replaced by an east-west string of three rooms set side by side. The western room is a dead-end enclosure. The central room is U-shaped, being open to the north, and contains in its floor a small, stone-lined bin filled with ground *Spondylus* shell. The eastern room gives access to the main ramp system, which consists of only two ramps. The first is a lateral incline along the north face of the platform, identical to the first component of a switchback series. The second ramp runs up to the south from the head of the first and is equivalent to the last member of a switchback system. The Type B forecourt (illustrated in Figure 5.1) occurs with the Bandelier and Laberinto platforms.

In Type C the forecourt is divided in half by a north-south wall. The principal half is the western one, which contains the entries to the entire platform complex and to the main ramp system. The latter is of the switchback type and is confined to the western half of the platform's north face. Type C forecourts characterize the Velarde, Uhle, and Gran Chimú burial platforms.

Type D is the simplest of the four. The single forecourt is an open space in which the only construction is the main ramp of the platform. The ramp is perpendicular to the north face rather than set along it. This variant occurs only in Squier.

Looters have virtually obliterated the forecourt of the Chayhuac platform, and its type is unknown.

Additions

Structural additions are of two types: primary-stage and secondary-stage.

Primary-stage additions take the form of a U-shaped block built around all but the north, or forecourt, side of the platform. This block contains further secondary cells. Additions of this type are visible in the Uhle, Chayhuac, Rivero, Laberinto, and Velarde platforms (see Figure 5.1). I believe them to be present in Gran Chimú and Tschudi, where they have simply been obscured, in the first case by looters' backdirt and in the second by the lack of looters' cuts into the sides of the platform that would reveal its original faces.

I have previously stated that the foundation of the Bandelier burial platform is much larger than its superstructure. In fact, the superstructure is only 15.5 meters wide. This measurement is far too narrow to be composed of the widths of the original platform plus two wings of a U-shaped addition. Accordingly, I conclude that this platform lacks a primary-stage addition. However, the foundation has ample space and the proper layout for the erection of a normal U-shaped primary-stage addition. Such an addition was apparently included in the original plan of the Bandelier burial platform, although it was never built.

In contrast, Squier lacks a primary-stage addition and was never intended to have one. The Squier platform abuts the east wall of its enclosure and is separated from the west wall by only four meters. There is simply no room for a primary-stage addition in Squier, and the original design of the platform must not have included one.

Secondary-stage-addition architecture appears in three basic forms. These are

(1) a small building set against either the south or west side of the platform;

(2) a larger elevated unit adjacent to the west side of the platform enclosure; and

(3) a simplified, miniaturized burial platform set in an enclosed unit immediately to the northwest of the main platform complex.

Structures of the first type occur in Bandelier and Tschudi; the second is found in Velarde (Figure 5.5) and Gran Chimú; the third occurs in Uhle.

Evidence for secondary-stage additions in Chayhuac, Rivero, and Laberinto is equivocal. Such additions might be buried under the large mounds of looters' backdirt on the south and west sides of the Chayhuac and Rivero platforms. A small, freestanding structure located between the Laberinto platform and the west wall of its enclosure could be a secondary-stage addition containing a single cell. Unfortunately, it is too heavily damaged to permit definite identification (and therefore has been omitted from Figure 5.1). Alternatively, these three platforms

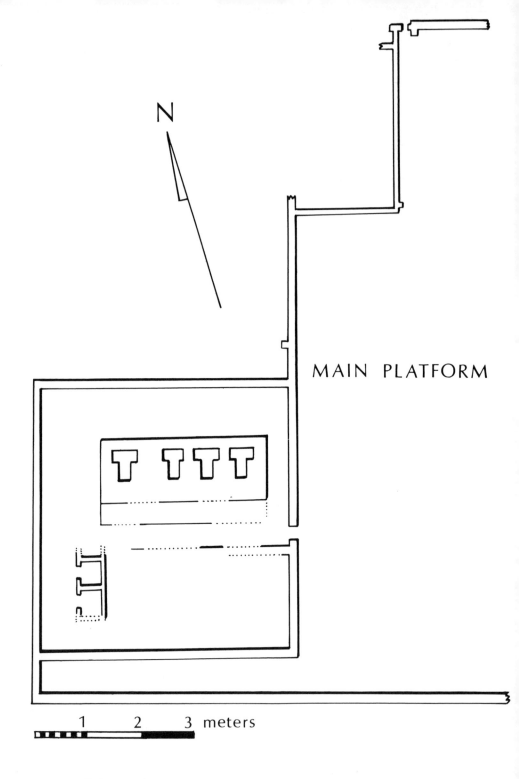

N

MAIN PLATFORM

1   2   3 meters

FIGURE 5.5. Secondary-stage structural addition to the Velarde burial plat-
his addition is a small mound containing four T-shaped cells.

may not possess secondary-stage additions. Squier definitely lacks a secondary-stage addition.

Cells in the secondary-stage structures are more elaborate than those in the primary-stage constructions. In at least two cases secondary-stage additions contain small replicas of the principal T-shaped chambers of the main platforms. All four of the chambers in Velarde's secondary-stage addition are T-shaped (Figure 5.5). There are 15 cells in the secondary-stage addition to the Tschudi platform; 12 are rectangular, but the central three are T-shaped.

Finally, there are two U-shaped rooms on the summit of the secondary-stage addition in Tschudi. Each of these rooms has in its floor a small, stone-lined bin filled with ground *Spondylus* shell. The bins are identical to the ones found in Type B forecourts.

All of this evidence argues that secondary-stage additions cannot be equated with their primary-stage counterparts. I therefore believe that the two types of structural additions served different purposes.

BURIAL PLATFORM CONTENTS

The content of the burial platforms has been established through intensive excavation of the Laberinto platform and testing in the platforms of Gran Chimú, Bandelier, Tschudi, Rivero, Velarde, and Squier.

This work revealed that the platforms contain large amounts of human bone and the highest concentrations of prestige items found to date in the city. Fine pottery, fancy textiles, carved wood, weaving equipment, and metal objects, along with whole and ground *Spondylus* shell, were all encountered in quantity. Moreover, these goods are merely the remains of what was once a much richer assemblage: the degree of looting and relooting of the platforms is in itself mute testimony to the vast quantities of high-status artifacts they once contained.

Further evidence of the special content of the burial platforms is provided by the human skeletal material excavated from the Laberinto platform. The remains of at least 93 individuals were recovered. However, while all 25 cells in the original platform and its primary-stage addition were tested, no more than one-quarter of the total volume of their fill was removed. Only one cell, the smallest, was completely cleared. It held 13 complete skeletons stacked like cordwood, with indications that 11 more bodies may once have occupied the chamber. (Twenty-four right calcanei were found in the cell.) Hence I estimate that the total number of burials in the platform was on the order of 200 to 300 or more. In every case where age and/or sex could be diagnosed the bones were those of adolescent and young adult females, which is certainly not a representative cross-section of the population of Chan Chan (T. Pozorski 1971:77–104).

Finally, an enclosed area adjacent to the west side of the Laberinto platform's forecourt contained the remains of a large number of sub-floor llama burials. Llama bones have been found near the other platforms as well.

BURIAL PLATFORM CHRONOLOGY

It is possible to arrange the burial platforms in temporal sequence if Kolata's adobe brick sequence is used (Kolata, Chapter 4). As Kolata has shown, the three types of bricks found in Chan Chan were made at different times. Flat adobes were the first type used in the city, square-ended adobes occupy an intermediate temporal position, and tall adobes are the latest type.

If the brick types are of different ages, then the burial platforms built with them must be of different ages. This fact suggests that it should indeed be possible to establish the sequence of the platforms through presence/absence seriation of their architectural characteristics.

The data to be used in the seriation have been discussed in the section dealing with formal variation among the platforms and in the above paragraph on brick chronology. Three of the architectural features discussed previously—size, cells, and additions—are not listed in the seriation. Size has been eliminated because of the lack of clear breaks in its range that would permit the definition of valid categories. Cells must be excluded since, due to the degree of looting, the absence of certain cell types cannot be proven in most cases. Neither primary-nor secondary-stage additions are included because they are not original elements of the platforms. (There is one minor exception to this last statement. The Rivero platform, which is made of tapia, has a primary-stage addition made of tall adobes and is enclosed by a wall built with tall adobes. I have used this information to bracket the platform within the time span of tall adobes.)

Information concerning the other characteristics—principal construction material, brick type, and forecourt design—is summarized and integrated in Table 5.2, which presents the seriation. Bandelier and Laberinto are paired because architectural characteristics indicate their placement relative to the other mounds but do not determine which of these two platforms was built first. The same statement applies to Tschudi and Rivero. In addition, two alternative versions must be offered because the data available at present do not completely resolve the position of Squier. Otherwise, an internally consistent picture of sequential construction emerges from the table.

TABLE 5.2
SERIATION OF CHAN CHAN BURIAL PLATFORMS

	Characteristic								
Platform	Principal adobe construction	Flat adobes	Square-ended adobes	Type C forecourt	Type B forecourt	Type D forecourt	Type A forecourt	Principal tapia construction	Tall adobes
Rivero							X	X	X
Tschudi							X	X	X
Laberinto	X					X			X
Bandelier	X					X			X
Squier	X				X				X
Velarde	X			X					X
Gran Chimu	X		X	X					
Uhle	X	X		X					
Chayhuac		X						X	

OR

	Principal adobe construction	Flat adobes	Square-ended adobes	Type C forecourt	Type D forecourt	Type B forecourt	Type A forecourt	Principal tapia construction	Tall adobes
Rivero							X	X	X
Tschudi							X	X	X
Squier	X					X			X
Laberinto	X				X				X
Bandelier	X				X				X
Velarde	X			X					X
Gran Chimu	X		X	X					
Uhle	X	X		X					
Chayhuac		X						X	

FUNCTIONAL INTERPRETATION OF
BURIAL PLATFORMS

Earlier Speculations

In the past, speculation about the nature and significance of the platforms has produced some widely varying interpretations. Tschudi and Rivero (1855:265–66) stated that the platforms in their eponymous compounds contained the tombs or apartments of Chimú concubines. Hutchinson (1873: Vol. II, 137) referred to the same structures as "square mounds of burying chambers." Squier (1877:159) and Peet (1903:171) also recorded the presence of burials in the Rivero platform. Squier (1877:156–58) identified the Tschudi platform as a prison; Holstein (1927:53) offered the same interpretation of the Gran Chimú platform, which both Squier (1877:142–43) and Horkheimer (1965:19) saw as the palace of the kings of Chimor. Rodríguez Suy Suy (1966:139–41) suggested the Tschudi platform might be a granary. Kroeber (1926:15) noted that these structures had been called chiefs' houses, but he remained noncommittal as to their true function. It must be stressed that none of these suggested interpretations were based on the results of excavations.

Pattern of Use

I am convinced that all of the information discussed in the preceding pages permits only one interpretation of the platforms: they served as the mortuary structures of extremely high-status citizens of the Kingdom of Chimor. The data suggest the following reconstruction of the pattern of preparation and use of a Chan Chan burial platform.

Each platform was one of the last buildings to be erected in its compound. However, it is clear that most of the great enclosures were designed and built with the knowledge that a burial platform would ultimately be included as one of their major features.

Evidence in support of these statements comes from Bandelier and Rivero. The foundation for a sizable burial platform was laid early in the history of Bandelier, but the superstructure was later built on a smaller scale. The reverse occurred in Rivero: its burial platform was finally erected on a larger scale than had originally been planned. Several earlier structures were razed in order to build the north end of the platform's forecourt.

Once a platform had been built, its use was occasioned by the death of a single highly important individual. The disposition of the cells in the platforms—a repetitive pattern of a central principal chamber, presumably T-shaped, surrounded by smaller secondary cells—argues that each platform was built in honor of one person, who was interred in the main chamber upon his death.

The death of this person served as the trigger for a series of complex funerary rituals extending over a considerable period of time. When the body of the principal individual was placed in the main chamber, vast quantities of offertory goods were installed with him and in some or all of the secondary cells. Included among these items were fine pottery, quality textiles, carved wood, weaving equipment, metal objects, and whole and ground *Spondylus* shell.

Ritual human sacrifice on a large scale must also have been an integral part of the ceremony. Such a practice is the most satisfactory explanation for the narrow demographic profile seen in the skeletal remains from the Laberinto platform. Epidemics, wars, and natural disasters do not kill so selectively. Age- and/or sex-specific cemeteries should hold a much greater number of bodies. Therefore, it is most probable that the Laberinto bones are those of young women who were killed ritually and then placed in some or all of the platform's cells to stress the importance of the individual interred in the main chamber. Considerable numbers of llamas were killed as further sacrifices and buried near the platform.

Some time elapsed after the completion of this first phase of the funerary rites (the interval may have been fixed by law). Then the person in whose honor the platform had been built was again celebrated by repeating aspects of the burial ceremony. A primary-stage structural addition was built around three sides of the original platform. As part of this second ceremonial phase, the new secondary cells in the addition were stocked with further prestige artifacts and human sacrifices, either all at once or serially over a number of years.[2]

In at least five cases, and possibly more, a secondary-stage addition was annexed to the platform after the construction of the primary-stage addition. The elaborate nature of the cells in the secondary-stage structures indicates that the persons buried in them held social positions that were high, though obviously not equal to those of the individuals interred in the principal chambers of the main platforms. The presence of T-shaped cells in secondary-stage additions argues that the persons for whom such structures were built were in some way connected with the individuals in whose honor the main platforms and primary-stage additions had been erected. All of this evidence leads me to contend that secondary-stage additions were the burial places of important persons closely affiliated with the individuals interred in the principal cells of the main platforms.

Specific Identification

The above recapitulation should be sufficient to demonstrate that the burial platforms of Chan Chan were the mortuary structures of a small number of extremely important citizens of the Chimú empire. I feel that it is possible to proceed further and identify those individuals as the kings of Chimor.

To confirm this assertion, the platforms must meet three criteria. First, they must be relatively few in number, as Chimor had relatively few kings. Second, they must have been built sequentially, as the empire had only one king at a time. Third, they must represent the highest-status funerary treatment in the empire because the king held the highest rank in the Chimú state.

The scarcity of large burial platforms and their sequential construction have already been shown: there are only nine such structures in central Chan Chan, and they were built one at a time.

Data also indicate that the platforms were the most prestigious funerary places in the Chimú empire. The individuals who were interred in the principal chambers must have been the most important residents of Chan Chan. No other persons in the city received such lavish mortuary treatment, either in terms of size and complexity of burial place, amount and quality of grave offerings, or grandeur of attendant funerary rites. Likewise, the rest of the empire has yielded no evidence of more elaborate mortuary practices.

Finally, the presence of ground *Spondylus* shell among the artifacts associated with the burial platforms suggests that these structures had a regal nature. Powder produced by crushing and grinding *Spondylus* was a symbol of royalty on the North Coast. The chronicler Miguel Cabello Valboa (1951:327) recorded a list of the courtiers of Ñaymlap, the founder of the pre-Chimú royal dynasty of the Lambayeque Valley. Among them was Fonga, the Preparer of the Way: he "scattered seashell dust where his lord was about to walk" (Rowe 1948:47).

In short, all available evidence argues that those individuals interred in the principal cells of the Chan Chan platforms were persons of paramount status in the Kingdom of Chimor, and the platforms have met all three criteria. I therefore conclude that they were in fact the burial places of the kings of Chimor.

FUNCTIONAL INTERPRETATION OF THE COMPOUNDS

If the burial platforms served as the royal tombs of Chimor, what was the function of the compounds with which those platforms were associated? This question has provoked considerable speculation in the past. Squier (1877:151, 159–60) identified the great enclosures as barrios, or wards, each occupied by a discrete group of people kept separate for social reasons. Kosok (1965:77) concurred with this view, listing the groups in question as clans, tribes, or more developed social units; some of the compounds, he felt, must have been reserved for the aristocracy. Rodríguez Suy Suy (1966:141) sees the enclosures as the seats of persons with specific primary duties (governmental, religious, economic, and so on) and secondary functions such as craft production. Tschudi and Rivero (1855:265–66) designated the compounds that now bear their names as palaces. Kroeber (1930:80) noted this interpretation but added that the real function of the enclosures was unknown, though probably connected with the position of Chan Chan as a late political center. Among those with more specific views, Bennett and Bird (1960:312–14) attribute the compounds to clans; Horkheimer (1965:19), to craft guilds; and Schaedel (1951a:232), to the urban elite and their retainers.

Most recently Day (1973) has argued cogently that the enclosures were the residences of the Chimú rulers. I am in complete agreement with him. The burial platforms have been identified as the royal mortuary structures of the Chimú empire, built to hold the kings of Chimor after their deaths. It seems most probable that the compounds with which the platforms are associated were designed to house the kings during their lives and were, in short, their palaces.

However, this interpretation is deceptively simple, and I suspect that it comes as a surprise to anyone whose models of kingship and empire are derived from the history of Western civilization. One palace in a capital city would be expectable, but not nine or ten. If Day's contention is correct, then the architecture of central Chan Chan must reflect some distinctly non-Western aspects of kingship. Can there really be a series of royal palaces in Chan Chan? If so, are there specifically Chimú, or more generally Andean, principles of social and political organization that would account for a pattern of multiple palaces?

ETHNOHISTORIC ACCOUNTS

Andean ethnohistory provides answers to the questions posed above. Information concerning both the Chimú and the Inca is relevant to the function of the great compounds and the organizational principles underlying them. A brief review of the pertinent ethnohistorical data will permit me to present a detailed hypothesis and then to evaluate it.

The Kingdom of Chimor

Like the Inca empire, the Kingdom of Chimor was a military expansionist state ruled by a dynasty of divine or semidivine despots. Fortunately, a list of the kings of Chimor is preserved in the so-called *Anonymous History of Trujillo*, written in 1604. This document provides a picture, albeit a sketchy one, of the political and territorial development of the state (Vargas Ugarte 1936:231–33; Rowe 1948: 39–40; Rostworowski 1961:54–55; Kosok 1965:73).

The Chimú dynasty was founded by a legendary figure named Taycanamo who was probably a mythical person, or at best a real individual whose exploits were later mythicized (Rowe 1948:40; Kosok 1965:73). Nine successors of Taycanamo expanded the dynasty's domain by military conquest. The last of these rulers was Minchançaman. His power extended over the entire coast from the Gulf of Guayaquil to the vicinity of modern Lima. Then, sometime between 1462 and 1470, Chimor came into conflict with the rising Inca empire and was defeated. Chan Chan and the lands it had governed fell into the hands of the Inca invaders (Rowe 1948:40).

The Inca Empire

Spanish chronicles relate that the conquest of Chimor was coincident with a reorganization of the Inca empire and had a major effect on subsequent Inca policy. Chimú administrative principles had been highly sophisticated, and certain aspects of the Inca state seem to have been restructured along Chumú lines (Rowe 1948:45–46).

One of the distinctive features of the revised Inca imperial system was a pattern of split inheritance among the royalty. By this term I mean a law of bequeathal based on two dichotomies: state office vs. personal wealth and principal vs. secondary heirs. In a pattern of split inheritance the principal heir receives the state office and attendant rights of the deceased; the latter's wealth and specific sources of income are granted to his secondary heirs as a corporate group.

Upon the death of the head of the Inca state the rights to govern, to wage war, and to impose new taxes on the empire passed directly to his principal heir, who became the next head of state. Future claims to revenue from taxes levied by the deceased emperor, along with his lands, buildings, servants, chattel, and the rest of his possessions, were bequeathed to a corporation (panaqa, or royal ayllu) made up of his other descendants. These secondary heirs managed their ancestor's property in his memory. They also cared for his mummy and maintained his cult. The new ruler was forced to acquire his own wealth by levying additional taxes in the existing provinces of the empire or by enlarging his domain through new conquests (Rowe 1967:61).

Around the time of the conquest of Chimor, the Inca emperor Pachacuti had Cuzco remodeled to befit its status as a major political and religious capital. In accordance with the law of split inheritance the "new" Cuzco was planned as a settlement in which each ruler built a palace to be the seat of his government and the center for control of his wealth. After his death his residence passed into the hands of his corporation, while his successor built the next palace (Rowe 1963:18; 1967:60–61).

THE HYPOTHESIS

Among the factors involved in the administrative and architectural patterns of imperial Cuzco were divine kingship, a view of property as a divine right, and military expansionism. The same phenomena characterized the Kingdom of Chimor (Rowe 1948:40, 49). Where governments and capital cities share the same bases and belong to the same general cultural tradition, we might expect them to show formal similarities.

Therefore, I propose that Chan Chan was built and governed under a system analogous to the one responsible for the form of imperial Cuzco and that the great compounds of the Chimú capital are equivalent to the palaces of its Inca counterpart. The hypothesis, then, reads as follows:

> The major compounds of Chan Chan were the palaces of the kings of Chimor. Each ruler built one such structure to house himself, be the seat of his government, and serve as the center for the management of his wealth. In accordance with a law of split inheritance the palace passed to the king's corporation of secondary heirs after his death. His principal heir became the next king of Chimor and built a new palace.

If the hypothesis is valid, the Chan Chan compounds should possess certain expectable features. Evaluation may consist of listing these properties and comparing them to those actually present in the archaeological data. Hence, if the hypothesis is to be accepted, the compounds must possess evidence of the following characteristics:

(1) They should have been built one at a time, since Chimor was ruled by only one king at a time.

(2) While the number of rulers given in the king list may be only an approximation, it is reasonable for the temporal duration of the Chimú empire. Therefore, the number of major compounds and burial platforms in Chan Chan should show some correspondence to the number of kings on the list—that is, the two figures should be of the same order of magnitude.

(3) The compounds should bear evidence of the control and management of wealth. As imperial rulers the kings of Chimor had access to, and control of, vast amounts of wealth in the form of prestige objects and rights to labor. Although a king's wealth need not have been stored in his residence, I presume that this structure would have been the center for the exercise of his royal property rights.

(4) Each compound should exhibit evidence for the continued posthumous exaltation of the king who built it. The royal dynasty of Chimor was held to be divine. Hence I assume that veneration of its members persisted after their deaths.

(5) Each compound should display indications of continued high-status occupation after the death of the king who built it. The inhabitants would be members of the corporation of secondary heirs honoring the dead king.

EVALUATING THE HYPOTHESIS

Expectation 1: The compounds should have been built one at a time.
It has already been demonstrated that the burial platforms were constructed sequentially. Since these platforms are architectural foci of their respective compounds, it would seem at first glance that the compounds themselves should have been built one at a time in the same order.

Unfortunately, matters are not quite so simple. In Chapter 4, Kolata has established that the compounds were indeed built one at a time. However, his sequence differs in several respects from the burial platform sequence presented in this chapter (Table 5.3). The specific disagreements lie in the placement of Laberinto and Squier.

TABLE 5.3
COMPARISON OF PROPOSED COMPOUND AND BURIAL
PLATFORM SEQUENCES*

Compound	Burial Platform
Rivero	
	Tschudi—Rivero
Tschudi	
	Squier?
Bandelier	Bandelier—Laberinto
	Squier?
Velarde	Velarde
Squier	
Gran Chimú	Gran Chimú
Laberinto	
Tello	
Uhle	Uhle
Chayhuac	Chayhuac

*Earliest at bottom; latest at top.

In Kolata's sequence, Ciudadela Laberinto is a relatively early structure—specifically, the fourth of the Chan Chan compounds. However, the seriation of architectural characteristics presented here assigns the Laberinto burial platform to a later position, that of the fifth, sixth, or seventh platform built in the city. While the placement of Squier in the compound sequence is ambiguous, it does seem to precede Ciudadelas Velarde and Bandelier. However, the burial platform seriation places Squier after Velarde, and perhaps after Bandelier.

The cause of these discrepancies is the fact that, in contrast to all other cases, the Laberinto and Squier platforms were built with bricks different from those used in the corresponding compounds. Ciudadela Laberinto itself and the external court in which its burial platform sits were constructed with flat and square-ended adobes, which are early types. However, the Laberinto burial platform was built with tall adobes, the latest type. Likewise, the Squier compound was built with adobes that are formally, and presumably temporally, intermediate between the square-ended and tall types. In contrast, the bricks in the Squier burial platform are unequivocally tall and late (Kolata, personal communication). This evidence argues that the Laberinto and Squier platforms were constructed at considerably later dates than their compounds.

Having stated these problems in some detail, I will now say that they are not as serious as they might seem. Strict sequential correlation between compounds and platforms is necessary only if we assume that the architectural adjuncts of Chimú government were fully developed when Chan Chan was founded. Such is not the case. As Kolata has shown, both U-shaped structures and the compounds themselves originally displayed considerable formal variation and were only gradually standardized. Significantly, both Laberinto and Squier occupy early to middle positions in the compound sequence. The later parts of the compound and platform sequences mirror one another and present no problems.

I shall return to this point in a subsequent section on developmental trends. For the moment, suffice it to note that the compounds were built one at a time and that all conflicts with the burial platform sequence involve relatively early compounds. Accordingly, I consider Expectation 1 to be confirmed.

Expectation 2: The number of compounds and burial platforms should be of the same order of magnitude as the number of kings on the traditional list. The usual interpretation of the Chimú king list includes ten rulers (most of them unnamed) from Taycanamo to Minchançaman. While the king list probably should not be taken as an exact historical record, the numbers of platforms, compounds, and kings are indeed of the same order of magnitude.

110

Expectation 3: The compounds should bear evidence of the control and management of wealth. The contents of the burial platforms show that the kings of Chimor did indeed have access to vast quantities of wealth. Strikingly, available evidence argues that control of those possessions was centered in the compounds: the majority of the smaller subdivisions of the great enclosures are units of storerooms protected by labyrinthine paths of approach. The goods deposited and guarded in these rooms were probably prestige items representing wealth. Every storeroom excavated to date had been completely and systematically emptied in Precolumbian times. Their contents seem to have been removed when the compounds were abandoned; some items may have been transferred to Cuzco. This uniform emptiness would be difficult to explain had all of the storerooms been filled with more mundane artifacts or foodstuffs (Day 1973:254–59).

The question of the role of wealth in the Kingdom of Chimor deserves more attention than I can give it here. However, some additional points concerning the topic are relevant to the purposes of this chapter.

I remarked earlier that in several instances burial platforms were eventually built to a different size than had originally been intended. A possible explanation for this phenomenon is differential availability of wealth at the beginning and end of the reign of the king who built each structure. That is, had Chimor prospered greatly during the reign of a certain king, he might have accumulated more possessions, and gained access to the services of a larger labor pool, than he had expected. He could then have built a platform larger and more elaborate than the one he had originally envisioned. Conversely, had the empire suffered political and economic reversals during his rule, his sources of goods and labor would have been limited. He might then have been forced to build his platform on a reduced scale.

Expectation 4: The compounds should exhibit evidence for the continued posthumous veneration of the kings who built them. The presence of commemorative primary-stage additions with new secondary cells containing further grave offerings and human sacrifices in every burial platform except those of Bandelier and Squier confirms the expectation.

The size, opulence, and perhaps even presence or absence of primary-stage additions may have depended upon the wealth available to the

111

members of a deceased king's corporation. A "rich" corporation, descended from a successful king who had left its members large, reliable sources of labor and income, might have been able to erect a large primary-stage addition and stock it lavishly. Members of a "poor" corporation, descended from a lesser king whose legacy consisted of small or unreliable sources of labor and income, might have had to limit themselves to a simple primary-stage addition. In extreme cases they might not have been able to build one at all.

Expectation 5: The compounds should display evidence of continued high-status occupation and use after the deaths of the kings who built them. The best evidence in support of this expectation is provided by the secondary-stage structural additions. The elaborate nature of the cells in additions of this type indicates that they were intended for the burials of individuals whose status was high, though not equal to that of the dead king buried in the main platform. The proximity of each secondary-stage addition to its respective platform argues that the persons interred in the former were closely affiliated with the deceased ruler. The presence of T-shaped cells in at least some secondary-stage additions strengthens this contention. Lastly, the association of ground *Spondylus* shell with the Tschudi secondary-stage addition suggests strongly that the individuals buried in these structures were themselves royalty. Hence I conclude that each secondary-stage addition was built for particularly important members of a dead king's corporation who resided in their ancestor's compound and were charged with maintaining his worship.

Again, the presence, size, and complexity of secondary-stage additions may have depended upon the wealth controlled by a deceased king's corporation.

Developmental Trends

Several problematical compounds and burial platforms argue that the architectural expressions of Chimú kingship were originally somewhat variable and were only gradually standardized during the occupation of Chan Chan. The most important evidence underlying this assertion is the difference between the compound and platform sequences (Table 5.3).

Reconciliation of the two sequences produces the following order of burial platform construction (earliest at bottom; latest on top):

112

Rivero
Tschudi

Bandelier $\begin{cases} \text{Squier?} \\ \text{Laberinto} \\ \text{Squier?} \end{cases}$

Velarde
Gran Chimú
Uhle
Chayhuac

The Laberinto and Bandelier platforms are thought to be roughly contemporaneous because the design of their forecourts is identical (Type B). Unfortunately, the design of the Squier forecourt (Type D) is unique, and at present it is impossible to determine whether the Squier platform was built before or after that of Laberinto. In either case, it is clear that the Squier and Laberinto platforms were built at a later date than their respective compounds.

To restate the matter in terms of my hypothesis, the Squier and Laberinto platforms were built well after the deaths of the kings who occupied the corresponding compounds. I therefore suggest that these two platforms were constructed as retroactive memorials to the kings in question during the reign of some later ruler. The mounds date to that segment of the occupation of Chan Chan represented by Velarde and Bandelier and were presumably built at the behest of a king who governed from one of those ciudadelas.

At least one incident recorded in the ethnohistoric literature makes this interpretation plausible. When Pachacuti remodeled Cuzco and its environs, he provided estates for eight previous Inca rulers, some of whom were probably mythical (Rowe 1967:61).

However, if this reconstruction of events is correct, why was a burial platform not added to the Tello compound as well? I can offer three possible explanations for the lack of a platform in Tello. The first is that Tello was functionally distinct from the other compounds. In other words, Tello was not a royal palace and should not be expected to contain a burial platform.

A second possibility is that Tello was the palace of a king who fell into disfavor for some reason—incompetence, palace intrigue, or the like. He may have been removed from office as a result; at any rate, he was not honored with a burial platform. Again, such an occurrence would have ethnohistoric parallels. Chroniclers name several Precolumbian Peruvian rulers whose power and prestige fell dramatically during their reigns. Fempellec, the last head of the pre-Chimú Lambayeque dynasty, was supposedly cast into the sea by priests as punishment for sacrilege (Cabello 1951:327–30; Rowe 1948:38–39; Kosok 1965:73). Likewise, several sources speak of Inca Urcon, an Inca ruler who lost his nerve in the face of an enemy threat and fled from Cuzco. His half-brother Pachacuti remained, defeated the enemy, and had himself crowned in Inca Urcon's palace. Pachacuti subsequently removed Inca Urcon's name from the official king list (Rowe 1946:203–4).

Still a third alternative is that the Tello king was interred in a previously existing burial platform—that is, in either Chayhuac or Uhle, the compounds preceding Tello in the sequence. This suggestion raises the possibility that in the early stages of Chan Chan's growth, palaces and burial platforms were designed to hold more than one ruler. For example, in later platforms primary-stage structural additions signify a repetition of the funeral ceremonies of the king buried in the original mound. However, did the primary-stage addition to the earliest platform, that of Chayhuac, serve this same purpose, or was it the tomb of one or more rulers who succeeded the king buried in the main platform? Similarly, in later cases secondary-stage additions are associated with important members of a deceased king's corporation. Yet Uhle, which seems to be the first compound with a secondary-stage addition to its burial platform, shows at least two major stages of construction (Kolata, Chapter 4). Does the secondary-stage addition in Uhle hold members of the corporation descended from the king buried in the main platform, or is it the tomb of a subsequent ruler who occupied, or at least enlarged, the compound?

The answers to these questions lie in specific historical events that are not archaeologically determinable, at least for the present. Nonetheless, some broader conclusions do emerge from the preceding discussion. On the whole, the archaeological data strongly support the hypothesized scheme of one king:one palace:one burial platform. Difficulties arise only in the interpretation of several relatively early compounds and their platforms. Furthermore, these problematical structures are understandable in a general sense if we posit that standardized visible expressions of Chimú leadership developed only after a period of experimentation with variable but broadly similar architectural forms. Therefore, I conclude that the major compounds of Chan

Chan were in fact the palaces of the kings of Chimor, just as the burial platforms were their mortuary structures, and that the great enclosures were built sequentially under a royal law of split inheritance. This pattern was incompletely developed during the early part of Chan Chan's history but gradually rigidified.

The exact time of crystallization is debatable. In Chapter 4, Kolata suggests that the pattern may have been codified with the construction of Laberinto, the first true ciudadela. However, since Laberinto originally lacked a burial platform, I am inclined to believe that standardization occurred somewhat later—specifically, in Velarde or Bandelier times, when burial platforms were finally added to the Laberinto and Squier palaces.

SYNTHESIS: ORGANIZATIONAL PRINCIPLES

Four governmental principles have been identified as common characteristics of the Chimú and Inca empires: divine kingship, a view of property as a divine right, split inheritance, and military expansionism. How were these factors integrated in Chimú society?

Sahlins (1970:83) and Service (1962:174–75) have argued that political power, the production and distribution of goods, and legitimized force form a functionally interrelated subsystem in society. Actually, complex societies contain a number of subsystems of this nature. In the case of the Chimú, Keatinge and Day (1973) have shown that the socioeconomic organization of the Moche Valley composed one such functional grouping. The rights and activities of the kings of Chimor formed another subsystem of this type.

In the specialized case of the Chimú royalty, the production and distribution of goods took the form of procurement of wealth. Thus the organizational principles underlying the rights and activities of the kings of Chimor may be seen as the basis of a functional subsystem in which political power was represented by divine kingship; the procurement of wealth, by the divine right to property and split inheritance; and legitimized force, by military expansion. These principles expressed themselves and were integrated in the following manner.

The king of Chimor was held to be divine. He was therefore separated from his subjects by his social status, governmental office, and position in the religious pantheon. In fact, the Chimú nobility were believed to have been created separately from the commoners (Rowe 1948:47). Hence the king was set apart from the general population by an insurmountable barrier that was at the same time social, political, and religious. This barrier was symbolized by his high-walled, labyrinthine palace, set in the heart of the capital city but inaccessible to anyone lacking the right to enter it.

Furthermore, the divinity of the Chimú ruler gave his procurement of wealth a religious sanction: that is, because the king was divine, his right to property was divine and presumably incontestable. Nonetheless, royal wealth may not have been inviolate: fear of theft was a Chimú preoccupation, and the punishment of thieves was severe (Rowe 1948:49). The royal palace, which served to separate the king from his subjects, also functioned as an elaborate safeguard for his possessions.

As both a political leader and a demigod, the king received the luxurious funerary treatment reflected in the burial platforms. Although he ceased to be ruler of the empire upon his death, his divine status did not end at that time. The primary-stage structural additions affixed to the burial platforms indicate that, as a member of the Chimú pantheon, a dead king continued to be a viable force in the world of the living. In fact, I think it likely, though unprovable, that the mummies of past rulers played a vital role in the important state ceremonies of Chimor. This phenomenon was observed among the Incas (Rowe 1946:308) and probably characterized the Chimú empire as well.

The continuing power of the dead king created certain problems with respect to his wealth. That is, in a sense, a legal conflict between the deceased ruler and his successor over control of the former's property was inherent in Chimú culture. Both men had a divine right to property; in the case of the possessions of the dead king, who was still a spiritual presence in the empire, their claims overlapped. This implicit dispute could not be settled on the basis of status, since the two contestants were equals; hence it was settled on the basis of priority. Because the dead ruler had the earlier claim to his wealth, it continued to be treated as his property and was given in trust to a corporate group of secondary heirs, who managed it for him. Accordingly, split inheritance may be seen as a legal principle formulated because the combination of divine kingship and the divine right to property in Chimor created an innate conflict that had to be resolved.

Resolution of this dispute in favor of the previous ruler forced the new king to exercise his property rights by amassing new possessions

116

that would be incontestably his own. As a divine being he was entitled to those possessions, and the most profitable way to obtain them was to conquer new territories, annex them to the empire as provinces, and levy taxes in them. Thus in the Chimú empire military expansion was a fully legitimized use of force and was probably not merely a right of the new king, but also his duty.

Accordingly, two principles most directly responsible for the design of the civic center of Chan Chan were divine kingship and split inheritance. Divine kingship made it possible for the Chimú rulers to construct palaces and burial platforms; split inheritance made it necessary for each ruler to build his own palace and burial platform. So, through time, the ring of compounds that dominates Chan Chan was formed.

One final point: all of the patterns described above were ideals that developed gradually and could be disrupted at any time by specific historical events. One complicating factor in the analysis of the platforms and compounds has been the fact that cases of disruption and/or incomplete development (for example, Laberinto) have been preserved equally with cases where full-blown ideals operated unhindered. Nevertheless, even in anomalous cases the ideal patterns asserted themselves recognizably, reaffirming their paramount importance in the social and political order of Chimor.

NOTES

1. The ten great compounds of Chan Chan may be separated into ciudadelas and cuadros. Ciudadelas have three major internal subdivisions: a northern entry sector, a central sector, and a rear sector, or canchón. Cuadros are also internally subdivided, but they lack the formalized tripartite plan of the ciudadelas. The ciudadela compounds are Gran Chimú, Bandelier, Tschudi, Rivero, Laberinto, and Velarde. The cuadros are Uhle, Chayhuac, Tello, and Squier.

2. Periodic repetition or recelebration of funeral rites is a persistent, well-documented tradition in the Andean area. Bandelier (1904), Cieza de Leon (1959:312), and Rowe (1946:286; 1962:131) discuss prehistoric and early historic examples; Valcárcel (1946:474) mentions modern practices.

6

Elite Compounds in Chan Chan

ALEXANDRA M. ULANA KLYMYSHYN
University of California, Santa Barbara

The central question addressed in this chapter is, Given that there are three major types of architectural remains in Chan Chan, what are the functional and social implications of the intermediate-size structures herein referred to as elite compounds?[1] The lines of evidence used in answering this question are (1) ethnohistoric records, (2) the layout of the site, (3) the data obtained through the excavation and survey of the structures, and (4) the results of related studies in Chan Chan.

INTERMEDIATE ARCHITECTURE: DEFINITION

The elite compounds consist of 35 structures, each enclosed by a wall which restricts access to the units. This concern with the control of access is further emphasized by the presence of one entry into each unit and of narrow corridors within over half the structures. The construction material is primarily adobe. Other than these defining characteristics, the other features of the units are marked by a high degree of diversity.

119

The degree of diversity characteristic of the elite compounds is immediately apparent from a comparison of sizes and internal subdivisions. The area of the individual units varies between 600 and 109,000 square meters. The internal subdivisions of some of the units are reminiscent of the interior sectors of ciudadelas, whereas other units contain closely packed rooms similar to the small irregularly agglutinated rooms, or SIAR (Chapter 7). The diversity is also evident in the number of wells contained within a unit (0–6), the percentage of storage space (0–5 percent), and the percentage of open space (less than 5 to over 90 percent per unit).

There are three main concentrations of these units: (1) within the central area of the site, bounded by the ciudadelas; (2) west of Ciudadela Rivero and south of Ciudadela Laberinto; and (3) south of Ciudadela Tschudi. Most of the elite compounds are located away from the immediate vicinity of the entries into monumental compounds. Rather they are usually located in the vicinity of SIAR.

The elite compounds have certain characteristics in common with both the ciudadelas described by Day (Chapter 3) and the small irregularly agglutinated rooms (SIAR) described by J. Topic (Chapter 7). The elite compounds are similar to the monumental ones in that they have restricted access and contain open courts, courts with benches and niches, U-shaped structures, storeroom courts, and wells. They differ from monumental compounds in their smaller size, less consistent internal planning, and the allocation of smaller percentages of the interior space to open areas and to courts with storerooms. Further, with one exception, elite compounds do not contain burial platforms.

Elite compounds are distinguished from the SIAR by their enclosing walls, restricted access, and a higher degree of planning. More U-shaped structures and storage rooms are found in the elite compounds than in the SIAR. And finally, though there is evidence for craft production in the SIAR, no such evidence has been found in the elite structures. The majority of elite compounds are either abutted by or are in close proximity to SIAR clusters.

ETHNOHISTORY

Information on the Kingdom of Chimor is sketchy. For this reason, most reconstructions rely heavily on the information available for the Inca empire. I will follow this procedure in discussing those elements of the ethnohistoric record which appear most pertinent to a sociopolitical and functional interpretation of elite compounds. First, the information specific to the Chimú.

In some ways, the most pertinent and important information is contained in the creation myth as recorded in Pacasmayo, which speaks of separate creations for nobles and commoners:

Ya dige en el tratado de Pachacamac, que estos Indios de los llanos, i costas del mar tenian por cierto, i oy lo piésan muchos, q́ sus primeros protoplaítos i progenitores no eran Adan i Eva sino quatro estrellas, que las dos precrearon a los Reyes, Caziques i nobles, i las otras dos a los plebeyos, a los pobres i a los mitayos, que en los relances del mundo es menester la Fé que profesamos, para no pensar que los ricos i potentado son dicendiétes de otros principios diferentes de los que tuvieron los pobres i umildes, pues aquellos miran sienpre a estos, *no como a iguales en la naturaleza* [italics mine], sino como a ultimos desprecios de la fortuna. (Calancha 1638:Bk. III, Ch. 2: 554)

This quotation is translated as:

It is said in the tract of Pachacamac that these people of the coastal plain had, and today believe in, as their original progenitors not Adam and Eve but four stars, two of which created the Kings, Lords and Nobles and the other two of which created the commoners, poor and laborers. Unlike faithful Christians who do not believe the rich and powerful are descendants of different beings than the poor and humble, these people always look upon themselves *not as natural equals to the privileged* [italics added], but as the scorned ones of fortune.

The ethnohistoric sources mention several occupational groups, the members of which held positions of prestige and authority and who, therefore, were probably members of the nobility rather than common people. Among these is a list of courtiers, whose titles indicate the service that they performed for the Chimú lord:

[Ñaymlap] brought in his company many people who followed him. . . . But those among them who were of the greatest bravery were their officials, who were forty in number. . . . Another very important official . . . was called Llapchillulli, and he wrought shirts and clothing of feathers. With this retinue, and with an infinite number of other officials and men of importance, he [Ñaymlap] brought his person and house, already adorned and established. (Cabello Valboa as quoted by Means 1931:51)

There is evidence that these courtiers were eligible for the cacicazgo (leadership of at least 100 men). First, during the reign of Cium, Ñaymlap's heir, Llapchillulli founded his own settlement in a place listed as Jayanca (Means 1931:53). And second, the cook of the cacique of Reque was elected to the cacicazgo (Rostworowski 1961:15). This clearly indicates that the courtiers were nobles rather than commoners, as the literature discloses that only nobles could become caciques.

The caciques and curacas (lower nobility) acted as the local governors and as collectors of the tribute (Rostworowski 1961). They were either members of the local indigenous nobility or nobles from Chan Chan, assigned to their post by the Chimú lord (Means 1931:53). Other members of the nobility included a hierarchy of military officers and the curers (Calancha 1638:Bk. III, Ch. 2:556). No doubt there was a group of functionaries who were engaged in the business of running and maintaining the empire, but whose duties and titles have not survived. It is, however, neither clear nor necessary that such a group consisted solely of nobles.

An indication of a concern with the maintenance of social order may be seen in the severe punishment meted out to thieves. The moon goddess, Si, who held the principal place in the Chimú pantheon, was the protectress of private property. She would go looking for thieves and hand them over to the stars for punishment (Calancha 1638:Bk. III, Ch. 2:552). Can this preoccupation with keeping objects with their rightful owner or in their proper place not be seen as symbolic of maintaining order in all aspects of life, including the social?

As we have seen, the ethnohistoric data are rather scanty and do not give a complete picture of the sociopolitical organization of the Chimú empire. However, the chronicles do point out the rigidity of the social organization, which comprised two distinct social groups, each created by a different set of stars. More information about the Chimú may be extrapolated from the Inca ethnohistoric record.

The Inca empire was organized along fairly strict lines with the social and political hierarchies paralleling one another. The highest position in both was, of course, held by the divine son of the sun, or Sapa Inca. All of the descendants of the emperors, including those of secondary wives, were members of the royal ayllus, or lineages. There were two classes of nobles: the Inca nobility and the local rulers.

The position of curaca or cacique was mainly hereditary, though successors were often chosen from among those eligible with an eye to their qualifications. The caciques had control of some of the land and of the surplus collected in taxes. Part of the surplus was used by them in "paying" the persons engaged in labor for the state (Cieza de León 1943:Chs. 18, 20; Rowe 1946:263–64; Rostworowski 1961:11–20).

Many of the administrative divisions of the Inca empire corresponded to the pre-Inca political and/or ethnic units (Rowe 1946:262) and therefore probably applied to Chimú organization. In these areas, the administration was often left in the hands of the indigenous rulers, once they had sworn fealty to Cuzco (Means 1931:293). It appears, then, that the conquered areas were allowed a certain degree of autonomy. There were, however, several mechanisms through which checks were maintained on the local rulers, whether indigenous or not. The curacas were required to maintain a residence in the capital and to attend certain ceremonies there (Garcilaso de la Vega 1966:Pt. I, Bk. 7). Further, local rulers were required to send their children to Cuzco for schooling (Zárate 1933:20, 34–35).

It seems probable that all of those who were permanently exempt from taxes and mit'a labor were also members of the nobility. In addition to the Inca ayllus and the curacas these were the priests, ministers, army officials, governors, and certain craftspersons (Rowe 1946:260–61; Garcilaso de la Vega 1961:Pt. I, Bk. 1, Ch. 15).

Kinship ties were the underlying principle of social organization. This is reflected in the structure of the parallel social, administrative, religious, and military hierarchies. Essentially, families were ranked; and their members could hold offices of similar importance within the different hierarchies. The evidence for this is in the kind of offices held by the close relatives of the Sapa Inca and in the list of those eligible for the cacicazgo (Rowe 1946:249–63; Rostworowski 1961:passim). Another line of evidence is that of liability, both in taxation and in legal punishments. The unit of taxation was not the individual but the family and the community (Means 1931:312–13); similarly, the whole family was punished for certain crimes committed by individual members (Means 1931:348). The basic residential unit appears to have been the extended family, though this might apply only to the nobility.

> Extended families seem to have lived by preference in a common enclosure (KANKA) containing three to six houses, if we may judge from the plans of such Inca sites as Machu Picchu and Ollantaytambo. (Rowe 1946:252)

Inca society can be summarized as strictly organized, with birth determining both positions and obligations. The social stratification was kept before the eyes of both the commoners and nobility through various outward means and sumptuary rules. Status and origin were reflected in both dress and the type of cloth used (Cieza de León 1943:Ch. 12; Murra 1962:passim). The use of certain other items and materials was also restricted. For example, gold could be used only by the nobility. Certain items and customs were restricted even within the nobility. The emperor could bestow the use of an item, whether on a noble or a commoner, as a privilege in return for some special service to the state, frequently military exploits (Rowe 1946:279–80).

A sociopolitical organization such as that of the Inca empire precludes the formation of a middle class. There are several reasons for this: (1) There was a basic split between two social groups—the nobles and the commoners. Membership in either was determined by birth and could be changed only by imperial decree. (2) Further, within the nobility, families were ranked. Members of the families held similar positions in the closely parallel hierarchies—social, political, and so forth. (3) The state, either directly or through its local representatives, the curacas, had control of the bulk of the surplus goods. (4) There was no monetary medium of exchange, and the use of certain luxury items was restricted, even within the nobility. Thus, the commoners and some members of the lower nobility would not have been able to amass the visible symbols of status. And (5), occupational specializations were correlated with social status in one or the other of the two main social groups and within these according to the inherited rank of one's family.

ELITE COMPOUNDS: CLASSIFICATION

The 35 elite compounds have been classified into six types. The classification was made on the basis of the standing architectural remains.

The criteria used in the classification reflect the degree to which the inhabitants and users of the structures controlled available resources. This degree of control over resources is in turn indicative of the occupants' social status. The criteria are (1) the number of wells enclosed within and/or closely associated with a structure; (2) size; (3) the number and characteristics of the internal subdivisions; (4) the percentage of open space (plazas and courts) within a structure; (5) the nature of the internal access patterns; (6) the number and types of courts within a structure; (7) the number, type and location of U-shaped structures; and (8) the percentage of interior space allotted to storerooms.

Wells are the primary criterion both because they are invariably visible on the surface and because they are good indicators of status, as will be discussed below. On the basis of the presence/absence of wells, the six types fall into two groups: Types I–IV either contain or are directly associated with wells, whereas Types V–VI neither contain nor are associated with wells.

Type I units are characterized by internal subdivisions similar to the tripartite division of ciudadelas. There are only three such units (see Figure 6.1).

Type II units are all over 150 meters long. Though they do not have subdivisions similar to those of ciudadelas and Type I units, they do contain features similar to those found in the first two sectors of ciudadelas, with the exception of burial structures. There are six Type II units. Two of these are characterized by large open courts and relatively small sections with standing architecture (Figure 6.2).

Type III units are marked by a high diversity of both size and internal planning. Each of them, however, contains at least one feature, which makes them similar to Type I and II units. These features, which are also associated with the first two sectors of a ciudadela, include U-shaped structures, storeroom complexes, and courts containing benches, ramps and/or niches. There are six units in this type (Figure 6.3).

Type IV units either contain or are associated with at least one well, but do not have any of the features listed above for Type III units. There are seven Type IV units (Figure 6.4).

Type V units neither contain nor are associated with wells. The units do, however, contain at least one of the other features found in Type I–III units. There are seven Type V units (Figure 6.5)

Type VI units are basically indistinguishable from the SIAR, except for the enclosing walls. That is, they contain neither wells nor any of the features listed under Type III above. There are six Type VI units (Figure 6.6).

ELITE COMPOUNDS: CHRONOLOGY

The discussion of chrónology is based on Kolata's adobe seriation (Chapter 4). It is summarized in tabular form in Table 6.1. The data

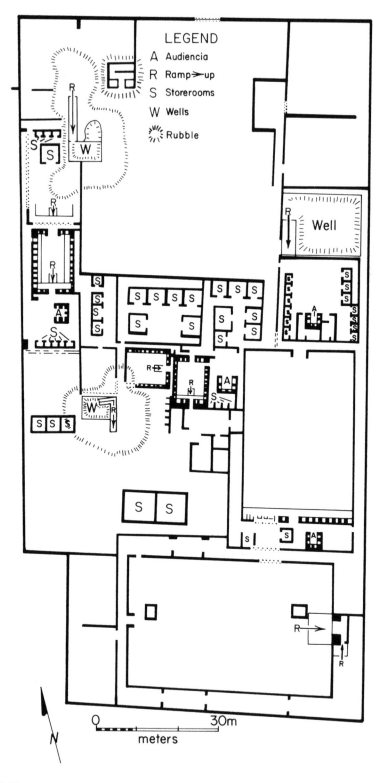

FIGURE 6.1. Unit 10, a Type I unit, with subsections similar to those found in ciudadelas. Type I units also contain architectural features (storage structures, audiencias) characteristic of ciudadelas.

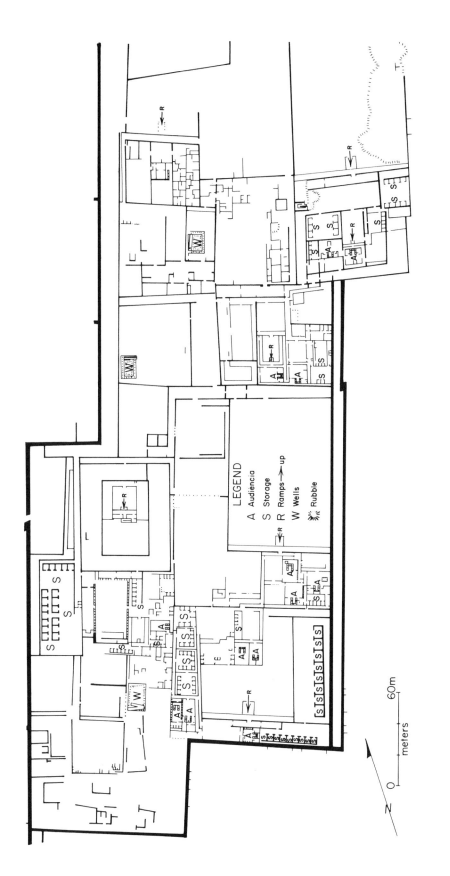

FIGURE 6.2. Unit 6, a Type II unit containing courts, audiencias, storage structures, and wells similar to those found in ciudadelas.

LEGEND

A Audiencia
S Storage
R Ramps → up
W Wells
☀ Rubble

N

0   60m

meters

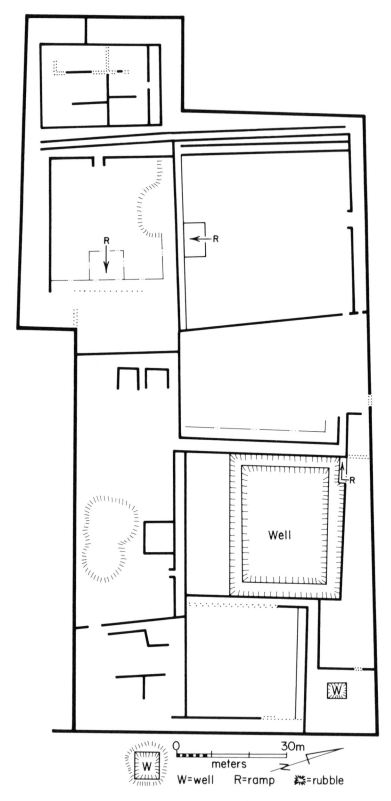

FIGURE 6.3. Unit 12, a Type III unit containing wells, corridors, and courts with benches and ramps.

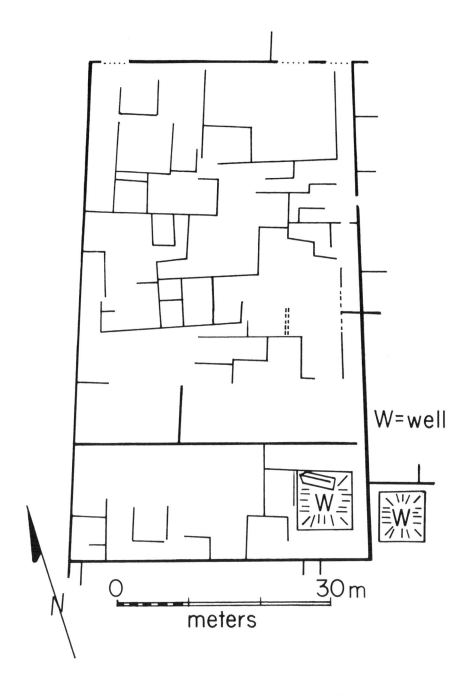

W=well

FIGURE 6.4. Unit 20, a Type IV unit that contains a walk-in well but no other architectural feature characteristic of ciudadelas.

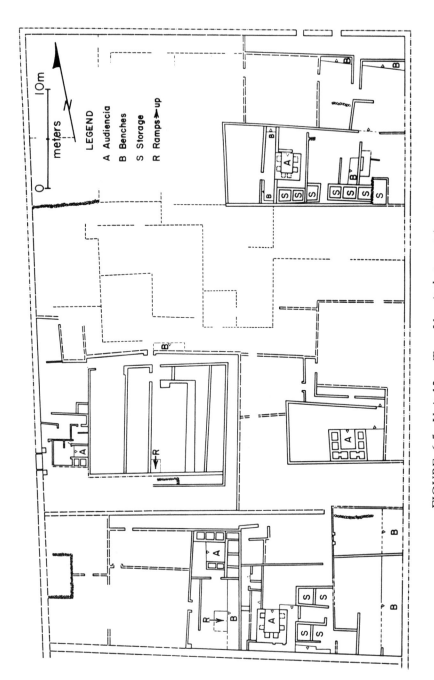

FIGURE 6.5. Unit 13, a Type V unit that contains storage structures, audiencias, and courts but does not contain a walk-in well.

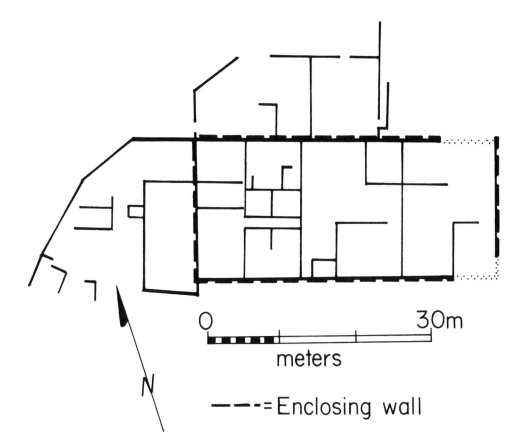

FIGURE 6.6. Unit 14, a Type VI unit that contains neither a walk-in well nor any other architectural feature characteristic of ciudadelas. This type of unit is distinguished from SIAR units by the presence of an enclosing wall.

on brick type are available for all but 9 of the elite compounds. Of these 26 structures, only 2 are in Phase I (early): Unit 5, north of Uhle, and Unit 21, south of Tello. These early units were probably associated with their neighboring monumental compounds, which are also early. Two structures, 3 and 4, are transitional between the Early and the Middle phases. They are located northwest of Laberinto, most of which is Early, but certain sections belong to the Middle Phase. Twenty units (88 percent of the units for which data are available) belong to the Late Phase. The remaining 3 units have bricks of mixed phases.

The units with mixed-phase adobes are 6 (east of Velarde and Laber-

TABLE 6.1
CHRONOLOGICAL CLASSIFICATION OF
ELITE COMPOUNDS

Compound	Phase I	I/II*	II	III	No data
1				x	
2				x	
3		x			
4		x			
5	x				
6**	x		x	x	
7				x	
8					x
9**	x			x	
10				x	
11				x	
12				x	
13				x	
14					x
15				x	
16					x
17				x	
18				x	
19					x
20					x
21				x	
22	x				
23				x	
24					x
25					x
26					x
27				x	
28					x
29				x	
30				x	
31				x	
32				x	
33				x	
34				x	
35				x	

*Transitional between Phases I and II.
**See text for discussion of these two units.

into), 9 (west of Uhle), and 31 (south of Tschudi). Units 6 and 9 have Early Phase adobes in the inner enclosing walls and Late Phase adobes in the outer wall. The structures inside Unit 6 (Figure 6.2) have adobes from all three phases, corresponding to the building sequence reconstructed on the basis of wall abutments and remodeling (Klymyshyn 1976:386–446). Unit 31 contains mostly Phase II adobes, with some Phase I bricks; it is not clear whether these Early Phase adobes are reused or not.

Most of the elite units can, thus, be said to belong to the later phases of construction in Chan Chan. It is interesting to note that all Type I ciudadelalike elite structures are Late Phase, as are all of the units south of Tschudi. Beyond this, there does not seem to be any correlation between chronology and typology, nor between chronology and the location of elite compounds.

ELITE COMPOUNDS: DISCUSSION

In this section, I will discuss elite compounds in relation to the other structures on the site and examine various features associated with the elite structures.

Location

As mentioned in the definition of elite compounds, there are three main concentrations of units. The breakdown by area of the site is: one unit in the north part of the site, northwest of Gran Chimú; three units among the SIAR northwest of Laberinto and southwest of Velarde; another three units in the east part—one north of Uhle and two between Uhle and Chayhuac; a cluster of ten units in the central core area within the rectangle formed by the monumental compounds; one unit between Tschudi and Rivero; nine units south of Laberinto and west of Rivero; three units south of Rivero; and five units south of Tschudi.

There is no clustering of units according to the classification in any part of the site. However, some of the types have a consistent pattern of association with units in one or all three major architectural classes. Type I units are found in close proximity to both elite compounds and SIAR architecture. They seem to hold important positions in that one of them, Unit 10, is located in the middle of the cluster of ten elite units in the central core area of the site; the other two, Units 25 and 32, are either abutting or close to huachaques in the south part of the site. Type II units are associated with monumental architecture. Three of them abut ciudadelas (Units 6, 27, and 29); one abuts the north annex of Rivero (Unit 15); one is a late intrusion into one of the large enclosures west of Gran Chimú (Unit 1); and one abuts Huachaque Chico (Unit 34). All but one of the Type II units are close to other elite units; all of them either abut or are close to SIAR. The units in Types III–VI have similar patterns of association: only 2 of the 26 units (one each in Types III and IV; Klymyshyn 1976:667–79) are neither abutted by nor close to SIAR. Fewer than half of these units are located close to monumental compounds. They are all in the vicinity of other elite compounds, with the exception of Unit 5, a Type VI unit.

Association with Monumental Compounds

Only one elite compound has connecting access with a monumental compound. This is Unit 6 (see Figure 6.2); the connecting access to Ciudadela Laberinto is through the outer court of Las Avispas (the burial platform associated with Laberinto, though outside of the ciudadela), and hence not direct. Further, access into the burial platform area would have been restricted to special personnel. This may mean, however, that the inhabitants of Unit 6 were involved in the maintenance of the platform and/or the memorial rites in honor of the person buried in the platform. The adobes on the outer court of Las Avispas are Early Phase, whereas those in the platform itself are Late Phase. The adobes in the other structures in this part of Unit 6 are from all three phases. This would seem to support the hypothesis that there was some connection between the burial platform and the rest of the unit, in that they were being remodeled or built at the same time.

Six units are located close to the entries of monumental compounds or their annexes and/or extensions. Of these, three either block or impede traffic into the monumental unit. Unit 8, a Type V unit, blocks the entry into Ciudadela Tello. Unfortunately, data on the type of bricks used in Unit 8 are not available. However, its construction is so different from and inferior to that of Tello that it seems almost certain the elite unit was not built as an annex of Tello but was constructed after Tello had lost its importance. The other two units impede access into the annexes of ciudadelas. Unit 12 impedes access into the annex of Tschudi; and Unit 15 contains the corridor leading into the annex of Rivero, thereby impeding access to the ciudadela. In both cases, the brick seriation discloses that both the ciudadela and the elite unit are Late Phase. As the residence of the king and the focal point of the city during his reign, each ciudadela shows a pattern of both restricted access from the outside and an internal access pattern that further emphasizes control and restriction of traffic. It seems, thus, that the people who were allowed to build elite compounds impeding access into a ciudadela would have had a fairly high social status.

Most elite compounds, particularly those in the south part of the site, are located away from monumental units. Even those units which abut Ciudadelas Rivero or Tschudi are more often than not located away from the main entrance into the ciudadela.

Association with SIAR

Most of the elite units are either abutted by or in close proximity to SIAR. It is not clear, however, what the relationship between the two types of structures was. And the data are not available for the dating of the SIAR on the basis of the brick seriation. In several cases (Klymyshyn 1976:667–79), entry into an elite unit is through the abutting SIAR. It might be, then, that these SIAR acted as some kind of annex of the elite compounds unit. The other possibility, of course, is that the SIAR were built after the elite compounds.

It is interesting to note that both the number and density of elite compounds and SIAR decrease toward the north end of Chan Chan. It may be that according to the canons of Chimú urban planning, all nonmonumental architecture had to be located in areas that had not been assigned to monumental architecture. The proximity of many of the elite structures and the SIAR to the cemetery at the south end of Chan Chan may have further bearing on the nature of the relationship between the inhabitants of these two types of structures.

Annexes/Extensions

Nine of the 35 elite units have possible annexes or extensions. Here, *annex* is defined as a structure abutting the unit and located so that a person must go through it in order to enter the unit. An *extension* abuts the unit, but is located away from the entry. Both have connecting access with the unit. Because the data were collected on the basis of survey, the access between the units and their annexes or extensions is not always clear. Thus, some of the structures labeled annexes or extensions may be other, usually smaller, elite compounds.

The units that have possible annexes and/or extensions are not limited to any one area of the site, except that three of them are located south of Tschudi. These units tend to be in Types I–III, with the exception of Unit 5, which is in Type VI. The, latter, however, is a very unclear situation, owing to erosion. It is significant that those units which have annexes or extensions are more similar to monumental architecture than to the SIAR.

Wells

Since Chan Chan is a desert city, water is a scarce commodity. A recent study by Rebecca Blanke (n.d.) indicates that of the over 140 wells in Chan Chan, more than 60 percent are located in the monumental compounds. Only 12 percent, on the other hand, are among the SIAR, which probably housed over 90 percent of the city's population.

Approximately 28 percent of the wells are either within or closely associated with elite compounds. Of these, 27 wells are in the main part of an elite unit; 7 are in an annex or extension of an elite compound, and another 7 wells either abut the exterior wall of a unit or connect directly with one.

Thirteen units, i.e., those which are Type V or VI, are not associated with wells. One of these, Unit 13, was excavated and found to contain a large, possibly communal, kitchen. This further supports Blanke's hypothesis that wells are as much indicators of status as of function.

Open Space

The percentage of open space within a unit is one of the main criteria used in classifying the elite compounds. In most cases, however, it proved quite difficult to calculate an exact percentage, since the calculation was done exclusively on the basis of surface evidence. Thus, under the heading of *open space*, I included all those areas of a unit that had no structural remains visible on the surface, as well as courts with colonnades, small platforms, niches, and benches and ramps. This means, of course, that open space encompasses areas comparable both to the entry courts of ciudadelas and to the canchones, and many kinds of areas in between. This presents obvious problems in assigning a function to an area designated as open space. It does not, however, negate the fact that the inhabitants or users of these units could mark off a relatively large area as their space.

The units which have open areas comparable to those in the ciudadelas are almost exclusively Type I and II, whether the open area be an entry court or a canchón. The other units are generally too small to have contained open areas of this type. The units which are most interesting in terms of open space are those which are characterized by large open courts (e.g., Units 27 and 34, both Type II units) or those which are almost without architectural remains (e.g., Units 9 and 33, Type II and VI, respectively).

U-shaped Structures

Only three kinds of U-shaped structures have been found in elite compounds: standard audiencias, arcones, and auxilios. The 55 audiencias will be discussed below. The four arcones were found in residential contexts in Type IV and V units: 7, 8, and 13—all in the central core area of the site. The five auxilios were found in Type I and II units: 6, 15, and 25. All but one (the one in Unit 15) are in a court with an audiencia. This one is on a bench in a court with storerooms. In addition, there are three U-shaped structures in Unit 34 and one in Unit 27, which are too eroded to determine the type.

The audiencias in elite compounds (see Table 6.2) are located in contexts similar to those in which they are found in monumental compounds, though not consistently so. They frequently cluster behind large courts or are accessible through courts with benches, ramps, and niches or through corridors. This means that they are located toward the back of a unit, i.e., away from the entry and/or entry corridor. The association of audiencias with both direct and indirect control of storerooms is less consistent than in the monumental compounds: there are many courts with storerooms which are not located close to audiencia courts. Further, most audiencia courts do not themselves contain storerooms. The audiencias are not located in the vicinity of wells. It is probable that many of the audiencias, particularly those in Type III and V units—a total of six—are in residential contexts rather than in administrative ones.

There are 18 units that do not contain U-shaped structures either in the main part or in the annexes and/or extensions. Of these, three units contain courts with storerooms (Units 1, 4, and 19). In addition to the Type IV and VI units, the units without U-shaped structures are in Types II, III, and V. This means that half of the Type III units (Units 9, 12, and 19) do not have any U-shaped structures. There is no clustering of units without U-shaped structures.

TABLE 6.2
AUDIENCIAS IN ELITE COMPOUNDS

unit number	6	7	10	13	15	16	17	22	24	25	27	29	31	32	35
in main part of unit	13	1	4	2	1		1	2	1	3	2	10	2	4	1
in annex or extension					5	1								2	
number of audiencias per court	1	1	1	1	1	1	1	?	1	1–2	1	1–2	2	1	1
with auxilio	3									2					
with ancillary structures	12											4			
with storerooms			3		1										
with storerooms and ancillary structures															
court entered through another court	2	1	1	2	1	1	1	?	1	1	1	1?		?	
court entered through corridor	11			2	4			?		?	1	3	2	?	1
on route to storeroom court	3		1		2							7		2?	
associated with a well			1?		1	?		?			1	1		?	
open side: north	6		3	2	4		1	1	1	2		1?	1	3	
south	4	1				1						5	1		
east												1	1	1	
west	3		1		2			1		1	1	4		2	1

138

Storerooms

Only nine (26 percent) of the elite compounds contain courts with storerooms. Only storerooms that are arranged in rows have been designated as such, owing to the obvious danger of assigning a function to small, isolated rooms on the basis of surface remains.

The percentage of storage space within units varies between 0.5 and 5.0 percent. The interior floor area varies between 1 square meter and 28 square meters. The units with the highest percentages of storage space are Type I, II, III, and V units. The latter two are exceptional cases. The Type III unit, 19, is very small and contains only six storerooms, all approximately 1 meter square. The Type V unit is the only one that was excavated, Unit 13 (Figure 6.5). In this case, many of the storerooms were not visible on the unexcavated surface.

As mentioned above, many of the storeroom courts are not con-trolled by audiencia courts, either directly or indirectly. Three of the nine units with storeroom courts do not contain audiencias. In the other six units only 7 of the 37 audiencias have a row or two of storerooms in the same court as the audiencia. Other than these, fewer than ten storeroom courts are directly controlled by an audiencia court. Also, most of the storeroom courts are located away from wells. The major exception is the east part of Unit 15, where there are eight storeroom courts directly south of a large well.

Given that there are so many elite compounds without storerooms (74 percent) and that those with storerooms devote little space to stor-age, we see that the primary function of elite units was not storage, nor did storage play as important a part in the function of elite compounds as it did in the monumental compounds.

CONCLUSIONS

Calancha's comments on the implications of separate creations for different segments of the population are similar to the salient features of the caste system:

> The caste system divides the whole society into a large number of hereditary groups, distinguished from one another and connected together by three characteristics: *separation* in matters of marriage and contact . . . *division* of labour, each group having, in theory or by tradition, a profession from which their members can depart

only within certain limits; and finally *hierarchy*, which ranks the groups as relatively superior or inferior to one another. (Dumont 1970:21)

Chan Chan is a preindustrial city, though perhaps not a typical one. It differs from Sjoberg's model at least in the lack of a developed market and trade system in the hands of a professional merchant class (Sjoberg 1960:Ch. 7). Nonetheless, the model applies to Chan Chan in reference to social structure:

> The preindustrial city is characterized by a bifurcated class structure comprising the elite or upper class . . . and the lower class. . . . The preindustrial city's class structure . . . is distinguished by its rigidity and lack of mobility. (Sjoberg 1960:110)

There are insufficient data to prove whether or not Chimú society was organized into castes or classes. But there is sufficient evidence to prove that Chimú society was marked by the rigidity and lack of mobility outlined by both Dumont and Sjoberg. The archaeological remains in the capital point to the possibility of a bifurcate social system and of heightened concern for social control. The most obvious evidence, of course, is in the high walls, single entries, and tortuous corridors found in the monumental compounds.

Enclosing walls and restricted access are the two main features which elite compounds have in common with monumental compounds. These are also the very features which clearly distinguish the elite units from the SIAR. In addition, because of the higher percentage of wells associated with elite units and the presence of storerooms in at least some of the units, the inhabitants of elite compounds seem to have had a greater control over resources than the inhabitants of the SIAR. It is this degree of control over resources which places the inhabitants of elite compounds in a higher social class than those of the SIAR. And, if one accepts that Chimú society recognized only two major social divisions, then the only higher social class that the inhabitants of elite structures could have belonged to is the nobility.

The main reason for considering the inhabitants of elite compounds as members of the nobility rather than as commoners is the evidence pointing to their access to and control over certain resources. The most important and indicative resource in these terms is water. Above, I mentioned that wells in Chan Chan are as much indicators of status as of function. With the exception of the Type V and VI units, all elite compounds have at least one well associated with them, if not within the compound. The enclosing wall itself is indicative of control over space, always a scarce commodity in an urban setting. All inhabitants or users of elite compounds were, by definition, capable of not only setting off some space as their own or for their own use, but were also able to include open areas within the enclosure. In the Type I–III units many of the open areas are similar to the entry courts of monumental compounds and could have served some public function. Other indicators of resource control are the storerooms and the audiencias. In the monumental compounds both of these types of structures are related to the storage and redistribution of goods.

It seems then, that the break between the nobility and the commoners coincides with the presence/absence of two features: enclosures and wells, in addition to the others mentioned above. It would be tempting to propose further subdivisions within both the nobility and the commoners and correlate these with the architectural remains. However, because of the lack of excavation particularly in the elite compounds, there is simply not enough evidence to do so. All that can be said is that the degree of closeness or similarity to monumental compounds decreases from Type I to Type VI units. It may be in fact that these types do reflect differences in social status, as much as differences in function.

The structural remains show that the inhabitants of elite compounds enjoyed some of the privileges which were the prerogatives of the nobility. The ethnohistoric records reveal that members of the lower nobility were responsible for the redistribution of goods and the payment of mit'a laborers on the local level. It may be that similar duties were performed by the lower nobility resident in the capital. Certainly the number of audiencias and storerooms found in elite compounds suggests that this was the case. Evidence of the kinds of goods placed in the storerooms was not recovered during excavation but consisted of foodstuffs and high-status items. These could then have been both for the personal use of the inhabitants and for redistribution.

A rather elaborate silver ornament was found during the excavation of Unit 13, a Type V unit. This would indicate that the inhabitants had the right to use objects of precious metal, especially since there was no indication that the unit was inhabited by artisans. And, finally, many of the units, especially Type I–III units, are so large and elaborate that they would have required mit'a labor for their construction. It is doubtful that commoners would have had access to mit'a labor, which they, after all, provided.

The questions remain, however, Who were the nobles who resided in elite compounds? And, Were all of the units residential?

Because of the degree of diversity that characterizes elite structures, it is doubtful that all units had the same function. Since there are wells associated with the SIAR, which are outside of both monumental and elite compound enclosures, neither would have served as sources of water for SIAR occupants, nor were these enclosures used in the control of water. Since the percentage of space alloted to storage is fairly small, even in those units that have a relatively high number of storerooms, elite units did not function primarily as storage facilities. Most of the units are too small to have served a public function either in the administrative or in the religious system. But the Type I and II units, as well as the larger Type III–VI units, might well have functioned as public meeting places. The units could also have had a role in the more mundane or routine administrative activities. Some of the units might have been workshops; and some might have been used for the payment of mit'a laborers, not necessarily in terms of goods to be taken away but, for example, for the distribution of food and chicha (maize beer) as immediate payment. Some might even have been used to house mit'a laborers, possibly under some kind of supervision. Just as not all the units need have had the same function, so, too, different sections of the same unit might have had different functions.

Since the ciudadelas have been identified as the royal residences, it would seem that the members of the immediate family of reigning lords and their descendants would not have lived in elite compounds. It is doubtful, however, that all members of the royal lineages would have fit into the monumental compounds. In addition to distant relations of the Chimú lords, probably all members of the lower or curaca nobility would have resided in elite rather than in royal compounds. Residences would have been needed not only for those nobles who were permanent residents of the capital but also for those in the outlying districts of the empire if curacas were required to maintain residence in the Chimú capital, as was the case in the Inca capital.

The interpretation of elite compounds is based on the present appearance of the site, and, of course, the latest phases of occupation are best preserved. It is interesting to note that most of the units, particularly those in the southern section of the site, in the vicinity of the most recent ciudadelas, are in the Late Phase. This may indicate that the elite units and the social group occupying them were a late development in the empire. What we may have, however, is a two-fold proliferation: an enlargement of the nobility both by simple population increase and through the expansion of the empire, concurrent with the proliferation of positions within the imperial polity that needed to be filled by members of the privileged class.

NOTE

1. Elite compounds have been labeled *intermediate architecture* in previous publications (Klymyshyn 1976; Moseley 1975a). In order to prevent confusion of the form with a time period, I decided to change the name to *elite compounds*. While the latter term has functional implications, I believe the evidence in this chapter is sufficient proof that the name is warranted.

7
Lower-Class Social and Economic Organization at Chan Chan[1]

JOHN R. TOPIC, JR.
Trent University

INTRODUCTION

Archaeologists have tended to view prehistoric cities from the top down. The organization, characteristics, and orientation of the elite segments of urban populations are generally examined in detail because they are viewed as the critical force in the evolution of social forms. The members of the urban lower class, however, are usually viewed as little more than a convenient supply of labor and services for the elite. Their presence is regarded as inevitable and not worthy (or susceptible) of explanation, and their role in causing or directing change in the urban scene is considered negligible. While it is usually assumed that a degree of occupational specialization exists among the urban lower class, archaeologists tend to be concerned less with the organization, activities, or makeup of this class than with the sheer numbers of lower-class residents they can claim for their particular site.

This view has been perpetuated even though historians and sociologists have long stressed the importance of the lower class in understanding urbanism. Pirenne (1925) emphasized the role of nonagricultural and nonelite segments of medieval society in the revival of urbanism and the destruction of the feudal order. Sjoberg (1960) and Wheatley (1963: 171–72) point out that the lower class in preindustrial cities tends to be highly organized and structured along guildlike principles. Anderson (1971, 1976) interprets common interest associations, of which guilds are one example, as adaptive mechanisms contributing to social stability in times of rapid social change. Studies such as Forrester's (1969) have shown that migration into the city is determined not by some elusive magnetism inherent in urban life but by distinctive economic and political signals that act selectively on different social segments.

Understanding the urban lower class and its role is prerequisite to understanding the preindustrial city. The purpose of this chapter is to present a model of the characteristics, organization, and orientation of the lower class within Chan Chan and to examine its articulation with other social segments in the Chimú state.

The data and interpretations that follow are based on an intensive program of research carried out intermittently at the site from 1969 to 1974. A surface survey of all the areas where small irregularly agglutinated rooms (SIAR) were found was undertaken, as these complexes housed the urban lower class, and excavation was carried out in selected complexes.

SURFACE INDICATIONS

The SIAR at Chan Chan cover an area slightly in excess of one square kilometer and housed approximately 20,000 people. The structures are grouped into units for ease of discussion (Figure 7.1; see also Moseley and Mackey 1974) and are designated with either letters or Roman numerals. Letters identify units in which excavations have been carried out, while Roman numerals refer to units that received only surface survey.

The surface survey of Chan Chan revealed that, with few exceptions, SIAR occurred in two locations and two contexts. The majority of SIAR units were concentrated on the south, west, and northwest edges of the site. Indeed, these units tended to merge into one vast sprawl, and the unit designations (Figure 7.1) are somewhat arbitrary. The remaining SIAR units were located in the center or along the eastern edge of the site; these were quite small and clearly isolated from each other.

146

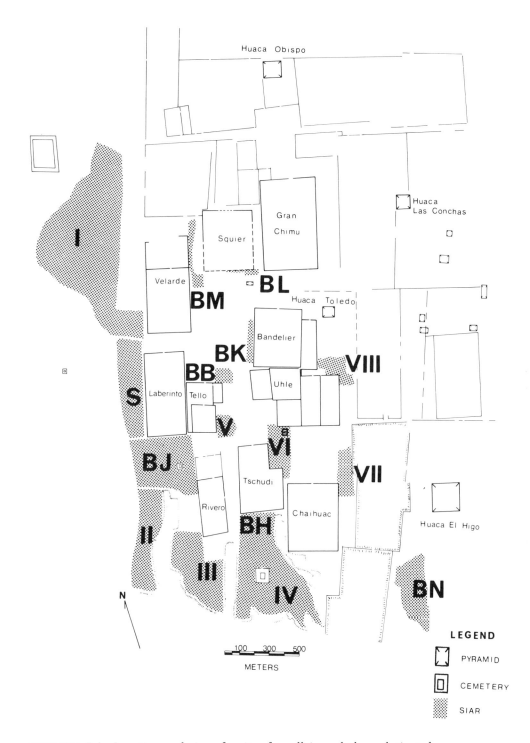

FIGURE 7.1. Location and size of units of small irregularly agglutinated rooms (SIAR).

This distribution is not the result of differential destruction. Repeated survey along the northern and eastern edges of the site revealed the presence of small sherd scatters and isolated SIAR structures, but these occurrences were sparsely distributed. In fact, the only example of large-scale SIAR destruction for agricultural reclamation is in Unit I in the northwest corner of the site, and this reclamation is recent.

The distributional evidence suggests that the Chimú conceived of the site as consisting of three parts. The ciudadelas occupied a central position, flanked by SIAR on the south and west and by huacas and large enclosures on the north and east. This concept of planning implies that those SIAR units located on the south and west peripheries were considered "typical," while those located in other areas were atypical in some way.

SIAR Context

Community patterning can also be considered in terms of the context within which the SIAR are located. The SIAR along the periphery of Chan Chan are associated with elite compounds (Klymyshyn, Chapter 6), wells, and large adobe-walled enclosures which apparently served as cemeteries. These units give the impression of being organized into relatively self-contained wards or neighborhoods, and are best described by the term *barrios*. Units BJ, II, and probably Unit III would together constitute one barrio. Units BH and IV would together constitute another barrio, while Unit VI forms still another, small barrio. Unit S does not contain a cemetery enclosure, but a possible cemetery enclosure is located west of the unit; taken together, these would form another barrio. A small cemetery enclosure is located within Unit I, and a larger enclosure, which may have been used as a cemetery, exists to the north. This last barrio seems to have fewer and less impressive structures of the elite-compound type and is less adequately serviced by wells than the other barrios.

In general, then, the distribution of barrios tends to be in the southern and western peripheries of the site. Minor exceptions are the inclusion of Unit VI as a barrio and the exclusion of Unit BN, which is explained below.

Another context in which SIAR are located is on top of artificial platforms. The *rooms-constructed-on-platforms* pattern includes Units BM, BL, BK, VI, VII, and VIII as well as the northeast part of Unit S

148

and the southeast part of Unit BJ. Most of the SIAR built on platforms are centrally located, and all are intimately associated with monumental enclosures. Still, the context of the platforms varies. Some platforms are freestanding; some abut the north annexes of monumental enclosures but carefully avoid abutting the walls of the enclosure itself; others abut or even partially overlie ciudadela walls.

Finally, three *anomalous* SIAR units (BB, V, and BN) fit neither of the patterns discussed above. The first two (BB and V) are rather centrally located, and each contains a small, heavily looted platform at one edge of the unit. The outstanding characteristics of Unit BN are its outlying location and the evidence for incomplete construction of both SIAR and wachaques (sunken gardens).

Access Patterns

A final way to view community patterning is in terms of access. Perhaps of most concern for the occupants of the SIAR on a daily basis was access to wells and water. SIAR residents would also have sought access to the center of the site, defined here as the large open area bounded by Ciudadela Bandelier on the east. Finally, within the perspective of the model of sequential occupations of ciudadelas (Kolata, Chapter 4), access to Rivero and Tschudi, the presumed centers of power during the late phase of the site, would have been important during the terminal occupation of Chan Chan.

The barrios, as stated earlier, are relatively self-contained. In these areas wells occur within both an elite-compound context and a more exclusively SIAR context. Internal alleys within each barrio clearly provide access to the general area of the wells, although specific details of access into the well itself are often difficult to reconstruct. Interestingly, the more centrally located SIAR are less self-contained with respect to water. For example, the only well in Unit BB is located within an elite compound; the implication is at once one of restricted access to the well and one of mutual interaction between lower-class and elite occupants of the unit around the well.

Chan Chan's streets were organized in a basically dendritic pattern and not in the grid pattern so often ascribed to the site (for example, Meggers 1972:88; Lumbreras 1974:183). This dendritic pattern is most pronounced in the central part of the site, while on the western periphery there is more of a tendency to rectilinearity. Even in this area, however, the pattern is a rectilinearized dendritic one rather than a grid system.

According to the model of sequential occupation of the ciudadelas, only one was fully functioning at any one time, while previous ciudadelas were maintained by a kin group and retainers. The overall access network visible on the ground at Chan Chan appears to date to the time when Ciudadela Tschudi was fully functioning, although the major approach route would serve Ciudadela Rivero as well (J. Topic 1977:Ch. 2). As the site grew, access to ciudadelas that were no longer active power centers became more difficult, as new construction blocked streets and rerouted traffic.

Summary

The surface survey investigated the location, context, and access patterns of SIAR, and indicated two basic patterns. The majority of SIAR were organized into self-contained barrios along the west and south peripheries of Chan Chan, with easy access to the seat of power. Some SIAR were located in the center or east of the site and were built entirely on platforms. Their context and access patterns suggested that they were not self-contained units but that their occupants had daily contact with members of the urban elite. Three anomalous units did not fit either pattern.

THE EXCAVATIONS

The purpose of the excavations was to test the patterning visible on the site surface, to correlate these patterns with variations in residential, economic, administrative, and refuse disposal patterns so that we could construct a socioeconomic model of the city, and to examine the site stratigraphy in order to construct a model of urban growth. To accomplish these aims, excavations were undertaken in samples of barrios, rooms-constructed-on-platforms, and anomalous architecture. The artifactual inventories associated with the different types of architecture can only be summarized very generally in this chapter, and space limitations preclude inclusion of plans of all the structures discussed. For more detail, the reader is referred to J. Topic (1977).

150

Barrio Excavations

Excavations in Units BJ and S were aimed at determining four levels of organization within the barrio: (1) organization of the residential complex, (2) the relationship between individual residences, (3) the relationship between barrio residents and the elite, and (4) the temporal and spatial aspects of urban expansion. With these aims in mind, the following will be presented: two concepts of planning based on different block structures, two types of kitchens, a pattern of architecture characteristic of shops, patterns of well access, and the results of the excavation of an administrative complex. Site stratigraphy will not be discussed in detail.

Barrios

Figure 7.2 illustrates four contiguous SIAR complexes in Unit BJ. Complexes 1, 2, and 3 were completely excavated, while Complex 4 was only excavated sufficiently to provide an accurate map.

The four complexes are located on the corner of one of the large blocks typical of this unit. Wall abutments and blocked doorways are indicative of the building and remodeling sequence. As the plan indicates, the complexes were not designed and built as individual structures. Instead, there was a tendency to enclose a large area first and to subdivide it later. Interior walls are much lower and less massive than the exterior walls, and the sealed doorways indicate that space within a block would fluctuate from one complex to another.

The entrance into each complex was designed to shield the interior from passersby in the alley, providing a degree of privacy. In Complexes 1 and 2, the rooms labeled A were clearly kitchens. Both contained a large hearth, and although they seem to have been swept out regularly, they were also liberally strewn with refuse. In each kitchen, one area of the floor consisted of heavily trampled llama dung, indicating that these animals were kept in the houses. The kitchen in Complex 1 also contained a cuyero (pen for keeping guinea pigs). Quantities of feathers and bird dung suggest that ducks or other birds were also kept. The kitchen in Complex 2 contained a low bench near the hearth in which a large batan, or milling stone, had been set. The kitchen in Complex 1 also held a low bench, but in this case there was only a large hole where the batan should have been. Room A of Complex 3 was origi-

151

FIGURE 7.2. Plan map of room complexes 1-4, Unit BJ.

nally a kitchen and still contained traces of the typical kitchen features, but remodeling had changed its function.

While the kitchens in these complexes formed a relatively standardized pattern incorporating the entrance, a hearth, and a bench, the other rooms were more variable. In general, however, they were cleaner and seem to have functioned as storage, work, and perhaps sleeping areas. Jars, the most common food-storage vessels, were placed either in bins or in a special storeroom. About half the storage space in Complexes 1, 2, and 4 and all the storage space in Complex 3 was occupied, at least at the time of abandonment, by artifacts relating to craft production. The items include ingots, scrap copper, hammers, beads, bangles, rings, and tweezers for metalworking; spindles, unspun and spun cotton for spinning; wool yarn in balls, skeins, and wrapped on spindles, loom parts, weaving tools, textiles, tapes, and tassels for weaving; wooden blocks, bone gouges, coral rasps, and wooden artifacts for woodworking. Similar artifacts were also scattered on the floors of some of the interior rooms, suggesting that these were work areas.

Although the interior rooms were kept clean and the kitchens were swept occasionally, deposits of refuse were common. Refuse was sometimes piled within a complex but frequently was dumped into the interior of the block or out into the alley. As a result, floor levels of both alleys and interior rooms are higher than floor levels in exterior rooms.

Although a variety of activities occurred in them, Complexes 1 and 2 are classified as single-family residential complexes mainly on the basis of the kitchen pattern, which will be referred to as a *formal kitchen*. Complex 3 was once a residential complex, but because remodelling destroyed the kitchen and because of the preponderance of evidence for craft production, it is classified here as a *shop*.

A somewhat different concept of residential planning in the barrios was encountered in excavations in a block of rooms located on the western edge of Unit S. Structures were again arranged in blocks, but these blocks were irregular rather than rectilinear in outline. They were separated by relatively large open spaces rather than narrow alleys and generally incorporated an alley in the interior of the block.

While in Unit BJ the blocks and alleys were delineated in the initial phase of construction, the wall abutments in Unit S indicate that no equivalent form of coordination was practiced. The complexes simply grew as more space was needed (see J. Topic 1970:Ch. 3 for a more detailed discussion of the construction sequence), and alleys existed wherever building did not take place. In this area of Unit S, refuse disposal patterns and kitchen type also contrasted with the practices in Unit BJ. A large amount of refuse was simply buried in pits within rooms, while the alleys, especially the interior alley, were kept relatively clean. A kitchen excavated here contained a standard hearth but lacked the low bench incorporating a milling stone; this type of kitchen will be referred to as an *informal kitchen*. These differences in planning and refuse disposal have been shown to correlate with a late phase of urban expansion and reorganization (J. Topic 1977).

Other features of the Unit S residence paralleled those discussed for Unit BJ. Most important, residences in this unit represent single family occupation, and well-organized refuse disposal was lacking. Evidence of the keeping of llamas and guinea pigs was encountered in the kitchen; an entrance antechamber provided a degree of privacy for the kitchen. An interior room included a special square firepit and a small bench and produced evidence of metalworking. A second interior room had once been a small storage area containing six bins but was remodeled to form a small benched room flanked by two bins.

Shops

Workshops are defined on the basis of both artifactual and architectural characteristics. Architecturally, the basic workshop was provided with narrow benches along one or more walls and a set of storage bins, which were usually arranged in a U-shaped configuration. These architectural features occurred both within residential complexes (for example, the Unit S residence just discussed and Unit BJ, Complex 1, Rooms D and E) and in separate complexes. Such structures contained little or no evidence of domestic activity, but produced quantities of material relating to craft production. The artifactual inventory included tools, raw materials, and partially or wholly completed finished products relating to metalworking, weaving, and woodworking. Most excavated shops tended to specialize in one of these activities.

The best example of a separate workshop complex was encountered in Unit S. This workshop specialized in metalworking and consisted of three small (roughly 3 by 3 meters) contiguous rooms. Two of the rooms were provided with low benches along three walls, and one of these benched rooms contained an arcón (a type of U-shaped structure with bins), which served as a supervisory structure. Activities in the shop included the melting of copper as evidenced by crucible fragments, large amounts of ash, and areas of burned earth. An ingot fragment, copper scraps, hammerstones, chisels, and a needle reflect other stages of the manufacturing process. Some evidence of weaving and spinning (two spindles, a comb, and two fragments of elaborate textiles) was also found.

Complex 3 in Unit BJ was previously discussed as a residence which had been remodelled into a shop. The artifactual evidence suggests a less specialized workshop than that in Unit S. Woodworking was an important activity, as indicated by a wooden block, five pieces of coral, and 63 wooden artifacts (including two eartubes) in various stages of completion. Wool and cotton yarn wrapped on spindles, copper needles and wooden stakes, several fragments of elaborate textiles, fringed tape, and seven tassels demonstrate the importance of weaving and spinning in the shop. Copper scrap, stone hammers and anvils, and completed products (beads, bangles, and needles) constitute evidence of metalworking.

It should be stressed here that shops varied in sophistication; they occurred within the same blocks as the residential complexes, and the degree of formality present in the residences of the block was reflected by the sophistication of the shop. The shop was simply one more characteristic feature of the block structure, providing communal work space for several nearby residences.

Administrative Features

Wells were a focus of daily activity which required a large initial labor investment and periodic maintenance work. They were the result of coordinated action by a large number of people. Although the construction and maintenance phases of the wells could not be studied directly, use of the wells could be approached by determining access patterns.

Access patterns to the wells located closest to the other excavations (in Units BJ, S, and BH) were studied. All three wells were enclosed by walls, and access was controlled by an arcón. Surface survey indicated that all the other wells in the barrios were probably also enclosed by walls which were not necessarily massive. The access pattern was most

155

clearly determined for a well in Unit BJ, located 60 meters southwest of the barrio excavations discussed above. In this case, the well was enclosed by a rectangular compound divided approximately in half by a north-south wall, and the well was located in the western half. The eastern half of the compound had direct access to the well via a large ramp. It could not be determined whether or not there was access directly into the eastern half of the compound from the alley system. The western half of the compound, however, could be reached from the alley system by following a branch alley that led to the well access-control structure via a doorway (now blocked), and past a square cobble-lined pit. The control structure proper consisted of a four-bin arcón flanked by a small benched room. Access was then through another door to a corridor (now blocked) leading to the well.

An administrative complex in a different kind of context was found in Unit S. The complex lacked any direct association with residences, shops, or wells. It included a symmetrically benched court, which resembled the ciudadela entry courts in bench arrangement and was five meters square. Four arcones were associated with the court. Artifacts in the bins of the arcones included metalworking tools and products, suggesting a close relationship between the administrative complex and the nearby metalworking shop; especially notable was a ceramic blowpipe for creating a draft (like that illustrated by Benzoni 1967:63), which had particles of copper embedded in its matrix.

The arcón was the single architectural feature common to residences, shops, well access, and administrative complexes. The basic form of the arcón is a three-sided or U-shaped structure that incorporates bins into one or more walls; the whole structure is often raised on a low platform. Formality in arcones is defined in terms of symmetry and elevation. The most formal arcón consists of an elevated, symmetrical structure with only two bins, both of which are located in the rear wall. Arcones are interpreted here as supervisory structures in which the bins serve organizational or information-carrying functions. The formality of arcones is viewed as increasing at higher levels of information processing.

Rooms-on-Platforms

Four examples of rooms-on-platforms were tested by excavation, and a wide range of variation in architectural patterns was encountered. While not markedly similar to each other throughout the site, rooms-on-platforms are distinct from barrios, shops, and administrative complexes.

A small excavation in a rooms-on-platforms complex at the eastern edge of Unit S produced the only formal kitchen found in this context. Units BL and BK both lacked any evidence of kitchens, while Unit BM contained what will be called a *communal kitchen*. The four units tested are characterized by a different pattern of refuse disposal than that found in the barrios. In the barrios, refuse formed the main body of fill between successive building levels. In contrast, the fill of the platforms was relatively sterile. The fill of the platforms in Units BL and BM was mainly sorted gravels. The fill in Unit BK was sterile sand, probably derived from the surface of the site in the immediate vicinity. The fill of the Unit S platform was a silty sand containing sherds but little organic refuse and probably derived from construction or cleaning of wells in the area.

Unit BK is a long rectangular unit running north-south along the west wall of Ciudadela Bandelier (Figure 7.1). It was divided into four or five blocks by alleys oriented east-west. Each of the blocks was in turn divided into several quadrangular complexes. Each complex contained 80 to 120 square meters of floor space, divided into three or four small rooms. Front rooms opening on the alley were carefully constructed with plastered floors and walls, but back rooms were less carefully finished. All the rooms were relatively free of refuse, but bins and storage areas in the back rooms yielded a few food remains (bone and seeds) as well as personal ornaments. The general plan of the Unit BK complexes, which incorporate many changes of elevation and formal bench layout along room walls, is interpreted by analogy with the ciudadelas as indicative of high status. Except for the lack of hearths, the complexes seem domestic in nature. Very little craft-related artifactual material was encountered.

Unit BL consists of a terraced platform flanked by a courtyard on the west and a storage complex on the east, located along the southern wall of Ciudadela Squier. This ciudadela was never completed; many internal features are lacking or rudimentary, and while northern sections of the enclosing wall are almost complete, the western and southern sections were built to a height of only two to four meters. The southeast section was hardly started. Some rooms of Unit BL are actually located on top of the south wall. Because of the storage facilities in Unit BL, the complex may have served as a staging area for the construction of the ciudadela. There is also some evidence of metalworking.

Unit BM consists of a platform paralleling the eastern wall of Ciudadela Velarde. The major excavation in the unit examined the multiroomed kitchen area of the platform. Access to the kitchen area is analogous to access to kitchens in the barrios, via an antechamber that served as a baffle. The kitchen area measured roughly 25 meters square and was subdivided by low walls into five rooms. One room contained two guinea pig pens, and two of the rooms each contained four-bin arcones. Material in the bins included gourd seeds, a gourd, sherds, and a few deer bones. A fourth room contained a hearth and a bench with three looters' pits (which presumably mark the original location of batanes); a low, well-worn spot on a wall provided access into a room with two more hearths. Although the area as a whole obviously functioned as a kitchen, artifactual evidence indicates that metalworking and weaving were also important activities.

A large cobble-lined pit was encountered under the junction of two interior walls. Six complete *Spondylus* shells in a hearth-blackened olla, nine pieces of slag, a fully grooved hammer, and a wooden stake were found in a layer of clean yellow sand at the bottom of a pit. The nature of the materials and the location of the pit suggest a dedicatory offering. The *Spondylus* shells in particular reflect the status of the occupants of the unit. It should be noted that this is the largest single cache of *Spondylus* reported from a Chimú context.

Other excavations in the unit revealed a U-shaped platform facing a small group of three bins, located just south of the kitchen, and two small well-constructed rooms located at the southern end of the mound. The former yielded evidence for metalworking, while the latter was associated with weaving and spinning artifacts.

Anomalous Units

As noted earlier, Units BB and BN fit neither the barrio nor the rooms-on-platforms categories of architecture, nor were they very similar to each other. Still, in both units the domestic architecture shared a general concept of planning and specific features of layout. Specifically, each unit was characterized by a high density of wide benches, which may have been used as sleeping platforms. More generally, in each unit there was a tendency to first enclose a large area with a wall and later to subdivide it into rooms. This concept of planning was of course similar to that described in the blocks in Unit BJ and was best illustrated by Unit BN, where the incomplete architecture allowed the archaeologist to reconstruct the process involved in SIAR construction.

Unit BN, located at the southeast margin of the site, contained areas with large numbers of pits separated by narrow balks. Many of these pits were rectilinear, and the backdirt from their excavation had been removed. It has been argued (J. Topic and T. Topic, in press) that these pits are evidence of ongoing wachaque (sunken garden) construction carried out by mit'a or corvée labor. Piles of unused cobbles were found among the excavated pits. Similar piles were found in and among the uncompleted SIAR. It thus seems reasonable to infer that as the wachaques were excavated, the laborers also sorted out suitable building stones. These stones were then moved to the area of SIAR construction and deposited in strategic locations. The SIAR were built using these stones by first laying out large, blocklike quadrangles with alleys and, as a final step, adding details such as benches. No kitchens were found in Unit BN.

The general layout (Moseley and Mackey 1974; Map 13) and details of wall abutments indicate that similar processes were involved in the construction of Unit BB, the anomalous unit located at the northeast corner of Tello. Excavation in the western half of the complex uncovered several benched rooms, rooms with ceramic storage vessels, and one large room (5 by 5 meters) with a concentration of llama dung in one corner. The only craft-related items in the excavated rooms were five copper needles and a spindle. The complex in general was quite clean. The central part of Unit BB contained a communal kitchen quite similar to that in Unit BM.

Perhaps the most interesting feature of Unit BB was the small platform located in the eastern part of the unit. This platform was about a meter high and was crowned by a small room with a well-constructed plastered bench at the south end. Both the room and the bench had been modified several times. Reconstruction of architectural features was complicated further by extensive looting of the platform.

Large numbers of llama bones were found in the looters' backdirt. Articulated llama burials were found in the floor and bench of the room. These burials had been cut into earlier architectural features but were presumably floored over during later remodeling. In the upper half of the platform fill under the room were other articulated llama bones. Accompanying the burials were strings of mishpingo beads and the remains of a macaw (*Ara militaris*). Two ollas were also found associated with the structure, and both contained mouse droppings. One of these ollas was resting on a pad of cloth, tassels, and skeins of wool yarn. The context of these two ollas suggests an offering, and the presence of mouse droppings in both imply that the offering consisted of vegetable food of some sort. While I do not suggest that the structure should be called "The Temple of the Llamas," a comparison of this structure with other, earlier structures which have been discussed under that rubric indicates that the significance of the llama to Unit BB was as great or greater than was the case at Huaca Prieta de Guañape or Aspero (see Willey 1953:56; Strong and Evans 1952; Willey and Corbett 1954; Moseley and Willey 1973:464).

INTERPRETATION

In this section, a model of the socioeconomic organization of the SIAR residents will be presented. The main points which will be made are:

(1) that the SIAR residents formed a distinct social class, the urban proletariat;

(2) that the urban proletariat was one of four hierarchical classes recognizable within the Chimú state;

(3) that within the urban proletariat, there was a range of variation in status and probably in social mobility;

(4) but that the classes themselves were rather rigidly defined and caste-like in nature; and

(5) that the classes were largely defined by the economic functions of the members.

Reconstructions of Inca socioeconomic organization served both as stimulation and general model for the reconstruction presented here (Rowe 1946; Murra 1956; Zuidema 1964).

The segments of Inca society most similar to the urban proletariat at Chan Chan appear to have been the tax-exempt class composed of the Kamayoq, the Yana-Kona, and perhaps the Aklya-Kona. All these groups worked full time for the state and thus were exempted from the usual labor tax. The first group, the Kamayoq, were skilled professionals, accountants, weavers, metalworkers, etc. The Yana-Kona seem to have been less specialized retainers of the king and other nobles and often were incorporated into the household as fictional kin. The Aklya-Kona, or chosen women, were trained by the state in weaving, maize beer production, and other household skills; they served as concubines of the king, secondary wives of favored nobles, or, in chastity, chosen women of the Sun deity.

Specific information on the tax-exempt class is vague or confusing. Although the groups were apparently hereditary, recruitment of new members by the state was constant and varied from being an act of punishment to a minor honor. There also appears to be some confusion about the exact duties of each of the groups, and little information exists on their organization. Certainly there is insufficient information with which to construct a detailed model testable against the present data. Yet evidence from the SIAR at Chan Chan suggests that aspects of the Inca organization operated as early as Chimú times (Rowe 1948).

Craft Production

Much of the reconstruction of socioeconomic organization is based on the evidence for craft activities within the SIAR. It is argued here that the urban proletariat consisted primarily of artisans. Evidence for the practice of crafts is not quantitatively overwhelming; there are no hoards of ingots or storerooms filled with textiles. Rather, the evidence occurs consistently, in significant quantities, in a number of different contexts in nearly all of the excavated SIAR units.

In assessing the significance of the evidence discussed here, several things should be kept in mind. First, evidence of craft activities—raw materials, tools, and products—consists mainly of portable and relatively valuable items. Thus, we might expect that as many of these items as possible would have been carried away when the site was abandoned. Second, the contexts of the artifacts suggest that the items had been left behind, not lost or discarded. The evidence cited here comes from inside storage bins, from room floors, and from work areas; evidence from alleys or middens is not cited here, although further data from these contexts could have been included. Third, evidence for subsistence activities such as farming and fishing is meager in the SIAR. While no tools which clearly relate to farming were found (digging sticks, points for digging sticks, hoes), the presence of three net fragments and two fishhooks suggests that fishing was a minor activity of SIAR residents. Finally, the quantity and quality of the evidence for craft production in the SIAR contrasts sharply with the available evidence from other parts of Chan Chan and from rural Chimú sites.

The presence of raw materials, tools, and finished or partially completed products within a single context is considered to be evidence for the practice of a craft within that context. In the section above describing SIAR excavations, some of the artifactual evidence for craft production has been detailed. This evidence will now be summarized in a more general way.

Copper smelting was evidently not practiced in the SIAR. Although crucible fragments, a blow pipe for creating drafts, ingots, and slag were found in SIAR contexts, these materials do not occur together within a single context. The evidence suggests that copper was imported to the site in an already smelted form, i.e., in the form of ingots. The distribution of slag does not conflict with this statement; except for one piece found in Unit S, the few pieces of slag encountered were found in elite SIAR contexts. The presence of the Unit S piece might be due to ideological rather than functional factors.

In contrast, metalworking, particularly copper and copper-arsenic bronze, was a major occupation of the urban proletariat. The artifacts most diagnostic of this activity are five stone anvils and 77 stone hammers uncovered in SIAR excavations. These tools vary widely in quality, with the best (four anvils and two faceted hammers from a single cache in Unit BJ) among the finest specimens known from Peru. Hammers in particular vary widely, from nicely shaped stones that fit the hand comfortably, to ovoid cobbles with one or more clearly defined facets, to cobbles that have only one slightly smoothed face. In general, the best quality hammers came from Units BL and BM, from the shop and administrative complex in Unit S, and, of course, from the cache in Unit BJ. Other tools associated with metalworking areas include stone chips, quartz gravers, awls, and chisels. The function of these tools is more problematical.

Although the tools found indicate that metalworking was done in all units except BK and BB, the artifacts associated with the tools demonstrate a certain degree of patterning within this industry. Thus, ingots tend to occur in single-family residences and especially in those with formal kitchens, while crucibles are concentrated in the shop in Unit S, and the blow pipe was found nearby in the administrative complex. These distributions, as well as the distributions in tool quality, are indicative of a degree of specialization. The preparation of sheet metal from ingots, and perhaps the fabrication of simple artifacts, was primarily carried out in single-family residences with formal kitchens. Areas lacking ingots (such as Units BL and BM) but having better quality tools probably concentrated on more delicate tasks. The shop in Unit S had the capability to perform a wider range of jobs, and one of its functions was probably the recycling of scrap copper by melting it down to new ingots. Single-family residences with informal kitchens seem to have been limited to more simple processes.

Both spinning and weaving were common barrio activities but are more poorly represented in the other types of SIAR units. Eighty-eight spindles were encountered in SIAR excavations, usually in association with unspun cotton; the fact that nearly all excavations produced spindles attests to the importance of spinning.

While cotton and wool yarn in both woven and unwoven format is common throughout the SIAR, unspun wool is rare. The only two lots of unspun wool found were mere wisps, while unspun cotton occurred often, in fist-sized or larger lots. It appears likely that wool was imported into the site already spun into yarn.

The quantity and quality of textiles encountered in the excavations was surprising. The materials included tapestry and brocade with complicated decorative motifs, fringed tapes that often border elaborate textiles, and tassels that consumed large quantities of rare wool yarn, as well as a variety of cotton plain weaves. While there are certainly better examples of weaving known from Peru, within Chan Chan the "elaborate" textiles from the SIAR compare in technical complexity to those found in a royal burial platform just east of Ciudadela Laberinto (T. Pozorski 1971; Anne Rowe, personal communication).

Relatively few weaving tools were recovered in the SIAR excavations, considering the quantity of textiles and yarn produced. Loom parts are obviously the best indicators of the presence of weaving, but only one end bar, four swords, and eight heddles were found, nearly all in Unit BJ, Complex 1. Other tools that may have been used in weaving include three combs (to beat down sectional wefts in tapestry weaving), 20 wooden stakes (for warping or anchoring looms), and eight wooden and 44 copper needles (which, along with the spindles discussed earlier, might have functioned as shuttles). Weaving was a common household activity in Precolombian Peru, and wood a scarce commodity; thus the scarcity of loom parts and weaving tools in the SIAR is probably due to the removal of these items at the time of abandonment of the site.

Good evidence for the production of wooden items was found only in Unit BJ Complexes 1, 2, and 3. The raw material for woodworking consists of cut blocks of wood planed smooth on one or more surfaces. Three such blocks were found, one each in the three Unit BJ complexes listed above. The tool used for planing and smoothing was probably coral, which functioned as a relatively efficient rasp (17 occurrences, 13 of these associated with wooden blocks). The cutting tools most directly associated with woodworking were bone gouges made from llama metapodials (four occurrences, two of which were associated with both wooden blocks and coral).

The three contiguous complexes of Unit BJ, which produced the tightest associations of raw material and tools, also produced 121 wooden artifacts. These ranged from figurine fragments, some of which had shell and copper inlays, to utilitarian items like spindles. It is impossible to say whether all these products were manufactured in Unit BJ, but certainly some utilitarian items as well as the more elaborate artifacts were produced there.

The evidence for the manufacture and distribution of one type of artifact, wooden eartubes, deserves further discussion. Eartubes are hollow wooden cylinders about two and one-half to four and one-half centimeters in diameter and four to five centimeters in length. Ten whole or partial eartubes were found in the SIAR. Three of these were associated with woodworking contexts in Unit BJ, while four came from other contexts in that same unit. One eartube was found in the Unit S excavations, in a bin of the arcón that controlled access to the well; one came from a bin in Unit BK; and one came from a storeroom in the western half of Unit BB. These artifacts have thus far been reported only from SIAR contexts and, in one case, from a royal burial platform (Conrad 1974) where the eartube was probably associated with the burial of a retainer. Ceramic vessels depict retainers (litter bearers, for example) wearing what appear to be eartubes, while main figures wear the more familiar ear spools (Margaret Hoyt, personal communication).

This brief summary provides a sampling of the evidence, or in some

164

cases the lack of evidence, for the practice of various crafts by the urban proletariat. Metalworking has the widest distribution, and there are indications that different areas of the SIAR specialized in different processes. Elaborate weaving and spinning of cotton yarn are restricted more to the barrios. Other minor crafts seem to be restricted to certain areas of the barrios; woodworking has been discussed as an example of this pattern, but the manufacture of stone spindle whorls is similarly restricted to parts of Unit S. Other crafts, such as the production of small ornaments and shell inlay pieces, were probably also practiced in the SIAR but are difficult to localize. Finally, there are a number of crafts, such as smelting, spinning wool into yarn, and pottery making, for which good evidence has not been found either in excavation or surface survey.

Time, Status, and Function

Most of the variation present within the SIAR seems to occur along three interrelated dimensions; these dimensions account for chronological variation, variation within the social and organizational hierarchy, and variation in activities performed by groups of people.

A detailed analysis of the history of the site lies outside the scope of this chapter, but a few comments on the chronological relationships of the SIAR units are necessary. Ceramic and stratigraphic data indicate that the SIAR and their inhabitants were present at Chan Chan from its inception. The history of the SIAR seems to involve periods of in situ evolution punctuated by phases of radical change and reorganization. The earliest occupation was centered around Chayhuac, in part in areas now occupied by wachaques. Expansion was for the most part gradual and northwesterly in direction. All the SIAR structures discussed in the preceding sections, however, represent the final occupations in their respective areas, and cross-dating of these various occupations indicates that the urban proletariat abandoned the site en masse. The quantity of raw materials, tools, and craft products left behind is indicative of abandonment under duress. This general abandonment probably correlated with the Inca conquest of Chan Chan and the removal of the skilled craftsmen to Cuzco and other Inca cities (Rowe 1948). The Incas were quick to recognize a major source of Chan Chan's wealth and power.

During Chan Chan's terminal phases, however, the site had been vigorously expanding. Mit'a laborers had been employed in Unit BN to excavate wachaques, sort building materials, and lay out large SIAR blocks. The similarities in the block structures of Units BN, BB, and BJ suggest that mit'a laborers had performed at least part of the construction in these other units also. The sorted nature of the gravel used in constructing the platforms of the rooms-on-platform type of SIAR, especially in Units BM and BL, is probably again indicative of corvée labor.

In part, the use of state labor in SIAR construction, especially in the barrios, is a chronological marker correlating with urban renewal programs late in the site's history. This renewal is best illustrated by the presence of the double-walled cemetery enclosures in Units BJ, IV, and VI, and along the western periphery of the site. These burial structures replaced the earlier cemeteries at the southern edge of the site. Where the cemetery enclosures occurred within a unit, they correlated with rectilinear block plans and indicate that the whole area had already undergone state-sponsored renewal. The enclosures along the western periphery occurred together with evidence of ongoing site expansion and a haphazard block plan, indicating that planned renewal programs had not yet been completed.

In part, however, differential access to labor signified differential status and is a pervasive theme in Chimú archaeology. Two other themes associated with status are the elevation of structures above ground level and the degree of formality present in an architectural plan; both of these themes correlate well with the use of mit'a labor in construction.

The ciudadelas provide an example of the correlation between access to labor, elevation, and use of formal concepts of planning in a high-status context. These monumental enclosures consumed labor conspicuously in the construction of walls and burial platforms, incorporated many changes of elevation along the route to seats of power, and adhered to rigid concepts of planning which included a formal court with benches of equal height along two walls and a slightly higher bench along a third wall (Moseley 1975b; Day 1973; Moseley and Mackey 1974; Day, Chapter 14). While all of these concepts are present in recognizable form in the SIAR, the difference in the quality of execution is vast; in rural communities such as Cerro la Virgen, these concepts cannot be recognized (Keatinge 1975b). Thus, while variations in status existed among the urban proletariat, the total range of variation present within Chimú society is not found within the SIAR.

Using the criteria of time and status and the evidence of craft production, three major categories that are functionally and locationally distinct may be defined within the urban proletariat: outsiders, proletarians attached to monumental enclosures, and unattached proletarians. There is, of course, a range of variation within each category.

Outsiders

Outsiders are characterized by a communal residential pattern; they were few in number and occupied architecture constructed by mit'a labor with barrackslike characteristics. Their residences were located in the three anomalous units described in the section on surface survey. These people performed activities appropriate to their status as outsiders, activities which did not include craft production.

One group of outsiders consisted of traders, best represented in Unit BB. Here they occupied a group of rooms significantly different from most of the SIAR architecture. The architecture is specialized, incorporating a large number of rooms containing benches, a few large corrallike rooms, and a platform with high-status characteristics. Artifactually, the unit is set apart by the lack of evidence for craft production as well as the presence of a large number of llama burials, a macaw burial, and the exotic mishpingo beads.

The similarities in architecture between Unit BB and the unexcavated Unit V suggest that the entire area along the east side of Ciudadela Tello was a trading terminal. This zone is advantageously located along the main access route to the center of the site.

The other group of outsiders was housed in Unit BN. Whatever the ultimate function of this unit was meant to be, at the time of general SIAR abandonment the completed rooms probably housed the laborers performing the ongoing construction. The unit was conveniently located at the construction site, and the architecture was specialized only to the extent that it provided basic housing.

While laborers serving their mit'a were certainly brought in from outside the site, as indicated by the provision of separate and distinctive housing, the single eartube found in Unit BB suggests that traders may have been considered a functionally specialized group within the urban proletariat.

167

Proletarians Attached to Monumental Enclosures

Although there was a wide range of variation in overall plan, context, and details of residential patterning, the rooms-on-platforms in some respects formed a consistent group. All, by definition, had at least one characteristic of high status—elevation above ground level—and the excavated examples all contained corroborating evidence of their relatively elite nature. Thus, Units BM and BL exhibit large outlays of labor in the preparation of the platform, while Unit BK and the kitchen excavated on the Unit S platform both had formal benches.

There is a clear correlation between the number of rooms-on-platform units and the number of monumental enclosures, as well as a clear locational association of the two architectural types. Undoubtedly, each king, in addition to providing himself with a burial platform, enlisted a group of retainers to serve him and, after his death, his descent group. These retainers performed a variety of activities, and at least some were craftsmen.

The variation present within the category of rooms-on-platforms conforms to the model of sequential occupation of the enclosures (Day 1973; Conrad 1974; Andrews 1974; Kolata, Chapter 4), and thus we can predict variation because of chronological factors. Although all the complexes were occupied during the terminal phase, many demonstrated planning and organizational concepts dating from earlier phases.

Unattached Proletarians

The barrios housed the vast majority of urban proletarians. Thus while the rooms-on-platforms provided an elite context and the anomalous units demonstrate functional variants, the occupants of the barrios should be considered typical urban dwellers.

Although there is variation in the size of houses, the formality of their plans, and the types of block they occurred in, the barrios are characterized by a single-family residential pattern. Several individual houses are grouped together in a block, and shared work areas are also incorporated into the block. The constant remodeling and the shifting of space from one household to another within a block suggest that each block consisted of several individual, but closely related, families. Endogamy within the urban proletariat is further suggested by the association of technically specialized crafts such as metalworking and the weaving of elaborate textiles within the same household; icono-graphic and ethnohistorical data indicate that metalworking was a male activity, while weaving was a female one. The apparent special-ization of some barrio areas, such as woodworking in Unit BJ and stoneworking and copper melting in Unit S, is again suggestive of the close relationship among families within a block. There was also a tendency for weaving techniques to be barrio-specific; brocade domi-nated in Unit S, while tapestry was more common in Unit BJ. It is impossible to determine, however, whether these relationships are due to marriage, to the organizational necessities of efficient craft produc-tion, or to a combination of these factors.

The major activity of the barrio population was certainly craft pro-duction. Evidence of metalworking occurred in almost every sizable excavation, and it also appears to have been the most highly organized craft. The greater emphasis on the organization of metalworking is reflected in the formal plans of areas which specialized only in metal work. In contrast, less formal plans were associated with other crafts. In general, however, all craft activities seem to have been hierarchically organized. Since much of the actual work was done in the home, the shop represented more than just workspace. On one hand, the pres-ence of arcones in shops implies a hierarchical relationship (master, journeyman, apprentice, for example) among artisans, and on the other hand, the shops and their control structures provided a conven-ient node in the distribution network of raw materials and finished products.

That the hierarchical arrangement referred to above involved some members of the urban proletariat supervising other members of this same class is most clearly demonstrated by the patterns of well access. At each of the wells tested, the artifacts found in the arcones indicate that the person occupying the structure was an artisan as well as a supervisor. The pattern suggests neither dictatorial control over people via the water supply nor a form of taxation based on access to water but simply a system of peer supervision of the wells to keep them functioning efficiently and to prevent pollution. By analogy to Inca practice, well supervisors may have been older people, respected because of their age but past their working prime, or they may have been employed only part-time on a rotating basis (Murra 1958:32). Whether the recruit-ment of supervisors was based on guildlike principles or age grades or

169

whether it was more egalitarian, it is clear that the barrio population was relatively autonomous. It was allowed to regulate its own affairs and organized to do so effectively.

In order to see how the urban proletariat in general, and the barrio population in particular, were integrated into Chimú society, it is necessary to compare them to other social segments.

The Economics of Class

It might be assumed because of the poor quality of both groups' architecture that the urban proletariat was essentially similar to its rural counterpart. I will demonstrate here that there was actually very little correspondence between the urban lower class and the rural peasantry's architecture, organization, economic orientation, and status.

The only rural site that has been studied intensively enough to be useful for comparative purposes is Cerro la Virgen (Keatinge 1975b). The houses at this site were basically one-room structures, although at times secondary rooms with large cobble-lined pits had been added on. The one room served as kitchen (sometimes with several hearths) and living area and also contained storage facilities in the form of large jars or urns buried in the floor. Other storage facilities, perhaps communal in nature, consisted of subterranean rooms clustered along the northeast edge of the site. There was no elite compound at the site, and there were no U-shaped structures. SIAR residences were much more spacious and architecturally more sophisticated, as evidenced by grinding platforms, multiplicity of rooms, and bins for storage.

The differences in storage facilities are especially significant. Those at Cerro la Virgen seem to have been designed for bulk storage of foodstuffs, while within the SIAR most bins were used for storing nonedible commodities. Certainly food was stored in SIAR houses, but storage was in smaller jars and took up proportionately less space than at Cerro la Virgen. Communal kitchens like those in Unit BM and probably Unit BB contained elaborate facilities to store a relatively small amount of food.

The differences in storage patterns certainly reflect the differing nature of the economic roles played by the two populations, but the differences also reflected the ways in which products were redistributed. SIAR residences simply did not have the facilities to store large quantities of vegetable food, and therefore they must have been able to

170

Traces of sinuous and straight furrows in the Canchon at the south end of Ciudadela Laberinto, Chan Chan. (Chan Chan–Moche Valley Project)

An area of unexcavated storage structures in Ciudadela Laberinto, Chan Chan. (Chan Chan–Moche Valley Project)

Oblique aerial view of Ciudadela Rivero (bottom) and Ciudadela Tschudi (top) at Chan Chan. (Shippee-Johnson)

Aerial view of the east side of Huaca del Sol, Moche Valley. (Chan Chan–Moche Valley Project)

The tangle of human bones left by looters in one of the chambers in Huaca Las Avispas, a small burial platform, Chan Chan. (Chan Chan–Moche Valley Project)

Excavations in progress in an area of Intermediate Architecture, Chan Chan. (Chan Chan–Moche Valley Project)

A U-shaped structure with bins in the walls in Intermediate Architecture, Chan Chan. (Chan Chan–Moche Valley Project)

Excavations in progress at El Milagro de San José, a Chimú rural administrative center north of Chan Chan. (Chan Chan–Moche Valley Project)

obtain supplies of food relatively frequently through an intermediary. In contrast, the rural residences seem to have had the facilities to stockpile food between harvests. The differences in storage patterns are also reflected in the different patterns of food consumption (see S. Pozorski, Chapter 8).

The inverse situation existed with respect to at least some craft products. This is best illustrated by metal objects and elaborate textiles. These items occurred at both Chan Chan and Cerro la Virgen, but seem to have been produced only at the former. Evidence for crafts such as spinning, weaving, and woodworking was found at both sites, but only at Chan Chan was a large proportion of residential storage space allocated to tools, materials, work-in-progress, and finished artifacts.

Differences in social organization are also apparent between the two sites. The barrios in Chan Chan consisted of single-family residences associated with shops. They were organized spatially into blocks; "neighborhoods" seem to have been relatively self-contained groups of blocks serviced by wells, cemeteries, and administrative complexes. In other words, the barrios consist of structured groups of features of various functions with the single-family residence, characterized by two well-defined types of kitchens, as the basis. At Cerro la Virgen, although different social groups may have been delineated by the road, alleys, or middens, there seems to have been very little inherent hierarchical structure. Judging from the variation in kitchen patterns, the basic social unit was less formally defined. Either the two populations had varying principles of organization, or they implemented the same concept of organization in quite different ways.

Finally, the various attributes associated with elite status defined from the ciudadelas (access to state labor, elevation of rooms, and formal plan) were associated with all the segments of the urban proletariat but are not recognizable in rural settlements. The lack of eartubes at Cerro la Virgen also seems to have distinguished the rural population from the urban. It should be noted that the Incas differentiated between the status of urban and rural populations in newly conquered territories (Zuidema 1964:42). Since the Incas were not an urban society at the time of their expansion, this distinction probably represented an acknowledgment on their part of the existing class structure.

While the SIAR residents were of higher, or at least decidedly different, status than the rural populations, they were obviously also the lower class of the urban population. Even when SIAR were closely associated with elite architecture, as in the rooms-on-platform group, they were locationally peripheral. Furthermore the inhabitants seem to have performed service functions, albeit these services were somewhat specialized. While all students of Chimú archaeology will agree that there was a vast social distinction between the urban proletariat and the urban elite, it is rather difficult to draw a distinct line between the two groups.

One method of defining this distinction is to examine the economic network that integrated the various segments of the Chimú population. While the rural population was basically engaged in food production, the urban population was oriented toward industrial production. The products of each segment, clearly, were distributed to the other segment. Because of the lack of evidence for a market economy, a state-controlled redistributive system probably served as the exchange network. Because the rural population appeared self-sufficient in terms of subsistence items and received only durable goods from the state, exchange would have been necessary only at infrequent intervals. The urban proletariat, on the other hand, relied on the redistributive system constantly to replenish supplies of raw materials as well as food. Thus we would expect to see a much more elaborate exchange network within the city.

From this viewpoint, the monumental architecture probably functioned largely as a warehousing facility. Food and raw materials were collected by the state and stored temporarily before being redistributed to the SIAR craftsmen. The overlap in locational patterns of elite compound and SIAR architecture, especially in the barrios, suggests that at least some of the elite units functioned as nodes in the exchange network. Raw materials, for example, could have been funnelled efficiently from the monumental enclosures through the elite architecture to administrative complexes in the SIAR such as the one in Unit S, and thence to shops and households; finished products would have returned through the same network.

Massive storage facilities and impressive architecture, which are indicative of capital accumulation and conspicuous labor consumption, were concentrated in the monumental architecture and in some elite units. The people who controlled or managed these units undoubtedly constituted the urban elite. U-shaped structures were the physical embodiment of this control (Day 1973; Andrews 1974; Moseley 1975b; Keatinge and Day 1973) and came in a variety of forms:

172

standard audiencias, audiencia variants, auxilios, trocaderos, trocadero variants, and arcones. Formal variation was at least partially chrono-logical in origin (Andrews 1974). However, since we are concerned with the final phase of Chan Chan, we need only refer to audiencias and auxilios, the types of U-shaped structures typical of Tschudi, and arcones. A close correlation has been demonstrated between the pres-ence of audiencias and auxilios and the presence of structures indica-tive of intensive capital accumulation (Day 1973; Andrews 1974), although not all audiencias conform to this pattern (Klymyshyn 1976). In contrast, arcones were found in both elite compound and SIAR contexts but were never found in association with large-scale storage. Moreover, burials were found only beneath audiencias (Andrews 1974; Klymyshyn 1976).

Based on this evidence from the redistribution network, I would recognize a class distinction between the occupants of audiencias and arcones, with the auxilios' occupants in an ambiguous position. A further status distinction may be drawn between the occupants of the audiencias and the king (Conrad 1974). The best evidence for the existence of the king is the style of his burial, which implies a semidi-vine aura (T. Pozorski 1971; Conrad 1974). While it is difficult to define a class with a single member, it is just as difficult to view the king as *primus inter pares.*

I would therefore tend to see a quadripartite class structure which paralleled, and was in part defined by, economic organization. The rural population was oriented toward food production. The urban lower class was involved mainly in craft production but also filled some supervisory posts and performed other specialized functions. The urban upper class was concerned with the management of production, the accumulation of capital, and the redistribution of materials and prod-ucts, while the king himself reaped the benefits of both the social and economic systems and served as their rationalization.

CONCLUSION

The SIAR did not house a monolithic, undifferentiated human mass. Instead, several distinct groups are recognizable. These groups varied from traders and mit'a laborers drawn from outside the ranks of the urban proletariat to personal retainers of the king. However, the overwhelming majority were semiautonomous craftsmen living in the barrios. The barrio population was itself highly organized, apparently in part on the basis of kinship, but also on the bassis of common occupational interests. This organization included hierarchical relationships among different members of the same residential or work block.

The urban proletariat can be distinguished from other social segments in the Chimú state. It was differentiated from the rural population by its specialized functions and by its direct and frequent access to state supplies and sources of labor, which was, of course, furnished by the rural population. It was distinguished from the urban elite by its role as producer rather than manager, lesser access to state sources of labor, and, especially, by the lack of burials beneath arcones. The king, in turn, was distinguished by the multitude of burials accompanying his own.

The creation myth which was recorded in the Jequetepeque Valley does not adequately describe the structure of the Moche Valley. This myth records separate creations of nobles and commoners and is interpreted as indicating a castelike division between the two groups (Rowe 1948). In Chan Chan, this division would presumably fall between the occupants of audiencias and arcones. While this ethnohistoric division can be confirmed archaeologically, a further social distinction, between urban and rural populations, is postulated archaeologically and confirmed ethnohistorically (Zuidema 1964:42). All these groups appear generally castelike in that they were rigidly defined status groups tending toward endogamy. The groups, in fact, fit the principles Leach (1960:6–7) outlines for Indian castes well.

I rather doubt that each of these four segments was viewed ideologically as a separate species. But economically each had its own characteristic privileges. In regard to the creation myth, moreover, while the king was gaining the privileges that distinguished him from the other nobles, the urban proletariat also accumulated privileges and principles of organization distinguishing them from other commoners. The result was the socioeconomic system that so impressed the Inca conquerors.

Generally, the structure of Chan Chan was comparable to the structure of other preindustrial cities (Sjoberg 1960; Wheatley 1963). Migration into the city, as indicated by the specialized functions of the urban population, appears to have been selective rather than indiscriminate in nature. Finally, the presence of a relatively large, well-organized population in the Chimú capital, performing a pivotal role in the state economy, suggests that the urban proletariat was a potentially powerful political force.

NOTE

1. The research that led to this paper was partially funded by NSF Dissertation Improvement Grant BNS7205515 and by a grant from the Committee on Latin American Studies, Harvard University. The study benefited from the aid of many people, including all the contributors to this volume. Special thanks are due to Dr. Gil Backer and Miz Becker, who analyzed the stone and textile artifacts, and to Eric Deeds, who helped survey parts of the SIAR. Dr. Raymond Paynter, Jr., of the Museum of Comparative Zoology, Harvard, kindly identified the macaw skeleton. I am also grateful to Margaret Hoyt and Ann P. Rowe for their critical comments on some of the ideas expressed in this paper.

8

Subsistence Systems in the Chimú State

SHELIA G. POZORSKI

Carnegie Museum of Natural History

INTRODUCTION

Food remains excavated from ten prehistoric settlements within the Moche Valley were analyzed for the purpose of reconstructing diachronic changes in prehistoric subsistence patterns. Major economic shifts and efficiency changes were pinpointed chronologically and culturally. Three such economic shifts occurred within the Moche Valley from the time of the first permanent Cotton Preceramic settlements until the end of the Late Horizon (see Table 1.1 for a diachronic chart of the Moche Valley). Each was marked by substantial changes in both the economic organization and the subsistence base of the communities involved.

Two of these shifts occurred very early in Moche Valley prehistory; one accompanied the local beginning of the Cotton Preceramic while the second was first documented in early ceramic (Initial Period and Early Horizon) times. The third coincided with the development of the Chimú state during the Late Intermediate Period. This paper focuses on the change in economic organization that characterized the final shift. First, subsistence patterns reconstructed for pre-Chimú sites are discussed briefly. Second, data from Late Intermediate Period and

177

Late Horizon sites are discussed as evidence of subsistence systems in operation within the Chimú state. Finally, general Chimú subsistence patterns are reconstructed and compared to patterns documented for earlier periods.

PRE-CHIMÚ SUBSISTENCE

The First Permanent Settlements

The beginning of the Cotton Preceramic in the Moche Valley is characterized by a shift from a nomadic way of life to a settled one. An economy based on wild plant gathering, hunting, and possibly shell-fish collecting was replaced by an economy based on marine resource use plus the cultivation of industrial and food plants. This shift was documented within the Moche Valley by data from two coastal sites, Padre Aban and Alto Salaverry (Figure 1.2).

Padre Aban dates to very early in the Cotton Preceramic when the change to settled life was in its final stages. The settlement may have been seasonally occupied, and the inhabitants were not as adept at marine resource use as later people of the area. Virtually all food consumed at the site came from the sea: small amounts of sea lion; many shore birds and shallow-water fishes such as sharks, rays, and mullet; and very large numbers of a large purple mussel (*Choromytilus chorus*). Two important industrial plants, cotton (*Gossypium barbadense*) and gourd (*Lagenaria siceraria*), as well as squash (*Cucurbita* sp.) were cultivated on the river flood plain.

Alto Salaverry was occupied near the end of the Cotton Preceramic. The site was a permanent settlement with both public and domestic architecture (S. Pozorski 1975, 1976:79–87; S. Pozorski and T. Pozorski 1977, 1979a). As at Padre Aban, the subsistence base was marine resources collected locally. Small amounts of sea lion and bird as well as substantial quantities of rock-perching shellfish were consumed at the site, but most of the animal protein came from fish. Compared to Padre Aban, a more developed fish procurement system was documented for Alto Salaverry. This increased emphasis on fishing was probably correlated with the apparent decline in local shellfish populations due to overcollecting. Major fish species taken include the same shallow-water sharks (*Mustelus* sp.), rays (*Myliobatis peruvianus*), and

178

mullet *(Mugil cephalus)* documented for Padre Aban plus two members of the croaker family *(Paralonchurus peruanus* and *Sciaena deliciosa)*, which were caught largely with nets and from the Salaverry rock mass. Plants were still cultivated on the Moche flood plain, but the three cultivated species noted for Padre Aban were supplemented by ají, or chili peppers *(Capsicum* sp.), lima beans *(Phaseolus lunatus)*, possibly common beans *(Phaseolus vulgaris)*, pacae *(Inga feuillei)*, cansaboca *(Bunchosia armeniaca)*, lúcuma *(Lucuma obovata)*, guayaba *(Psidium quajava)*, and avocado *(Persea americana)*. While most food plants were present in very small amounts, the industrial plants, cotton and gourd, as well as squash, continued to dominate the inventory.

Both of the first permanent communities within the Moche Valley were characterized by an essentially marine economy complemented by small-scale flood plain cultivation. The industrial plants, cotton and gourd, were consistently among the main species because these plants were extremely important to people without pottery containers and to fishermen needing nets and floats. This suggests that plant cultivation was primarily viewed and accepted as a means for obtaining essential raw materials and secondarily as a source of food. Also, toward the end of the Cotton Preceramic, when flood plain land was used to its fullest extent, more of this limited area was devoted to essential industrial crops than to food species. This is reflected in the Alto Salaverry floral inventory.

The Advent of Irrigation Agriculture

Irrigation agriculture was first practiced on a significant scale during early ceramic times. Initially, it was more feasible upvalley, where the incline was greater and short canals were adequate. In conjunction with this practice, early ceramic sites were situated inland—their location predicated upon water control and the use of local fields (T. Pozorski 1976). Yet marine resources continued to be very important. Eventually, irrigation systems were improved and expanded, and an upvalley location was no longer crucial. By then, meat from inland mammals supplied virtually all the animal protein necessary. Within the Moche Valley, sites within the Caballo Muerto complex provide evidence of early agricultural endeavors coupled with a heavy reliance on marine products supplied by coastal sites, exemplified by Gramalote (S. Pozorski and T. Pozorski 1979b). The later centers of the Moche,

179

Huaca de la Luna and Huaca del Sol and Galindo, document an economy dominated almost completely by reliable local inland production systems.

With the location of Caballo Muerto inland, the shift from floodplain to irrigation agriculture was complete, yet the site still relied substantially on animal protein from the coast. In this sense, the site reveals one aspect of the transition to a predominantly inland focus. At the early Caballo Muerto mound tested, almost half the animal protein consumed came from deer (probably *Odocoileus virginianus*) and a domesticated camelid (probably llama, *Lama glama*), with deer furnishing slightly more. The remainder, slightly over half, came mainly from large shellfish collected in the vicinity of Gramalote in exchange for agricultural products. Although no plant remains were preserved at Caballo Muerto, the generally contemporary Gramalote plant inventory indicates that two new cultigens, peanut *(Arachis hypogacea)* and maize *(Zea mays)*, were added to the species already identified for the Cotton Preceramic. Maize remains were rare; the plant was apparently not an important food. Industrial plants continued to be very important, but for the first time, several food species occur in comparably high frequencies. This increase in food plants correlates well with the cultivation of larger areas through irrigation, thereby providing sufficient space and water for both food and industrial plants. Larger average seed size for some species may also reflect the regular and adequate water supply possible with irrigation.

By the time the polity based at Huaca del Sol and Huaca de la Luna dominated the valley in the Early Intermediate Period, irrigation agriculture was very well developed, and an inland source for animal protein had been secured. Domesticated llamas, which were coming into importance in early ceramic times, supplied virtually all the animal protein consumed at the Moche center. Numerous efforts were made to increase the efficiency and productivity of the agricultural system. More area was opened up to irrigation. Field crop species, especially storable commodities, were emphasized at the expense of fruits. Important crops included cotton, gourd, peanuts, common beans, and especially maize and squash. Seed and plant-part size changes suggest that artificial selection may have been practiced to increase overall yield. Plant species data from Moche reflect both this emphasis on agriculture and the large local population employed in agricultural activities (S. Pozorski 1976:113–26).

The Middle Horizon site of Galindo continued to function much as the Moche Huaca del la Luna and Huaca del Sol had within the valley. However, the survival of a small community such as the Early Chimú occupation of the Moche Huaca de la Luna and Huaca del Sol indicates that the valley was only incompletely controlled (S. Pozorski 1976:127–50). Subsistence patterns documented for Galindo are more typical of the period, and they closely parallel patterns reconstructed for the earlier Moche center. Again the domesticated llama furnished virtually all the animal protein consumed. The population of Galindo largely consisted of agriculturalists concerned with irrigating and farming local fields. Field crop cultigens were far more abundant than fruits. Of the crop cultigens, the common bean and especially maize were most frequent; therefore agricultural production at Galindo may have focused on these two storable species.

In early ceramic times the focus on irrigation agriculture and the corresponding move inland indicate a change of values because plant production had become more important than the marine resources that had reliably supplied so much food. Gradually both agricultural production and animal protein production increased in efficiency until virtually all meat came from a single source and field crop cultigens dominated the plant species inventory. After the initial increase in efficiency that made field cultigens, especially maize, gain prominence and llamas become the reliable meat source, basic inventories remained unchanged while the valley was dominated by a succession of centers through the end of the Middle Horizon.

CHIMÚ SUBSISTENCE: CHAN CHAN AND SATELLITE COMMUNITIES

During the Late Intermediate Period and Late Horizon, Moche Valley economy was efficiently controlled by the Chimú state centered at Chan Chan. As part of Chimú domination, influence was exerted over greater distances, new production and procurement zones were made accessible, and communities were established strictly to provide specialized goods or services. A state redistribution system complemented this emphasis on specific settlements with specific functions by moving products to where they could best be used.

Subsistence patterns documented for Chan Chan and three satellite communities, Caracoles, Cerro la Virgén, and Choroval, reveal much about how the Chimú economy functioned. Despite their general contemporaneity, the locations of these sites within the valley vary greatly. Two of the satellite communities are situated near resources they were established to exploit; the third lies near a construction project for which it supplied the labor.

Chan Chan

A group of ten rectangular enclosures dominates Chan Chan, but substantial areas of middle-range architecture (elite compounds) and peripheral small irregularly agglutinated rooms (SIAR) are also present. Most of the population was concentrated in areas of SIAR that fringed the central area of compounds. Excavations designed to recover subsistence data concentrated on this portion of the site. A single sample was collected from a reoccupied portion of one of the walled compounds.

J. Topic (Chapter 7) established that the SIAR housed artisans who practiced a form of cottage industry in order to supply high-ranking personages with products such as metal objects and textiles. Therefore, this sector of the population of Chan Chan was essentially nonagricultural and necessarily dependent mainly on food brought into the city. The remai..s of this food were dumped into alleyways or small rooms in densely settled SIAR areas nearer the core or in heaps on the site periphery, forming middens. Refuse from all three contexts was sampled.

Animal remains. Faunal remains analyzed from all four cuts within the Chan Chan SIAR indicate a dependence on land animals for most of the dietary protein (S. Pozorski 1976:152–58, Tables 32, 34, 36, 38). This correlates well with meat procurement patterns documented for the earlier population centers of Moche and Galindo. About 20 percent of the animal protein consumed in Chan Chan SIAR was marine-derived. This frequency is considerably higher than those documented for earlier sites with an inland focus.

Herds of domesticated llamas provided most of the meat consumed in the Chan Chan SIAR. The dietary contribution was consistently between 55 and 80 percent of the total protein. Such emphasis on a single species is reflected in the large sample of bone collected during SIAR excavations. Like the samples from Moche and Galindo, this bone from Chan Chan was adequate for a detailed analysis aimed at reconstructing meat processing and procurement systems (S. Pozorski 1979).

In addition to llama bone, dog bones *(Canis familiaris)* in all four SIAR cuts and guinea pig bones *(Cavia porcellus)* in three cuts indicate that these domesticated animals may have been kept locally. Relative to the llama, neither was an important protein source, but meat from both could have served to supplement or break the monotony of llama meat. Small amounts of sea lion bone (probably *Otaria byronia*) were recovered from two cuts, and the meat represented adds up to about 10 percent of the total meat for each cut. Apparently these marine mammals were still occasionally available along the coast.

Bird bone was collected in only two of the four excavations. Fish, especially one croaker species *(Paralonchurus peruanus)*, were more substantially represented. The proportion of fish protein documented for each cut varied from just over 3 to over 5 percent. This suggests that fish was one of the more important groups of minor dietary items. The prevalence of a single fish species indicates that specialized methods for capture were used or that this species was supplied in considerable quantity to SIAR workers from fishing communities—or perhaps both.

The total contribution of marine shellfish to the SIAR diet varied widely—from over 32 percent documented for one cut to less than 5 percent for another. Data from all excavations reveal that the tiny tidezone clam *(Donax peruvianus)* was the main molluscan staple. A variety of other species were collected, but none approached *D. peruvianus* in frequency.

Plant remains. An analysis of plant material from the SIAR excavations revealed many coincidences in plant frequencies for the four cuts (S. Pozorski 1976:158–63, Tables 33, 35, 37, 39). Compared with earlier samples, the proportions of some species had changed markedly. Perhaps more important, a new species had been added to the inventory and had become very prominent.

All of the plant cultigens identified for earlier periods were still part of the total inventory during Chimú times. These include maize, common beans, squash, gourd, cotton, peanuts, and ají. Tended trees include cansaboca, lúcuma, avocado, and pacae, identified for earlier periods, plus a new species, guanábana *(Annona muricata)*. When species frequencies are considered, several features are evident that make the Chimú sample different from the earlier data from Galindo and Moche. First, the field crop cultigens that dominated earlier inventories are less frequent. Only maize is present in even moderate amounts. Second, tree fruits, which were consistently subordinate in earlier inventories, are extremely abundant in the Chan Chan SIAR sample. Lúcuma leads all the species in abundance except the new plant, guanábana. The condiment, ají, is also unusually frequent in two of the cuts.

Wild plant remains were common in the Chimú refuse. Important species include cane (*Gynerium sagittatum*), which was used in construction, and *Tillandsia* sp., a major source of fuel. Algarrobo (*Prosopis chilensis*), local grass (*Panicum* sp.), and burrs (*Cenchrus echinatus*) were probably accidentally brought to the site. The small amount of seaweed certainly accompanied fresh live mollusks. Several examples of an exotic wild species commonly called mishpingo (*Nectandra* sp.) were also collected at Chan Chan. These single cotyledons had been perforated for stringing, a procedure that served to hold large quantities together for transport.

Some time after Ciudadela Rivero was no longer in active use as a redistribution center, small numbers of Chimú people apparently reoccupied portions of its front section. Although some of the ash and food remains may have been associated with the main period of compound use, the refuse sampled by this study was clearly not associated with original compound use because the tiny hearths had been cut into portions of plastered floors and benches. Also, the reoccupation does not postdate compound use by a great length of time. Ceramics and subsistence remains are consistent with data from much of the Chan Chan SIAR.

Animal remains. The general frequencies of animal species consumed by the Rivero squatters point to similarities with the Chan Chan SIAR as well as Galindo and Moche (S. Pozorski 1976:163–65, Table 4). Again, most meat was supplied by land mammals, while marine sources were insignificant.

Also in keeping with earlier data, domesticated llamas were the main protein source during the Rivero reoccupation. Guinea pig and dog bones were also identified in the refuse, but their dietary contribution was minor. Remains of a very young dog were found wrapped in a textile and buried within the refuse. Bones of one rat and one mouse complete the mammal inventory.

No bird bone was recovered, but the same fish species that dominated the SIAR fish inventory also supplied most of the fish protein during the Rivero reoccupation. However, the total contribution was minimal.

A number of shellfish species were identified in the Rivero inventory. The species that contributed the most meat was a large clam *(Semele corrugata)*, but the number of individual clams actually taken was quite small. In fact, the amount of meat furnished by all shellfish was almost insignificant.

Plant remains. The frequencies and types of plants present in the squatter refuse link this occupation most closely to the Chan Chan SIAR sector (S. Pozorski 1976:165–66, Table 41). Including the continued use of the new fruit, *guanábana*, the basic plant inventory was essentially unchanged.

An examination of plant frequencies and estimated food yield reveals that, with the exception of maize, field crop cultigens are underrepresented while tended fruits occur consistently in significantly greater amounts. *Lúcama* and the new fruit, *guanábana*, are especially substantial contributors to the total plant food diet.

Wild plant remains present in the Rivero squatter material include the same accidental inclusions of algarroba, grass, and seaweed. Cane, an important construction material, and possibly *Tillandsia* sp. were the only wild plants brought into the compound intentionally. A single seed of the exotic plant maichil *(Thevetia peruviana)* was found near the dog burial.

Caracoles

A second Late Intermediate Period to Late Horizon settlement composed largely of nonagriculturalists was the site of Caracoles, located along the nonarable northern margin of the Moche Valley (Figure 1.2). The site's inhabitants had apparently been relocated for the purpose of constructing nearby roadside structures as well as possibly a walled cemetery. Late Horizon elements in the ceramic assemblage place it late in the time span under consideration here. No architecture was present; therefore excavations within the site focused on areas of concentrated midden. Four such site areas were carefully sampled to provide data used in this study.

Animal remains. Virtually every aspect of the faunal inventory defined for Caracoles contrasts with the previously described inventories for Moche, Galindo, and Chan Chan. Two major differences are especially important. First, reconstructed total quantities of animal products consumed fall far below the proportion of food supplied by plants. Second, in contrast to the essentially inland focus of the major centers, most of the animal protein consumed at Caracoles came from the sea (S. Pozorski 1976:168–71, Tables 42, 44, 46, 48).

The domesticated llama was of minor importance at Caracoles. Remains were encountered in three of the four cuts, but only one cut yielded an appreciable amount. A small amount of dog bone was identified in two of the four cuts; even rodents were absent from the Caracoles midden. The only other mammal bone present was sea lion, and the small sample was restricted to a single cut.

Shore birds, specifically pelican (*Pelecanus* sp.) and gull-sized species, consistently accounted for between 5 and 10 percent of the total animal protein. Even this relatively small quantity represents a substantial increase relative to bird protein consumed at other post–Early Intermediate Period sites.

Fish were the main animal protein source. Data from the four cuts indicate that the percentage of meat supplied by fish ranged from just over 70 percent to just under 45 percent. The low frequencies for nonbony fishes suggest that reed boats were being used to reach the slightly deeper neritic zones frequented mainly by these fishes.

The molluscan inventory for Caracoles provides clear evidence of a singularly unproductive subsistence system. The site's surface is crowded with thousands of gastropod shells —hence the name Caracoles. Every test excavation and major cut hit thick bands in which these mollusks were concentrated. However, a close examination revealed that a large proportion still contained the bodies of hermit crabs that had reoccupied empty shells. Hermit crabs are not generally considered edible, and the quantities of shells at Caracoles with intact crabs indicate they were not used for food there either. Apparently the people of Caracoles had hauled immense quantities of these crab-infested shells up to the site for use as food without realizing they were worthless! These species are not considered in the reconstruction of total animal protein sources. Without the gastropod species, the total shellfish inventory is greatly reduced. However, marine mollusks and occasional crustaceans still account for between 16 and 30 percent of the total protein consumed. The small tide-zone clam and a thin-shelled mussel (*Semimytilus algosus*) far surpassed other species in total meat yield.

Plant remains. In contrast to the disparity between reconstructed animal procurement systems for Caracoles and for Chan Chan, the types and frequency of plant species at the two sites are very similar. Despite the fact that plant remains are often underrepresented and hard to quantify, data from Caracoles indicate that the site's inhabitants relied much more on plants than on animals (S. Pozorski 1976: 171–74, Tables 43, 45, 47, 49).

The cultivated plant inventory is essentially consistent with data from both earlier sites and other Late Intermediate Period and Late Horizon sites. A single seed of a new cultigen, caigua (*Cyclanthera pedata*), was also identified in the Caracoles plant material. Compared with data from Chan Chan, several field crop cultigens occurred more frequently at Caracoles. Squash was noticeably more abundant, as were gourd and cotton, and all were present in amounts comparable to maize. One fruit species, lúcuma, consistently dominated the inventory in frequencies ranging from 45 to over 80 percent of the reconstructed plant food quantities. Guanábana continued as an important food plant, but the reconstructed frequencies are highly variable. Lower overall percentages suggest that it was less significant in the Caracoles diet than in the Chan Chan diet.

Wild plant species identified in the Caracoles material were both abundant and varied. Among the more useful species, cane and totora reed (*Scirpus tatora*) were probably brought from low coastal areas or near the river for use in construction while algarrobo and espino (*Acacia macracantha*) were available nearer the site. Grass plant parts and burrs were certainly accidentally brought in as was the seaweed that probably accompanied live mollusks. Important rare species include wild tomato (*Solanum peruvianum*), which may have been collected for food, and the imported medicinal seeds of maichil (*Thevetia peruviana*) and mishpingo (*Nectandra* sp.).

Cerro la Virgen

The Cerro la Virgen village lies about five kilometers northwest of Chan Chan near Huanchaco Bay (Chapter 1, Figure 1.2). The settlement was apparently established by the Chimú state to maintain and farm the extensive areas of regularly laid out irrigated fields in the vicinity of the site. Major components of Cerro la Virgen include agglutinated rooms with storage facilities, alleys, midden accumulations, and a road through the site connecting it with Chan Chan.

Cerro la Virgen middens were sampled to provide subsistence data complementary to information resulting from major excavations by R. Keatinge. More specific aspects of both the site and subsistence data have been described elsewhere (Keatinge 1973, 1974, 1975b; Griffis 1971). However, as part of this study, Cerro la Virgen is evaluated in terms of its place in the Chimú economic system.

Animal remains. The faunal inventory of Cerro la Virgen generally reflects the proximity of the site to the coast (S. Pozorski 1976: 178–80, Table 50). Much of the animal protein consumed was marine in origin. However, more traditional inland systems were also in operation to supply a substantial portion of the meat consumed.

The domesticated llama was the greatest single meat source for Cerro la Virgen, but the animal protein supplied by this species constituted only about 35 percent of the total meat consumed. A small sample of recovered guinea pig bone indicates that this domesticated species was also present in small amounts. Occasional rat bones were the only other mammal remains identified within the midden.

Cerro la Virgen refuse contained very few bird bones, and most of these were from gull-sized coastal species.

Fish contributed nearly one-third of the total animal protein consumed at Cerro la Virgen. The dominance of members of the croaker family parallels the situation at Chan Chan and especially Caracoles. However, several other species were also identified from the refuse. The virtual absence of shark and other cartilaginous fishes from the Cerro la Virgen species inventory is noteworthy because these shallow-water fishes dominated species inventories of early sites in the vicinity. This change reflects the use of reed boats by later people to reach deeper portions of the neritic zones further offshore.

Artifacts recovered at Cerro la Virgen also reflect the importance of fishing (Keatinge 1975b: 323; Griffis 1971: 71–73). Small-mesh net (8–11 millimeters) and net weights (which were often unshaped rocks tied with string) document the continued use of haul seines along the nearby sand beach. Net fragments of very large mesh (85–115 millimeters) indicate that gill nets were also used. Finally, several copper fishhooks provide evidence of a fishing technique not documented for other sites.

Plant remains. Two aspects of the Cerro la Virgen plant inventory and species frequencies are especially significant. First, the consistent abundance and generally high frequency of several field crop cultigens correlates well with the generally agricultural function of the site.

188

Second, the plant species assemblage for Cerro la Virgen also shares several important features with inventories from the nonagricultural communities of Chan Chan and Caracoles, and therefore also reflects the site's participation in the Chimú plant redistribution system (S. Pozorski 1976: 180–82, Table 51).

In addition to the species documented for contemporary sites, at Cerro la Virgen a single shriveled tuber was tentatively identified as sweet potato *(Ipomoea batatas)*. Several field crop species were especially abundant at Cerro la Virgen while other species were under-represented. Remains of cotton in all forms (seeds, bolls, and fiber) were extremely abundant at the site. Both bean species are difficult to quantify, but their consistent frequent occurrence in the Cerro la Virgen midden argues for relative frequencies much higher than those documented for Chan Chan or Caracoles. Ají also occurred in an unusual amount. Of the crop cultigens, maize is consistently present but does not account for much of the total diet. In contrast to the high frequency of cotton, squash and gourd occur in greatly reduced amounts. The high frequency of lúcuma and guanábana in the Cerro la Virgen inventory correlates well with data from Chan Chan and Caracoles. Cansaboca is also consistently present, but the overall yield is quite low.

Cane and totora reeds were the most widely used wild plants, and both are important construction materials. Other useful wild species included *Tillandsia* sp., an important fuel, and algarrobo, valued for its wood. Both were probably available near the site. Seaweed and small amounts of local grass are seen as accidental inclusions.

Choroval

The site of Choroval lies in a low coastal area between Las Delicias and Salaverry, south of the Moche River (Figure 1.2). The site is part of a series of small settlements established to maintain and farm large-scale sunken garden construction in low areas of the valley mouth. Sunken gardens supplemented canal irrigation by bringing slightly more land area under cultivation. Sites such as Choroval sit atop ridges formed by earth piled up during excavation of the garden areas to a depth where moisture was supplied by groundwater seepage. None of the sites had a significant architectural component; therefore testing and, ultimately, controlled excavations focused on areas of dense re-

189

fuse. Within a single elongated site, two such areas were sampled to obtain data on local subsistence.

Animal remains. Over two-thirds of the animal protein consumed by the people of Choroval came from the ocean, a fact easily explained by the site's coastal location (S. Pozorski 1976:186–89, Tables 52, 54. The remainder, a substantial portion, was furnished by land mammals, the meat source characteristic of inland systems. However, no single species dominated the inventory. These data closely parallel the proportions reconstructed for Cerro la Virgen.

The amount of meat supplied by domesticated llamas represents a substantial contribution for a single species, but many marine products approach it in meat-yield frequency. No other domesticated animals were documented from Choroval. Even rodents were so rare that only a single rat bone was collected. The only other mammal identified at the site was the sea lion, and bones from this animal were present in both cuts. Such evidence indicates that these animals continued to be taken along the coast.

Shore birds, including pelican, were consumed in small amounts. Scattered fragments of a small lizard were the only other land vertebrate remains.

Fish supplied a substantial amount of animal protein for the site. Three members of the croaker family were again the dominant species. These bony fishes may have been taken using reed boats or with gill nets staked away from the shore. However, the presence of mullet, a vegetarian, as well as three cartilaginous inshore species also documents the use of haul seines. Archaeological remnants of the local fishing technology include a copper fishhook and some small-mesh net (8 millimeters).

Shellfish, especially mollusks, contributed a portion of the dietary protein equal to that of fish. Most by far came from the tide-zone clam, which was abundantly represented in the vicinity of the second cut. However, limpets *(Fissurella* sp.) and crab *(Platyanthus orbignii)* were present in small but significant amounts in the collections from both cuts, while the thin-shelled mussel and a small striated mussel *(Brachidontes purpuratus)* were substantially represented only in the first and second cuts respectively. Variations in the frequencies of these minor species may reflect fortuitous concentrations resulting from a single collecting foray or even a single meal.

Plant remains. Data for Choroval indicate that the frequency for several species differs from amounts observed for other Late Intermediate Period and Late Horizon sites. However this deviation is still consistent with the predominantly agricultural function of the site. In general, field crop species were very well represented and probably reflect the manner in which the local sunken gardens were used (S. Pozorski 1976:189–94, Tables 53, 55).

Cultigens identified at Choroval are generally consistent with the species present at other contemporary sites. Within the sample, squash and especially maize are consistently abundant. The industrial plants (cotton and gourd) as well as two food plants (peanut and pepper) also occur in unusually large amounts, though not in quantities approaching maize or squash. Relative to the increased crop plant frequencies, fruits appear less significant in the diet. However, lúcuma and guanábana remains are still as relatively common as those of most crop plants.

Among the wild plants identified, seeds of algarrobo were the most consistently abundant. These trees may have grown naturally in the vicinity. Cane was also very common, and may have been used to construct small dwellings at the site. The small amount of totora reed may have been similarly used. Additional high frequencies of grass, burrs, and other wild plants, which still grow on the ridges, certainly reflect their proximity in prehistoric times as well. Wild tomatoes may also have been available locally. A single soapberry seed (*Sapindus saponaria*) was also recovered from one of the cuts.

The Sites Compared

Evidence from the Chimú capital of Chan Chan and three dependent, or satellite, communities was used to reconstruct subsistence patterns characteristic of the Late Intermediate Period and Late Horizon within the Moche Valley. Though the sample is incomplete, the data available reveal both general and specific features of the economic organization of the Chimú state. This is true on two levels. On a specific level, differences observed in local subsistence data from site to site reflect facets of the internal economic function of the Chimú state. On a general level, subsistence systems common to a majority of sites studied probably represent patterns characteristic of the Late Intermediate Period through Late Horizon as a whole.

Many features of the Chimú state provide evidence of an internal economic organization which was largely dependent on efficient systems of redistribution. For example, the architectural plan of the Chan Chan compounds reflects the need for generous storage facilities to which access could be easily controlled. On another level, the existence of highly specialized satellite settlements, both agricultural and nonagricultural, argue conclusively for such a redistribution system because no such community could benefit the state—and some could not even exist—if goods and services did not move within the state.

In an attempt to partially reconstruct the redistribution system central to Chimú economy, the capital city of Chan Chan and the three satellite communities were evaluated in terms of their component subsistence activities. Working under the assumption that animal and plant remains from sites with a nonsubsistence focus are products of the Chimú redistribution system, the Chan Chan SIAR and Caracoles were examined first in order to assess the composition of a diet provided largely by the state. Second, sites specializing in goods (agricultural products) rather than services were examined to determine which commodities were produced locally in quantities adequate for redistribution and which products were brought into each site.

Subsistence data from the Chan Chan SIAR best documented all aspects of a diet furnished essentially by the state. Animal protein came mainly from the domesticated llama, a source well documented as reliable and long subject to polity control. The SIAR plant inventory was dominated by two fruits, lúcuma and guanábana, while crop cultigens, including maize, were present in greatly reduced amounts. Animal and plant remains from Caracoles revealed a vegetal diet component consistent with that of Chan Chan but a reduced meat protein component that was locally acquired by people who appeared inept at marine exploitation. Certainly, the similarities between plant frequencies at Chan Chan and Caracoles are an indication of the type and proportions of vegetal products distributed to these populations. However, the discrepancy in the quantity, nature, and source of animal protein consumed at the two sites reveals that a modified redistribution system was in effect to supply Caracoles. In this case, possibly because of status differences or because llamas could not be feasibly kept near the site, no meat allotment was provided. Instead, the inhabitants of Caracoles received a larger total quantity of plant food to compensate. Therefore, the unskilled marine exploitation probably reflects local initiative to supplement a vegetarian diet.

The existence of both Cerro la Virgen and Choroval was predicated on the nearby arable land which the sites were established to maintain and cultivate. Despite its agricultural orientation, Cerro la Virgen apparently did not supply comestibles to the state. A study of plant species frequencies revealed that most local fields were devoted to cotton production. Food plants may have been grown locally, but the coincidences of Cerro la Virgen frequencies with comparable frequencies from both Chan Chan and Caracoles suggest that most were brought into the site. Plant data from Choroval indicate that food plants, especially maize and squash, were the main crops produced in the sunken gardens. Other plants such as peanuts, ají, gourd, and cotton may also have been grown locally, and this is reflected in species frequencies which differ considerably from those of other contemporary sites. While some food plants, namely fruits, were probably brought to Choroval, the overall quantity was small, presumably because so much plant food was produced locally. With respect to dietary meat protein, similar allowances were apparently made for the marine resources locally available to both Cerro la Virgen and Choroval. As a result, neither site received large amounts of llama for food. Instead, local marine procurement systems were sufficiently developed to provide most of the animal protein consumed at each site.

CHIMÚ SUBSISTENCE

A consideration of the specific evidence available concerning Chimú redistribution reveals portions of a complex valley-wide network of sites that provided both goods and services. Chimú control was exerted over long distances to govern the establishment, maintenance, and operation of these satellite communities. The sample of settlements considered here confirms that many of these sites performed highly specialized functions and at the same time were provided with commodities not within the realm of their production. Yet the Chimú system for compensation was neither indiscriminate nor inefficient. The potential of an area was evaluated in terms of resources available locally, and the quantity and nature of goods distributed to the site were adjusted accordingly.

When the features of subsistence common to a majority of Late Intermediate Period and Late Horizon sites are grouped, it is possible to characterize subsistence patterns for this time span on a general level. This facilitates a focus on factors unique to the period of Chimú domination and makes possible comparisons with subsistence patterns documented for earlier periods.

Data from the two agricultural sites and especially Chan Chan indicate that the keeping of llamas was still the "officially sanctioned" and most reliable manner of insuring a meat supply during the Late Intermediate Period and Late Horizon. In this respect the main animal protein source for Chan Chan and the earlier centers of Galindo and Moche is identical. However, the meat production system employed to supply non-subsistence-oriented Chan Chan was not established indiscriminately with the founding of satellite communities. Instead, some llamas were provided, but the development of local procurement systems was encouraged to the extent that some sites such as Choroval and Cerro la Virgen became largely self-sufficient in this respect. There is some evidence that relatively small amounts of marine products moved from coastal sites to Chan Chan. However, the amount of fish and shellfish consumed there is also easily accounted for by individual efforts and local forays.

A consideration of the food plant inventories of Cerro la Virgen, Caracoles, and Chan Chan reveals that the vegetal diet was dominated by fruits such as lúcuma and guanábana while maize, beans, and squash occurred in reduced amounts. This contrasts markedly with the situation documented for the centers of Moche and Galindo. At these earlier sites, maize, squash, and, at Galindo, also beans, were the principal dietary items, while fruits were secondary. For the Late Intermediate Period and Late Horizon such dietary proportions are paralleled only at the food-producing site of Choroval. The Choroval diet, like the diets documented for Moche and Galindo, reflects both the major crops grown in local agricultural areas and the agricultural orientation of the population.

In the Late Intermediate Period and Late Horizon sample, several new food species were identified. These represent the first new additions to the plant inventory since maize and peanuts were documented for the early ceramic periods. Two of the species, guanábana and caigua, were domesticated, while the third, tomato, grew wild locally. Of the three, only guanábana attained widespread popularity, and it was apparently widely consumed almost immediately after it joined the inventory. Guanábana probably became available when new areas were opened up during Chimú expansion. Its sudden popularity suggests that areas where large amounts of guanábana and possibly other fruits were grown were incorporated by the Chimú and the products redistributed immediately. Once the new species was introduced, local land may have also been devoted to its production.

SUMMARY AND CONCLUSIONS

To recapitulate, the economic history of the Moche Valley was marked by three major shifts. The beginning of the Cotton Preceramic was characterized by the establishment of the first permanent settlements. These were coastal in location and orientation, but small-scale flood plain cultivation was practiced mainly to provide industrial raw materials.

The second economic shift was correlated with the advent of irrigation. Initially, during a period of adjustment to this revised economy, sites were located upvalley where canal construction and water control were easier. Despite this new focus on irrigation agriculture, marine resources continued to be important in the diet; therefore inland sites maintained contact with the coast.

After the initial period of adjustment, irrigation systems and field systems became increasingly organized and better developed. This is reflected in the emphasis on field crop cultigens documented for the Early Intermediate Period and Middle Horizon sites. A concurrent focus on domesticated llamas to supply meat made such sites largely independent of marine resources. Settlements generally housed large agricultural populations, and the agricultural products present at a site generally reflected crops grown on land controlled and worked by a given site.

This developed economic system, characterized by large-scale irrigation agriculture and llama use, persisted unchanged through the several ceramically defined cultural periods of the Early Intermediate Period and Middle Horizon. This stability largely reflects the efficiency of such a system as a means of adapting to and exploiting a Peruvian coastal valley. However, despite its efficiency, this economic system was dependent upon the recognition and use of only a very few large ecological zones within a valley. There is no indication that additional zones were systematically exploited during either the Early Intermedi-

195

ate Period or the Middle Horizon. Consequently, to a polity such as Moche, expansion meant gaining control over only those zones which were considered useful within a series of valleys outside Moche.

In contrast, the subsistence shift and resulting economic patterns reconstructed for the Late Intermediate Period and Late Horizon were characterized by the systematic additional exploitation of resources in zones which were not previously recognized as useful or accessible. This was accomplished through the establishment and control of highly specialized satellite communities, each of which performed a narrow range of functions for the state. An efficient system of redistribution was essential to the success of such an economy in order to provide a balance of goods and services among sites within the jurisdiction of the state.

Such an effort to use new resources resulted in the addition of several new species to an inventory which had persisted virtually unchanged since early ceramic times. It may also be correlated with the observed emphasis on fruits in the plant diet and the corresponding lesser use of maize. The most significant of these fruits was guanábana, which became available and immediately popular as new land areas were opened up. Also because of the recognition and use of new resource zones, Chimú expansion resulted in the incorporation and use of more resource zones in the series of valleys which came under state control.

9

The Chimú Empire in a Regional Perspective: Cultural Antecedents and Continuities[1]

RICHARD W. KEATINGE

Columbia University

A regional perspective can provide considerable insight into the processes that culminated in the development of the Chimú empire. In particular, examination of data from the Jequetepeque Valley emphasizes the importance of the cultural traditions shared by the Moche Valley with the rest of the North Coast region. While our current knowledge of the Chimú empire is based largely on evidence from the Moche Valley heartland, preliminary data from other parts of the North Coast provide evidence concerning the nature of Chimú organization and administration of conquered territories. The data further suggest that the rise of the Chimú expansionist state was the culmination of a general trend of cultural evolution that developed out of traditions characterizing the region as a whole.

The purpose of this paper will be to integrate a number of lines of archaeological evidence provided by an extravalley perspective, utilizing as a baseline data on the socioeconomic organization of the Moche Valley during the Late Intermediate Period. With the aim of emphasizing the utility of a broader view of North Coast cultural development, particular attention will be paid to the role of the audiencia as it is found in varying contexts in the Jequetepeque Valley. Additional attention will be directed toward a consideration of the nature and function of religious pilgrimage centers in the coastal cultural tradition.

THE SOCIOECONOMIC ORGANIZATION OF
THE MOCHE VALLEY DURING THE
LATE INTERMEDIATE PERIOD

The analysis of data on Late Intermediate Period architecture, settlement pattern, ecology, and ethnohistory in the Moche Valley makes it possible to discuss the administration of land, water, and labor resources as primary socioeconomic factors in the maintenance of Chimú hierarchical social organization. Since the model generated by the integration of these data has been presented in detail elsewhere (Keatinge and Day 1973, 1974; Keatinge 1974), only a brief outline will be given here.

An examination of the valley's settlement pattern reveals that the region was tightly controlled by a Chimú elite who lived in the huge enclosures at Chan Chan. As discussed elsewhere (T. Topic 1971; Kus 1972; Farrington 1974; Moseley, Chapter 1), the rural areas of the Moche Valley during the Late Intermediate Period were characterized by massive hydraulic networks consisting of primary and secondary canals, field systems, and aqueducts. These irrigation networks opened up considerable areas of land that otherwise would have been unsuitable for agriculture. Furthermore, given the highly organized nature of these field and canal systems, it is evident that these areas were planned, operated, and maintained as state enterprises. Rural residence appears to have been restricted to a small number of nucleated villages such as Cerro la Virgen which were very likely established for the purpose of farming specified agricultural zones (Keatinge 1975b). In the case of Cerro la Virgen, the site architecture does not provide evidence of state administrative structures or storehouses associated with the village itself. Rather Chimú state management of agriculturally productive regions seems to have been maintained through auxiliary administrative units located in nonmetropolitan areas of the valley and completely unassociated with nucleated population centers.

198

The Chimú Empire in Regional Perspective

Rural Administrative Centers

If current interpretations are correct, three major sites designated as Chimú rural administrative centers constituted focal points of the state economic control headquartered in the Chan Chan ciudadelas. They were El Milagro de San José, Quebrada del Oso, and Quebracha Katuay. Analysis of architectural attributes and topographic features exhibited at these three sites suggests that they did indeed represent "state presence" in rural areas of the valley and probably had as their primary function the maintenance of state control over land, water, and labor resources (Keatinge and Day 1973:286, 1974:233; Keatinge 1974:67). Moreover, tentative archaeological evidence suggests that there may have been a hierarchy of such structures (at least in terms of size) situated throughout the agriculturally productive areas of the valley (Farrington 1974:91; Moseley, Chapter 1). However, only the three largest of these structures have been excavated and mapped to any reliable degree. As a result, a clear delineation of the rural hierarchy of administrative structures as well as the relationship between them must for the time being remain hypothetical.

Since the three administrative centers discussed here have been described elsewhere (Keatinge 1974), only the briefest of characterizations will be given. The three sites are all isolated complexes of mass labor constructions surrounded by extensive abandoned field systems, and they are all located near major irrigation canals. The main structure at each of these sites consists of a rectilinear compound oriented north whose interior organization shares many of the architectural attributes found in the much larger ciudadelas at Chan Chan. Each of the structures has a single main entry at its northern end, flanked by two parallel walls that extend outward. Like the Chan Chan ciudadelas, the interiors of these rural enclosures are characterized by entry courts, pilastered doorways, baffled entries, tortuous passageways, and symmetrical apportionment of rooms (see Day, Chapter 3). At El Milagro de San José, the main structure contains a kitchen located off the first entry court in relatively the same location as the posited kitchens in the ciudadelas at Chan Chan. Evidence for the existence of kitchens in the main structures at the other two sites is less conclusive. However, of even greater significance is the fact that the main structures at each of the sites have or probably had one or more audiencias as the focal point of the structure.

In comparing the audiencias at these rural sites with those at Chan Chan, Andrews (1972, 1974) has termed them "rural audiencia variants." Though they differ in construction material and technique (that is, the rural structures are built in stone while those at Chan Chan are built of adobe brick), these rural audiencia variations share many of the attributes of the audiencias at Chan Chan. El Milagro de San José contains five audiencias in the main structure and one in Structure A-5, a small attendant structure. All of these audiencias contain differing numbers of niches in their walls and conform to slightly different plans. In addition, the main structure at El Milagro de San José is also characterized by banks of niched walls and an entry court containing parallel niched walls.

Such banks of niches or niched courts do not occur at Quebrada del Oso or Quebrada Katuay, neither of which appears to have been as architecturally elaborate as El Milagro de San José. However, the focus of the main structure at Quebrada del Oso is toward a niched audiencia that is located at the rear of the building and is identical in plan to one of the audiencias in the main structure at El Milagro de San José. Due to the tremendous amount of wall fall in the southern end of the compound at Quebrada Katuay, excavated in what was essentially a salvage operation (the site has since been completely destroyed by gravel miners), the existence of an audiencia at the site could not be proven. By analogy with the plan of the main structure at Quebrada del Oso, it is assumed that if an audiencia originally existed at the site, it would have been situated at its southern end.

In terms of their associated features, all three sites are isolated and completely unassociated with any nearby population concentration dating to the Late Intermediate Period. The only other architectural features at the sites are the small attendant structures that occur at El Milagro de San José and Quebrada del Oso. The auxiliary structures at these two sites, while sharing architectural attributes with the main structures, apparently functioned as dwellings of individuals primarily concerned with the actual workings of the field and canal systems.

Dating of these rural administrative centers is based on complementary evidence from architectural, ceramic, and radiocarbon analyses. In comparing the audiencias at the rural administrative centers to those at Chan Chan, Andrews (1974:262) places the construction of the rural administrative centers solidly within the Imperial Chimú

200

Phase of the Moche Valley sequence, a chronological placement that has also been confirmed by more recent research on the adobe brick sequence at Chan Chan (Kolata, Chapter 4).

Analysis of ceramic collections from El Milagro de San José (Keatinge 1973) in conjunction with collections from two other rural sites, Cerro la Virgen (Keatinge 1975b) and Medanos la Joyada (Kautz and Keatinge 1977), clearly establishes an early Imperial Chimú date for the occupation at El Milagro de San José. In fact, El Milagro de San José is evidently one of the earliest rural Chimú sites yet discovered for the Late Intermediate Period in the Moche Valley. Radiocarbon analysis of charred plant remains taken from firepits in the main structure and Structure A-5 also confirms the Imperial Chimú time period, giving uncorrected dates of A.D. 1255 ± 80 (I-7911) and A.D. 1325 ± 80 (I-7910) respectively. Correcting for the C^{13}/C^{12} ratio gives dates of A.D. 1225 (I-7911) and A.D. 1135 (I-7910). Taking the new radiocarbon half-life as well as other correction factors into account tentatively places the occupation of the site during the late twelfth century. While similar information on the chronological placement of Quebrada del Oso is not available, preliminary analysis of the ceramic collections suggests that this site may date even earlier than El Milagro de San José. Analysis of ceramic collections from Quebrada Katuay was inconclusive due to the small size of the sample. Since no organic material suitable for radiocarbon dating was encountered during the brief excavations, the site can only be placed on the basis of its shared architectural pattern with the two other rural administrative centers.

The evidence presented on the dating of El Milagro de San José and Quebrada del Oso strongly contradicts Farrington's contention (1974:91) that these sites date to the Chimú-Inca Period, having been constructed during the Late Horizon (A.D. 1476–1534) after the conquest of the Chimú empire by the Inca. On the basis of the evidence, there is no question that the major irrigation and construction projects on the Pampa El Milagro as well as the Pampa Cerro la Virgen were undertaken completely within the Imperial Chimú Phase and are in no way related to Inca domination of the region. Farrington's contention appears to be the result of a misinterpretation of both ceramic and architectural evidence and should be discounted due to the preliminary nature of his published statements.

In conclusion, the repetitive topographic situation of the three rural

administrative centers discussed above together with their obvious architectural affiliations with the ciudadelas at Chan Chan suggests that
the Chimú were responsible for organizing and maintaining state control over rural agricultural and irrigation resources. The occurrence of
audiencias in rural areas serves to substantiate further the importance
of these sites in the Chimú socioeconomic system. Audiencias at Chan
Chan are most often associated with banks of contiguous rooms hypothesized to have been storerooms or with other restricted areas of the
ciudadelas. It is therefore assumed that the occurrence of this particular architectural form in a rural context is symbolic of the regional
extension and economic unity of the state control that was centered at
Chan Chan. The planned layout of both the structures and associated
field and canal networks strongly suggests that the Chimú state developed, maintained, and controlled the land and its produce surrounding these centers. Since there are no nucleated population concentrations
within the immediate vicinity of any of these sites, it is assumed that
some form of tribute labor such as the mit'a system described for the
Inca (Rowe 1946:267–68) and more recently suggested for the Moche
and Chimú as well (Day 1973:130–31; Moseley 1975a, 1975b, 1975c)
was employed in constructing and maintaining the fields and associated irrigation canals (Keatinge 1974:79). These tribute labor forces,
which may have been housed and fed at state expense during their
period of employment, could have been drawn directly from Chan
Chan, from the few villages in the Moche Valley located outside of
Chan Chan, or from other regions that were once part of the Chimú
empire.

Summary

The archaeological evidence from Chan Chan and its rural sustaining area in the Moche Valley strongly suggests that Chimú society was
characterized by a hierarchical social order and a powerful elite that
exercised absolute control over the production, storage, and redistribution of goods. By their ability to call upon large numbers of laborers for
the construction of public works, canals, and field systems, the elite
effectively maintained control over the two most basic resources in the
Chimú economy: land and water. This tight control over the socioeconomic system is exemplified, on the one hand, in the community
settlement pattern at Chan Chan, where three stratified types of archi-

tecture undoubtedly imply differences in social status, and, on the other hand, in the state policy of restricted rural settlement (Keatinge 1975b:227) combined with state-administered agricultural lands and hydraulic networks typifying Chan Chan's hinterland. By their ability to plan huge canal networks and organize the labor crews to build them, the Chimú elite were able to bring into production large expanses of land that otherwise would have remained uncultivated desert. Through control of these lands, all wealth resulting from agricultural productivity accrued to the state. Thus, while construction of canals and the management of rural production were organized through rural administrative centers, which may themselves have exhibited site stratification, responsibility for the overall functioning of the economy together with the administration of storage and redistribution was centralized in the ciudadelas at Chan Chan. The capital city can thus be seen as the nucleus of administrative authority in the valley from which agricultural production was organized and managed through an institution of satellite administrative centers. As suggested elsewhere (Keatinge and Day 1973:292–93), such a model for the organization of rural production and administration of economic resources may perhaps be extended to other valleys of the Chimú-dominated North Coast.

THE AUDIENCIA AS SYMBOL

The occurrence of audiencias in different contexts within the monumental, intermediate, and SIAR (small irregularly agglutinated rooms; see J. Topic, Chapter 7) architecture at Chan Chan as well as in rural administrative centers suggests that this architectural form may have had a variety of functions. However, it is noteworthy that audiencias located within the ciudadelas at Chan Chan show evidence of subfloor burials, indicated by the consistent pattern of looters' pits with their floors together with the scattered remains of human bone, textile, fine blackware ceramics, llama bone, shell beads, and *Spondylus* shells (Andrews 1972, 1974). Often, but not always, these audiencias are associated with contiguous rooms thought to have been storerooms and are located in such a manner that anyone wishing to gain access to these rooms would have had to pass in front of one or more audiencias. This association of audiencias and possible storerooms has led to the hypothesis that the audiencias were administrative offices of persons charged with overseeing the storage and distribution of goods thought to have been placed in the storerooms. In plan and elevation the audiencias bear a strong resemblance to many architectural depictions occurring on funerary ceramics of the Late Intermediate Period and earlier periods, suggesting that these may be the same buildings. Elaborately garbed individuals are depicted standing or sitting in structures represented on these vessels. Thus, whether occurring in the ciudadelas at Chan Chan or in a rural context at the administrative centers described above, the audiencia seems to represent a symbol of state authority and administration.

Further data relevant to the importance of the audiencia as a symbol in the expansion of the Chimú state, as well as information bearing on the contextual evolution of the audiencia as an architectural form, can be found in an examination of recently recovered evidence from the Jequetepeque Valley.

COMPARATIVE DATA FROM THE JEQUETEPEQUE VALLEY

Within the North Coast setting, the Jequetepeque Valley represents an important though largely neglected area of research (Figure 9.1). Situated some 150 kilometers north of the Moche Valley, the Jequetepeque Valley (sometimes referred to as the Pacasmayo Valley) is the third largest valley on the Peruvian coast in terms of total area (56,184 hectares) (Ortega 1962:3; Robinson 1964:166–67). Unlike most of the other valleys on the North Coast that specialize in the production of sugarcane, the Jequetepeque today is characterized by the cultivation of wet rice on approximately 70 percent of the arable land (Ortega 1962:10). The agricultural productivity of the valley was noted as early as 1547, a mere fifteen years after the Spanish Conquest, by Pedro Cieza de León (1959:321–22), who described it as one of the most fertile and thickly settled of the coastal valleys.

As for many valleys in Peru's coastal zone, the prehistory of the Jequetepeque is little known. A number of large sites in the valley have been mentioned in general surveys of the North Coast region (Kroeber 1930; Schaedel 1951a; Ishida et al. 1960; Kosok 1965; Conrad 1974); however, only the sites of San José de Moro (Disselhoff 1956, 1958a, 1958b) and Pacatnamú (Ubbelohde-Doering 1951, 1959, 1960, 1967) have

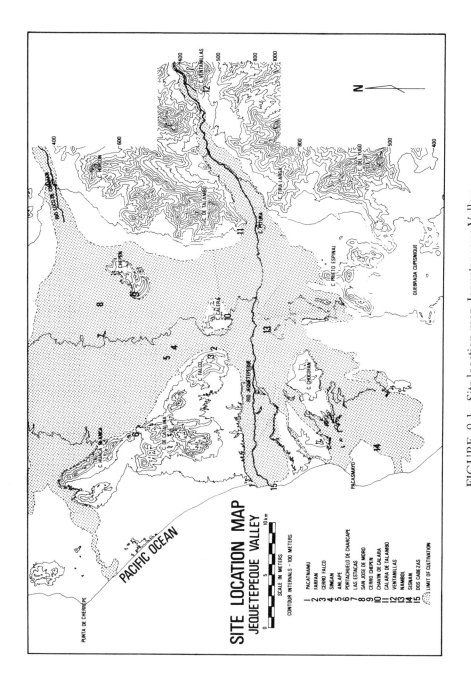

SITE LOCATION MAP
JEQUETEPEQUE VALLEY

SCALE IN METERS
0   5   10 km
CONTOUR INTERVALS - 100 METERS

1   PACATNAMU
2   FARFAN
3   CERRO FALCO
4   SIMGAN
5   ANLAPE
6   PORTACHUELO DE CHARCAPE
7   LAS ESTACAS
8   SAN JOSE DE MORO
9   CERRO CHEPEN
10 CHAVIN DE CALARA
11 CALARA DE TALAMBO
12 VENTANILLAS
13 NAMBOL
14 SISNAN
15 DOS CABEZAS
    LIMIT OF CULTIVATION

FIGURE 9.1. Site location map: Jequetepeque Valley.

been the focus of published archaeological excavations. Moreover, only Kosok's work (1965:115–28) begins to approach a comprehensive overview of the archaeological problems inherent in a study of the area. Unfortunately, Kosok's research, which centered on the nature of the prehistoric irrigation works in the valley, involved only surface survey and did not include excavations.

Given the limited nature of previous research and the paucity of published information, an initial valley survey was undertaken by the author and several students during the summer of 1974. The purpose of this fieldwork was to gather sufficient data for the development of a research design for a long-term archaeological investigation. This survey was concerned with a general reconnaissance of the valley together with intensive mapping and survey of two of its largest sites, Farfán and Pacatnamú. No excavations were undertaken and no surface collections of ceramics were made. Thus, the hypotheses presented here are designed to provide a focus for future research and should therefore be treated as such.

Farfán

Located right on the ancient intervalley highway near its junction with the main road to the highlands, the site of Farfán stretches along the eastern side of the modern Panamerican Highway near the center of the valley (Figure 9.1). Covering a total area of about one square kilometer, the site is approximately three and one-half kilometers long but never more than a quarter of a kilometer wide, having been destroyed on the west by construction of the Panamerican and on the east by encroaching farmlands. The major architecture at the site consists of six compounds strung in a line next to the highway. Like the much larger compounds at Chan Chan, these structures at Farfán are constructed of sun-dried adobe. Much of the terrain outside these compounds has been disturbed by gravel miners and cultivation. Nevertheless, a number of additional features including looted cemeteries, platforms, small structures, and canals are still preserved.

Like many of the archaeological sites in the Jequetepeque Valley, Farfán has been largely neglected by archaeologists. In Schaedel's survey of the North Coast the site is assigned to the Chimú empire on the basis of the "Chan Chan–like" architecture and surface sherds (1951:234–35). Kosok (1965:123) makes brief mention of the site in

206

his work as well. However, with the recent work at Chan Chan, Farfán takes on crucial importance in terms of our understanding of the politicoeconomic organization and administration of the Chimú empire.

Results of an intensive survey of the site indicate that Farfán represents a Chimú site unit intrusion into the Jequetepeque Valley (Keatinge et al. 1975; Keatinge 1977). According to the chronicle of Father Antonio de la Calancha (1638), the Jequetepeque Valley was annexed to the Chimú empire when an expeditionary force sent north from Chan Chan by a Chimú ruler conquered the valley under the leadership of a general whose name was Pacatnamú. Means (1931:56–57) provides the following summary translation of the pertinent parts of Calancha's chronicle (Book 3, Chapters 1 and 2). After deciding to conquer the Jequetepeque Valley, the Chimú ruler

> sent a very brave captain of his, chosen for his skill from among his most warlike men, into that valley. After much difficult fighting the victory rested with the captain, and twelve leagues of territory were thereby added to the realm of his master, the Chimo. The name of the captain was Pacatnamú. . . . After his victory, the Chimo made him governor of the territory which he had conquered and . . . the valley was named Pacatnamú in his honor, being today called corruptly Pacasmayo. The hill upon which the captain built his house, the remains of which are still to be seen, is called Pacatnamú to this day. . . . Near this river, and close beside the sea, rise some mountains three leagues long, quite treeless and, indeed, entirely sterile, even in the season of rains and mists when other mountains of the region produce grass and bring forth flowers. The mountain nearest to the river is that called Pacatnamú, and today it displays a large number of buildings and ruins, some of which were the palace of the Chimo's Goveror and his household. . . .

Kosok (1965:123) has suggested that it was the largest compound at the site of Pacatnamú that served as the palace of the governor referred to in Calancha's chronicle. However, as argued below, the results of the 1974 survey of Pacatnamú indicated that the compound to which Kosok refers is neither an anomaly nor does it bear the striking resemblance to the compounds at Chan Chan seen in the compounds at Farfán. Of prime importance is the fact that one of the compounds at Farfán contains a flat-topped burial platform and administrative architecture consisting of storerooms in assocation with one-binned audiencias.

207

This association located within a large rectangular compound containing a burial platform is precisely the pattern that has been found at Chan Chan and would seem to indicate that Farfán represents an important politicoeconomic outpost of the Chimú empire.

Returning to Calancha's chronicle, a careful reading indicates that there is also considerable room for interpretation of the location of Governor Pacatnamú's palace. The "mountain nearest the river," which is part of a chain of mountains "three leagues long" (a Spanish league is equal to approximately five kilometers) on which Pacatnamú is supposed to have built his palace, could easily be a reference to the chain of mountains formed by Cerro Faclo and Cerro de Catalina (Figure 9.1), which coincidentally is about fifteen kilometers long. The compound that contains the burial platform, storerooms, and audiencia is located at the southeastern foot of Cerro Faclo, nearest to the Jequetepeque River.

Finally, the choice of Farfán as the "real" Pacatnamú would seem to be strengthened by the fact that Farfán is ideally located for the exercise of politicoeconomic control of the valley. Given the Chimú pattern of centralized control over strategic resources and the organization of production and distribution, the location of Farfán fits the Chimú administrative pattern much better than does the site of Pacatnamú which is located some thirteen kilometers away on a bluff overlooking the ocean. Thus, considering Calancha's chronicle, architectural features, and location, the site of Farfán seems to represent a much better candidate for Governor Pacatnamú's administrative center than does the site that is today referred to as Pacatnamú. Furthermore, it should be possible through examination of the audiencias, brick types, and other architectural features located in the administrative architecture at Farfán to correlate the construction of the compounds at Farfán with specific compounds at Chan Chan. Such a correlation could then provide a chronological gauge of Chimú imperialistic expansion.

Just as the rural administrative centers in the Moche Valley reflect the institutionalized pattern of Chimú intravalley socioeconomic organization headquartered at Chan Chan, Farfán represents an imperial administrative center also modeled along the lines of the Chimú capital but established as a base for the organization and consolidation of a conquered territory. Of particular importance in both architectural patterns is the occurrence of audiencias as a hallmark of the

Chimú state. Study of Farfán and its associated hinterlands should thus provide important information on the nature of Chimú imperial administration. Excavation of the site would also, one hopes, yield information on the effects of foreign imposition of an extractive economic system on the indigenous culture of the Jequetepeque Valley.

Pacatnamú

While Farfán represents an intrusive administrative center entirely foreign to the Jequetepeque Valley, the site of Pacatnamú reflects the indigenous cultural tradition that characterized the valley prior to the expansion of the Chimú empire. Located in a spectacular setting overlooking the mouth of the Jequetepeque River (Figure 9.1), Pacatnamú is situated on a high bluff that drops off steeply to cultivated rice fields on one side and the Pacific Ocean on the other. The main site area (Figure 9.2), covering somewhat less than a square kilometer, encompasses 37 truncated pyramid mounds. Nonetheless, the site has been mentioned only sporadically in the archaeological literature (Kroeber 1930:88–89; Garcia Rosell 1942:123–24; Schaedel 1951:235; Ishida et al. 1960:435; Kosok 1965:123). The first overview of the site was undertaken by Kroeber (1930:88–89), who drew a sketch map of a small part of the western portion of the site when he made a brief visit there in 1926 (1930:Plate XXVIII). However, except for the few circumscribed excavations conducted by the three German expeditions to Peru (1937–39, 1952–53, 1962–63) undertaken by the late Heinrich Ubbelohde-Doering (1951, 1959, 1960, 1967), the site has never been extensively excavated.

The information pertaining to Ubbelohde-Doering's excavations, obtained primarily through museum research in Munich, West Germany (Keatinge 1978), combined with data from the 1974 survey of Pacatnamú, suggests that the site may have an occupational history beginning in the late part of the Early Intermediate Period (200 B.C.– A.D. 600). Of particular importance are indications that evidence relating to the Moche-Chimú transition may exist at the site. This transition, about which little is known, probably took place during what has traditionally been defined as the Middle Horizon (A.D. 600–1000). Research in the Moche Valley has suggested the importance of this transitional period; however, since stratified deposits containing later Moche (Moche V) and early Chimú ceramics have not been discovered in the Moche

FIGURE 9.2. Plan map of Pacatnamú showing the location and relationship between the three types of architectural complexes.

Valley, a clear definition of the nature of this period has yet to be formulated. Examination of Ubbelohde-Doering's collections suggests that the delineation of this transitional phase may be possible through further work at Pacatnamú.

The major work in the excavated cemetery at Pacatnamú was undertaken by Ubbelohde-Doering in collaboration with Hans Disselhoff in 1938, when some 61 graves were discovered. Ubbelohde-Doering attributed the most spectacular of these tombs (EI, MXI, and MXII) to the "Mochica-Gallinazo culture" (1959:6–26; 1967:22, 24), or to a period of time when Moche and Gallinazo pottery were used together in grave offerings. However, Rowe (1963:14, 23; note 30) has noted that Ubbelohde-Doering was incorrect in his assessment of the vessels in these graves. Rowe dates the vessels to the Middle Horizon I (Moche V). Examination of the rest of the collections from Pacatnamú stored in Lima and Munich indicates that among the other graves excavated by Ubbelohde-Doering and Disselhoff, there may have been several containing vessels of Moche IV style which were apparently unassociated with later vessels. However, except for these several additional graves and the spectacular tombs mentioned above, the majority of the 61 graves in the cemetery were Late Intermediate Period (Chimú) in date. Surface survey of the site also suggests a Chimú occupation at the site, or, more precisely, what would be called Chimú if it were found in the Moche Valley.

In addition to the chronological information available from the ceramics excavated by Ubbelohde-Doering, the textiles recovered from the same cemetery offer evidence that the occupation of the site may have spanned the Moche-Chimú transition. These textiles represent the finest collection with unequivocal site provenience yet reported for the North Coast (William Conklin, The Textile Museum, personal communication). While most of the textiles lack specific grave associations, some of the unpublished ones as well as the few outstanding examples published by Ubbelohde-Doering (1967) are clearly Early Intermediate Period (Moche). On the other hand, the majority of the unpublished examples studied in Munich (c. 300 pieces) seem to be Chimú. Of primary importance, however, is the fact that in most cases the iconographic motifs represented on the unpublished textiles indicate that they are very likely early Chimú and may in fact be representative of the Moche-Chimú tradition.

The currently available information relating to chronology supports the supposition that the initial occupation at Pacatnamú dates prior to the occupation of Chan Chan. Furthermore, in comparing Pacatnamú and Chan Chan, it is evident that although there are some striking similarities in detail, the overall picture is one of sites with generally different orientations. At Chan Chan the architectural focus is on ten large compounds; at Pacatnamú the major architectural features are formed by large truncated pyramid mounds, or huacas, the largest of which rise to over 13 meters in height.

Architectural Complexes at Pacatnamú

Based on intensive survey, the huacas and associated architecture at Pacatnamú were divided into A complexes, B complexes, and C complexes. An A complex (Figure 9.3) is defined by a large elevated huaca one or more terraces high, the top of which is reached by one or more ascending ramps. Associated with this huaca is a side platform located in front and to the east of the huaca on what is usually a large open plaza with one or sometimes two small mounds (referred to as monticulos) situated toward its center. A compound of varying size is always part of the complex, usually located to the rear or south of the huaca. This pattern of huaca, associated side platform, and compound, which was first noticed by Ubbelohde-Doering (1959, 1960, 1967) and amplified by our fieldwork, is repeated 16 times at Pacatnamú and includes the largest mounds at the site. It is perhaps noteworthy that this use of a repetitive architectural layout represents the same concept of urban planning also found in the ciudadelas at Chan Chan. Except for Pacatnamú and Chan Chan, no other large sites on the North Coast are known to be characterized by single plans that form the basis for a repetitive pattern of monumental architecture.

The second type of complex, the B complex, consists of all 21 remaining elevated huacas and their associated architecture. For a mound to be classified in this group it must *not* be associated with a side platform but it must be elevated to the extent that a ramp is necessary for access. As with the A complexes, a compound is usually located to the rear of the huaca and often, but not always, there is a small monticulo located in the plaza in front of the huaca.

The third and final category, the C complex (Figure 9.4), contains 69 small mounds which are not elevated, i.e., which can be approached at ground level or, if a terrace should exist, are so low that a ramp was

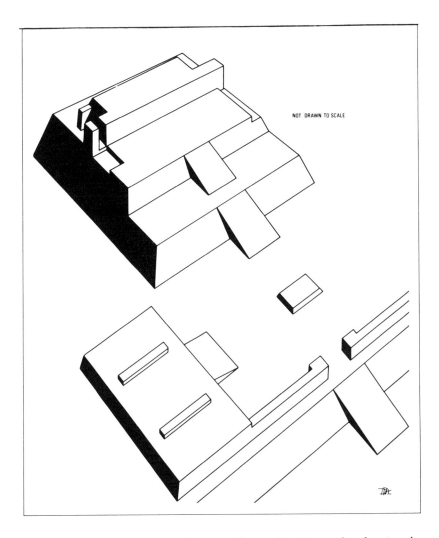

NOT DRAWN TO SCALE

FIGURE 9.3. Reconstruction drawing of part of an A complex showing the location of the huaca, the side platform, and the monticulo. Not shown is the associated compound located to the rear of the huaca.

not necessary for access. Of the 69 mounds, only 9 are associated with other huaca complexes, usually as an integral aspect of a compound. The remaining mounds are defined as separate architectural entities, though several may be found grouped within close proximity.

Though both Chan Chan and Pacatnamú are characterized by compound architecture, the enclosures at Pacatnamú are clearly adjuncts to their associated huacas, while the ciudadelas at Chan Chan consti-

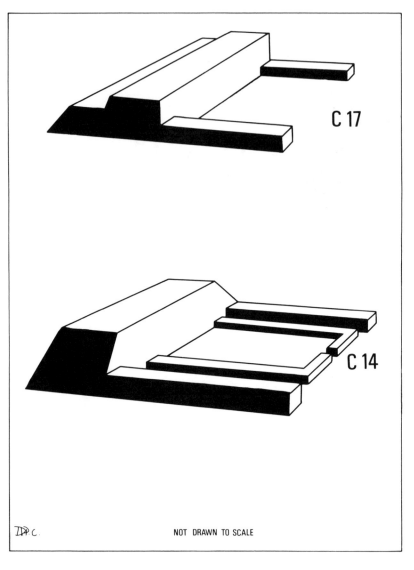

FIGURE 9.4. Reconstruction drawings of two C complex mounds. Note that C17 has only flanking walls while C14 has both flanking walls and enclosing walls.

tute the basic architectural focus at the site. The few huacas at Chan Chan are totally separated from any connection with the ciudadelas. Furthermore, there is little evidence of storage facilities at Pacatnamú; at least there is not the proliferation of contiguous rooms that defines the pattern of storage facilities at Chan Chan. Finally, the multiple func-

214

tions represented by the monumental, intermediate, and SIAR archi-tecture at Chan Chan do not appear to be replicated at Pacatnamú in any major way. While the architecture at Chan Chan represents the complexity of functions appropriate to the capital of an expansionist empire, the site of Pacatnamú seems to have been geared primarily toward the celebration of religious ritual.

Interestingly, however, there are indications that the North Coast as a whole may have participated in a common religious or cultural tradition. A notable feature of all three types of complexes found at Pacatnamú is evident in Table 9.1. The overwhelming majority of mounds, regardless of size or classification, face north. In fact, all mounds classified as A complexes face north, while among the other types of complexes only a small percentage face in the other cardinal directions. It is perhaps noteworthy that the ciudadelas at Chan Chan as well as the compounds at Farfán all face in a northerly direction. Further comparison with other large sites on the coast dating to the Early Intermediate Period and later may well show similar directional preferences, with north the preferred orientation and west the predict-able second choice.

TABLE 9.1
DIRECTIONAL ORIENTATION OF ARCHITECTURAL
COMPLEXES AT PACATNAMÚ

	Orientation				
Complex Type	North	West	East	South	N
A	16(100%)				16(15%)
B	18(85.7%)	3(14.3%)			21(19.8%)
C	58(84%)	7(10.1%)	3(4.3%)	1(1.4%)	69(65%)
Totals	92(86.7%)	10(9.4%)	3(2.8%)	1(.1%)	106(100%)

Audiencias at Pacatnamú

The possibility of a shared religious and cultural tradition between the Moche Valley and Jequetepeque Valley is further supported by the occurrence of audiencias at Pacatnamú. Unlike their counterparts at Imperial Chimú sites, audiencias at Pacatnamú are not niched and exhibit a much thicker rear wall of solid adobe with two smaller paral-lel walls extending perpendicularly from it. Moreover, audiencias at Pacatnamú are unassociated with banks of contiguous rooms which, at Chan Chan, would qualify as storerooms. However, entry into the courts in which the audiencias are located follows a similar pattern to that found at Chimú sites, involving access through a baffled corridor and pilastered doorway.

Of particular interest is an audiencia which is located in its own court opposite a pilastered doorway in the rear of the largest compound at the site (Figure 9.5). The floor of this audiencia is littered with crushed *Spondylus* shell. Ethnohistoric sources record that the retinue of a Chimú ruler included a specific courtier, Fonga, who as "Preparer of the Way" scattered crushed sea-shell dust before the path of the ruler (Rowe 1948:47). The discovery of subfloor burials containing *Spondylus* shells in the audiencias at Chan Chan suggests the hypothesis that excavation of this particular audiencia would yield a burial beneath the floor. If such a burial is found, the accompanying grave goods will help date the audiencia and the compound in which it is located.

Of additional importance is the fact that there are far fewer audiencias at Pacatnamú than at Chan Chan, with only 6 definite examples so far discovered in comparison to the more than 178 audiencias known from Chan Chan. Moreover, at least 2 audiencias at Pacatnamú are located on top of huacas (Figure 9.6), a location entirely unknown at Chan Chan.

Numerous Moche and Chimú vessels depict elaborately garbed individuals sitting in structures that are clearly located on top of huacas. Often, these scenes include other lavishly dressed individuals standing on the ramp in front of the huaca. The research at Pacatnamú suggests that these individuals are either sitting in or standing in front of an audiencia. It thus seems possible that audiencias originally evolved in the highly religious ceremonial context of the huacas, such as those found at Pacatnamú, and through time became increasingly associated with the socioadministrative activities of the compounds, activities that are represented in their most developed form by the audiencia/storage complexes at Chan Chan.

Even though found in a more bureaucratic context, the audiencias associated with storerooms in the ciudadelas at Chan Chan continued to have a religious aura about them; virtually all of them had dedicatory burials located beneath their floors (Andrews 1974:250). Major interments at Chan Chan are confined to the burial platforms. However, there are indications that earlier precursors of burials in the floors of the audiencias are represented at Pacatnamú, particularly with respect to the two instances where audiencias have been found on top of

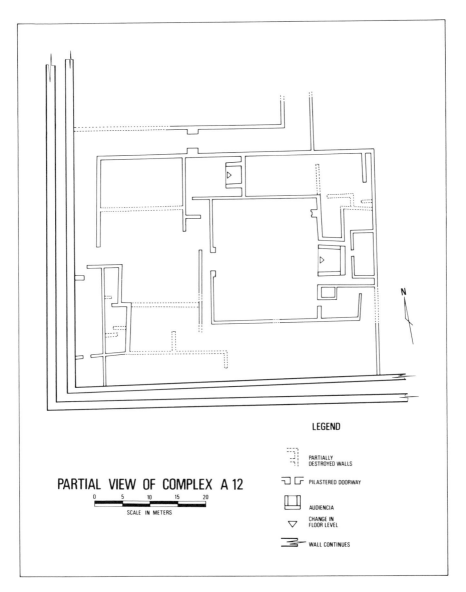

LEGEND

PARTIAL VIEW OF COMPLEX A 12

0 5 10 15 20
SCALE IN METERS

PARTIALLY
DESTROYED WALLS

PILASTERED DOORWAY

AUDIENCIA

CHANGE IN
FLOOR LEVEL

WALL CONTINUES

FIGURE 9.5. Plan map showing the location of one or possibly two audiencias located in the rear of one of the compounds. Notice that entry into the court in which the larger audiencia sits is through a baffled entry and pilastered doorway. This access pattern together with the small room behind the audiencia is also found at Chan Chan.

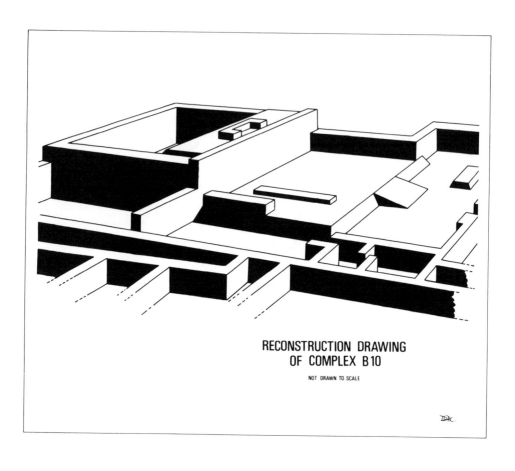

RECONSTRUCTION DRAWING
OF COMPLEX B 10

NOT DRAWN TO SCALE

FIGURE 9.6. Reconstruction drawing of a small B complex showing a huaca with an audiencia situated on its summit, a small compound to the rear, and a ramp and monticulo to the front.

huacas. Most huacas at Pacatnamú apparently contain cells or chambers located directly beneath the part of the huaca on which the audiencia sits and which may possibly contain burials. If future excavation confirms this hypothesis, the occurrence of burials in the floors of audiencias at Chan Chan could be interpreted as a vestige of an earlier practice

218

represented at Pacatnamú, that is, the location of an audiencia on top of a huaca in which chambers were constructed to hold the dead.

Pilgrimage and Oracle Worship

Ubbelohde-Doering (1967:22) has suggested that Pacatnamú may have been a regional pilgrimage center, perhaps directed towards the veneration of the moon, known from the chronicle of Father Antonio de la Calancha (1638) to have had special significance in the Jequetepeque Valley. Pilgrimage, oracle worship, and divination were important aspects of Inca religion at the time of the Spanish Conquest. However, there seems to be little question that oracle worship and pilgrimage represent a long-standing practice in Andean religion, one that predates the advent of the Incas by a considerable period. The oracle at Pachacamac located in the Lurín Valley just south of Lima was known to be so ancient and powerful that when the Incas conquered the coastal region they did not dare to destroy it. Instead, they ordered that a temple to the sun be erected alongside the temple housing the oracle (Cieza de León 1959:329, 336). Rowe (1946:302) notes that only a limited number of sites had oracles which were held in such esteem that they were consulted by people from throughout the Inca empire (also see Cieza de León 1959:150–53). The hypothesis that Pacatnamú was a regional pilgrimage center drawing on a wide spectrum of populations is given additional weight by Brundage (1963:53) who, in referring to famous oracles on the Peruvian coast, notes that in addition to the oracle at Pachacamac and the one in Rimac (Lima) there was also a famous oracle in Pacasmayo (Jequetepeque).

Work conducted at Pachacamac (Uhle 1903; Strong and Corbett 1943) has provided a model of a Precolumbian Peruvian pilgrimage center that can be used in assessing the data obtained from Pacatnamú. In fact, there are a number of things that Pachacamac and Pacatnamú share in common, not the least of which is their similar topographic locations. Just as Pacatnamú is located next to the ocean on a bluff overlooking the mouth of the Jequetepeque River, Pachacamac is situated on a promontory near the mouth of the Lurín River some 300 meters from the sea (Uhle 1903:2, 10). In addition, at both Pachacamac and Pacatnamú a high adobe wall defines the northern limit of the main site area and in each case may have served to demarcate a sacred precinct. In addition to the temple of the oracle located within this precinct, Means (1931:185) believes that the Spanish chronicles indicate that there were also lesser huacas within the site of Pachacamac that were important to specific villages, provinces, and kingdoms. Means notes that the chronicle of Calancha (1638, Bk. 2, Ch. 19) "leads us to think that certain families (perhaps those of other coastland rulers) were in the habit of maintaining shrines at Pachacamac. . . ." Such a practice at Pachacamac suggests the possiblity that the B and C complexes at Pacatnamú may have served similar functions.

The area outside the north wall at both sites also presents a number of similarities. Uhle (1903:62) states that beyond this wall at Pachacamac there are sherd fragments everywhere, cemeteries in various locations, and the whole area is "occupied by extensive quarters of huts which have now disappeared, being merely cane shacks, and only their foundations of adobe brick remain." The same situation obtains outside the wall at Pacatnamú, where heavy sherd scatters are found for over one kilometer, along with many looted cemeteries and the remains of a variety of different constructions. In both cases, these remains outside the wall may well represent the temporary camps of pilgrims who came to visit the site. This interpretation is supported by the eyewitness account of Miguel de Estete who visited Pachacamac in 1533 as a member of the first Spanish expedition to reach the site. According to Estete (1872:82–83), "They come to this Devil, from distances of three hundred leagues [c. 1500 kilometers], with gold and silver and cloth . . . from the town of Catamez [Atacames, on the coast of Ecuador], which is at the commencement of this government, all the people of this coast serve this mosque with gold and silver, and offer tribute every year."

Additional substantiation for the pilgrimage nature of both sites is also provided by artifactual evidence. At Pachacamac, Uhle (1903) and Strong and Corbett (1943) discovered a diversity of ceramic styles. Uhle's work is of particular importance since it included excavations of graves containing Chimú and Chimú-influenced vessels (1903:42 and Plate 8, Nos. 5, 7–9; Plate 13, Nos. 8–12; 94 and Plate 18, Nos. 11, 12), a wooden idol in Chimú style (1903:Plate 13, No. 18), and ceramics (1903:42, and Plate 8, No. 10) and ear spools (1903:70 and Plate 13, Nos. 19a, 19b) diagnostic of the Lambayeque region of the Peruvian North Coast. At Pacatnamú this same pattern is represented by the presence of artifacts that point toward the visitations of people foreign to the immediate valley area. Included in Ubbelohde-Doering's collections are numerous examples of Lambayeque and Cajamarca style ceramics, suggesting the possible pilgrimage nature of the site as well as providing evidence of a strong and continuous contact with the highlands.

Finally, textile collections from Pachacamac and Pacatnamú provide yet further evidence for the relationship between the two sites. Schmidt (1929:488, center; 489; 490, upper right; 491–96; 511, right; 512; Plates XII, XIII, XIV) illustrates a number of textiles supposedly obtained by looters from unrecorded graves at Pachacamac. Though this kind of loose provenience calls for extreme caution, the fact that Uhle (1903:44 and Plate 8, Nos. 17–19) also excavated at least three textiles at Pachacamac that are executed in the same North Coast style as those found at Pacatnamú suggests that the provenience recorded by Schmidt may actually be correct. Of major significance is the fact that two of the textiles found at Pacatnamú by Ubbelohde-Doering are virtually identical to two of those illustrated by Schmidt (1929:496, lower left and lower right) from Pachacamac.

All of these similarities together with the striking affinities of the textiles suggest the possibility of some kind of close relationship between Pacatnamú and Pachacamac (Keatinge 1978). The situation on the coast of Peru during the Middle Horizon and Late Intermediate Period may have been similar to that described by Childe (1951:143) for Sumer. There, temples were not isolated units and the priests were not isolated individuals but were part of corporations that administered the accumulated resources of the temples. The temple gods were not exclusively local deities but were common to the whole land, like many of the saints to which Christian churches are dedicated. Perhaps Pacatnamú and Pachacamac represented shrines of different deities who nevertheless were part of the same religious tradition. We do know that the part played by pilgrimage worship was so important in Peru that persons journeying to Pachacamac were guaranteed safe conduct through normally hostile territory (Brundage 1963:53; Squier 1877:72).

It may well be that a coast-wide religious tradition characterized by pilgrimage to centers of oracle worship played an important if little-studied role in Peruvian prehistory. In this view, an oracular center such as Pachacamac or Pacatnamú could have functioned in an essentially autonomous manner similar to the famous Greek oracle of Apollo located at Delphi. The Delphic oracle was consulted by emmissaries from all over the Hellenic world and by the sixth century B.C. had achieved an unrivaled level of prestige and influence that continued for centuries in the otherwise fragmented political and social life of Greece. Thus, except when confronted by outright conquest (as occurred from 356–46 B.C. when it was forcibly occupied by the Phocians) Delphi maintained its preeminence even during major political upheavals. If the model provided by Delphi is applied to Pacatnamú, it suggests the hypothesis that while the center of North Coast political power may have shifted from time to time, the essentially theocratic character of Pacatnamú allowed the site to maintain its independence from the effects of political turmoil. By functioning in such a manner, it could continue as a focal point of religious activities and a source for dissemination of ideas throughout the region.

CONCLUSIONS

In examining the archaeological evidence available for Chan Chan and Pacatnamú, it is apparent that religion was of basic importance in the functioning of both sites. The audiencia represents a particularly significant example since it apparently evolved in a highly religious context such as that found at Pacatnamú. It is later found in the more bureaucratic context represented by the contiguous banks of storerooms at Chan Chan. It would appear that at some point the growth of ceremonial redistribution, which functioned as an integral part of theocratically organized chiefdoms, reached a level of complexity necessitating the development of storeroom complexes. As Adams (1975: 236) argues, the importance of ceremonial redistribution and the concomitant emphasis on economic organization was that it served as a source of independent power for the priesthood beyond that allocated to it on the basis of belief alone. Drawing on his inquiry into early Mesopotamian political development as interpreted from texts, Jacobsen provides a particularly good example of the early interrelationship between economy and religion. Jacobsen notes that the term for "lord" (en) appears in the earliest texts where it is apparent that

> the political side of the office is clearly secondary to the cult function. The en's basic responsibility is toward fertility and abundance, achieved through the rite of the 'sacred marriage' in which the en participated as bride or bridegroom of a deity. . . . Whether male and politically important as ruler, or female and only cultically

222

important, the *en* lived in a building of sacred character, the *Giparu*. Where the *en* was male and a ruler that building in time took on the features of an administrative center, a palace. (Jacobsen 1957:107, note 32)

The nature of the *Giparu* is indicated by an important text which translates:

At the lapis lazuli door which stands in the *Giparu* she (Inannak) met the *en*, at the narrow [?] door of the storehouse which stands in Eannak she met Dumuzid. (Jacobsen 1957:107, note 32)

Jacobsen adds:

The connections between the *en* and the *Giparu*-storehouse are made clear by the text as a whole, which, dealing with the 'sacred marriage' shows it to be a rite celebrating the bringing in of the harvest. . . . Summing up we may say that—at least in Uruk—the *en* lives in the storehouse, the *Giparu*, because the crops are in the storehouse and the *en* is the human embodiment of the generative power. . . . (Jacobsen 1957:108–9, note 32)

Viewed somewhat more pragmatically, it could be argued that the en was the embodiment of the generative power *because* he lived in the storehouse and became an important cult figure due to his control over storage. Jacobsen's interpretation tends to ignore the significance of this economic control over a basic resource. For it is this economic power base that gives the en more than symbolic importance. Thus, on the basis of solid textual evidence it is clear that in its original form the Mesopotamian temple was not only the focus of religious activity but also a storage and administrative center as well.

Though we do not yet know at what point control over storage and redistribution augmented the religious responsibilities of a Precolumbian priesthood, it is nevertheless clear that religion represented a crucial cohesive force in North Coast society. Its importance arose out of the fact that religious ideology provided the basis for an organization that could transcend individual polities and unite society through common allegiance to a set of supernatural beliefs (Worsley 1957:27; Adams 1975:231–32). As Wheatley notes,

kings no less than priesthoods subscribed to the all-pervading norms of religion. What distinguished the two power groups were their political goals, rather than the methods employed to attain them. Kings and corporate warrior groups tended to pursue aims not subsumed under, and indeed alien to, the values of kin-structured society. Whatever their precise relationship to the deity, they were prone to use religious authority not only as a means for consolidating their own social position, but also as a primary instrument for the achievement of autonomous political goals. . . . (1971:315)

In this sense, religious ideology probably always formed a fundamental basis of legitimacy for actions taken by the elites of centralized societies.

In attempting to obtain a better understanding of the processes at work in North Coast prehistory, a regional perspective can provide critical insights into both the development and the functioning of the Chimú empire. Archaeological evidence from the Jequetepeque Valley promises to fill important gaps in our knowledge of Chimú expansionist policies and the cultural traditions out of which the Chimú empire evolved. The appearance of audiencias in different contexts at Farfán and Pacatnamú reflects both geographic and temporal continuities in North Coast cultural traditions. It is the delineation of the precise nature of these continuities that remains one of the more important problems for future research.

NOTE

1. Partial support for field research in the Jequetepeque Valley during the summer of 1974 was provided by grants from the Columbia University Council for Research in the Social Sciences and the Columbia University Institute of Latin American Studies. Support for museum research in West Germany during the summer of 1975 was provided by grants from the Columbia University Council for Research in the Social Sciences and the L. S. B. Leakey Foundation. Funds from the Institutional Scientific Research Pool of the Department of Anthropology, Columbia University, covered drafting, reduction, and photographic-related expenditures. Special thanks to David Chodoff, Deborah Phillips Chodoff, Helaine I. Silverman, and Murray Marvin for their assistance with the fieldwork in Peru. I am also grateful to Luis G. Lumbreras, who was not only of considerable general assistance but also allowed us to study and photograph the collections from the late Heinrich Ubbelohde-Doering's 1962–63 expedition to Pacatnamú. Oscar P. Lostaunau, Conservador del Centro Zonal de Pacatnamú–Valle de Jequetepeque, Instituto Nacional de Cultura, deserves special consideration for his constant support both in directing us to archaeological sites and in solving logistical problems. In West Germany, research on the collections of Ubbelohde-Doering was facilitated by the help and hospitality of Else Ubbelohde-Doering and by the cooperation of Otto Zerries, Angelika Neudecker, and Ala Seeberg, of the Museum für Volkerkunde, Munich. Thanks also to Japhet Rosell of Trujillo, Peru, for his continuing assistance and for drafting Figures 9.1, 9.2, and 9.5; to Deborah Phillips Chodoff of New York City for drafting Figures 9.3, 9.4, and 9.6; and to Sarah Whitney Powell of the Peabody Museum, Harvard University, for final preparation of all the illustrations for publication.

10

Early Social Stratification and Subsistence Systems: The Caballo Muerto Complex

THOMAS POZORSKI

Carnegie Museum of Natural History

INTRODUCTION

The earliest site of great size and importance in the Moche Valley is a complex of mounds known as Caballo Muerto, which dates between 1500 and 400 B.C. Many of the data gathered from this complex suggest that the principles of subsistence orientation, architectural layout, and social organization seen in later cultures occupying the Moche Valley were first present in Caballo Muerto.

The Caballo Muerto complex was discovered and named in 1969 by members of the Chan Chan–Moche Valley Project. Prior to this time, its existence was unknown, or at least unreported, probably owing to the amount of attention paid to other important sites in the Moche Valley such as Chan Chan. Once the complex had been dated to Cupisnique or Chavín times, preliminary excavations under the auspices of the Chan Chan–Moche Valley Project were undertaken by Luis Watanabe of the University of San Marcos early in 1972. His excavations revealed, among other things, that at least one mound, Huaca de los Reyes, contained a number of impressive mud friezes.

My own investigations at Caballo Muerto were carried out between June 1973 and December 1974. Six weeks of this time were spent excavating at Huaca de los Reyes.

THE CABALLO MUERTO COMPLEX

The Caballo Muerto complex (Figure 1.2; Figure 10.1) is located at the mouth and partially within the Río Seco quebrada (dry ravine) between the Cooperativa Laredo and its old annex of Galindo on the north side of the Moche Valley. The complex consists principally of eight platform mounds, made of cobbles and boulders wet-laid in a mud matrix, which are distributed over an area of about two kilometers north-south by one kilometer east-west. Individual mounds vary in size from 24 meters by 25 meters by 2 meters high (Huaca San Carlos) to 120 meters by 100 meters by 18 meters high (Huaca Herederos Grande), though in terms of overall area and components, Huaca de los Reyes is the largest (Figure 10.1).

Each mound bears or probably bore the shape of a U, consisting of a central large mound and two flanking parallel wing structures projecting from its principal face. Each mound is large enough to be a corporate labor structure, that is, a product of the labor of several individuals working collectively under the authority of one person or a few people (Moseley 1975b:79–80). All but one of the mounds are clustered on the south side of the complex; however, the exception, Huaca San Carlos, seems to be connected with the other mounds by a wide road. The construction and use of the mounds were sequential, with no more than two or three mounds being used at any one time. Huaca de los Reyes was built and used during the middle of the sequence.

Economic Base of Caballo Muerto

The inland location of the Caballo Muerto complex argues for extensive cultivation of the desert by means of canal irrigation. Because of later reworkings of the canal system, no direct canal evidence survives, but the complex is clearly situated where it is so that its inhabitants could control the irrigation takeoff points and be close to agricultural fields. This inland location and dependence on agricul-

226

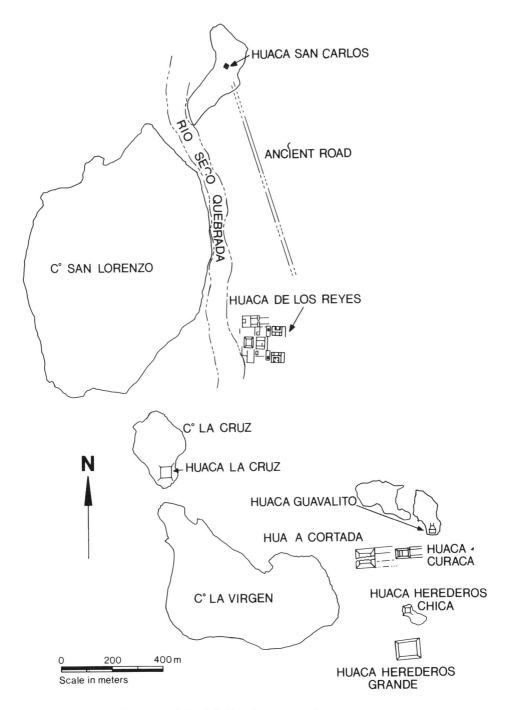

FIGURE 10.1. Site map of the Caballo Muerto complex.

227

ture represent a shift from the coast where in earlier, Cotton Preceramic times, sites such as Alto Salaverry south of the Moche River relied principally upon marine resources for their subsistence base. The move inland was a conscious effort to expand arable land for growing both industrial and food plants, probably motivated by population pressure.

The shift to the valley neck was made largely because the gradient at this point is sufficiently steep so that only short leadoff canals are needed in order to water relatively large tracts of land. Attempting to build canals near the river mouth would require canals of much greater length than at the neck since the gradient is much less. Granting this labor-saving mechanism, it is easy to see why the Caballo Muerto complex is situated near the neck. Close proximity to canals both for initial construction and maintenance is really nothing more than a matter of common sense. Inland shifts based on irrigation agriculture have been noted in the past for several other valleys such as Chicama (Larco Hoyle 1941:145), Virú (Willey 1953:392), Nepeña (Proulx 1968:25), Casma (Fung 1969:196–98), Supe and the Ancón-Chillón-Rimac area around Lima (Moseley 1974:77–82; 1975b:107–9; Patterson and Moseley 1968:125; Patterson 1971:202–3, 1973:71), Chilca (Engel 1966:72–76), and Ica (Wallace 1962:312–14).

Direct plant evidence at Caballo Muerto is lacking due to relatively poor preservation, but at the contemporary site of Gramalote there are remains of cultigens. Gramalote (Figure 1.2) is an early ceramic (Initial Period and Early Horizon) site located some 50 meters northeast of the coastal settlement of Huanchaquito on a series of bluffs overlooking the ocean. Refuse and vestiges of architecture are spread irregularly over a series of dune tops, covering a total area of approximately 16,500 square meters. The architecture is generally deeply buried in refuse, but exposed areas revealed elaborate structures of wet-laid, double-faced boulder-and-cobble walls with rubble fill. Most of the architecture was filled in and often covered over by refuse. Combined with its form, this practice suggested that the site was largely domestic in function. Abundant stratified midden, the only other site component, reaches a maximum depth of 195 centimeters and is spread over the entire area. It was the basis for the definition of the site boundaries. Chronologically the site dates to the first half of the Caballo Muerto complex and was probably abandoned sometime during or shortly after the use of Huaca de los Reyes.

Cultigens present at Gramalote include squash (*Cucurbita* sp.),

228

gourd *(Lagenaria siceraria)*, cotton *(Gossypium barbadense)*, common bean *(Phaseolus vulgaris)*, peanut *(Arachis hypogaea)*, pepper *(Capsicum* sp.), and some maize *(Zea mays)* as well as tended fruits such as lúcuma *(Lucuma obovata)*, cansaboca *(Bunchosia armeniaca)*, and avocado *(Persea americana)*. Since this is not close to irrigable land and since, as will be shown later, shellfish from the area near Gramalote are present at Caballo Muerto, it appears that the cultigens at Gramalote were brought in from Caballo Muerto (S. Pozorski 1976: 110; S. Pozorski and T. Pozorski 1979b: 429). Increased quantity and relative frequency of the cultigens plus increased seed size for both squash *(Cucurbita* sp.) and gourd (L. *siceraria)* argue that they are the products of a regular canal irrigation system rather than less regular floodwater farming (S. Pozorski 1976:109; S. Pozorski and T. Pozorski 1979b:430). From this evidence, it can be safely assumed that the cultigens present at Gramalote were used by the inhabitants of Caballo Muerto.

The next question is, If irrigation took place, how much land was under cultivation? This, of course, is difficult to answer, as no direct early canal evidence is extant. However, again, settlement pattern would suggest that rather soon after the initial move up the valley, one or two short canals corresponding roughly to the initial parts of the Moro and Vichansao canals (Farrington 1974:88–89) could have been dug rather quickly, opening up large tracts of land immediately adjacent to the complex. The present-day Vichansao passes just north of Huaca Herederos Chica and Huaca Herederos Grande, but during the time of use of the Caballo Muerto complex, it probably passed a bit south of Huaca Herederos Grande since this was an integral part of the complex during the initial centuries of its existence. The location of sites away from irrigable land at the time of their construction is a time-honored Prehispanic tradition (Farrington 1974:84–85), especially noted for sites of later time periods up to the Spanish Conquest (Schaedel 1966b:7). It allowed for maximum use of precious agricultural land while at the same time utilizing nearby but otherwise unproductive land.

The Moro Canal at that time probably only extended to the south side of the later site of Galindo or perhaps a bit beyond, watering the land above the Vichansao level (Farrington 1974:88–89). The total effect of these two short canals would be the irrigation of approximately 600 hectares from the narrow valley neck at the end of Galindo out to and even with the land contours just below Huaca Herederos Grande (Figure 10.1). Using a low figure of only two people supported per hectare of farmed land (a bit lower than Schaedel's 1971:2, 29 figure of one person per acre), a population of 1,200 people could have been attained and maintained within a few generations of the initial settlement of Caballo Muerto. Use of land south of the river up to the same end point of the Vichansao, just past Huaca Herederos Grande, is also entirely feasible, especially since the gradient is even better on that side. If farmed, this area would add almost 400 hectares to the 600 hectares north of the river.

One question that remains is, If 1,200 or more people were sustained by the irrigated land adjacent to the Caballo Muerto complex, where did they live? One site that is definitely contemporary with part of the Caballo Muerto occupation is Gramalote on the coast. Recent investigations at Cerro Orejas on the south side of the valley opposite Caballo Muerto indicate the presence of an early occupation contemporary with that of Caballo Muerto. The areal extent of this deeply buried occupation, however, is unknown. Intensive survey of the whole lower Moche Valley failed to reveal any other habitation sites of comparable date. This brings one to the possibility that the bulk of the sustaining population for Caballo Muerto actually lived at the center. Survey of the granitic hills within the complex, including Cerro la Virgen, shows indications of early occupation in the form of sherds and conical adobe fragments, but these data are mixed with remains from various later Prehispanic cultures that lived on the hills for another two millennia. The other possible living area within the complex is the land between and among the platform mounds. Excavated evidence from Huaca Herederos Chica revealed a 100-centimeter-thick band of refuse deep within the mound fill. Unfortunately, the fill was not particularly stratified, so it possibly was laid down rapidly as part of the construction fill rather than as a gradual midden buildup. Still, the extent and depth of the band indicate that somewhere in the vicinity there were people living and producing normal domestic refuse. The Herederos excavations as well as others in nearby mounds also show that the base of several Caballo Muerto mounds is buried under several meters of alluvium. Hence, while it is possible that numbers of people lived among the irrigated fields in small, perishable structures which were destroyed long ago, it is equally possible that many lived adjacent to the large mound sites at the center. The latter possibility seems more likely for the majority of the people, since it generally agrees with Prehispanic policy of living away from agricultural land, and it also coincides with lack of other contemporary sites away from agricultural land within the lower Moche Valley.

Though the primary subsistence base of the Caballo Muerto complex was inland agriculture, the center did not completely shed its ties with the coast. On the contrary, excavated evidence from both Caballo Muerto and the coastal site of Gramalote shows that the two places had a symbiotic exchange relationship.

As noted above, Gramalote contains ample remains of a variety of plants that probably indicate that they were grown under expanded land conditions of irrigation agriculture. At Caballo Muerto, especially in two deep cuts within Huaca Herederos Chica, abundant remains of shellfish were found, indicating that, at least during the early part of the Caballo Muerto occupation, more than 50 percent of the animal protein was supplied by this means. Major protein-producing species are the mussel *Choromytilus chorus* and clams *Semele aff. corrugata*, *Protothca thaca*, and *Eurhomalea rufa*. Area-specific shellfish have been documented for the littoral zone of the Moche Valley (S. Pozorski 1976:95; S. Pozorski and T. Pozorski 1979b:424); therefore the existence and predominance of the three large clams, *S. corrugata*, *P. thaca*, and *E. rufa*, indicate that they came from the Huanchaco Bay area. Since Gramalote is located near Huanchaco Bay and since it contains plant food probably grown near Caballo Muerto, it seems evident that the people of Gramalote gathered shellfish to exchange for plant foods grown by the people of Caballo Muerto. Early ceramic deposits containing molluscan species characteristic of Gramalote are known to exist within the town of Huanchaco. Such settlements may also have contributed marine products.

Consistent breakage patterns on shells plus the high frequency of large meat-yielding clams and mussels at Gramalote indicate the efficient manner in which they were collected. Other sea food, such as birds, fish, and sea lion, were also shipped up to Caballo Muerto, though they were of much less dietary importance. Hence, the people of Caballo Muerto made indirect use of Huanchaco Bay, a mixed rock-and-sand littoral zone, by means of a mutually beneficial exchange system.

Given the fact that Caballo Muerto was so much larger than Gramalote, it is entirely possible that Gramalote was set up as a satellite or colony of Caballo Muerto for the express purpose of supplying shellfish to the inland settlement. It seems that Caballo Muerto was transitional in the sense that it could not completely break away from its coastal heritage. Even after the abandonment of Gramalote, probably sometime during or shortly after the use of Huaca de los Reyes, shellfish and other marine resources continued to be supplied by the Huanchaco Bay area up to the termination of the complex as a viable center.

The remainder of the meat supply for Caballo Muerto was provided by two sources. During the use of both Huaca Herederos Chica and Huaca Cortada, deer, probably *Odocoileus virginianus*, were hunted enough to supply almost 20 percent of the total meat intake for Caballo Muerto inhabitants (S. Pozorski 1976:101; S. Pozorski and T. Pozorski 1979b:428). Deer probably inhabited the environment near the Moche River both near the center and upvalley. Bones of deer, however, do not appear at any of the other sites within Caballo Muerto. Since Cortada and Herederos Chica are among the earliest mounds within the complex, it seems that this protein resource was either hunted to extinction or driven to other regions by alteration of their natural habitat.

The second alternative source of meat, camelids, probably llamas *(Lama glama)*, proved to be an important and steady meat source throughout the existence of Caballo Muerto. In the early stages of the center, revealed by the refuse deposits in the two deep cuts of Huaca Herederos Chica, llama ranked third in meat importance, behind shellfish and slightly behind deer. Later on, when deer were gone, llamas probably replaced that portion of the diet, rivaling and perhaps even surpassing shellfish in dietary importance. In any case, llamas, providing meat, wool, and possibly means of transportation, probably grazed along the river or irrigation canals. Cardozo (1954:66–67) states that llamas prefer the wild plants of the altiplano; therefore, in the past they probably preferred wild plants on the coast to cultivated ones. Some foraging may have occurred upvalley. Most likely there were never so many llamas that special cultivated fields were needed to feed them.

Huaca de los Reyes

This mound is the best preserved and most elaborate, in terms of decoration and layout, of all of the mounds within the Caballo Muerto complex. My excavations here were guided by information gathered during the previous excavations and mapping. My focus was primarily on entrance and access patterns within the site and the clarification of several relationships that were architecturally unclear. A secondary focus was the partial clearing of certain rooms in an attempt to ascertain functional aspects of the site. During excavation, several new and different friezes were discovered, adding considerably to the group discovered in 1972 by Watanabe (Moseley and Watanabe 1974).

Huaca de los Reyes (Figure 10.2) is located with its back face along the east side of the latest cut of the Río Seco quebrada. This was presumably intentional, probably to restrict access to the mound area. The layout of the site consists of two main bilaterally symmetrical contiguous platform mounds. Each mound has a pair of lateral wings extending eastward, each opening N85°E. The upper or west platform mound (F) stands about six meters high with its pair of lateral wings (D and D') bordering a central plaza (III); these wings rest on top of the lower or east platform mound (E), which serves as a foundation. The lateral wings (A and A') of mound E extend to the east from its face and also border a plaza (II) that is somewhat larger than Plaza III. The height of mound E is about five and one-half meters, but since it is built on a much lower level than mound F, the perceived difference between the heights of the mounds is greater. Also included in the layout are two sets of side platform mounds, one set (B and B') flanking the east face of mound E and the second (C and C') flanking the lateral wings D and D' of mound F, and a large rectangular plaza (I), east of Plaza II, partially outlined by a single row of boulders. Additional features include various walls and benches to the south and north of mound F, walls and a small eastward-looking platform (G) with at least two plazas north of mound F, a small two-room structure just west of mound F, and a few rooms at the eastern end of wing A. Friezes are present on the east faces of both mounds E and F as well as on the entire sides of their corresponding lateral wings (A and A', D and D') that face inward toward the centers of Plazas II and III. Also, friezes exist on the east faces of all the lateral wings of mounds C and C' and on the summit of mound F.

Excavations in several places revealed two construction phases. The evidence remains scanty for the first phase as extensive excavations would have called for the destruction of the second construction layer. Unless otherwise indicated, the following description is of the second construction phase.

233

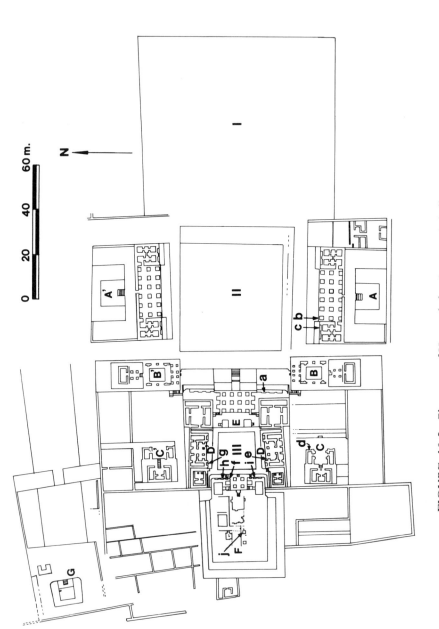

FIGURE 10.2. Plan map of Huaca de los Reyes at Caballo Muerto.

A mere glance at Figure 10.2 suggests symmetry and great regularity. Indeed, a closer inspection of general layout and actual field measurements reveals some interesting relationships. Each wing of mound E has 12 pillars and two niches at each end; each wing of upper main mound F has 2 pillars or one-sixth the number of pillars of wings A and A' and only one niche at each end. The east face of mound E contains eight pillars while the corresponding face of mound F has four pillars; the same 2:1 relationship exists when comparing the total lengths of each of the faces. In addition, each face is divided roughly into thirds, one-third for the colonnade, and a third each for the two niched ends (each of which, by the way, contains three niches). As one can see, a pattern is set for various architectural features within the site based on the number 12. Fractional relationships of one-half, one-third, one-fourth, one-sixth, and one-twelfth exist not only in linear but also in areal dimensions. For example, Plaza III is one-sixth the size of Plaza II, which in turn is one-third the size of Plaza I. The "magic" or symbolic number 12 is probably correlated with a solar calendar of 12 months. More detailed astronomical correspondences such as with solstices or equinoxes are not evident. However, both Kirchhoff (1949) and Zuidema (1964) note the importance of 3 and 4 in social groupings of the Inca *ceque* system, all within the context of a solar calendar. If the correlation of the number 12 of Huaca de los Reyes with the solar calendar is correct, then the use of this time measure dates as early as or earlier than the lunar calendar in the Andean area (Kosok 1965:49–62).

These were ideal relationships, however, and should not be confused with today's ideas of standardization. Field measurements of smaller, analogous units, such as niches and pillars, reveal a standard error of about 10 percent. These measurements also indicate the standard minimum unit of measurement was from 25 to 30 centimeters, or about the length of a man's foot. Certainly Huaca de los Reyes was not a Great Pyramid of Cheops for exactness of measurement, but there was a good deal of planning and organization behind its construction.

Adobe Friezes Found in Huaca de los Reyes

A total of 39 out of 58 friezes present were excavated at Huaca de los Reyes. Each frieze is made of adobe laid over a matrix of cobbles, boulders, and mud mortar. An intact frieze surface is distinguished from the rubble by a yellow finishing clay and, occasionally, by faint white paint which probably acted as a base for other colors.

In Plaza II (Figure 10.2), there are two basic types of friezes: (1) large adobe heads and (2) standing bipedal figures, usually associated with smaller design elements. The first, and more impressive, type of frieze is the large adobe head (Figure 10.3) bearing human as well as feline characteristics. There are six of these set in niches along the east face of mound E, three to the north and three to the south of the central colonnade area. Each head varies slightly in details, but basically each faces east and has a frowning mouth with interlocking canines, a broad, flat nose, and rectanguloid eyes apparently looking straight ahead. Each head measures about 170 centimeters across, 60 centimeters deep, and probably once stood at least 2 meters high.

The second, and more numerous, type of frieze is the bipedal, presumably human, figure (Figures 10.4, 10.5). Along each lateral wing (A and A′) of mound E, there is a bipedal figure adorning the plaza-side face of each of the pillars in the front row. Each of these figures stands on the floor of the colonnade with its feet parallel and slightly apart, the toes pointing toward the plaza. The feet extend out from the face of the pillar an average of 20 centimeters. Often, but not always, there is a fanged, outward-looking profile head to the left and right of the feet. Preservation varies, but usually about 30 centimeters of the height of each frieze has been conserved. Exceptions to this are the end pillars which, preserved up to one meter high, reveal the rest of the figure's legs, part of a belted vestment, and a pendant snake head.

Each six-room structure at the ends of wings A and A′ has two wide niches that also contain bipedal figures. To each side of the upper portions of the legs are a snake head, apparently emanating from the body of the figure, and some other pendant ornamentation (Figure 10.6).

Bipedal figures are also present along the colonnade area of the east face of mound E on all four plaza-side faces of the front row pillars and form the two entrance panel friezes off the extreme ends of this front row. These figures differ in that the feet are less three-dimensional than the ones on the lateral wings and are situated on top of elements of each of the outward-looking fanged profile heads to the left and right.

For mounds C and C′, each of the lateral wings contains a niche with a mud frieze. Each is of a standing feline with clawed feet and a tail which has been elaborated into a serpent head (Figure 10.7). The friezes are arranged in a bilaterally symmetrical manner with respect to

FIGURE 10.3. Large adobe head in a niche on the east face of mound E, Huaca de los Reyes.

20 cm
0

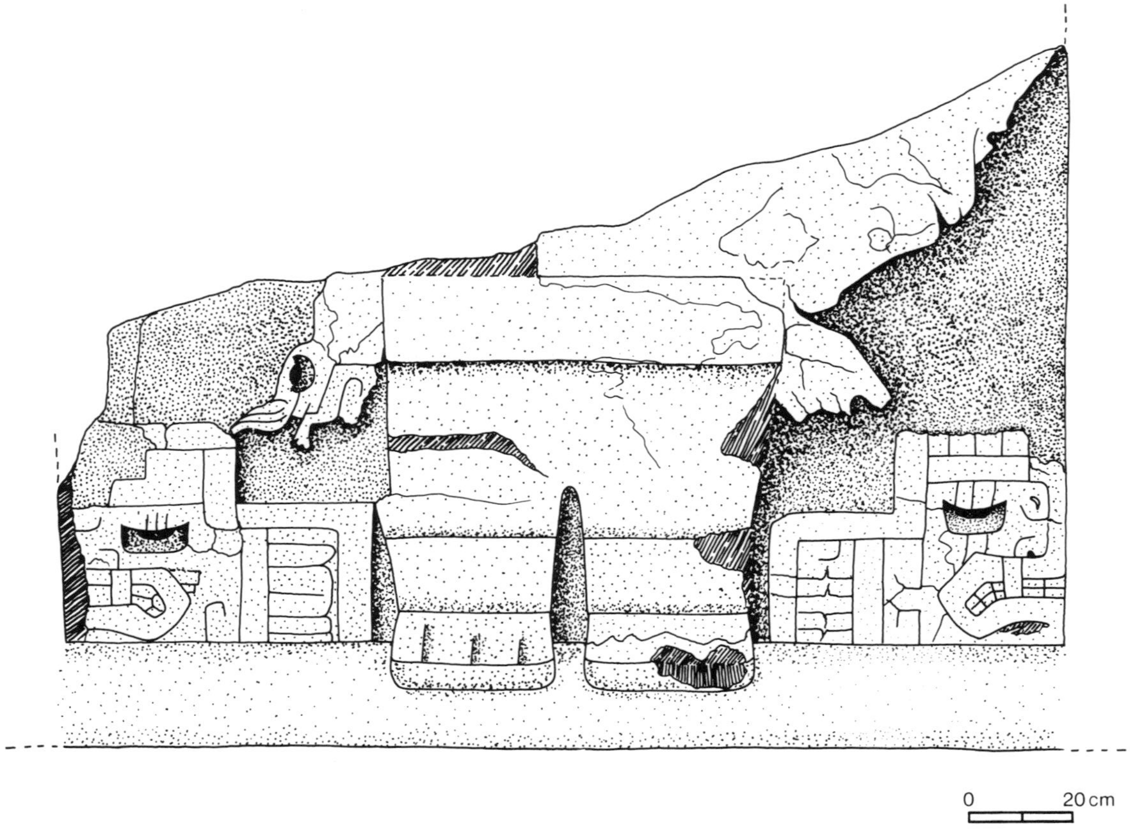

FIGURE 10.4. Bipedal figure fragment on a pillar of wing A, Huaca de los Reyes.

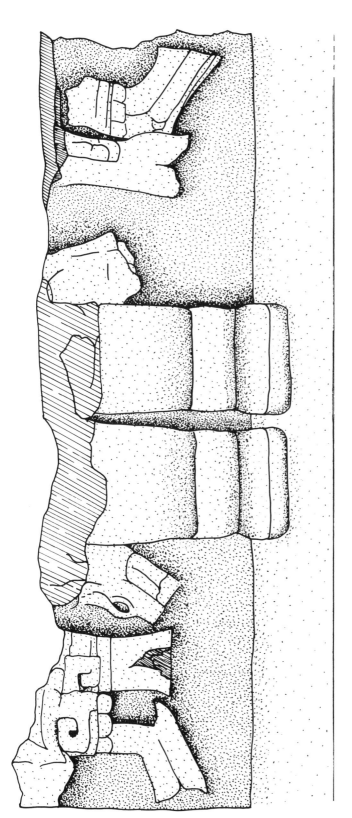

FIGURE 10.5. Bipedal figure fragment in a niche of wing A, Huaca de los Reyes.

0   20cm

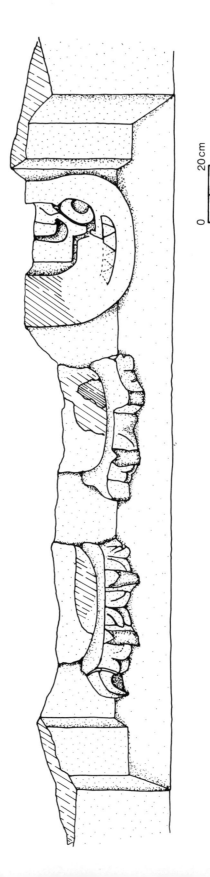

FIGURE 10.6. Fragment of a feline with a serpent-head tail in a niche of mound C, Huaca de los Reyes.

0   20 cm

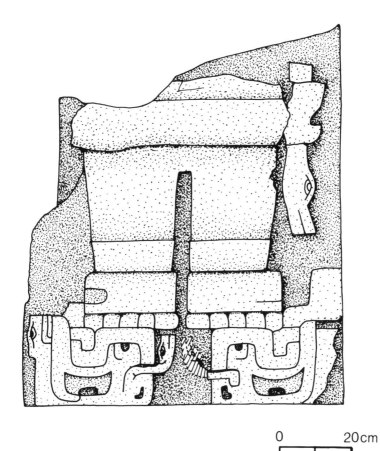

0   20cm

FIGURE 10.7. Bipedal figure fragment in an entrance panel of wing D, Huaca de los Reyes.

the east-west axis of each mound. This means that for each mound, the south wing has the head to the north and the tail to the south while the north wing is just the opposite.

For Plaza III, there is more variety. On each of the lateral wings, there are two central pillars with friezes, two entrance panel friezes adjacent to the pillars, and two niches with friezes, one on each side of the colonnade area. Along the east face of mound F, there are two central pillars with friezes, two entrance panel friezes adjacent to the pillars, and four niches with friezes, two on each side of the colonnade area.

There are standing bipedal figures on each of the plaza-side pillar faces of wings D and D' and on the east face of mound F. These figures are situated on top of a decorated border of two profile heads,

241

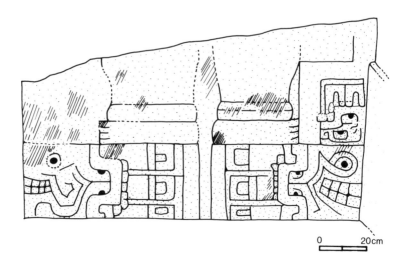

FIGURE 10.8. Bipedal figure fragment in an entrance panel on the east face of mound F, Huaca de los Reyes.

one to the right and one to the left of the figure (Figure 10.8). The same is true for all of the entrance panel friezes of wings D and D' and of mound F, though quite often the profile heads differ markedly.

Each niche of wings D and D' contains a frieze pattern consisting of two side elements of either downward-looking or inward-looking agnathic heads, plus a central element of two upward-looking agnathic heads joined at the top of their heads (Figure 10.9). The central element is a semirectangular projection from the plane of the two side elements, in which all of the projection is decorated by frieze designs. The total width of each niche is about 1.7 meters, with each element, the two sides and center, occupying roughly one-third of the total width. The best-preserved frieze stands about 40 centimeters high, but undoubtedly each frieze was originally much higher.

The niches along the east face of mound F have about the same dimensions and form as those of the lateral wings. However, all frieze designs differ from each other (Figure 10.10). Central elements basically appear to be different forms of feet, while side elements vary from upward-looking heads to inward-looking heads to downward-looking heads.

These are descriptions for the upper set of friezes only, however, for below the floor level of each niche lies another stratigraphically earlier

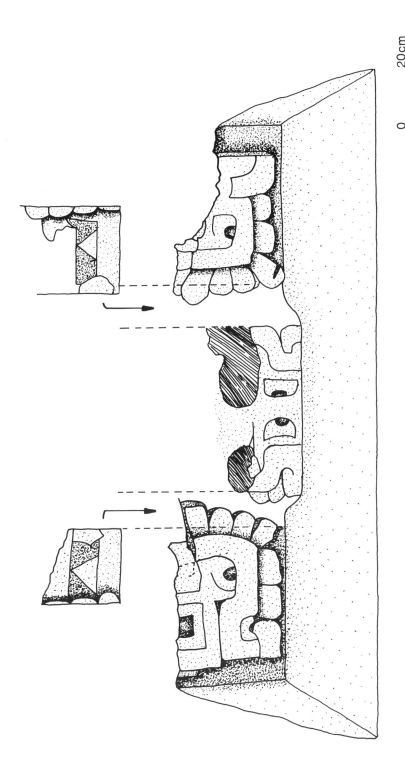

FIGURE 10.9. Fragment of a frieze depicting agnathic heads in a niche of wing D', Huaca de los Reyes.

20cm

0

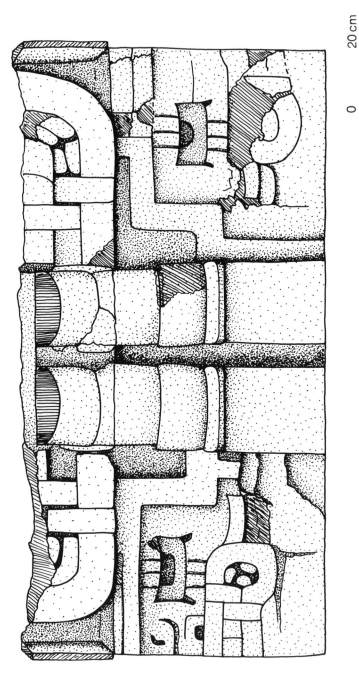

FIGURE 10.10. Superimposed friezes in a niche on the east face of mound F, Huaca de los Reyes. The upper frieze depicts two inward-looking heads, of which only the fanged mouths are preserved, separated by the fragmentary remains of a bipedal figure. The lower frieze shows two outward-looking profile heads flanking a bipedal figure that stands on two cylindrical pedestals.

20 cm

0

frieze. The basic earlier design is a bipedal figure standing on two cylindrical pedestals flanked on each side by an outward-looking fanged profile head. Three of the early niches follow this pattern, but a fourth (Figure 10.11) has the bipedal figure standing on two sculptured heads accompanied by two very different, more curvilinear, profile heads to each side.

With respect to the summit of the upper main mound F, one full, round, adobe head (Figure 10.12) was found in situ on the northwest corner of a rectangular pillar located on the south side of the summit. Its condition is far from perfect, but it seems to have faced the interior of the mound, probably looking over a sunken room.

Fuller, more detailed descriptions of the friezes of Huaca de los Reyes can be found elsewhere (T. Pozorski 1975; 1976). These references include not only the ones found during my excavations but also those uncovered by previous excavations.

Style of the Friezes

Style, defined as the representation of certain forms and motifs in a prescribed manner, varies considerably at Huaca de los Reyes. While certain figures are common and repetitive, their manner of execution differs markedly. The best example of this is the bipedal figure, which is generally depicted in a three-dimensional, almost fully round manner but also is portrayed in both bas-relief and engraving. If depth of execution is used as a criterion for style definition, then there are at least three styles, or three variations of the same style, represented at Huaca de los Reyes.

Most figures are repetitive at the site and differences among them can probably be attributed to individual artistic variation. However, in certain places there is more variation than artistic license allows. This is especially true for Plaza III. Of the four entrance panel friezes on wings D and D', three depict a bipedal figure standing on inverted agnathic heads while a fourth figure stands on an upright head. Along the east face of mound F, three of the four friezed early niches have regular, somewhat rectangular fanged profile heads. The fourth also depicts a fanged profile head, but it is done in a much more curvilinear, high-relief style. Lastly, in addition to a distinctive incisionlike technique, the entrance friezes and pillars of mound F depict profile heads containing nonfanged mouths and circular noses. Hence, if

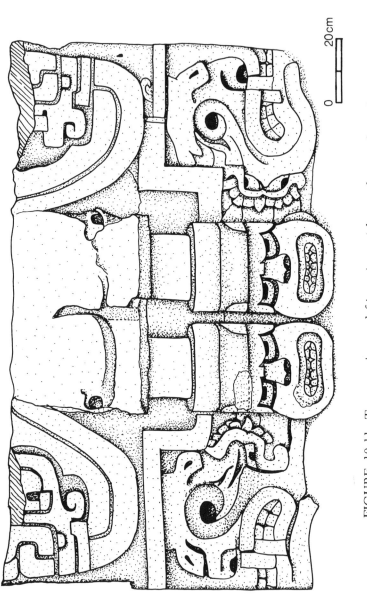

20 cm

0

FIGURE 10.11. Two superimposed friezes in a niche on the east face of mound F, Huaca de los Reyes. The upper frieze represents two agnathic, upward-looking heads flanking the stylized feet of a bipedal figure. The lower frieze shows two curvilinear profile heads flanking a bipedal figure that stands on two sculptured heads.

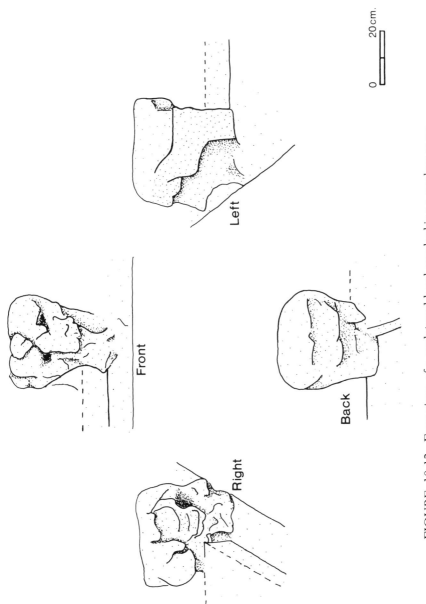

FIGURE 10.12. Four views of a sculptured head overlooking a sunken room on the summit of mound F, Huaca de los Reyes.

style is defined by spatial correspondences, then there appear to be at least three styles or an extremely wide variation of one general style.

Dating Huaca de los Reyes and its Friezes

Relative intrasite dating makes the stylistic interpretations of the friezes even more interesting. Careful excavation revealed that the majority of the friezes, including all of those surrounding Plaza II, those of mounds C and C′, those of wings D and D′, and all the upper ones on the east face of mound F, are contemporaneous, contrary to the hypothesis of Moseley and Watanabe (1974:161). This is based on architectural connections of floors and walls plus symmetrical architectural layout (especially for wings A and A′). This dating is supported by ceramic evidence. Though certain areas have concentrations of vessels, apparently ceremonially broken, all architectural units contain the same types of ceramics. The stratigraphically earlier friezes of the face of mound F are probably not much earlier than the upper friezes because (1) architectural construction techniques and layout are the same, and (2) the ceramics are the same for both sets of friezes. The stylistic ties between the common profile fanged heads of the older mound F niches and the later ones of Plaza II are closer than the ties among the contemporary older friezed niches themselves.

The following conclusion for the Huaca de los Reyes friezes presents itself: A large number of friezes, largely contemporaneous, have been found in situ. If found as isolated examples and then compared, several friezes would probably be classified as stylistically and chronologically distinct. However, since they are known to be contemporaneous, they must represent either (1) an extreme variation of one style, a stand which, if taken, calls into question the very definition of style; or (2) several styles being used at one point in time (T. Pozorski 1980: 108). In either case, great chronological change is not present.

Absolute dates for Huaca de los Reyes are also available. Four cane samples, taken from burned post holes of the first construction phase on the summit of mound F, were submitted to the radiocarbon laboratory of the University of Texas at Austin. The results, uncorrected and based on the 5,568-year half-life, were 850 B.C. ± 60 (Tx-2181), 1190 B.C. ± 60 (Tx-1973), 1360 B.C. ± 80 (Tx-1972), and 1730 B.C. ± 80 (Tx-1974). It is possible that the 850 B.C. date was contaminated, and the 1730 B.C. date seems a bit early. This leaves a range of 1400 to 1200 B.C. for beginning and use of construction phase 1.

248

The second construction phase, containing the majority of the friezes, probably does not follow too much later than this time. The dates might seem early to some people, but they are supported by relative dating of ceramics. A majority of the ceramics are crude utilitarian types with a relatively small percentage of finer wares. Fine ware decoration is limited to broad-line and fine-line incision, punctation often delimited by incised lines, appliqué bumps, combing, raised bands bearing incision, and graphite or manganese decoration found in incised lines and in zones or bands on flat surfaces. The use of graphite may be correlated with the Chavín phenomenon, since all of the other techniques are present at mounds that predate Huaca de los Reyes. Major forms are neckless ollas, jars, open bowls, and stirrup spout bottles. The wares, some decoration, and some forms correspond to those found at the early coastal site of Gramalote on the north side of the Moche Valley and to other early sites on the Peruvian coast. The radiocarbon dates from Gramalote also correspond well with those from Huaca de los Reyes.

CORPORATE LABOR AND SOCIETAL IMPLICATIONS

Focusing on the use of corporate labor at Huaca de los Reyes, one can reach certain conclusions about the nature of the society that built it and other mounds at Caballo Muerto. Based on estimates of volumes and weights of rocks and mud, plus the amount of individual labor needed to haul and use these materials, it is estimated that 100 men, working full time, would need 11.43 years to build the second construction phase of Huaca de los Reyes. The time estimate, of course, would vary according to the amount of men working on the mound at any one time. However, the symmetry, planning, and careful execution of the site suggest that it was built under the direction of one person who supervised construction within his generation of leadership, about 25 years. A longer construction time would have been interrupted by the death of the original planner, resulting in changes in the site layout. Fifty to 100 individuals working full time could have easily built the second phase of construction at Huaca de los Reyes within 25 years.

Societal ranking has already been implied by the existence of a planner and perhaps a few associates who directed the overall operation and labor group serving him. However, within the labor group a number of artisans existed who specialized in the finer aspects of mound construction, such as architectural wall and floor finishing, stair construction, and frieze design. Ceramic specialists were probably also part of this artisan group. The bulk of the labor—digging, collecting, and hauling of clay and stones—could have been the work of full-time specialists but more likely was done by common laborers taken from the supporting population. If later Andean examples are analogous, then perhaps a form of labor tax or mit'a-like system was used to construct the mounds of Caballo Muerto. Hence, the 100 or so individuals needed to complete Huaca de los Reyes within 25 years or less could have in fact consisted of considerably more than 100 individuals taking turns throughout the year who in effect did the work of 100 individuals working full time.

The exact source of the labor force remains a moot point. The evidence for a domestic component of Caballo Muerto is scanty. The inland position of the complex suggests an agricultural base, and land area between the complex and the river was more than adequate to support a population base large enough to construct Caballo Muerto. However, the possibility of labor forces derived from outlying areas, such as from the Chicama and Virú valleys or other areas of the Moche Valley, cannot be discounted. At the very least, there was most likely a labor tax put on the inhabitants of the coastal site of Gramalote.

One of the surest markers of the existence of a ranked society such as a chiefdom in an archaeological context is site stratification, that is, the presence of a clearly larger site in conjunction with several other smaller sites of the same time period within a given area (Sanders and Price 1968:52). Though the sample size is small, this relationship exists between Caballo Muerto and Gramalote. Equally valuable, however, is the presence of internal site stratification, which gives evidence of status and rank within a site. Huaca de los Reyes is an example of this. Plazas I and II could hold a great quantity of people and were probably used by common people, visitors, and pilgrims. The awe-inspiring giant friezes found there, which may once have been painted, would certainly be in accord with this view. The restricted Plaza III and the plazas of mounds C and C', being smaller, held fewer people and were probably used by a more elite clientele, persons of higher status. The variety of friezes in Plaza III and the distinctness of the feline figures of mounds C and C' argue for a more complete knowledge of the religious pantheon and mythology, knowledge perhaps restricted to certain status groups. Furthermore, the inner sanctum of the mound F summit could very well have been restricted to the most elite members of the society. Certainly the small size of the room dictates limited group visitation, and the air of secretiveness, possibly akin to that found in galleries in highland Chavín sites, adds to the supposition (T. Pozorski 1980:109).

The overall plan of Huaca de los Reyes shows that passage from one area to another within the site is from more open areas to smaller ones by means of narrow restricted entrances. This is especially evident for the passageways to Plaza III and to the plazas associated with mounds C and C'. Restricted entry is strongly indicative of status differences. If this were not the desired effect, then wider, more accessible passage-ways would have been built for easier traffic flow.

Internal site stratification does not begin with Huaca de los Reyes or even with the earlier mounds within the Caballo Muerto complex. At the Cotton Preceramic site of Alto Salaverry (S. Pozorski and T. Pozorski 1977, 1979a) south of the Moche River there is evidence of an incipient ranked system. There, common domestic, higher status semidomestic, and simple ceremonial architecture are all present in a site covering only 19,200 square meters. On the west part of the site is the main area of domestic refuse and house remains, which are often buried by refuse up to one meter of the preserved height. Included in this section is a small corporate labor platform built of large boulders and small cobbles. On the east portion of the site is a large multiroomed structure associated with a smaller area of refuse at its west end. Considering the size of the rooms and their association with refuse, it seems likely that the structure was used as a house for the head man of the village and also as a meeting place for secular affairs. At the north end of the site, isolated from any other structures and barren of refuse, is a circular stone-lined structure, nine meters in diameter and two meters in depth, built inside a hollowed-out sand dune. In the center of the floor is a small hole, presumably once for a pole, used as a roof support. At opposite ends of the structure are two stepped entrances. Considering its isolation and unique configuration, this structure seems to be ceremonial in nature.

Beginning with such evidence in the preceramic, internal site stratification is seen to continue in later periods. Though Caballo Muerto lacks a definite domestic component, the layout of Huaca de los Reyes is highly suggestive of a continuation and an elaboration of the three-rank system.

It is tempting to correlate this system with the one reflected in the planning and use of Huaca de los Reyes:

Plazas I and II —
> large open areas used to impress common people and laborers who provided the subsistence base of the complex.

Plaza III and the plazas of mounds C and C' —
> smaller restricted areas used by the artisan group with a possible subdivision for a feline cult.

Summit of mound F —
> small sunken gallery used by the corporate labor leader(s) who probably also directed canal construction and maintenance as well as other community and religious activities.

Evidence from other mounds within the complex, though not as extensive as at Huaca de los Reyes, also suggests a similar system, showing a continuity of social organization from the initial settlement of the complex to its demise well after the final use of Huaca de los Reyes. Specific activities within plazas at Huaca de los Reyes and other mounds were undoubtedly religious in nature, consisting of gatherings and processionals perhaps similar to those still seen at religious festivals in Peru today. Within smaller rooms of wing structures off open plaza areas, more private activities took place such as specialized craft production and esoteric religious ceremonies involving only a few individuals.

CONCLUSION

Caballo Muerto was the center of a chiefdom. External and internal site stratification is present, implying the existence of a ranked status system. Site planning and corporate labor suggest the presence of a single leader or ruler, probably a hereditary chief whose lineage is represented by the sequential construction of the mounds and their various reconstructions. Hereditary rule represented by sequential construction is analogous to a later pattern postulated for the Chimú capital of Chan Chan. At Caballo Muerto, there is no evidence of defensive works or warfare—further evidence of its chiefdom status.

In a chiefdom, there is centralized extrafamilial authority, but there is no coercive force to back up the leader's will (Service 1975:15–16). Rule is by charismatic leadership and persuasion.

The roots of Caballo Muerto extend back into the late Cotton Preceramic. Even after the inland move, the center never did break ties with the coast completely but still depended greatly on marine resources for much of its animal protein supply. In terms of social organization and governmental structure, the beginnings also lay back in Cotton Preceramic times, as evidenced at Alto Salaverry. This correlates well with the observations and hypotheses made by Moseley (1975b) for the Central Coast of Peru. The tradition of mound building at the Caballo Muerto complex, and probably architectural decoration as well, date to pre-Chavín times. Subsequently, Caballo Muerto was definitely connected with the Chavín phenomenon as seen in the friezes at Huaca de los Reyes.

Compared with other early ceramic centers along the North Coast, such as Sechín Alto in the Casma Valley to the south, Caballo Muerto cannot be considered the most important center of the time period. However, on a smaller regional basis, for the Chicama–Moche–Virú Valley area, Caballo Muerto emerged as the most important center and reflected the complexity of North Coast societal development at that time. Within the Moche Valley, Caballo Muerto represented the beginning of the trend of one-site dominance for any given time period.

11
The Early Intermediate Period and Its Legacy

THERESA LANGE TOPIC

Trent University

INTRODUCTION

This chapter will focus on the Early Intermediate Period of the North Coast of Peru, especially as it is manifested in the Chicama, Moche, and Virú valleys. The area's history during this time period is imperfectly known, but the information that is gradually accumulating indicates that the Early Intermediate Period (hereafter abbreviated EIP) was a time of particularly rapid and vital change. The social units into which the inhabitants were grouped increased steadily in size and complexity, and the increasing political complexity was paralleled by growing economic sophistication. These changes were not temporary; they provided the organizational foundation for later Middle Horizon and Late Intermediate Period events in the area.

I will first briefly review the EIP in the three valleys which formed the core area of the North Coast in prehistoric times. I will then present a more detailed look at Moche culture, drawing on the results of excavations and other studies carried out by myself and several colleagues[1] at the site of Moche in 1972 and 1973. These studies produced important new information on the history of the site, its growth, and the activities carried out there. These results will be discussed not just in terms of the functioning of this one site but also as they relate to the structure of Moche society in general. While data relevant to early occupations at the site will be presented, the emphasis will be on the florescent Moche III and IV subphases.

I will conclude with an analysis of the major structural continuities and discontinuities between Moche and Chimú cultures. It will be argued that most of the forms that characterize Chimú political organization and economic structure have recognizable antecedents at the site of Moche.

THE EARLY INTERMEDIATE PERIOD

The Early Intermediate Period (EIP) on the North Coast is not well dated in absolute terms, but the dates 400 B.C. to A.D. 600 are reasonable estimates for its inception and conclusion. More important, the EIP includes the Salinar and Gallinazo cultures and the first four subphases of Moche culture (see Bawden, Chapter 12, for a discussion of the terminal Moche V subphase, which falls in the Middle Horizon).

The EIP in general is frequently characterized as a time of regional autonomy, in which political entities of varying sizes exerted authority free from any pan-Peruvian political or ideological influences. The EIP is also described as a time of regional differentiation, during which minimal interaction encouraged each culture to develop along distinct lines. The result of this regional autonomy and differentiation was, presumably, an increase in the frequency and intensity of warfare. It is also argued that the EIP saw the rise of the first Peruvian cities, artistic florescence, population peaks, expansion of irrigation systems, and the emergence of craft specialization and social stratification (see, for example, Willey 1971; Lanning 1967; Lumbreras 1974).

Generalizations of this sort are of course designed to illuminate the most important and distinctive features of a given culture or time period in order to facilitate their comparison. We should not expect the generalizations listed above for the EIP to be equally applicable to all parts of Peru, and indeed this is not the case. The first appearance of cities, for example, is usually credited to the South Coast and the

256

Southern Sierra. But the other broad statements about EIP events do seem most applicable to that time period on the North Coast, and more specifically to the Chicama-Moche-Virú area.

Even within this small area, certain qualifications and reservations are necessary if we are to appreciate the diversity of EIP cultures and the ways in which these cultures evolved within the thousand-year time span under consideration.

Salinar and Gallinazo

The Salinar culture was first described by Larco Hoyle (1944) on the basis of gravelots from the Chicama Valley. The identifying characteristic of the culture was and remains the pottery, especially the White-on-Red painted fine wares. The most common shapes include stirrup spout jars, cylindrically spouted jars with wide strap handles, and false double-spout-and-bridge jars. Human and animal figures are often modeled, and the modeling is frequently embellished with simple incised or white painted designs. The skill with which Salinar pottery is modeled varies, but technically the fine wares are very good.

The distribution of Salinar is apparently limited to the Chicama-Moche-Virú area. The population was agricultural and tended to live in agglutinated villages scattered along the margins of valleys.

Only cemeteries are reported from the Chicama Valley, but the Virú Valley is quite well known. Willey's (1953) settlement pattern survey of that valley located 83 sites with a Salinar (Puerto Moorin) occupation. Settlement was concentrated in the Huacapongo, the narrow valley of a tributary several miles from the coast. Forty sites were located in this section of Virú, and the effect was a high population density in this relatively small area. Nine of the 14 mounds dating to Salinar times are also found in the Huacapongo. There was a considerable population in the lower valley, but it was scattered over a much larger area. None of the Virú Salinar sites were especially large; many of the sites discussed by Willey were individual farmsteads, and the largest agglutinated villages would probably not have had populations of more than 100 people.

One site category defined by Willey, the "fortified stronghold or place of refuge," had a profound effect on the interpretation of EIP events. Willey discusses two hilltop redoubts of Salinar date from Virú. In both cases, a hill crest was ringed by a wall, and room complexes and low mounds were built inside the wall. Both sites were located in the lower valley, and both could have sheltered large numbers of people. In addition, four hilltop platform complexes are discussed, three in the Huacapongo, and the largest in the lower valley south, between the two hilltop redoubts. These four sites were not walled, but are classed as defensive because of their location (Willey 1953:92–100).

These six sites have been construed as evidence that warfare was frequent during Salinar times. The two hilltop redoubts certainly represent a considerable investment of labor, and the difficult access to the other four sites mentioned above contributes to the impression that defensibility was a major factor in site location and planning for some Salinar groups. It is less clear, however, where the potential threat came from. The Huacapongo defenses might be viewed as a reaction to the possibility of raids from the sierra, while the defenses in the lower valley would offer some protection against intruders from neighboring coastal valleys. But given the location and nature of the defenses, it is more likely that conflict existed between the different segments of the Virú population itself.

No single site is preeminent in Virú during Salinar times, and the defensive sites extant during that time period could have effectively protected only a small proportion of the valley's population. These facts lead to the conclusion that there was no political unity in Virú. While individual settlements were undoubtedly linked to varying degrees by kinship ties and common economic concerns, there is no indication that formal political authority united any part of the valley.

The situation is somewhat different in the Moche Valley to the north, which contains the largest Salinar site known, Cerro Arena. This site, located on the south side of the river, consists of hundreds of stone-walled houses strung out on and below the north-south trending ridge of the hill, in close proximity to the area irrigated by the Orejas-Arena S2 canal (see Chapter 2). Mujica Barreda, who excavated at the site in 1973, confirmed the existence of a large and dense population (easily in the thousands, although no population estimate has yet been made). There is no evidence yet that the site maintained any effective political control over the entire valley, but none of the other much smaller settlements in the Moche Valley could have challenged its importance.

The markedly different situations in the Moche and Virú valleys may reflect the responses of the residents to the geography of each valley. The Virú Valley consists of two very different zones. The Huacapongo, because of its restricted size and steeper gradients, would have been more favorable for early irrigation agriculture than the valley below. This advantage, though, could be enjoyed only by some, and those forced by population pressure to settle in the lower valley may have been in periodic conflict with their more prosperous Huaca-pongo neighbors. There is no such geographic division in the Moche Valley; the narrow upper valley does not form a distinct geographical unit, and while it offers the advantages of steep gradients, it contains only a very narrow ribbon of arable land. The south side of the lower valley was apparently most suited to irrigation, and the valley popula-tion was concentrated here until the end of the Early Intermediate Period. From an early date, a large part of the Moche Valley popula-tion was cooperating in the use of a single irrigation system.

Like Salinar, the Gallinazo culture has thus far been encountered only in the Chicama, Moche, and Virú valleys, and, as is the case for Salinar, only a handful of cemeteries and mound complexes are reported from Chicama, while the Virú Valley has been studied well. In Virú, the Gallinazo culture has been divided into Early, Middle, and Late subphases. The Early and Middle Gallinazo subphases corre-late with Gallinazo occupations in the Moche Valley, while Late Gallinazo is probably contemporary with Moche I and II in Moche and Chicama.

In the Virú Valley, the greatest change between Salinar and Gallinazo times is a major shift in settlement, as the Huacapongo was virtually abandoned and population concentrated in the lower valley (Willey 1953:102). The Late Gallinazo subphase was especially important in several respects. The population of the valley hit the highest point it was to achieve in prehistoric times, and the irrigation system reached its maximum extent (Willey 1953:393). The Gallinazo Group and the site of Gallinazo itself achieved prominence at this time. This cluster of sites in the northern part of the lower valley held the largest population concentration up to that time on the North Coast, with an estimated 30,000 rooms in an area no more than five kilometers square (Bennett 1950:68–69). This group of sites was situated to take advan-tage of irrigated land, the Virú River delta, riverine lagoons, sandy beaches, and rocky headlands. During this time, too, a new concept of fortification emerged. Individual sites were no longer defensively located or protected; instead, large and impressive fortifications were placed on hilltops at strategic points. The narrow passage from the lower valley to the Huacapongo was particularly well defended, with four castillo complexes of Late Gallinazo date overlooking it. The implication of this configuration is that the greatest threat to the valley emanated from higher elevations—from the sierra or from groups still living in the Huacapongo.

A high degree of political cohesion characterized the Virú Valley during Gallinazo times, particularly in the Late Gallinazo subphase. A large proportion of the valley's population was concentrated at or near the site of Gallinazo, which could quite reasonably be regarded as the "capital" of the valley. Fortifications were located in such a way that they defended the entire lower valley rather than individual settlements, although the coastal approaches into the valley were not defended at all. The irrigation system was a coherent valley-wide network, almost certainly controlled by one central authority.

The Gallinazo occupation in the Moche Valley is not well enough studied yet for a similar postulation of central authority to be made with complete confidence. There was certainly no pre-Moche site in the valley to rival the Gallinazo Group, although Cerro Orejas had a large population. This site was located on the south side of the valley, eight kilometers northeast of Cerro Arena, at the point where the valley narrows. It included a series of agricultural terraces climbing the steep lower slopes of the hill, stone-walled houses on platforms above the S1 canal, and a small fortified platform perched on the almost vertical hillside above the settlement. Although Cerro Orejas is smaller than Cerro Arena, the site was probably the most important Gallinazo settlement in the valley and may well have exerted some form of authority over the rest of the valley. The degree of political organization in the Moche Valley at this time was on a level with that of the Virú Valley during its Early and Middle Gallinazo subphases. However, complete cohesion and extravalley expansion were achieved only by the succeeding Moche Culture which, I will argue below, conquered the Late Gallinazo peoples of Virú.

The early part of the Early Intermediate Period in the core area of the North Coast can be characterized as a period of growth. Populations grew, irrigation systems expanded, and there was an increasing centralization of political authority. The Late Gallinazo subphase of the Virú Valley was the culmination of this period of growth and change, but the growth and change did not stop here. At the same time that the Gallinazo Group was becoming the Virú Valley power center, a potential rival was taking shape at the site of Moche 25 kilometers to the north.

Moche Culture

The Moche culture of the North Coast is an outgrowth of the two preceding Early Intermediate Period cultures discussed above. Moche spans the latter part of the EIP and at least the first part of the Middle Horizon. A very useful five-part subdivision of the Moche phase has been made by Larco Hoyle (1948) based on changes in the shape and proportion of spouts and stirrups on stirrup spout jars. Moche remains are found from the Lambayeque Valley south to the Nepeña Valley, with some enigmatic occurrences farther north and south.

Much of our familiarity with the culture stems from studies of Moche art, particularly as it is expressed on ceramics. Moche ceramic art has been frequently discussed in the literature, with many writers outlining the interpretive possibilities of the realistically painted and modeled fine wares (Larco Hoyle 1938–39, 1946; Sawyer 1966; Kutscher 1948, 1950; Benson 1972). More recently, Donnan (1976) has posited that the art depicts mythical, rather than cultural, reality, and must be used cautiously as a source of information on Moche life. Donnan's elegantly argued interpretation of Moche art will undoubtedly provide a wholesome rein on attempts to reconstruct Moche society solely from iconographic evidence, but it need not disallow use of this evidence for testing archaeologically derived interpretations. Certainly Moche potters depicted people, plants, animals, activities, scenes, and concepts with which they were familiar, although the aim was not to create a historical chronicle.

Very little controlled excavation and survey was directed at Moche sites until quite recently. The largest and most impressive Moche sites have frequently been discussed (Uhle 1913, Kroeber 1925, 1930, and Bennett 1939 for Moche; Kroeber 1930 for Huancaco; Schaedel 1951b and Bonavia 1961 for Pañamarca). The Virú Valley survey (Strong and Evans 1952; Willey 1953) provided data on settlement patterns and sites in the valley. More recently Donnan (1973) has surveyed sites in the Santa Valley, and Proulx (1973) has done the same in the Nepeña Valley.

The combination of archaeological and iconographic data allowed a number of generalizations to be made concerning the nature of Moche society. It was known that Moche society was based on irrigation agriculture, a wide variety of plants having been grown. Fish, sea mammals, mollusks, deer, and many other animals were hunted, collected, or taken from the ocean. The farming population was distributed in small villages located near fields. The society was stratified, and some occupations were in the hands of specialists. Fortifications were not especially common in Moche times, but the people were probably familiar with warfare. The best known examples of Moche architecture are the adobe platform mounds found throughout the Moche sphere of influence. Individual platform mounds tend to be rectangular, are built of rectangular mold-made adobes, and are often approached via a ramp. The largest sites (Mocollope, Moche, Pañamarca, Huancaco) combine one or more mounds into a complex with walled courtyards, plazas, and low platforms. The largest single adobe mound, Huaca del Sol, is located at the site of Moche.

Recent excavations at the site of Moche have provided a variety of new information which has helped to clarify and refine this reconstruction.

THE WORK AT MOCHE

Site Description

The site of Moche is located on the southern edge of the Moche Valley, six kilometers inland from the ocean and 600 meters from the present bed of the Moche River. The valley plain south of the river is much narrower than that north of the river, and Moche is located at a point where the hills that define the southern boundary of the valley protrude sharply northward. Thus the site is close to the center of the valley and close to the river, but is not located on prime agricultural land and has its back against Cerro Blanco, a hill that rises sharply to a height of over 500 meters above sea level.

The boundaries of the site at its maximum extent can be defined accurately in three directions. To the north, the site is bounded by a small hill and by a bend of the Moche River. The steep slopes of Cerro Blanco to the east of the site limited expansion in that direction. While

Moche ceramics are found scattered for great distances on the sandy plain south of the site, the architecture designated AA 2 and AA 3 on Figure 11.1 marks the most southerly occupation at Moche.

To the west, the boundaries of the site cannot be fixed. In 1602 the river was diverted by the Spaniards to the foot of Huaca del Sol in an attempt to find the gold which supposedly was hidden there. Well over half of the huaca was flushed downstream by this singularly ambitious undertaking, and it is impossible to determine how much of the site might have lain to the west of the huaca and met the same fate.

The site as it exists today is dominated by two man-made features, Huaca del Sol and Huaca de la Luna. Huaca de la Luna is a complex of platforms, walls, and courtyards constructed of adobe, resting on the steep lower slopes of Cerro Blanco. The western face of the main mound has been heavily looted, but it still rises 30 meters above the plain and gives the appearance of a sheer adobe cliff. Huaca del Sol dominates the view on the opposite side of the plain. The remnant of this adobe platform towers 40 meters over the plain at its highest point, and is 380 meters long. Viewed from any part of the settlement, it is a truly impressive sight.

The two major constructions bracket the 500-meter-wide plain which was the most densely occupied part of the site. Run-off from Cerro Blanco during infrequent but heavy rains has affected subsurface preservation adversely. Organic material is very poorly preserved in deposits on the plain, and in some locations percolation of moisture from the surface has badly damaged the adobe construction material and hardened both adobe and fill into an extremely hard matrix. In addition, the drainage of considerable amounts of water over the site has scoured the surface of the plain, leaving very little architecture visible. In light of the very poor surface preservation at the site, it is not at all surprising that Moche has traditionally been classified as an empty ceremonial center (Schaedel 1951a).

In discussion of Moche occupation, the site will be divided into five sectors, as illustrated in Figure 11.1. Sector 1 consists of Huaca del Sol, and this designation includes the huaca itself and the occupation remains under, in, and on top of it. Strata cuts 1 and 2 are located on the huaca. Sector 2, the northern plain, is the part of the site lying north of a line drawn perpendicular to the northern top of Huaca del Sol, running eastward to the foot of Cerro Blanco. Strata cut 3 is located on the river bank in this sector, and testpits 1 and 2 are nearby.

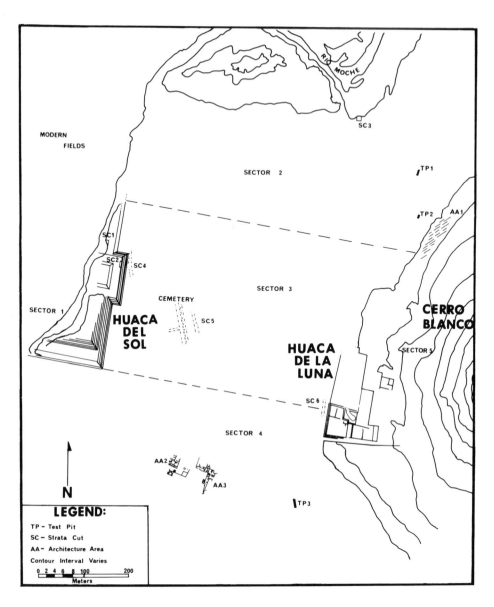

FIGURE 11.1. Plan of Moche, showing locations of excavations and other features mentioned in the text.

Occupation in this part of the site was shallow, and there is no major occupation preserved. Sector 3, the central plain, is the part of the site which shows the longest and densest occupation. Strata cuts 4, 5, and 6 are located here, as is a large cemetery with Moche and Chimú burials. Sector 4, the southern plain, lies south of the central section of the site where the terrain becomes much sandier. This has resulted in

264

better preservation of architecture in this area, particularly Architecture Area 2, which was in excellent condition. Occupation of this section of the site was late, and does not extend far south of AA 2 and AA 3. Indications of a ceramic workshop (testpit 3) were found here. Sector 5 includes the lower slope of Cerro Blanco, which consists of aeolian sand and occasional outcrops of bare rock. In addition to Huaca de la Luna, there is an extensive area of domestic occupation to the north, Architecture Area 1, which has been badly destroyed by erosion and looting. From the extent of huaquero activity, it seems that there was also a large burial area upslope from Huaca de la Luna and on the hillside south of it.

The necessity for a concentrated program of excavation at the site became apparent in 1972. The Chan Chan–Moche Valley Project had up to that time concentrated its attention on the Late Intermediate Period. As that period became better known, the question of precedents arose. What organizational principles embodied in Chan Chan had local antecedents in earlier cultures, and to what extent had the Chimú been innovators rather than borrowers? Moche was clearly an important and influential site, and might be expected to provide information on continuities and discontinuities between the Early Intermediate and the Late Intermediate periods. Excavation and architectural studies began at Moche in June of 1972 and continued for a year (see T. Topic 1977 for a more detailed report of the research at the site).

The excavations at the site revealed a longer period of occupation than expected. Although Uhle's gravelots had included vessels from Subphases I and II (Kroeber 1925), no significant occupation was thought to date to this period. But beneath the thick mantle of III–IV remains, evidence was found of earlier habitation. The occupation of the site began in Gallinazo times. The lowest levels of strata cuts 1, 2, and 4 contained Gallinazo sherds; the distribution of these remains probably reflects two contemporary settlements, one underneath the present location of Huaca del Sol, and another a few hundred meters to the northeast on the bank of the river. The Gallinazo style was quickly supplanted by Moche I, but the site was still small. The riverbank settlement (SC 2) was probably abandoned before Moche II times (a stratigraphic discontinuity caused by flooding makes this unclear), but the SC 4 occupation expanded east, and Moche II remains are found in the lowest levels of SC 5.

Very little can be said about early occupation of the site, other than that it existed. Only a few square meters pertaining to this occupation were uncovered, and this sample consisted mostly of midden and a few areas of domestic habitation. A much larger sample of architecture and artifacts would be necessary to postulate what kind of settlement early Moche was. But clearly it was small, and evidently there was no monumental construction at the site.

Moche III marks the turning point for the site. Remains of this period were found in every excavation. This period also sees the first stages of construction on Huaca del Sol and Huaca de la Luna. There was an influx of population to the site, and the new construction indicates that the site had achieved power and prestige. Moche III and the succeeding Moche IV subphase witness the florescence of the site, at a time which corresponds to the period of greatest Moche expansion, influence, and complexity.

Because of the variety of studies carried out at the site, the III–IV occupation is relatively well understood. This is fortunate, as it is this stage of Moche development which can most fruitfully be compared to Chimú society. Before undertaking this comparison, however, florescent Moche culture will be outlined in more detail.

Moche society during Phases III and IV was a stratified, expansionist state, with wide-flung trade networks, a high degree of occupational specialization, economic sophistication, and a bureaucracy capable of conceiving and carrying out large-scale public projects. I will discuss each of these assertions separately, citing the new evidence from Moche which supports these long-held assumptions.

Social Stratification

The hypothesis that distinct social classes existed within Moche society is not new, but evidence from burials and domestic architecture encountered during the excavations at Moche augments the iconographic interpretations on which the interpretation formerly was based.

Moche burials conform to the pattern predictable for a class-structured society. Most are single, extended, and primary, with no particular orientation being favored, but there is considerable variation in the grave location and quantity of burial goods. Some individuals were buried with no goods at all, and these burials occurred most frequently in deposits which were probably middens. Two such burials (adults) were found associated with III–IV refuse. Both bodies appeared to have been unceremoniously dumped; they were face down, in awkward positions, with no grave goods. A third adult was more carefully interred, fully extended and face up, in a small excavation in a minor adobe platform. Again however, no grave goods accompanied the burial.

In contrast to this pattern, other burials were found in midden areas but were carefully buried with a number of goods. At the base of Huaca del Sol for example, 80 centimeters below the present ground surface, an infant burial was found accompanied by a shell necklace and a fabric-wrapped copper ingot.

In AA 1, the hillside architecture north of Huaca de la Luna, evidence was found of an adult burial under the floor of a house. The burial had been disturbed by huaqueros, but the association of human bone with probe-broken fine ware stirrup spout jars and floreros in the fresh backdirt indicates that goods accompanied the burial, which had been placed under a low bench and then plastered over.

Two Moche burials were also found incorporated in Huaca del Sol. One was a double burial with dozens of pots, and the other was a more modestly endowed single burial. These burials were incidental inclusions in the huaca; almost certainly the main purpose of Huaca del Sol was not to serve as a burial mound.

A high-status burial area was discovered by project workers in the center of the plain between Huaca del Sol and Huaca de la Luna. Dozens of Moche burials were found here, and all were provided with a few ceramic vessels. Many of the burials also contained copper ingots and ornaments; several of the burials were so rich that one must infer that this was an especially high-status cemetery (see Donnan and Mackey 1978).

There were of course other burial grounds at Moche. Uhle reported a large expanse of burials on the slopes of Cerro Blanco south of Huaca de la Luna. This cemetery had already been depleted by huaqueros when he worked at the site in 1900.

Of the dozens of burials uncovered at Moche, the majority were individuals of evidently high rank, buried in high-status areas, accompanied by several pots, often a few pieces of copper, and occasionally some beads and pendants. Considerably fewer burials were found in domestic or refuse contexts, with few or no grave goods. But I doubt that this can be construed as evidence that individuals of high rank made up most of the population at Moche. There was a very conscious bias built into the obtaining of this sample. When the high-status cemetery was found in the center of the site, it was excavated to exhaustion. The less rich burials were found only by accident, in spatially restricted strata cuts which represent only a minute percentage of the total site fill.

Status variation can be inferred also from domestic architecture. Several different excavations at Moche indicate a considerable range of variation in quality of housing.

The architecture in AA 1, AA 2, and AA 3 was shown to be domestic by the presence of hearths, milling stones, food remains, and the layout of the structures. AA 1 and AA 2 probably housed persons of relatively high status. This inference is based primarily on the quality of construction; these structures were solidly built, well finished, and exhibited frequent architectural elaboration. Floors were level, well plastered, and in good repair where they had not been disturbed. Walls were built of adobes and stone to unusual heights. One well-preserved wall segment was 1.9 meters high. Most of the walls were sealed with mud plaster, although the construction underneath was quite good. In one room in AA 2, plaster in contrasting shades of brown had been applied to the walls in two broad horizontal bands. Individual domestic complexes were multiroomed, with two to six smaller subdivided areas per structure. Two of the AA 2 domestic complexes contained storerooms, bins, and niches, and one had an adobe platform provided with a head rest. AA 1 was constructed on a moderately steep hillside, and individual structures were frequently built on two or three levels, with well-made stairs of two or three steps connecting the different levels. Preservation in AA 3 was poor, and most excavation was directed to ascertaining room outlines.

In general, the fill in AA 1 and AA 2 was richer than in other parts of the site. Proportionately more floreros and stirrup spout fragments were found, as well as less utilitarian ware. Small objects of value were frequent; stone, copper, and modeled ceramic beads, figurine fragments, pieces of clay (red and white—possibly cosmetics), copper implements including tweezers and knives were all found associated with the architecture. A few craft-related implements were also found, including hammerstones and polishing stones, needles and spindle whorls, paddles and other wooden items. The evidence is too sparse, however, to support an argument for craft production in any of the architecture areas.

The architecture associated with Subphases III and IV in the deep cut at the base of Huaca del Sol, SC 4, differs greatly in construction, layout, and associated remains. Three superimposed domestic units were uncovered in the cut at depths of 1.6, 2, and 3.5 meters. The two uppermost were simply unremodeled floor/wall configurations, but the third was a quite complicated affair consisting of at least three separate structures which had seen considerable remodeling. All the rooms and structures share a number of similarities: construction techniques and layout are less imposing than in the three architecture areas discussed above. Floors are usually packed dirt with considerable garbage ground into them, and are often sloping and uneven. Walls are of cobblestone set in mud or of worn, pirated adobes. The walls are seldom preserved for more than one or two courses of their original height; the lack of rubble within or around rooms, and the deteriorated condition of the building materials, suggest that the remaining wall stubs represent the entire height of imperishable materials in these walls and that the remainder of the walls consisted of mats, reeds, or some other organic materials. This of course implies that construction in this part of the site was less permanent and less imposing.

The assertion that these structures at the foot of the Huaca del Sol housed people of relatively low status is supported by the artifactual evidence. Material remains included many of the same kinds of artifacts as were found in AA 1 and AA 2, but in different proportions and of different qualities. Some fragments of fine decorated pottery were found, but the vast majority of the ceramics were thicker, less finely finished, simpler in shape, and usually undecorated. Copper was found, but was less abundant and most frequently occurred in the form of needles and small bangles. For the amount of fill moved, far fewer beads or pendants of any material were found. More shell (especially *Donnax*) was found in association with the SC 4 floors, but this may reflect different patterns of refuse disposal rather than any differences in diet.

The three areas of architecture discussed above and the cemetery in the middle of the plain represent a very small and skewed sample of the site's occupation, and it is hazardous to speculate too freely on the nature of the site's occupation during Moche III and IV on the basis of this evidence. Nevertheless, a few significant conclusions can be drawn from the data. The domestic architecture and the burial patterns both imply the presence of at least three distinct classes of people inhabiting the site.

The burials can be grouped into three classes as follows: burials with no grave goods; burials with grave goods placed in middens and under floors; burials with grave goods in cemeteries. No extreme high-status burials, like that at Huaca de la Cruz in Virú (Strong and Evans 1952), were encountered at the site.

The domestic architecture can similarly be grouped into three classes. The lowest status domestic units would include the SC 4 architecture, characterized by unplastered floors and walls of perishable material. The second group would include the AA 1 and AA 3 architecture, which was well constructed and relatively spacious, but lacking in architectural elaboration and ornamentation.

Two domestic complexes in AA 2 can be identified as the highest status domestic structures, because of the complexity and quality of the architecture, the amount of space they control, and the storage capacity included in both (Figure 11.2). Each of the multiroomed complexes was provided with a variety of bins, niches, and small storerooms, providing in each case a total of 8.7 cubic meters of storage space. The multiplicity of bins and niches is peculiar to this part of the site; only a few niches were found in the AA 1 area, and while AA 3 contains bins and niches, no individual domestic unit evidences so high a capacity. No evidence was found in the AA 2 bins which would suggest what goods were being stored, but certainly the residents of these two units were controlling a disproportionately large amount of goods.

The AA 2 structures housed wealthy and probably elite members of Moche society, but it is unlikely that the individuals of highest status lived here. The most elite residence was probably located in the Huaca de la Luna complex.

Moche as an Expansionist State

A growing body of evidence supports the interpretation of Moche culture as an expansionist state, with the site of Moche as its political center.

The spread of Moche influence south into the Virú, Santa, and Nepeña valleys of the North Coast fits the expected pattern of conquest and political domination from an external area. Moche III pottery appears suddenly in Virú and Santa, superimposed on local styles which are displaced by the new pottery. This new pottery is similar in most respects to Moche pottery in the heartland (the Moche and Chicama valleys) and comes into use in all levels of the local cultures

270

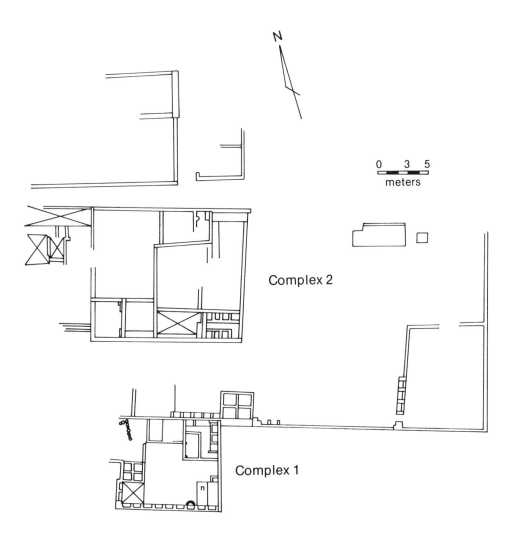

N

0   3   5
meters

Complex 2

Complex 1

FIGURE 11.2. Detailed plan of architectural area 2, the best preserved domestic architecture at Moche.

(Willey 1953; Donnan 1973). In addition, there are settlement pattern changes in both valleys correlating with the appearance of Moche pottery; population is concentrated in fewer, larger settlements after the beginning of Moche influence, and the settlements are more widely dispersed over the valleys. The sudden appearance of Moche materials and the subsequent reorganization within each valley implies conquest. Only Moche IV pottery appears in the Nepeña Valley, and Moche sites are restricted to a small zone around Pañamarca in the middle valley. The short duration and limited extent of the Moche presence in Nepeña imply a late and tenuous occupation of the valley, perhaps in an effort to protect the southern border of the state. The obviously militaristic orientation of much of Moche art (and by extension, history and/or mythology) suggests that the conquest of Virú and Santa was military, and that the occupation of part of Nepeña was predicated on military and strategic requirements.

The argument for the site of Moche as the political center of this Moche expansion derives from several lines of evidence. The presence of the two large huacas at the site argues for Moche's prominence. Huaca del Sol is built of some 143 million adobe bricks, laid up in discrete columns (Hastings and Moseley 1975:197). Most columns are identified by one of the more than 100 makers' marks found on adobes at the site, and Moseley (1975c:192) argues that the makers' marks identify the labor of distinct work parties, fulfilling tax obligations by constructing particular sections of the huaca. The size of the huaca and the number of marks suggest that it was necessary to draw on labor from outside the valley. Undoubtedly work parties from the Chicama Valley (larger and presumably more populous) were recruited to work on the Moche huacas; this would be a clear indication that the elite at Moche during Subphases III and IV were in a politically dominant position over their northern neighbor, as well as the three southern valleys.

The increasing size of Moche itself during Subphases III and IV (both in terms of population and total area covered) and the rise in quality of some domestic architecture also argue for a significant increase in the site's wealth and power during this period. Chronologically, this increase correlates with Moche expansion into the three more southerly valleys, and domination over these neighboring valleys may be invoked as the source of the new wealth and prestige of the site.

The abandonment of the site also supports the argument for an expansionist state. Moche V remains are almost completely absent from the site, and there are Moche IV burials in abandoned architecture, indicating that the site was abandoned at the end of Subphase IV. This correlates with the loss or weakening of Moche influence in Nepeña, Santa, and Virú, implying that the Moche sphere of influence was crumbling. This crumbling may well have been in part a reaction to Middle Horizon events in Central Peru. With the disintegration of Moche power comes the founding of Galindo, farther up the Moche River, and a significant shift in North Coast power to the Lambayeque Valley. The Huaca del Sol symbolized the power of the Moche Valley and the primacy of the site of Moche; the abandonment suggests a hard fall indeed.

In summary, because of the patterning of the appearance and disappearance of Moche influence in the three valleys to the south, I argue that Moche was expanionist. I argue that Moche was the center of this expansion, because of the wealth and power exhibited by the site, unrivaled by any site in Chicama. And I argue that Moche was a state—that formal government, law, and institutionalized force were part of the political structure. Power and influence had been centralized by the Moche, and participation in the Moche social order was not voluntary.

Economics

Economic sophistication and the existence of trade networks are difficult to document for the Moche Phase. Evidence is fragmentary and indirect, and economic arguments must frequently be based on negative evidence.

Moche obviously traded with neighboring areas. This is not at all remarkable, since the steadily accumulating archaeological evidence indicates that Andean cultures from an early date participated in trade though on a small scale. Moche society, particularly in Subphases III–IV, was no different. That the culture was not isolationist is witnessed by the discovery of Moche artifacts in the guano deposits of the Chincha Islands off the south coast of Peru (Kubler 1948:40).

Exotic items occur at Moche and other contemporary sites, usually in burial contexts or as offerings. *Spondylus* from Ecuador is found in many graves, usually in the form of beads or pendants. Feldman reports surface scatters of partially worked *Spondylus* and mother-ofpearl fragments near the summit of Cerro Blanco east of the site (personal communication). Copper, gold, and silver are of course found in Moche burials, and copper also occurs in domestic contexts. While Lechtman (1976) has demonstrated the existence of outcrops rich in copper ore on the North Coast, the other metals presumably would have a sierra source.

Another link to the sierra is provided by Cajamarca pottery, which occurs infrequently in Moche IV contexts. Kroeber (1925: Plate 63) illustrates some sherds from Uhle's Site A excavations on top of the southernmost platforms of Huaca del Sol which are probably Cajamarca III. One Cajamarca II sherd was found in the SC 4 excavation, in a Moche IV context.

We have only a few pieces of evidence with which to attempt a reconstruction of internal Moche economic organization. There are clear indications of a labor tax during Moche III–IV times. The segmentation and the patterning of makers' marks on adobes at Huaca del Sol are undoubtedly the result of labor performed by discrete labor parties drawn from different communities or kin groups. These workers would have advance knowledge of the amount of work required of them on a particular project (Moseley 1975c). The same pattern of construction in segments has been reported from Huaca Brujo in the Chicama Valley (Kroeber 1930:84) and from Huancaco and Tomoval in Virú (Willey 1953:163–64, 206). The building of other monumental structures and complexes, and the expansion of the Moche irrigation system, were probably carried out by workers paying their labor tax according to the same organizational principles.

Taxation of labor continues into Chimú and Inca times, but in these societies the tax paid by the populace is balanced by the major role taken by the state in redistribution. There is no evidence for this kind of reciprocity in Moche society. If the Moche economy were organized like that of the Chimú, with governmental intervention in the redistribution of many commodities, we would expect to find storerooms. At Moche, because of the poor surface preservation, it would not be surprising if all traces of such structures had been destroyed. The only storerooms found at the site were in the areas of domestic architecture, AA 2 and AA 3. Several small storage complexes occur, but only in a domestic context; given the nature of the surrounding architecture, they cannot possibly be interpreted as public storage or redistribution points.

If public storage complexes had existed at Moche in a part of the site now destroyed or buried, we would still expect them to be present at other important Moche sites in other valleys. No such evidence has been found. Recent reconstructions of the Chimú economic system (Andrews 1974; Keatinge and Day 1973; J. Topic Chapter 7) have been based in large part on the association of U-shaped structures and storerooms at Chan Chan and some rural Chimú states. If these features were not present during Moche times, the conclusion must be that the means of collecting and redistributing goods was not the same in the two societies, and that the state had fewer responsibilities to groups paying their labor tax. I will return to these very important points later.

Occupational Specialization

Occupational specialization can be dealt with briefly here; no one doubts that it existed in Moche society. I will review some of the arguments for its presence, however, in order to interdigitate a few new data.

Most of the people in Moche society were undoubtedly full-time agricultural specialists. The numerous small villages and isolated homesteads in the Moche region point to this, as well as to a relatively high degree of self-sufficiency for these farmers.

Ceramic and metal production were probably specialized occupations on the North Coast well before Moche times. The presence of ceramic specialists has long been argued for Moche, because of the fine quality of the best pottery and evidence of mass production (Rowe 1971; Donnan 1965). Two hundred meters south of the densely inhabited area of Moche, a ceramic discard pile was found which sheds some light on ceramic specialization at the site.

The cache (testpit 3) was found in soft, clean sand, with occasional flecks of ash but no evidence of habitation. If we can assume that the discard pile was close to the shop area, then the shop must have been on the outskirts of the site. We found no trace of the shop itself.

The cache is interpreted as a discard pile and not as an offering of some sort because each of the 29 pieces found in the cache is flawed. The cache is Moche IV in date, and includes three floreros, seven jars, eight handled bottles, three bowls, three stirrup spout jars, and five figurines, all neatly stacked. All pieces were damaged during firing. Florero rims and stirrup spouts drooped asymmetrically, and jar and bottle walls had collapsed or split. Some pieces were cracked, chipped, or broken, but most were whole. None of the vessels was extremely fine; painting was very simple and somewhat sloppy. Many were exact replicas of each other; all handled bottles, for example, were identical. In this same excavation, testpit 3, a vast quantity of sherds was found, especially of large, thick storage jars with no signs of use. An extraordinary number of broken figurines and broken figurine molds was also found.

The shop in this area seems to have been producing large urns, smaller-sized utilitarian ware, figurines, and low-quality fine ware. If there was a master potter in the shop, he left no evidence of his presence in the discard area.

There is additional evidence for craft specialization at Moche, but this evidence is more tenuous. Sector 3 northeast of strata cut 4 includes an area with relatively high surface concentrations of turquoise in the form of beads, bead blanks, and unworked fragments. The fact that all stages of the manufacturing process are represented in the surface finds suggests the presence of specialized craftsmen in the immediate vicinity. Stone tools similar to those found in metalworking shops in the SIAR (small irregularly agglutinated rooms) of Chan Chan occur in strata cut 4 and AA 1, but these finds are few in number and apparently unpatterned.

The presence of needles and spindle whorls in domestic contexts implies that simple weaving and spinning was done in most households, but there is also evidence that some weaving was done by specialists. A frequently illustrated florero (see Benson 1972:103) portrays several female weavers working under the supervision of an overseer.

In addition to craft and agricultural specialists, Moche society included religious and administrative specialists. These specialists are discussed in the next section.

Bureaucracy and Political Structure

I asserted earlier in this chapter that Moche society had a bureaucracy which was capable of conceiving and carrying out large-scale public projects. This assertion needs little explanation. A variety of large construction projects were carried out in Moche times. A new maximum elevation canal was built in the Moche Valley. Huaca del

Sol and Huaca de la Luna were constructed at Moche. Pañamarca and Huancaco were built in Nepeña and Virú, probably to serve as valley administrative centers. Many smaller huacas were constructed in the Chicama, Virú, and Santa valleys. These are all projects which required planning. Their presence alone is evidence for a skilled administration, capable of visualizing the result of a planned project, dividing the project into smaller segments, and organizing the large work crews necessary to carry out such projects.

But reconstructing the details of Moche political structure has presented an array of problems, and the best current reconstructions are not nearly as complete as they are for Chimú or Inca society. In part, we can blame this lack of specificity in the reconstruction of the Moche power structure on the lack of ethnohistoric information. But the poor quality and limited quantity of architectural information from many Moche sites has also been a hindrance. In later Chimú society, specific architectural forms are associated with different levels of the political hierarchy and different administrative functions. Incomplete architectural preservation at major Moche sites raises the possibility that we may be missing entire classes of architecture associated with the bureaucracy. Thus, interpretations of Moche political structure must be considered tentative; as new evidence accumulates and new analytical methods are applied, we may see considerable changes in the interpretations.

The data currently available support the existence of a hereditary kingship in Moche III–IV. There is ample iconographic evidence for the concept of a preeminent individual in Moche society. The presentation scene which occurs frequently on Moche pottery and on wall paintings illustrates this concept graphically. In the presentation scene, an individual who is seated alone on a raised dais is honored in various ways. In addition, all evidence indicates that power in the Moche state was centralized at the site of Moche. Thus, we can assume that the king lived at the site.

Kroeber (1930:Plate 27) reports the presence of a dais (now destroyed) similar to that in the presentation scene in one of the interior courtyards of Huaca de la Luna. The location of this U-shaped structure in one of the more inaccessible parts of the Huaca de la Luna complex has several important implications. The dais provides evidence for the existence of a Moche ruler, and suggests that he was housed at Huaca de la Luna, segregated from the rest of the population and viewed only on formal occasions. The dais associates the U-shaped structure (as a general architectural type) with power and prestige at a very early date. It also implies a division of some sort in authority. If Huaca de la Luna is to be identified as the residence and audience chambers of the ruler, Huaca del Sol must have fulfilled a different set of functions.

Huaca del Sol, like Huaca de la Luna, was constructed in several stages during Subphases III and IV. But unlike Huaca de la Luna, habitation remains are found under, around, in, and on top of Huaca del Sol. The remains under the northernmost segment of the huaca (strata cut 1) predate the expansion of the huaca in that direction, and the Moche IV and Chimú refuse atop the huaca (strata cut 2) apparently postdate the effective functioning of Huaca del Sol. But the lenses of refuse between the different building stages and the habitations clustered at the foot of the huaca (strata cut 4) suggest that while the huaca may have symbolized the power of the Moche state, everyday activities were carried out in its immediate vicinity. Huaca del Sol appears to have been the focus of community life, providing the actual interface between ruling class and populace, while Huaca de la Luna, isolated and exclusive, may have been the locus of policy making.

This pattern, then, would require the Moche bureaucracy to be associated with huacas, which are usually accorded a nonsecular function. There is obviously a great disparity between this pattern and the later Chimú tendency to associate administrators with U-shaped structures and storerooms. But the reason for the disparity becomes clear when the function of the Moche bureaucracy is considered. Unlike their Chimú counterparts, Moche administrators are not involved heavily in redistribution within the society. They apparently play little or no direct role in the organization of production or movement of goods. They function more as planners, leaders, labor organizers, and agents of social cohesion. It follows that the administrative class would be smaller and less diverse than in Chimú society, and could be expected to provide both religious and secular leadership. In this sense, Moche society is in an intermediate stage between Chavín society (whose justification is entirely religious) and the Chimú state (where redistribution and manipulation of the economy are the rationale for the existence of the administration). In short, unless we assume that we have missed an entire class of architecture, not only at Moche but in the provinces, we must equate huacas with political control.

278

A recent article by Conrad (1978) shows that this equation is reasonable. His application of locational analysis to Virú Valley settlement pattern data for the Moche occupation shows a hierarchical patterning of huacas and associated architecture. He has been able to identify the valley administrative center as well as secondary and tertiary centers, and has shown that the locations of these centers are predictable on the basis of administrative efficiency. Interestingly, the valley administrative center combines elements of both Huaca del Sol and Huaca de la Luna. A large huaca is associated with several platforms, courtyards, and compounds clustered against a steep hillside. Since the smaller sites which have been identified as secondary and tertiary centers in the valley have suffered proportionately more damage, it is impossible to tell whether all administrative sites combined both types of architecture.

A similar pattern can be inferred from Donnan's (1973) report on the Santa Valley. Fifteen huacas are reported from the valley. Some are free-standing, some are associated with minor architecture, and some are grouped into complexes. The largest huaca firmly dated to Moche times (PV28-138) measures 95 by 95 by 18 meters, and is associated with elaborate formal architecture, an area of domestic habitation, two smaller huacas, and several cemeteries (Donnan 1973:38). This is the largest concentration of Moche architecture in the valley, and can unhesitatingly be identified as the valley administrative center. A closer examination of the remaining huacas and their associated architecture might well reveal the presence of a hierarchical administrative organization in that valley too.

The evidence from Nepeña is less straightforward. Pañamarca is the largest Moche complex in the valley, and undoubtedly served as the administrative center for the valley. But it is not clear what the site administered. Only 22 Moche sites are reported from the valley, and 13 of these are cemeteries. Five huacas are probably of Moche date, but these are clustered within a few hundred meters of Pañamarca (Proulx 1973). Either the Moche had only a small foothold in the valley, or they were using principles of administration different from those used in other valleys.

At present, the evidence from Moche public architecture suggests the following chain of command. Decisions made by the ruler at Huaca de la Luna which affected the site of Moche or the Moche

Valley were communicated to the administrators functioning at Huaca del Sol, whose responsibility was to transform the decision into action, or to pass the decision on to more minor officials. Decisions affecting other valleys were communicated to valley administrative centers. The elite administrators at these sites could take action directly, or could pass information on to secondary centers. Secondary centers would be responsible for a group of small tertiary centers of only local importance. At each descending level of the hierarchy, fewer and less important decisions were made by less powerful individuals in less impressive architecture.

This hierarchical arrangement of administrators would be very efficient, allowing much decision making to take place at the local or regional level, and providing a mechanism for major state-level decisions to be communicated and executed. The arrangement would also facilitate taxation. Decisions about state projects requiring labor would be passed down the chain of command, and groups of laborers would be passed in the other direction. This arrangement, of course, would be efficient only so long as communications between local, regional, and state officials were rapid and accurate. We have considerable evidence for Moche messengers; there are many paintings, on pots, of runners carrying small bags of specially marked beans which, quipulike, may have conveyed information to those able to understand their meaning (Larco Hoyle 1942).

Huacas have traditionally been classed as "ceremonial" architecture and associated more with religious aspects of a society than with its secular functioning. But there is no reason to presume that the Moche drew any kind of distinction between religious and secular, much less maintained two separate hierarchies to manage the two spheres of activity. While events of a "ceremonial" nature undoubtedly occurred at Moche huacas, it is quite likely that they also served as the loci of more mundane functions. The Moche administrative structure and religious hierarchy were probably the same organization in most particulars.

THE QUESTION OF CHIMÚ ROOTS

The data from Moche, as I have interpreted them, argue for strong ties between the Moche and Chimú traditions. Similarly, the evidence helps to illuminate some of the unique aspects of Chimú society. I will discuss the similarities between the two societies first and will then turn to three specific institutions that distinguish the Chimú from their predecessors.

Structurally, Moche and Chimú were very similar. Both were centralized expansionist states with internal class divisions and ruled by an elite. In both societies, the hierarchy's apex was a ruler who was segregated from most of the population in a special compound, and shown great honor and respect. Class structure and primacy of the elite were probably structural tenets that were carried unbroken into Chimú society, rather than reinvented at the beginning of the Late Intermediate Period. A cogent argument could be made (but not in the space available here) for the transfer of Moche power to Pampa Grande in the Lambayeque Valley at the close of Moche IV as a result of the loss of the southern Moche territory, and the return of the ruler to Chan Chan a few centuries later. We may actually be witnessing an unbroken dynasty from Moche to Pampa Grande to Chan Chan.

This hypothesis is supported by the fact that Chan Chan is located in the Moche Valley. I do not think that this is historical accident, and I doubt if it is due to any overriding geographical advantages offered by the Moche Valley. I suspect that a tradition of Moche as a center of power and prestige was kept alive during the Middle Horizon when Galindo had only regional importance. The high-status Chimú burials discovered at Moche evidence the respect the Chimú had for the site. This respect was probably not rooted simply in an appreciation of the site's architectural grandeur; it is more likely that Chimú tradition recognized Moche as a historical precedent, ancestral to Chan Chan itself.

Another thread of similarity between Moche and Chimú lies in the economic orientations of the two societies. Both were oriented inward economically. Neither appears to have been a great trading nation, and neither appears to have had a significant merchant or trader class. Both imported exotic materials from outside their territories, but these imports represent a restricted range of goods, and were primarily for elite consumption. The economic basis of both societies was agriculture, made possible by the carefully maintained irrigation networks. Economic growth in both societies was predicated on the expansion of those irrigation networks. Neither society apparently made any real attempts to dominate the sierra; their focus was exclusively coastal.

There are three institutions which underscore the differences between the Moche and the Chimú. These are split inheritance, the secularized bureaucracy, and the redistributive economy.

Split inheritance is the principle which produced the architectural form most specific to Chan Chan—the sequentially constructed ciudadelas divided into three segments, containing storerooms, audiencias, and the king's burial platform. When a king died, his principal heir founded a new lineage and constructed his own ciudadela to be the seat of the new government and his eventual tomb. His predecessor's ciudadela (and perhaps much of its contents) housed and supported the descendants of the dead king.

There is no evidence at Moche for the pattern of split inheritance. The development of the pattern may be a result of the Middle Horizon sojourn in the Lambayeque Valley. Some support is given to this view by oral histories of the Lambayeque Valley recorded by Father Miguel Cabello de Balboa in the sixteenth century (discussed in Kosok 1965:73, 148), detailing the successive division of the realm into smaller parcels as each son was given his own territory to rule. A brief period of such fragmentation of power would provide ample stimulus for the appearance of the split inheritance pattern, whose effect was both to codify the obligations and rights of heirs and to distribute the benefits of a king's death more equitably. The evidence from Chan Chan is unclear as to whether split inheritance and the one king: one ciudadela pattern were present during the early phases of the site.

The Chimú bureaucracy was more secular, more formalized, more numerous, and more complex than its Moche counterpart. The trademark of the Chimú bureaucrat was the audiencia, the elevated U-shaped structure located in a variety of contexts but always controlling access to someone or something. This removal of administrators from huacas and their repositioning in more practical situations with only a hint of elevation implies that prestige of the elite bureaucracy was now derived from the power of the state as a whole, and not from any association with the supernatural. The audiencia as a locus of power may have dated back to the "throne" at Huaca de la Luna, but it underwent immense changes before the final occupation at Chan Chan. The Middle Horizon saw an increase in the total number of such structures as well as an increase in the kinds of contexts in which they occurred (see Bawden, Chapter 12). This proliferation continued at Chan Chan.

The increase in the number of administrators and their responsibilities reflected their increasing participation in the economy. Towards the end of the Chimú occupation of Chan Chan, the state was apparently directing a great deal of agricultural activity as well as playing a role in the production of nonagricultural commodities (J. Topic, Chapter 7). Agricultural communities were provided with goods produced by the craftsmen at Chan Chan, and the craftsmen were provided with food and with raw materials. A very sizable bureaucracy managed this redistribution. The bureaucracy (which has clear Moche antecedents) was located in audiencias (with possible Moche antecedents), and controlled vast quantities of storage space (with tenuous Moche antecedents). But the bureaucracy worked according to a principle which had no apparent Moche precedent—economic reciprocity between those governing and those governed.

There is no evidence for Moche state intervention in the economy, other than its probable role in the construction of irrigation systems. While the Moche paid a labor tax, their return on the investment appears to have been mostly the advantage of being governed, probably defended, and perhaps cared for in some very indirect ways. The most significant change made later by the Chimú in this pattern of general reciprocity was the control of goods circulating in the state. Those laboring for the state full- or part-time apparently received more tangible evidence of the state's concern for their welfare than did their Moche forebears. The most direct evidence for this state control of the economy is the abundance of storerooms, bins, niches, and the like at Chan Chan and at rural administrative centers. This centralized economic control must have been achieved step by step, paralleling increases in the size, power, and skill of the bureaucracy. The presence of storerooms in association with monumental architecture is probably a good marker for the appearance of state-managed redistribution. This marker was absent in the Early Intermediate Period, made its entrance in the Middle Horizon, proliferated during the Late Intermediate Period, and provided the economic basis for the Inca Empire.

Moche society invented the centralized expansionist state, experimented with hierarchical secular authority, and formalized the labor tax. In these particulars, Moche was ancestral to Chimú and probably served as a model. But these precepts were refined during the Middle Horizon and the Late Intermediate Period. By the end of the Late Intermediate Period a much more complex, organized, and rigid social order had evolved on the North Coast.

SUMMARY

During the Early Intermediate Period on the North Coast of Peru, the resident peoples underwent great change, especially in the area of political organization. At the beginning of the EIP, the political unification of even single valleys was a rarity. By the end of the Moche IV Subphase a thousand years later, the North Coast was united by a single central authority which had spread its influence by military force. This state had developed a simple but efficient system of administration and taxation which maintained order and guaranteed completion of state projects but without a great deal of interference in the everyday lives of its subjects.

The Chimú empire of the Late Intermediate Period was a direct descendant of the Moche state. Like their predecessors, the Chimú centralized authority at a conspicuously preeminent site in the Moche Valley, and invested one individual with ultimate authority. Like the Moche, the Chimú assured the smooth functioning of the state by maintaining a class of professional administrators and levying a labor tax. But the Chimú increased the complexity of their political organization to an unprecedented level by taking control of the economy and overseeing all levels of production, redistribution, and consumption of a wide range of commodities. This intervention in the economy was made possible by three institutions which evolved after the Early Intermediate Period—split inheritance, which assured political stability; the secularized bureaucracy, which provided managerial competence; and control of redistribution, which gave the state the necessary rationale for usurping economic authority.

NOTE

1. Shelia Pozorski, Claude Chauchat, Michael Moseley, Charles Hastings, Robert Feldman, Dennis Heskel, and Chris Donnan were most generous in sharing information and ideas with me, and I extend my thanks to all of them. I alone, of course, am responsible for the inferences which I draw from their data in this paper.

12

Galindo: A Study in Cultural Transition During the Middle Horizon

GARTH BAWDEN

Peabody Museum

INTRODUCTION

The purpose of this paper is to describe and analyze architectural form and settlement plan at the site of Galindo in the Moche Valley. This Moche V site dates to the earliest phase of the Middle Horizon period and thus temporally represents the final stage of the long-lasting Moche cultural hegemony of the North Coast. Innovations in architectural form and site configuration reflect changes long attributed to Huari intrusion. Examination of the nature of these innovations provides important information regarding the period of transition from Moche to Chimú domination of the region.

THE SETTING: MOCHE CULTURAL DEVELOPMENT AND DECLINE

During the Early Intermediate Period the Moche culture represents the primary development on the northern Peruvian coast. It is through architectural and ceramic accomplishment that Moche culture is best known. The most impressive architectural remains are the adobe huacas common to all valleys within the Moche culture area. These structures consist of large rectangular platforms approached by ramps. They form the bases for architectural superstructures of varied character. In several instances such edifices are arranged in complexes, usually regarded as constituting ceremonial centers. Such sites as Pañamarca in the Nepeña Valley and Mocallope in the Chicama Valley contain several huacas (or platform mounds).

Knowledge of Moche domestic residential patterns is as yet incomplete owing to insufficient investigation and destruction of sites. On the basis of surveys so far conducted (Donnan 1973; Proulx 1973), however, it appears that most of the population lived in agglutinated villages spread throughout the coastal valleys. Many of these were situated on hillslopes bounding the narrower sections of the valleys. It is probable that few such settlements existed on the irrigable valley floors due to the pressure toward utilizing these areas for irrigation agriculture. The site of Moche, with its large concentration of domestic habitation, and the later urban centers of Galindo in the Moche Valley and Pampa Grande in the Lambayeque Valley (see Figure 1.1) demonstrate the continuing tradition of urbanism in the Moche cultural phase.

Apart from the great architectural complexes, the aspect of Moche material culture best preserved is ceramic art. The versatility of Moche potters has long been recognized, encompassing on the one hand naturalistic, plastic art, and on the other an accomplished painting style which extends from simple geometric forms to intricate fine-line designs. The most notable Moche ceramic products are the stirrup spout vessels. These forms first appeared in the Andean area in the Early Horizon and constitute a long-lasting component of the North Coast ceramic tradition. In Moche times they formed the medium for an artistic expression that included all aspects of culture.

Representations on Moche pottery suggest some important features regarding social content and organization. A high level of social stratification is indicated by the deference accorded elaborately garbed individuals in contrast to those performing menial tasks or captives. Persons of high status were often depicted carried on litters or sitting on raised daises. Sometimes these daises were situated on the tops of platforms approached by ramps.

Of equal importance to the study of Moche historical development is the use of stirrup spout vessels as chronological markers. Rafael Larco Hoyle, deriving his conclusions primarily from cemetery excavations in the Chicama Valley, formulated an internal ceramic seriation for Moche culture based on the evolution of the stirrup spout form. He divided vessels into five distinct sequential groups, I–V, using as his criteria changes in shape, decoration, and relative proportion of spouts, stirrups, and vessel bodies. By relating these specific ceramic substyles to archaeological remains, it has been possible to reach some understanding of the nature of Moche geographical and historical development on the North Coast.

The Moche state, centered for most of its existence in the Moche Valley, passed through a complex historical development. Initially the area of hegemony seems to have been confined to the Chicama and Moche valleys, although the appearance of Phase I vessels in the Piura Valley far to the north raises unanswered questions regarding Moche origins (Larco Hoyle 1965). By Phase III, Moche ceramics and architecture are found in valleys to the north and south of the Moche-Chicama heartland, and it can be assumed that during Phases III and IV the Moche state attained its greatest power. Throughout this period the great site of Moche expanded and flourished as the center of the state. It probably represented the focal point of administrative and ideological power and in this sense may be regarded as the Moche equivalent of a state capital.

By the end of the Early Intermediate Period, corresponding to the end of Moche Phase IV, the pattern of expansion was being reversed. The southernmost valleys, from Nepeña to Virú, no longer showed evidence of Moche occupation. Furthermore the reduced state underwent a radical internal reorganization. The center was moved from the Moche Valley to Pampa Grande in the Lambayeque Valley far to the north (see Figure 1.1). In the Moche Valley the focus of local authority shifted to the newly created settlement of Galindo, almost 20 kilometers inland from Moche. This major reconstitution clearly marked the presence of great stress in the Moche culture toward the end of the Early Intermediate Period, the result of which was unusually rapid change encompassing many aspects of Moche cultural organization.

Following this drastic rearrangement, the Moche V state maintained its autonomy for a considerable period of time. Although the terminal date for this phase is as yet uncertain, it is clear that it did not occur until well after the commencement of the Middle Horizon (see Table

287

1.1). In its final stages, therefore, the Moche state was contemporary with the significant changes taking place farther south and usually ascribed to the expansion of the Huari empire.

The nature of the Middle Horizon as it pertains to the North Coast is not as yet clear. As research continues, it appears, however, that the chronological hiatus formerly posited as separating the Moche and succeeding Chimú cultural phases was minor; indeed, its very existence is now open to serious question. Thus the nascent Chimú state of A.D. 1000 shared significant continuity with the Moche, chronologically as well as culturally. In its political expansion, urban base, and artistic personality, the Chimú empire of the Late Intermediate Period represented the culmination of the trends noted in Moche cultural development.

PROBLEMS IN INTERPRETATION

Moche V material remains offer some difficult problems regarding the development of North Coast culture. Ceramic technology, architecture, and settlement pattern all evidence change between Moche IV and V in the Early Intermediate, and between Moche V and Chimú in the Middle Horizon.

Until recently the final Moche phase was known solely through its ceramic component. Historical interpretation was based on cross-comparison with other Peruvian styles. Such an approach, although valuable in identifying the general cultural patterns of a defined time period, result in an overly simplistic view of cultural development.

Menzel (1964) described, through ceramic analysis, the initial consolidation of the Huari empire in southern and central Peru during Epoch 1 of the Middle Horizon. This was followed by a temporary check during Epoch 2A and a further period of expansion and ultimate fall during Epoch 2B. During Epochs 1 and probably 2A the Huari empire was contemporary with the Moche V state of the North Coast, while in Epoch 2B Moche hegemony was apparently replaced by that of the intruding Huari. However, evidence for this development rests on the presence of small quantities of Huari-related pottery in scattered sites along the North Coast. The emergence of the Late Intermediate Chimú empire is seen under this approach as an amalgam of regional traditions with strong Huari influence.

This interpretation sheds no light whatever on the significant changes which occurred within Moche culture at the close of Moche Phase IV. At this time, as previously noted, radical reorganization of the state was effected, with traditional centers abandoned and new ones appearing. The hypothesis of Huari conquest can only apply to the end of Moche V, not the much earlier transition between Phases IV and V when internal reconstitution occurred (see Table 1.1).

Thus the problems associated with late Moche culture are twofold, involving two instances of profound change: one between the final Moche phases and one at the end of Moche V. The site of Galindo provides an excellent opportunity to study the changes that occurred at the end of the fourth Moche phase. The study assumes that problems of cultural transition cannot be solved by the formulation of single simplistic theories such as that of invasion. Instead, the complex nature of the Moche V changes visible at Galindo is examined as a precondition to considering their significance.

GALINDO: GENERAL DESCRIPTION

Galindo was a large urban settlement, approximately six square kilometers in surface area, in the Moche Valley. Like other Andean valleys, the Moche is cut by a river which, in its upper courses, falls abruptly down steep mountain slopes, gouging out a narrow gorge. It reaches its lower course approximately twenty kilometers from the sea. At this point the hills that flank the upper courses curve away from the river to the north and parallel the coast. To the south, hills continue adjacent to the river, although at a gradually increasing distance. The resulting coastal plain is asymmetrically fan shaped, the largest segment of level, irrigable land lying north of the river.

Galindo stands at the point of juncture between the upper and lower courses of the River Moche. Above it tower the peaks of Cerro Galindo, faced across the river by Cerro Orejas. The other hills curving to the north are pierced by several large dry valleys opening on the coastal plain. One of these, the Quebrada Caballo Muerto, penetrates the hills adjacent to Galindo, significantly affecting the form of the settlement.

On the basis of extensive ceramic surveys Galindo dates almost entirely to the Moche Phase V, with only a minor earlier component.

Galindo consisted of large areas of residential occupation and elaborate complexes of enclosures, huacas, and other nondomestic architecture (Figure 12.1). Residential areas were divided between hillside and plain segments by a massive adobe wall and parallel "moat." Several roads run into the site, converging on its central area. Huacas generally followed the pattern of earlier Moche structures although with some important functional changes, which will be discussed. The innovative architectural features were large complexes of adobe-walled enclosures situated in the center of the settlement. Large clusters of structures used primarily for corporate storage and sites of industrial activity indicate the diverse activities encompassed by the settlement. Upon these many architectural forms was imposed an overwhelming aspect of rigid planning, with internal functional segments strictly defined and separated from each other.

Galindo, then, presents the aspect of a well-organized and tightly controlled urban settlement containing all of the features basic to such forms. The nature of this configuration will be examined in order to reach greater understanding of Moche V social and political structure and the historical processes which defined it.

THE SITE: PHYSICAL CONFIGURATION

In order to avoid confusion in describing the topography and settlement configuration of Galindo, prominent natural and artificial features and divisions will be assigned locational symbols. In the case of physical features these are given either names (Cerro Galindo) or geographically derived titles (northern tributary). Topographical titles combined with letter symbols represent natural divisions within the site (hillside A, plain B), while man-made structures are designated by numbers (structure 3).

Galindo is located on the lower slopes of Cerro Galindo, the neighboring hills, and the fan-shaped plain at their base (Figure 12.1). Two natural water-cut channel systems cross the site. The larger of these systems—Quebrada Caballo Muerto—possesses three main tributaries that converge in a single trunk running between Cerro Galindo and Cerro Muerto. The smaller channel system—Quebrada del Norte—crosses the northern fringe of the site. Ancient downcutting activity associated with these channels has resulted in the formation of terraces which

290

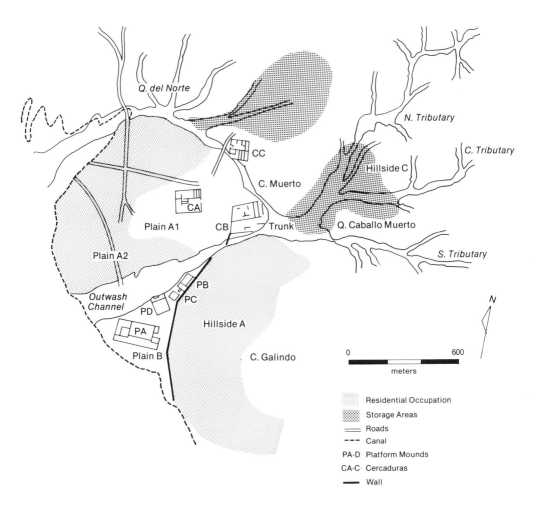

Q. del Norte

N. Tributary

C. Tributary

CC

Hillside C

C. Muerto

CA

Plain A1

CB

Trunk

Q. Caballo Muerto

Plain A2

S. Tributary

Outwash
Channel

PB

PC

PD

PA

Hillside A

Plain B

C. Galindo

N

0   600

meters

Residential Occupation
Storage Areas
Roads
Canal
PA-D Platform Mounds
CA-C Cercaduras
Wall

FIGURE 12.1. Site map of Galindo.

were later used for architectural construction sites. At the base of the slopes of Cerro Galindo and Cerro Muerto is a relatively level plain, bounded to the south by the present high-level irrigation canal. The outwash channel of Quebrada Caballo Muerto crosses this plain, dividing it into two unequal portions—plain A and plain B (Figure 12.1). The only significant topographical feature associated with the plain is a low spur which projects from the base of Cerro Muerto into the center of plain A.

The foothills adjacent to the plain naturally constitute distinct topographical segments which play important roles in determining the nature of site planning. The slopes of Cerros Galindo and Muerto form discrete settlement components and are here designated hillsides A and B respectively. Hillside C includes the terraced flanks of the tributaries of Quebrada Caballo Muerto above the quebrada trunk.

Thus Galindo's settlement pattern incorporates several quite distinct topographical areas, each naturally segregated from the others. The importance of this configuration will become clear when distribution of architectural classes is discussed.

ARCHITECTURAL COMPOSITION

Investigation at the site revealed that architectural forms fell generally within two main categories, domestic and nondomestic. Within each of these groupings it was possible to detect subcategories. In addition, a relatively small number of structures possessed attributes of both major architectural classes. The architecture of Galindo will be discussed according to this categorization.

NONDOMESTIC ARCHITECTURE

Nondomestic architecture includes those structures whose functions were not primarily residential. Thus the forms do not contain the attributes characteristic of the domestic residence such as hearths and kitchen refuse. Nondomestic architectural structures are numerous at Galindo and span a wide range of configuration and usage. They are best described in terms of their apparent function. This approach leads logically to a further architectural categorization, formal and non-formal architecture. Formal architecture refers to structures that functioned within the cultural subsystems pertaining to settlement control. Administrative and religious architecture fit this category and in general aspect display careful planning, accomplished building technique, and often elaborate form. Nonformal architecture served as the context for more mundane activities connected with industrial, agricultural, and redistributive activities in the settlement. This type of architecture was usually less well constructed and more haphazard in form.

Formal Architecture

There are two main classes of formal architecture, each possessing its own distinctive structural and locational characteristics. First there is a group of structures closely related to the traditional Moche huaca. A second architectural category consists of complexes of walled enclosures containing numerous rooms and benches; such complexes, for the purposes of this study, will be termed cercaduras.

In addition to these primary formal classes there also appear architectural units, much smaller in size, which occur both as independent structures and as components of the two major classes. For descriptive purposes they are named tablados.

Platform Mounds. In the segment of the site designated plain B (Figure 12.1) stand four huacas, A–D. As mentioned previously, this area is segregated from the rest of the site by both topographical features and the presence of a massive adobe wall with accompanying moat which skirts the base of Cerro Galindo.

In basic form, the platform mounds reflect the traditional Moche huaca, which originated in earlier cultural phases on the North Coast. Platform A (Figure 12.2) measures 50 meters square and is 8 meters high. It stands in a complex of adobe-walled compounds whose perimeter measures approximately 250 meters in length and 130 meters in breadth. By contrast, platform B is not surrounded by compounds. It was built on the lowest hillslopes of Cerro Galindo in the northern part of the plain B segment and measures 70 meters by 50 meters. At its western, downhill side, platform B stands almost 5 meters high, the eastern side having been built into the hillside. The top of

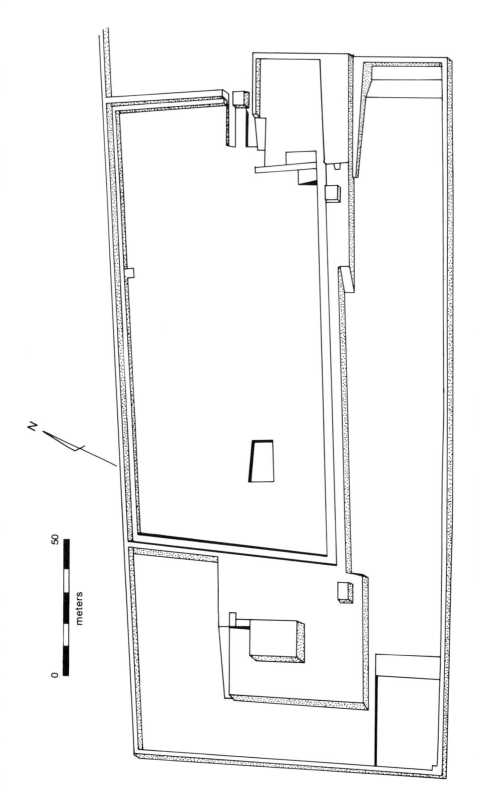

FIGURE 12.2. Plan map of platform A complex. Isometric projection.

this structure is terraced, with low ramps connecting the different levels. Standing on these terraces are several tablados, also approached by ramps.

Directly to the south of platform B is a small structure—platform C—10 meters square and 3 meters tall. Nearby is a fourth structure, badly damaged, which backs onto the steep bluff overlooking the quebrada. This structure, platform D, has surface dimensions of 40 meters by 35 meters and at its highest point only stands 1.5 meters above the natural ground level. While in plan it repeats the typical Moche huaca with terraced summit holding architectural superstructure and centrally placed access ramp, it largely constitutes a modeling of the natural topography. The body of the huaca, so massive at Huaca del Sol at Moche, has, in this structure, shrunk to the bare minimum necessary to achieve the shape required by this architectural form.

When the huacas of Galindo are compared with their predecessors in Moche culture, it becomes clear that significant changes have occurred in this architectural form. Earlier huacas generally dominated the countryside in which they stood. In their great size they represented major enterprises, requiring the mobilization of very large work forces for their construction. By contrast, the Moche V huacas at Galindo appear as mere rudimentary forms; even the larger examples, platforms A and B, are minuscule in comparison with the majority of their antecedents. It seems probable that this trend reflects changes in the role of the huaca, in the capacity of the community to erect large structures, or a combination of both elements.

The three smaller Galindo huacas, platforms B, C, and D, reflect earlier Moche huaca architecture. They share with the earlier structures their characteristic freestanding pattern, independent of adjoining architecture, and a near identical surface configuration. It seems reasonable to assume that such similarity of form in the context of direct chronological and cultural continuity indicates functional uniformity between Moche huaca architecture of Phases IV and V as expressed by platforms B, C, and D. Platform A, however, possesses features that set it apart from the three neighboring structures. Unlike the latter, it is a component of a large architectural complex which also contains adjoining adobe-walled compounds. Access to the complex is limited to a single elaborate entrance in the compound wall farthest from the huaca. The huaca itself is approached by an indirect route from ramps leading to side benches. From the side benches, laterally placed ramps provide access to the platform (Figure 12.2).

A moderate amount of kitchen refuse occurred within the compounds surrounding platform A, suggesting that domestic activity played a role in the function of the complex. This contrasts with the situation at other huacas where no such refuse was present.

Thus the architectural configuration and artifact associations of platform A distinguish it from its counterparts at Galindo. Conrad (1974) has pointed out that this architectural complex deviates from the traditional Moche huaca plan in features which suggest an antecedent relationship to the great Chimú compounds at Chan Chan. The rectangular compounds, the location of huacas in their own compounds as far away from the entrance as possible, the presence of domestic refuse, and the indirect access routes are all features present in the Chan Chan ciudadelas, although in a more complicated configuration. This presumably indicates a functional similarity between the platform A architectural complex and the Chan Chan ciudadela form, namely that both constitute elite residences.

In summation, the huaca architecture of Moche V Galindo suggests certain important changes in both sacred and secular cultural spheres. The situation of the structures in plain B (Figure 12.1), a peripheral location relative to the site as a whole, suggests a less important role. The great reduction in huaca size is compatible with such an interpretation. Furthermore, the appearance of an elite residential complex, incorporating the huaca, signifies functional diversification associated with this architectural form.

Available settlement pattern and ceramic evidence from Moche Phases I–IV suggests that all aspects of control were concentrated around the great huacas. At Galindo, however, administrative authority was diversified. This change is manifested in architecture, some forms of which diverge from the traditional Moche huaca. Platform A and its adjoining compounds represent one example of this trend. In its secular role as the site's most elaborate elite residence, the complex evinces the nature of the change—functional diversification and increase in the importance of secular authority over sacred. The huaca remains as a symbol of Moche societal integration. This authoritative function is now, however, expressed in an increasingly diverse manner. On the one hand the traditional huaca, as in platforms B, C, and D, remains the religious focus. On the other hand, the elite residence, with the huaca as a component, suggests rising importance of secular rulers in Moche V administration, a trend which was to continue in Chimú culture. Whereas at the site of Moche a single vast structure, Huaca del Sol, appears to have served as the locus of administrative authority, at Galindo this aspect of control was shared among previously unseen architectural forms. The huaca with surrounding compounds was one of these new forms. Others will now be discussed.

Cercadura architecture. Located centrally, in the plain A segment of the site nearest Cerro Muerto, stand three large architectural complexes, cercaduras A, B, and C (Figure 12.1). This area is mainly free of other architecture, although a few elaborate residential structures stand in the vicinity of the cercaduras. The latter consist of series of adjoining, internally divided rectangular compounds. These compounds are delineated by high adobe walls allowing limited access. Within the compounds stand groups of adobe-walled rooms and benches, some of which support tablados. In general the Galindo cercaduras have been badly damaged by earth-moving equipment, but enough remains to make possible a fairly accurate reconstruction of their form and plan.

The largest architectural complex of this class, cercadura A (Figure 12.3), stands on the low spur which projects from the base of Cerro Muerto into the center of the plain. Because of the relatively low level of the surrounding ground, the cercadura, from its central, elevated position, dominates the core of the settlement.

The overall dimensions of cercadura A are 170 by 135 meters. The eastern section of the complex consists of a large compound, to the south of which stand the remains of a group of small rooms (Figure 12.3). The eastern compound is bounded by a tall adobe wall abutted interiorly by a wide bench. Access to the total complex is obtained by means of a narrow opening in the northern wall. This entrance is flanked by two tablados. The remainder of the architecture stands nearer the summit of the spur, thus at a higher elevation. This segment of the cercadura consists of three terraces which descend in height toward the south with the natural slope. A single ramp leads from the eastern compound to the terraced area. The two southern terraces, now largely destroyed, contain the remains of numerous adobe-walled rooms. The northern terrace, smaller than the others, is reached by three wide steps supporting small central ramps. This area is nearly free of architecture except for the remains of a tablado standing near the rear of the terrace.

There is evidence of cooking activity in the rooms adjoining the eastern compound but none on the ridge terraces. Many fine pottery fragments were, however, found in the latter area, together with numerous pieces of copper, including a miniature axe. Some decorated textile

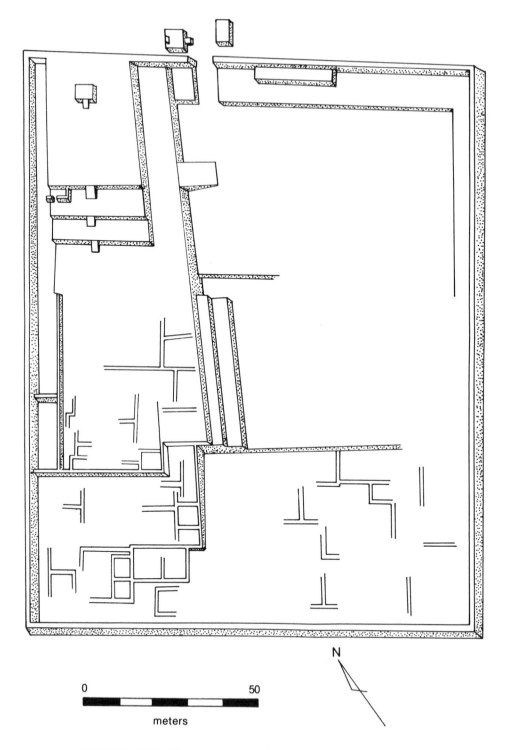

0   50

meters

FIGURE 12.3. Plan map of cercadura A. Isometric projection.

was also present on the northern terrace. Artifactual evidence indicates functional differentiation between various areas of the cercadura, with domestic activities occurring in the rooms adjoining the eastern compound and more formal activities associated with the terrace architecture.

Located on the level ground between cercadura A and the outwash channel of Quebrada Caballo Muerto is a small, isolated area of elaborate residential architecture. Although it is not possible to demonstrate a relationship between this architecture and the cercadura, it seems probable that they were functionally linked. Such a relationship involves individuals concerned with the activities of the cercadura living in exclusive neighboring dwellings. Evidence gathered from a similar locus, cercadura B, strongly indicates this type of connection and will be discussed in the following section.

Cercadura B stands at the base of Cerro Muerto (Figure 12.1). Like cercadura A, it basically consists of a series of leveled terraces and divided compounds surrounded by a high adobe wall pierced by a single narrow entrance flanked by tablados. In surface dimension this cercadura measures approximately 150 meters square. The entrance opens into a large compound, free of architecture, which in turn leads by means of steps and ramps to smaller compounds and terraces farther up the hillside. Much of this architecture has been almost totally destroyed recently, but in air photos it appears to have contained room complexes. The presence of kitchen refuse in these rooms suggests that cooking occurred here. The area farthest from the entrance comprises a series of small ramped terraces supporting tablados and containing a large quantity of fine decorated pottery fragments.

Immediately to the south of cercadura B runs the trunk channel of Quebrada Caballo Muerto at the base of a steep bluff (Figure 12.1). A massive adobe wall, continuous with the perimeter wall of the cercadura, extends across the quebrada floor, cutting off access from the plain and isolating the quebrada trunk and the structure it contains.

The ancient terraces which adjoin the quebrada channel in the trunk provide the setting for an important component of the settlement. In this isolated area stand several primarily residential structures of great elaboration and complexity. They contain numerous storage areas, elaborate benched rooms, large kitchens, and rooms apparently formal in nature, containing tablados mounted on benches which abut the walls. The latter features indicate the presence of activities of administrative or religious import. Their occurrence in a primarily domestic setting suggests that these structures represent the residence of personages involved in activities concerned with settlement control.

In addition to the elaborate character of the structure in the quebrada trunk, the relationship of this architecture with nearby construction also emphasizes its significance. A flight of steps runs up the face of the bluff from the residential architecture and gives direct access into a side compound of cercadura B. It thus seems probable that the residential area which adjoins it is functionally related. Individuals who participated in the activities of the cercadura lived in a special residential area and enjoyed exclusive access to the site of their activities. By contrast, access to the cercadura from the rest of the site is strictly controlled by the walls which segregate both the formal architectural complex and its associated residential structures.

A third, smaller cercadura, cercadura C, better preserved than the others, stands on the lower slopes of hillside B. This structure flanks the main route leading from the center of the site to the extensive architecture situated on hillside B. Cercadura C measures 60 by 45 meters. It differs from the other structures of this class in that its walls are of stone rather than adobe construction.

In plan, cercadura C is an almost rectangular enclosure with a single L-shaped entrance (Figure 12.4). It is subdivided into two main spatial units connected by two openings in the dividing wall. Each segment consists of stone terraces connected by ramps and steps. The northern segment contains a large empty compound into which opens the sole entrance of the cercadura. Adjoining this compound are a series of terraces and rooms, some of which contain kitchen refuse, repeating the pattern of the other cercaduras. The southern segment of cercadura C contains a series of ascending terraces. On the highest of these—the most inaccessible section of the cercadura—stand two small tablados. As was the case with the two larger architectural complexes of this class, only fine ceramics are present in the areas which appear more exclusive in character, cooking remains being confined to areas near the entrance. However, unlike cercaduras A and B, cercadura C has no residential architecture in its immediate vicinity.

The significance of the cercadura architectural form lies in both its plan and locational pattern. It has been noted that at the earlier site of Moche the structures strategically located to command the settlement were the two great huacas. At Galindo this role is assumed by the cercaduras, which stand at the center of the site and utilize natural topography to rise above and dominate the settlement. In configura-

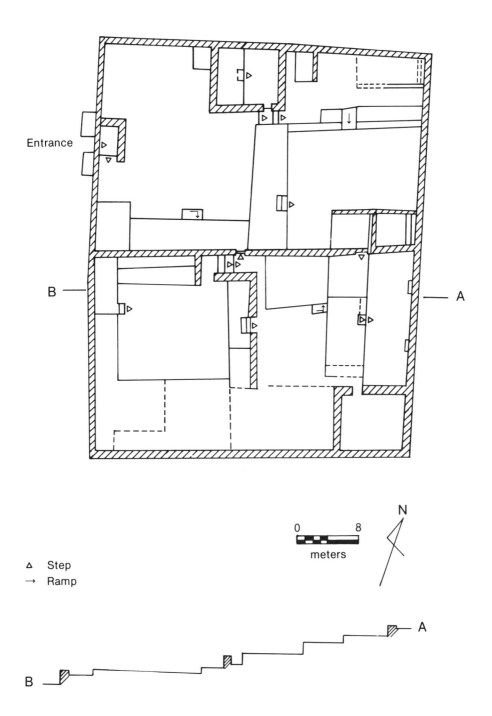

Entrance

B

A

N

0   8

meters

△   Step

→   Ramp

A

B

FIGURE 12.4. Plan map and profile of cercadura C.

tion these cercaduras are quite different from the Moche huaca. Rather they resemble the later Chan Chan ciudadelas, which also consist of large subdivided enclosures containing room complexes in which evidence of mundane activity is found. The evidence suggests a similar function, with the new Galindo architectural forms inheriting much of the secular administrative role previously incorporated in the Moche huaca and creating a partial antecedent to the Chimú pattern.

Both the cercadura and the huaca with surrounding compounds as seen in platform A indicate a departure from traditional architectural patterns. Together they represent the development of secular-oriented authority in its various aspects. The cercadura represents the main seat of administrative activity with its functionaries, the ruling elite who resided in inclusive dwellings nearby. The huaca compound architectural complex served as the most elite residence in the settlement and possibly housed a supreme ruler as did the later Chimú ciudadela. This development left the traditional huacas, as represented by platforms B, C, and D, shorn of secular function, as specialized religious loci. They no longer incorporated all elements of societal integration as had Huaca del Sol at Moche.

Tablados. The tablado is a raised daislike platform approached by a perpendicular ramp; it is thus a miniature of the large Moche huaca, although, unlike the larger structure, it carries no architectural superstructure. The platform is flat-topped and varies in size between 1.25 meters square and 10 meters square. It rarely exceeds 1 meter in height.

Tablados occur both as parts of larger structures such as platform mounds and cercaduras and as independent architectural units. In the former case they stand on benches and terraces within such structures (Figure 12.5a). As separate architectural units, tablados may be single or double tiered, both levels being approached by ramps (Figure 12.5b). However, even in the latter instance they are placed adjacent to elaborate formal architecture or flank strategic access routes within the site. The tablado thus consistently appears in locations concerned with control and can be regarded as playing a role in this aspect of intrasettlement integration.

This small structure most probably represents the dais form commonly portrayed on Moche painted pottery, where it is shown supporting dignitaries who are overseeing ritual and secular activities.

Although evidence for the existence of the tablado in earlier Moche cultural phases is largely of a graphic nature, later development is

302

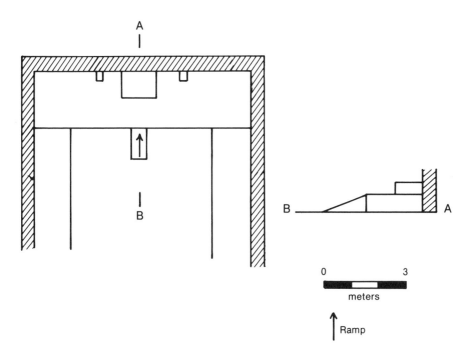

FIGURE 12.5a. (Upper) Plan and profile of a tablado as an architectural component of a larger structure.

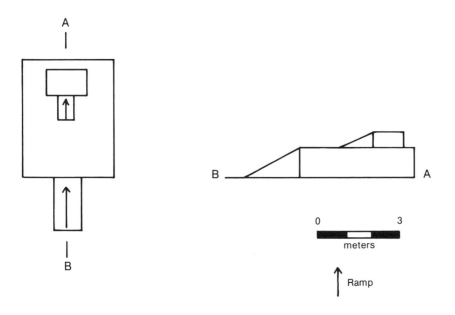

FIGURE 12.5b. (Lower) Plan and profile of a free-standing tablado.

almost certainly marked by the U-shaped structures of Chan Chan. Like the tablado, these structures appear in many different contexts, all concerned with aspects of control. The two forms demonstrate continuity of this element of social ordering from Moche to Chimú culture.

Nonformal Architecture

Storage Facilities. The section of the site designated as hillside B (Figure 12.1) is covered by an extensive area of terraces supporting small stone structures. This area stands well away from the residential sections of the settlement. It is reached by a single path which traverses the Quebrada del Norte directly adjacent to cercadura C. This cercadura and a large free-standing tablado farther up the hillslope command access to hillside B.

A second terraced hillside area—hillside C—similarly contains a large number of stone structures. As in hillside B, access is strictly controlled. In order to reach the hillslope architecture in this segment it is necessary first to traverse the bluff on which stands cercadura B. From here a series of wide steps flanked by tablados lead to hillside C. Thus access to both areas of hillside terracing appears indirect and strictly controlled. Such control is facilitated by the natural configuration of the ground.

The form taken by the hillslope architecture is variable in detail but presents an aspect of overall uniformity. The nature of this consistency distinguishes this class of architecture from residential hillside construction at Galindo and strongly suggests a specialized function.

At the hill bases, stone structures of rough construction are built directly on the gently sloping terrain. Higher up the hillside, however, this pattern gives way to architectural terracing. The structures themselves consist generally of complexes of small interconnecting rooms, rarely more than five in number (Figure 12.6). There is usually a single entrance. Contained in the rooms are numerous stone-walled storage bins and narrow benches which abut the walls. On the steeper slopes a single structure may extend over several terrace levels, these being interconnected by stone steps.

Throughout the area represented by hillsides B and C there is a total absence of domestic refuse and cooking facilities. Likewise there is very little fine Moche pottery or small ceramic vessels of any type. In short, it appears that residential usage of the area was negligible.

Material remains consist almost entirely of roughly made storage

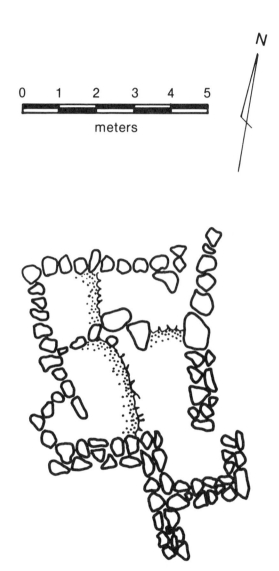

FIGURE 12.6. Plan map of a storage structure on hillside B.

vessels. These vary in size but are in general very large. Few structures are without such vessels, some containing a considerable number, which appear to have stood in rows on the wall benches. There is no evidence as to the original content of the vessels, these invariably being empty.

In spite of the lack of information regarding the contents of the storage vessels, the nature of the architecture in which they occur is clear. The stone structures which extend across hillsides B and C represent an area of large-scale storage. Virtually no other activities took place in this extensive section of the settlement. Possibly each structure contained a specific commodity, although evidence for such a pattern is lacking. The presence of formal architectural complexes athwart the access routes to the storage area together with the great size of this area and its remoteness from the rest of the settlement suggest a more specific function. It appears probable that hillsides B and C comprise one area of storage, used and controlled by the ruling authorities of the settlement.

Supporting this interpretation is the presence on the hillsides of other specialized architectural forms. Interspersed among the extensive areas of roughly built stone architecture are several structures of greatly superior quality of construction. These structures extend over several terrace levels, are larger than the surrounding architecture, and apparently conform to a formal plan. Instead of small, irregularly shaped rooms and storage bins, stone-faced terraces, mostly free of architecture, are connected by finely constructed stone steps. In rare examples tablados are located on the terraces. By contrast to the storage structures few large ceramic vessels are found, but fine ceramics and copper fragments including miniature axes occur. This architectural form presumably served a different purpose from that which surrounds it. In view of their formal nature, elaborate content, and location, it is probable that such structures served as control points for activity related to the large storage area. Movement of commodities to and from the storage buildings could be easily regulated by officials located in these formal structures.

The importance of the storage area to the settlement is clearly indicated by its placement in the overall site plan. It represents approximately a fifth of the surface area of the site. It is situated so as to constitute the most inaccessible portion of the settlement. Quebrada channels and elevated bluffs naturally segregate the storage areas while artificial obstructions emphasize this separation. It thus appears that circulation of stored materials was deemed of great importance, so much so that stringent measures were taken to regulate it. Most probably the capital represented by stored materials was vital to the economic system pervading the Moche Valley and centered at Galindo. This system was in the hands of the ruling elite, almost certainly the same class who controlled settlement administration from the cercaduras. The settlement was so organized that access to public wealth was barred to the population in general and movement in this important area rigidly ordered by means of an elaborate control system.

The pattern of controlled storage is also observed in the contemporary, larger Moche V settlement of Pampa Grande in the Lambayeque Valley. Here storage architecture is of a considerably more elaborate nature, possibly reflecting the greater significance of the settlement as a whole to Moche V culture. By the period of Chimú hegemony on the North Coast, this system had developed to the extent that storerooms were incorporated into the great palace compounds of the kings—the ciudadelas of Chan Chan. Within these huge structures, access to the storage areas was regulated by individuals located in U-shaped structures, the Chimú counterparts of the Galindo tablados and their related architecture. Although the Chan Chan pattern displays greater formalization, it surely represents a more evolved stage of the redistributive system evidenced by the storage areas at Galindo. Such a development depicts another aspect of the long and consistent process of cultural evolution on the North Coast.

Ceramic Workshop. The one industrial area to be securely identified at Galindo is a ceramic workshop. This was fully excavated and revealed much information regarding the nature of pottery production at the settlement.

The workshop is situated on the plain A segment of the site on a high bluff overlooking Quebrada del Norte. It thus stands at the extreme northern edge of the settlement. Although this area is generally one of well-constructed residential architecture, there seems to have been no formal attempt to separate the workshop from the structures standing in the vicinity.

The workshop area consists of a large floor, roofed with cane along its eastern side (Figure 12.7). Very little construction was involved other than a low stone wall and two stone-walled storage bins abutting the east wall.

The main feature of the workshop floor is an extensive circular area of dense ash containing fragments of wood, manure, and rough pottery. Lenses of burnt earth are present in the ash layer. In a small area

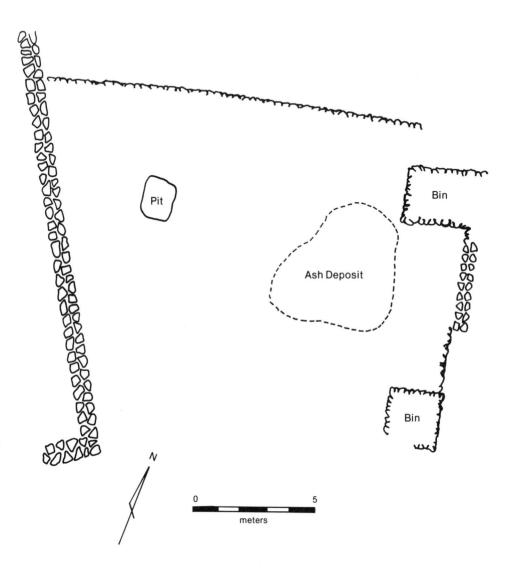

Pit

Ash Deposit

Bin

Bin

N

0   5
meters

FIGURE 12.7. Plan map of ceramic workshop.

in the northwest corner of the floor lie the fragments of several ceramic molds. Various pottery forms are present, all of them fairly small, ranging from face neck jars to figurines. All of these forms are typically Moche in aspect. Elsewhere on the work floor is a deep storage pit containing vegetal material, mostly cane and wood, and a considerable amount of llama manure.

Adjoining the workshop to the west, separated from it by a stone wall, is an enclosure free of architectural features. The floor of this enclosure is covered to a depth of 20 centimeters by llama manure. Also present are numerous pieces of rope, gourd, cane walling material, and many ceramic fragments.

Together the workshop and adjoining enclosures formed the functional unit for pottery production. In the workshop the pottery was formed and fired. The molds and ash pit mark the actual locus of these activities. Pottery was fired in open pits with manure and wood used for fuel. The lenses of earth probably mark discrete firing pits which were covered when filled with unfired pottery in order to control degree of oxidation and thus the quality of color.

The adjoining enclosure was a llama corral. The significance of this area lies in its depiction of the mode of transportation used to convey raw materials to and finished products from the production site. The nearest source of clay necessary for pottery production is the Río Moche, approximately one and one-half kilometers distant. It is, of course, quite possible that supplies adequate for quantity production at Galindo necessitated transport of clay from more distant sites. Clay was presumably carried to the settlement by llamas who were unloaded and corralled in the enclosure which adjoins the workshop. Numerous rope fragments recovered from the enclosure are the remains of material used to secure the animals and their loads.

The presence of small quantities of pottery not in the Moche style in the workshop area and elsewhere at Galindo suggests contact between the settlement and areas beyond the Moche cultural sphere. Such pottery fragments bear no resemblance to contemporary forms of the North and Central Coast. On the basis of negative evidence it may be tentatively proposed that contact, probably commercial in nature, occurred between Galindo and the nearby sierra, whose ceramic sequences are imperfectly known at present. Galindo, situated as it is at the neck of the coastal plain of the Río Moche, commands the route from the lower valley settlement to the highlands. It is therefore reasonable to assume interaction between the two regions and that evidence of this activity would be present at Galindo.

Other Nonformal Architecture

Although other nonformal architecture is present at Galindo, especially in the vicinity of the ceramic workshop and its nearby residential structures, insufficient investigation has been performed to make specific identification possible. It may be assumed, however, that some of this architecture is concerned with the production of commodities commonly used at the site. Thus workshops which produced woven, metal, wooden, and ceramic items await recognition.

DOMESTIC ARCHITECTURE

The domestic architecture at Galindo includes those structures which display a configuration and content primarily reflecting residential activity. Extensive excavation reveals the basic domestic structure as consisting of a three- or four-room complex with cane walls set into stone bases (Figure 12.8).

The most strictly defined functional component of these complexes is a food preparation area. This is a rectangular room, devoid of architectural elaboration, containing one or more hearths. Hearths are sometimes stone-lined but usually consist of a shallow circular pit roughly 30 centimeters in depth. Large quantities of ash fill the hearths and cover the surrounding floors. Within this ash level are numerous fragments of food refuse and utilitarian pottery. Cuy dung is prevalent in food preparation areas, marking the presence of these animals, also found in present-day Peru. Usually one or two large grinding stones occur, often mounted on low adobe pedestals. More rarely small stone or adobe storage bins are present; vegetal and ceramic remains of varied character are found within. Food preparation areas were usually roofed with cane roofing material supported by wooden posts.

The second usual component of a domestic structure consists of a room, formally planned, containing benches with stone faces. These benches abut at least three of the walls and form a central enclosed patio. The bench surfaces and patio floor are usually covered with smooth mud plaster. Relatively little food refuse or dung appears in these benched rooms, and hearths are never present. Material remains are chiefly of a ceramic nature with a higher proportion of fine wares and forms which do not pertain to cooking activity. The benches carry

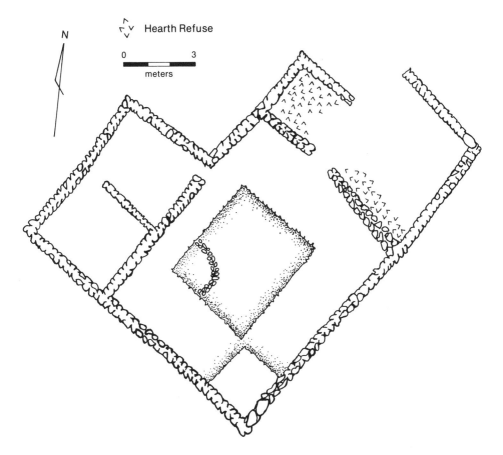

FIGURE 12.8. Plan map of a domestic residence on Plain A.

the remains of cane roofs which were originally supported by wooden posts set.into the patio floors, the patios themselves remaining open.

It is logical to suppose that the physical differences between the two room types are defined by their differing functions. It is probable that the rooms lacking hearths represent the main social focus of the inhabitants and their sleeping area.

The third component characteristic of domestic architecture is a storeroom. This is a small, rectangular room walled by cane set into stone coursing, usually roofed, and often with no obvious means of access. It possesses no architectural embellishment, and its contents consist almost entirely of fragments from large storage vessels. This room usually adjoins the larger benched area.

Access patterning in the domestic architecture is remarkably consistent. There is a single main entrance, usually a simple opening in a wall of the food preparation area. Inside the residential structure another well-defined opening leads from this area into the benched room. Access to the small storerooms is obtained from one of the benches, either through a formal entrance or more frequently by surmounting the low stone wall-base which defines these rooms.

In general the domestic architecture at Galindo presents a strong impression of careful planning and internal differentiation of function. This is emphasized by limited and consistently directed access, features which have been observed to characterize the overall settlement configuration. Each functional component is clearly distinguished from its neighbor. Within each residential unit the storage facilities are most isolated. Thus storage appears to fill an important role in the individual residence just as in the settlement as a whole. More mundane domestic activities such as cooking are thus more accessible.

Although all domestic architecture contains these components, there is a wide variation in actual plan. There appears to be no formal rule as to the alignment of the rooms relative to each other. Likewise size and elaboration vary widely, with architecture ranging from small, simple hillside terrace structures to large, elaborate complexes. The latter may contain numerous rooms, those components most commonly represented being the benched rooms and storage areas. Such structures may even incorporate stone-walled passageways to aid access from one area to another. There also appear architectural complexes which contain a number of domestic residences abutting each other, as in a modern city block. These residences share walls, although each remains a discrete unit with no means of intercommunication with the others. Furthermore, a small number of structures contain architectural features primarily nondomestic in nature. These will be discussed at greater length in the following section.

In spite of great variability in architectural detail, clear trends appear when the residential areas are examined relative to general settlement configuration. First, there is a well-defined arrangement according to size and quality of construction. The residential sectors are broadly confined to two distinct areas of the site—the western two-thirds of plain A and hillside A (Figure 12.1). Those structures situated on the plain are generally well constructed, of moderate size, and well spaced. In addition there are a few extremely elaborate structures, already discussed, which are apparently related to the cercaduras. These are segregated from the greater part of the residential sections and probably represent the dwellings of the ruling elite. By contrast the architecture of hillside A is poorly constructed, of random plan, and consists mainly of small, crowded terrace structures which extend for a considerable distance up the slopes.

Such difference in architectural quality suggests a corresponding social variation, with inhabitants of higher class and wealth level living on the level plain. Such a hypothesis is supported by the contents of the structures. Excavations in the dwellings on the plain provide a much higher proportion of fine ceramics and luxury items than do those in the hillside terraces. It is also evident that individuals living on the plain had far better access to other areas of the settlement and to the irrigated area adjoining it. This includes access to the vital commodity of water. Acquisition of water was relatively easy for the plain dwellers (the high, level canal borders the settlement at this point). However, for the inhabitants of the hillside, water gathering involved a long haul up steep slopes. Further, it appears from the available evidence that commercial activity and industry was centered on the plain within the general area of residential occupation. This suggests that the inhabitants of the area were involved in such activities even if overall control was exercised by the small ruling class. There is no evidence of industrial or commercial activity in the hillside residential areas. The implication is that any participation of the inhabitants was of a subservient character, like unskilled labor.

Finally, hillside A is separated from the rest of the settlement by a large adobe wall paralleled on its downhill side by a ditch. This wall skirts the base of Cerro Galindo and is pierced by a few openings which provide access to the residential area above. The wall is open at both ends and possesses no rampart. These factors, together with the location of all important site structures in a vulnerable position on the plain, indicate that the well and ditch were not intended as fortifications. Most probably these features were an elaborate means of internal social delineation. The basis of such segregation was social level, with a large lower class being confined to a barrio and the upper classes occupying relatively spacious dwellings in an area of better facilities from where they participated in the operation of the economic activities of the

313

settlement. Such clearly defined segregation reveals the high degree of social and functional differentiation reached in Moche V Galindo. Moreover it forecasts the equally rigid situation visible in the Chimú state and thus presents a cultural antecedent for this later development (see J. Topic, Chapter 7).

MIXED-FUNCTION ARCHITECTURE

The final architectural class to be discussed includes a number of structures which, although possessing features of the domestic residence, also incorporate nondomestic elements. They differ from those formal architectural complexes which contain evidence of domestic activity in that their basic plan includes the characteristic residential pattern described in the preceding section. Three distinct forms were revealed during excavation. Although it is clear that these do not constitute the total inventory of this architectural class, they do provide a general idea of the functional variety related to residential occupation at Galindo.

Several residential structures of typical plan adjoin stone-walled enclosures that are usually empty of architecture, sometimes partially roofed, and contain much llama manure and domestic refuse. They rarely possess direct access from the adjacent domestic residence, entrance being obtained from the exterior by means of simple wall openings. These enclosures are all located on the southern part of the plain A area, near the perimeter of the site. They probably represent llama corrals used also as refuse dumps for the adjoining dwellings. Such structures reveal the regular presence of llama at the settlement and suggest that functions involving the use of these animals were in the hands of individuals who lived on the plain, probably in the dwellings attached to the enclosures. No such enclosures appear in the elaborate architectural complexes inhabited by the ruling elite. It can thus be assumed that the elite were primarily concerned with overall administrative duties rather than specific tasks pertaining to the functioning of the various socioeconomic cultural systems of the settlement.

The second form of mixed-function architecture is represented by a single example, again located in the residential area of plain A. In plan it consists of a large domestic residence with two additional rooms and an enclosure (Figure 12.9). These rooms contain rows of storage bins approximately one and one-half meters square lining one wall; the

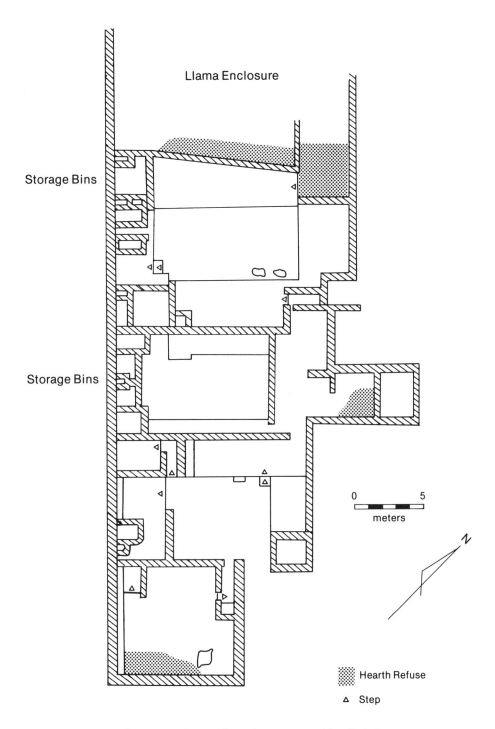

Llama Enclosure

Storage Bins

Storage Bins

0   5
meters

N

Hearth Refuse

△ Step

FIGURE 12.9. Plan map of a residential structure with adjoining storage facilities and llama enclosure, plain A.

other bins are abutted by benches. All are roofed with cane and their surfaces plastered. In addition, two other small rooms contain hearth and food remains; this rather crude domestic area is separated from the main residential segment of the structure, seemingly relating more directly to the rooms containing benches. At the extreme end of the architectural complex is a large llama corral.

Small quantities of materials, mainly of a dietary nature, were found in the storage bins. Separate bins contained corncobs, seeds, shells, animal bones, and fragments from large storage vessels.

This complex structure seems most easily explained as a site of redistributive activity. The bins apparently served as storage facilities for materials which in quantity far exceeded that needed by the inhabitants of the adjoining domestic residence. The secondary cooking area was probably used by individuals primarily concerned with the activities centered in the storage rooms; they do not appear to constitute part of another residential component. The presence of a llama corral reveals the means by which substances stored in the benched rooms were transported. Such structures as this, again supervised by persons of high status, may well have controlled the flow into the settlement of commodities required for subsistence. Whether they served merely as clearing houses in a more complex redistributive scheme that included the large storage areas or represented actual distribution centers remains a matter of conjecture.

Finally, there are several domestic structures of extremely elaborate construction and plan, apparently the residence of the ruling elite class. These structures also incorporate elements atypical of domestic activity. The close relationship of such architecture to the neighboring administrative cercaduras was discussed above. Specifically nondomestic features occurring in this type of architecture are of a formal, ideologically oriented nature rather than a commercially oriented one as in the other structures of mixed function. Here the tablado, which usually relates to loci of religious or administrative control, appears in conjunction with elite residential structures. The dichotomy between this architecture and the other forms discussed in this section is emphasized by its differential location pattern. Those forms which have been defined as pertaining to redistributive or industrial activities are situated in areas of apparently nonsegregated internal configuration: large numbers of residential structures are interspersed in an informal manner with nondomestic architecture in plain A. This arrangement contrasts vividly with that of the elite structures. The latter are located well away from the main residential areas, possess limited access, and contain no evidence of commercial or industrial activity. Thus their exclusiveness and elaboration point to the probability that the ruling elite lived there.

CONCLUSIONS

It has been seen that a large number of architectural forms appear at Galindo. These forms vary in structure according to status and function. The same factors determine the differential location of architecture within the settlement. Consequent separation of architectural classes is enforced by the rigid limitation of access between the various sectors, the controlling agents consisting of topographic divisions and special architectural features. This overall configuration suggests a settlement in which an emergent secularized administration ruled from the large cercaduras. A ruling elite was supported by traditional religious beliefs whose related activity was centered around traditionally shaped Moche huacas. Major reduction in the size of the huacas and their location at the periphery of the site suggest transferral of authority from the religious aspects of social integration to the secular, represented by the now-central cercaduras. The ruling class dwelled in exclusive residential areas and was probably headed by a paramount ruler who lived in a large huaca-compound "palace." Control of the extensive storage areas found at Galindo was in the hands of the administration. These areas were so restricted in access as to imply that they were of great economic importance to the settlement and the surrounding valley.

This complex administrative structure headed a population in which social stratification was rigidly enforced. The wealthier classes lived in relatively large and well-constructed dwellings situated in the choicest areas of the settlement. They also operated most industrial and commercial activities. By contrast a larger lower class was confined to an area of crowded hillside occupation away from the centers of public activities. This segregation was enforced by a large adobe wall and ditch.

In sum, Galindo possessed the attributes of a settlement in which diverse cultural systems are integrated by a strong centralized administration. This administration based its authority partly on long-standing traditional control forms and partly on innovative factors which at Galindo were emerging from the tradition.

Temporally Galindo has been seen to represent one link in a chain of intensive occupation centers in the Moche Valley. This chain extends back in time at least as far as Salinar times and probably can trace its origin to the Cupisnique Phase. Galindo was thus part of a long-lasting trend towards urbanism that culminated in the Chimú state with the vast city of Chan Chan. An investigation of the nature of this trend in the Early Intermediate Period indicates, however, significant changes within the developing urban tradition (see T. Topic, Chapter 11).

Galindo, as the center of valley political and economic power in the Moche V Phase, was successor to the site of Moche, which filled this role during earlier Moche cultural phases. The question arises as to why Moche was abandoned at the end of Moche IV and replaced by Galindo, a settlement of very different character. While both settlements were of considerable size and complexity, Moche overshadowed Galindo in significant architectural features. The great Moche huacas were many times larger than even the largest Galindo example. They obviously reflected the ability of the administration of Moche to organize huge labor forces. The magnitude of these huacas and the high degree of elaboration of other architectural forms infused Moche with a quality of size and dominance which totally exceeded that of contemporary sites on the North Coast. Indeed such factors strongly suggest that Moche served as the focal point of Moche culture till the end of Moche Phase IV. The location of the site near the coast, thus close to the intervalley roads and canals, likewise facilitated such a role. It is more difficult to ascertain whether this focal role denotes Moche as the capital of a political state or a great religious center. However, the frequent representations of warfare on Moche III and IV pottery suggest political conflict, a factor which strongly argues for the former designation, that is, that Moche was indeed the capital of an expansionist state and as such also incorporated ideological control.

A similar overview of Galindo leads to very different conclusions regarding its status. Although the architectural forms are complex, they lack the dimensions and extreme formal quality seen at Moche. Such reductions may well indicate a lessening of power at the government level, the Galindo administration not possessing the widespread control necessary for erecting edifices of the magnitude of the Moche huacas. Although Galindo was rigidly subdivided in terms of functional and social differentiation, within these defined areas there was little sense of formal planning. When compared to its Moche IV predecessor, Galindo appears to have been a provincial center as regards formal internal arrangement and architectural quality and size. This status is supported by the location of the site. Galindo developed from an earlier small Moche hillside settlement at the neck of the valley, far from the coast with its strategic importance for intervalley communication and control. The settlement was thus most satisfactorily located to exert control over the Moche Valley alone.

Finally, when Galindo is viewed in the context of the Moche V culture area, its role as a secondary center becomes even more evident. The site of Moche flourished in a valley which by Phase IV lay in the heart of an extensive Moche-dominated region. This reached at least as far south as the Nepeña Valley and probably north to the Lambayeque Valley. By Phase V, however, the Moche Valley marked the extreme southern border of the area of dominance, the southern valleys having been lost. Galindo therefore represented the southernmost center, an exposed position in view of the development ascribed to Huari expansion along the central coastal region.

In fact the main center of Moche culture in its ultimate phase lay far to the north, in the Lambayeque Valley. Here the site of Pampa Grande rivaled Moche itself in its architectural quality and formal planning. Like Moche it possessed a vast central huaca surrounded by an extensive occupation area exhibiting a high degree of internal ordering. In general the site suggests the presence of a strong centralized administration, one which held power to control and utilize the resources of a large region. In this latter quality it differed significantly from Galindo.

Thus, a general study of Galindo in context of its temporal and spatial cultural setting suggests that at the end of Moche IV, developments occurred which resulted in a significant reorganization of the political structure. This reorganization consisted of the shrinkage in territory under Moche hegemony and the abandonment of the vast site of Moche, the center of the Moche culture sphere subsequently moving to the north. This left the Moche Valley as a frontier area controlled by the newly developed settlement of Galindo. The new center was located well away from the coast and displayed major signs of internal adaptation to the events which caused the transformation. Indeed, the magnitude of innovations in Galindo architectural form and settlement plan indicates the emergence of a new social integrative system at this time. The new system was secular in nature, led by an elite class and probably headed by a paramount ruler. Traditional religious authority was greatly modified. It must be stressed, however, that these changes constitute internal reorganization in the face of danger rather than foreign intrusion. While the loss of the southern Moche territories and the removal of the largest Moche center to the Lambayeque Valley indicate strong external pressure, possibly deriving from expanding Huari influence, there is no indication that such events involved invasion of the Moche Valley. Rather, the innovations apparent at Galindo represent internal adaptive response to severe stress in a frontier settlement possibly menaced by foreign incursion.

In terms of on-going development on the North Coast, the cultural situation reflected by Galindo proved transitional. The site represents a single phase of occupation—that of Moche V—and was abandoned after approximately two centuries. Following a period of poorly understood cultural fluctuation after the end of the Moche V Phase, the focus of valley authority returned to the coast with the rise of the Chimú state and the establishment of its capital of Chan Chan. However, the architectural and related administrative innovations which appeared first at Galindo continued in the Chimú period, being utilized at Chan Chan to integrate the social, ideological, and political structure of a great empire.

13

The Middle Horizon as Viewed from the Moche Valley

CAROL J. MACKEY

California State University, Northridge

The Middle Horizon is identified as the time when the Huari state spread from its capital in the southern sierra of Peru and influenced the entire Andean area stylistically and culturally. As more archaeological research is undertaken, it is becoming increasingly clear that the nature and degree of Huari influence varied greatly in different Andean regions. This chapter will elucidate the nature and extent of Huari influence in the Moche Valley, the heartland of the important Early Intermediate Period Moche and Late Intermediate Period Chimú cultures on the North Coast of Peru, and then discuss other geographic areas that may have influenced the Moche Valley during the Middle Horizon. Although there are still many unanswered questions concerning the Middle Horizon, it is felt that an initial statement should be made to pave the way for future research.

TRADITIONAL NOTIONS ABOUT HUARI INFLUENCE

During the Middle Horizon, the Moche Valley witnessed the demise of the Moche culture and the rise of the Chimú culture (see Table 1.1 for a time chart). It has been postulated that Huari influence

321

on the North Coast was so strong that it created a three-and-one-half-century hiatus between these two cultures. Categories of evidence used in defense of intrusive Huari influences are the development of urbanism, changes in architectural features, and changes in ceramic styles. Recent work in the Moche Valley, however, suggests that several of these categories exhibited long antiquity on the North Coast and that Huari influence was only one of several influences felt in the valley.

The Development of Urbanism

The view that urbanism is linked to Huari intervention can be traced to Kroeber (1930). In Kroeber's brief 1925–26 visit to the North Coast, he did not notice any large sites which predated the Middle Horizon. He also observed that Middle Horizon ceramics represented a break with the previous Moche style and that this stylistic break was due to invaders from the sierra (1930:111). These observations were reinterpreted by other scholars to mean that Huari invaders were responsible for urbanism during the Middle Horizon.

Recent excavations and survey in the Moche Valley reveal that the foundations for urbanism were developing locally in the Early Intermediate Period. From these data it appears that urbanism did not suddenly arise without antecedents but shows a continuous indigenous development. Nucleated sites with domestic architecture were present in Salinar settlements. The site of Cerro Arena, located on the south side of the valley, was a terraced hillside settlement with well-preserved domestic architecture that extended for over two kilometers (Mujica Barreda 1975; Brennan 1977). A second Salinar site, in the northern portion of the valley, was a terraced, hillside settlement over one kilometer in length. The wide distribution of the Salinar population is evidenced by smaller beach sites located at Huanchaco, northwest of the modern city of Trujillo.

The subsequent Gallinazo Period is characterized by nucleated sites with domestic and corporate-labor architecture. The Gallinazo occupation continued to be greatest at the valley neck and along the south side of the valley. The most extensive Gallinazo settlement, at Cerro Orejas, extended for over three kilometers. There may have also been a sizable Gallinazo settlement at the pyramid site of Huaca del Sol and Huaca de la Luna. The construction of Huaca de la Luna may even have begun during the Gallinazo occupation of the valley (Hastings and Moseley 1975).

The Moche pyramid site of Huaca del Sol and Huaca de la Luna exhibits the densest occupation of the Early Intermediate Period. The site exceeds one square kilometer and has cultural deposits up to six meters in depth. Evidence for cultural complexity is shown by the different classes of domestic structures, the burials, and the corporate-labor architecture (T. Topic, Chapter 11).

The final phase of Moche occupation in the valley is represented by the settlement of Galindo. This site, located on the north side of the valley near the valley neck, became the new urban center after the pyramid site was abandoned at the end of Moche Phase IV. The Galindo settlement, which extended for over five square kilometers, contained various classes or architectural units and appears to have been urban in all respects (Bawden, Chapter 12). Thus the density which characterizes urban sites was already developing during Salinar culture, and by Moche times society was well oriented to the urban concentrations which typify the succeeding Late Intermediate Period city of Chan Chan.

Architectural Features

Similarities in architectural features at the type site of Huari and at the Chimú capital of Chan Chan have also been used as evidence of Huari intrusion. However, the sites are difficult to compare since Chan Chan is well known archaeologically whereas a thorough archaeological assessment of Huari has not been undertaken. Therefore, the discussion will focus mainly on the antiquity and function of the two features most often attributed to Huari and Chan Chan: the building technique called "columnar construction" and the architectural use of large enclosure walls.

The first feature, columnar construction, is the erecting of adjacent columns of bricks for building of walls or other structures. At Huari, the walls were built in columns of some length and were joined at the wall intersections by interdigitated bricks (Rowe, Collier, and Willey 1950:122). In the Moche Valley the adjacent brick columns were *not* bonded. Each segment was separated from the next unit by a narrow gap. Moseley (1975c) has referred to this type of construction as "segmentation." This construction can be traced from Gallinazo to the Colonial Period and is found in functionally different architectural units such as platforms, walls, and canals. Segmentation is found at both Huaca del Sol and Huaca de la Luna (Kubler 1962; Moseley

1975c) and the compound walls of Chan Chan (Day 1973). This technique may be a manifestation of the labor tax. According to Moseley (1975c), each segment corresponded to the separate work party which was responsible for constructing that unit.

The second feature, which has been equated with both Huari and Chan Chan construction, is the use of great rectangular enclosures which contained planned architectural units. At Huari the form of the enclosure varied from trapezoidal to rectangular (Isbell 1973), whereas the enclosures at Chan Chan were more rectangular.

In the Moche Valley, enclosure walls predate the Middle Horizon. The earliest known example is the Moche pyramid site. Huaca de la Luna, a complex of several platforms and plazas, was enclosed by a peripheral adobe wall which created the rectangular enclosure. The bricks in this wall are dated to Moche Phase IV (Moseley, personal communication). The Moche V site of Galindo also exhibits several structures which can be classed as rectangular compounds (Bawden, Chapter 12). The enclosed platform mound of Galindo, in both formal and functional characteristics, appears to have been antecedent to the large walled compounds at Chan Chan (Conrad 1974). In fact, the adobe bricks used in the enclosure walls of Huaca Galindo are typologically similar to the adobe bricks used in the construction of the earliest compound at Chan Chan, Chayhuac (Kolata, Chapter 4). Therefore, the use of compound enclosure walls clearly predates the Middle Horizon and shows continuity from one culture to the next.

Pottery and Art Styles

In the Moche Valley there are two pottery traditions said to be associated with Huari. The first, called "Huari polychrome," is an oxidized ware distinguished by its highly polished polychrome decorations which emphasize Huari mythological themes. The second, "Red, white, black," is an oxidized ware which utilizes three slip colors for its geometric decorations. Huari polychrome is associated with the type site of Huari and is manifested in the styles of Conchapata, Robles Moqo, and Vinaque (Menzel 1964). Huari-derived styles as well as Huari polychrome are found on the South and Central coasts in the Nazca, Ica, and Supe valleys and at the site of Pachacamac. However, it is the latter site, Pachacamac, which was ultimately the most influential on the coast (Menzel 1964). The most distinct mythical figure of

324

Pachacamac was a griffin with winged feline body and an eagle head (Menzel 1964). The ceramic forms associated with the Huari motifs include face neck jars, bowls, double spout bottles, and the kero (beaker).

Four keros have been found in various excavations at the Moche pyramid site of Huaca del Sol and Huaca de la Luna. Two keros were uncovered by Uhle from site A at Huaca del Sol. Although the stratigraphic context is unclear, it was thought that the two keros were from graves intruded into the rear of the huaca. Stylistically, one kero can be ascribed to the category of Huari polychrome and the other corresponds to the three-color (Red, white, black) geometric motif (Kroeber 1925:Plate 63). Found with the keros were sherds from Cajamarca tripod bowls. Recent reexcavation of site A at Huaca del Sol established that the graves with the keros are associated with a well-defined Chimú occupation. In the reexcavation, a third kero was found which is blackware with a press-molded square head on the body of the cup. The fourth kero, which was excavated from the cemetery situated between Huaca del Sol and Huaca de la Luna, has a Pachacamac-like eagle head design executed in Red, white, black style (Donnan and Mackey 1978).

Site survey of the Moche Valley has revealed fewer than a dozen sherds which could be ascribed stylistically to Huari polychrome. The same evidence was noted for the Virú Valley by Collier (1955: 185), who stated he found only 14 sherds of Huari style.

The second ceramic tradition is the Red, white, black ware associated with the early Chimú occupation of the valley. The design motifs of the tricolor ceramics were mainly geometric in nature and painted in a crude and sloppy manner. Certain geometric elements used in the Huari style did survive in this style; the most prevalent were the checkerboard pattern and the large circle, which could be a local version of the Huari circle-and-dot motif. Huari-related shapes existed in the Red, white, black style and included face neck jars, double spout bottles, and the kero. The most common bowl shape associated with Red, white, black pottery was the ring base bowl, which resembled the bowls found in the Supe Valley. Thus far, only the keros (mentioned above) exhibited religious/mythological motifs as found on Huari or Huari-related ceramics. The design motifs on the Red, white, black ceramics found in the Moche Valley were filler elements used in the Huari-style ceramics and not the mythical/religious motifs described by Menzel (1964).

325

Recently 14 whole vessels of this tradition were excavated from two cemeteries: one cemetery was located between Huaca del Sol and Huaca de la Luna and the other was found to the south of the pyramids (Donnan and Mackey 1978). Associated with these vessels were ollas, jars, and bowls which were decorated with press-molded designs and composed of both oxidized and reduced wares.

From surface survey and excavation it appears that Red, white, black ceramics were not stylistically significant in the valley. Twenty sites yielded this style, and they are localized within two main areas of the valley: on the south side of the river, in and around the area of Huaca del Sol and Huaca de la Luna, and on the north side of the valley on La Esperanza plain. There was only one site on the north side of the river near the Moche V site of Galindo. The total ceramic sample from these 20 sites is 2,360 sherds, and of this total, .02 percent or 52 sherds were in the Red, white, black style.

It would seem apparent that the Red, white, black ceramics did not represent a strong cultural influence from either Huari or Pachacamac. This observation is based on the almost total lack of vessels carrying religious/mythical themes. The Huari elements which seem to have penetrated into the Red, white, black style were vessel forms and some of the abstract filler elements.

Discussion

The evidence presented points to an indigenous development of urbanism in the Moche Valley. Just as the city developed from a local base so did the architectural canons and construction techniques which, in the past, appeared to be the work of Huari architects (cf. Lanning 1967:139). Huari or Huari-derived ceramics are not numerous in the valley. Red, white, black ceramics exhibit forms associated with Huari ceramics but do not carry the religious/mythical motifs typical of the Middle Horizon pottery found on the South and Central coasts. There have been no reports of Huari or Huari-derived pottery or Red, white, black pottery found at the Moche V site of Galindo, and excavation and survey have not uncovered any of these styles in Chan Chan. Only Kroeber (1926:34–35) reports four Red, white, black vessels attributed to Chan Chan. The majority of Red, white, black vessels found in tombs are localized in and around the Moche pyramids of Huaca del Sol and Huaca de la Luna.

EXTERNAL INFLUENCES IN THE
MOCHE VALLEY

Although the evidence presented thus far indicates minimal Huari influence, this is not to say that the Moche Valley was in a cultural vacuum during the Middle Horizon. Throughout this time period there were cultural influences from several regions: the Central and South coasts; the Far North Coast; and possibly the Northern Sierra.

Central Coast Influence

One of the most obvious changes which occurred during the Middle Horizon was the change in burial position. Burials for this time period were interred in a seated, flexed position, a major change from the extended position which had existed before this time. This new burial custom persisted in most regions until the arrival of the Spaniards.

The practice of flexed seated burials was introduced on the Central Coast at the beginning of the Middle Horizon (Menzel 1964:32). At this same time in the Moche Valley several lines of evidence point to the extended burial as the dominant pattern. According to Donnan and McClelland (1979), Moche V vessels depict a burial scene which shows a corpse in an extended position being lowered into a tomb. Bawden (personal communication) found evidence of looted burials beneath the floors of domestic dwellings at the Moche V site of Galindo. The size and shape of the tombs indicate extended burials.

By Epoch 4 of the Middle Horizon, which would be contemporaneous with Chimú culture, the practice of flexed burials is well documented, and it is found with burials of all ages and classes of society.

Far North Influence

The Moche Valley shows strong affinities with the Far North Coast, especially the region from the Jequetepeque to the Lambayeque valleys. The evidence for contact is seen in the architecture, art styles, and mythology of the Far North Coast.

As is discussed elsewhere in this volume (T. Topic, Chapter 11; Bawden, Chapter 12) the Moche state underwent a reduction in size at the end of the Early Intermediate Period or the beginning of the Middle Horizon (that is, between Moche Phases IV and V). Moche power decreased in the valleys to the south: Virú, Santa, and Nepeña. This shrinkage caused the Moche Valley to become the southern border of the Moche state. At the same time that power was waning in the south, power in the Far North was strengthened. Pampa Grande, in Lambayeque, became the major Moche V settlement on the North Coast and presumably the capital of the state. Whether these shifts in Moche polity were in response to the incursion of Huari forces elsewhere in Peru is not entirely clear at this time.

Architecture

There are features at the site of Pampa Grande—for example, pyramid plan and construction—which did not appear in the succeeding Chimú culture in the Moche Valley. However, one important architectural feature did. This was the audiencia, a three-sided, U-shaped structure associated with most of the compounds of Chan Chan. It has been identified with the ruling elite and the control of valuable commodities. The antecedent form to this structure was absent in the Moche Valley but existed at Pampa Grande (Day, Chapter 14) and also at the site of Pacatnamú in the Jequetepeque Valley (Keatinge, Chapter 9; 1975a). At Pampa Grande these structures were associated with control of goods and were also situated atop pyramids. Keatinge (1975a) has suggested that the association of the audiencia with the pyramid mounds at Pacatnamú may indicate that the structure evolved in a religious-ceremonial context. This important structure seems to have evolved, at least at Pampa Grande, in a secure Moche context and later diffused to the Moche Valley from the Far North.

Art Styles and Mythology

One of the purposes of this chapter is to account for the origin of the corporate art style employed by the Chimú. The ceramics generally lack any mythical representations related to either Huari or Moche styles. In this respect it is valuable to look at the Chimú friezes which were associated with either pyramid mounds or elite structures. The friezes portray two human figures. One represents a man with a pointed cap, his legs and head drawn in profile. The pointed-cap men from the

328

frieze at Huaca el Dragón are almost exact images of figures painted on textiles from Pacatnamú (Fang 1975:17). Further, in the Tule Boat Frieze from Chan Chan described by Fang (1975), the figures on the boats have backward-trailing headdresses. This attribute was shared by several of the figures on the frieze at Huaca el Dragón, and is similar to the figures on Huaca Chotuna in the Lambayeque Valley. Although the evidence is fragmentary, this feature may be a further indication that the Chimú friezes in the Moche Valley have incorporated stylistic and cultural elements from the Far North.

The validation for the ruling elite of Chan Chan is the mythology, and this too has Far North origins. *The Anonymous History of 1604* (Rowe 1948) relates an origin myth for the Moche Valley. In this legend, a man named Tacaynamo comes to Chimor (Chan Chan) by sea, presumably from the north, since his balsa raft was the type found in the region of Guayaquil in Ecuador. The dynasty which ruled Chan Chan is believed to have been descended from him. Further work may prove the assertion that Chimú art and mythology have their origin in the Far North.

Discussions of Huari Influence

The clearest case for Huari influence is the change of burial position associated with the spread of the Huari state. This major change must have been related to ideas concerning the afterlife (Moseley, Chapter 1) and should be viewed as further proof of Menzel's proposition that the impetus for Huari expansion was based on religious motivation (Menzel 1958, 1964). Menzel's hypothesis on the religious nature of Huari was drawn from the mythical representations which appear on the pottery. Huari religion is represented in ceramic art in a variety of mythical themes which are recognizable even when altered by local imitation. If the change in burial practice indicates a change in religious beliefs, we would also expect some loan features of Huari mythology to be found in the Moche Valley associated with the change in burial practice. However, Huari iconography does not appear to have penetrated either the Moche or the Chimú style to any appreciable degree. When religious/mythical figures are found, as on the friezes at Chan Chan, they do not appear to be Huari-related but instead seem to stem from the Far North Coast tradition.

A CHRONOLOGICAL INTERPRETATION
OF THE DATA

Several interpretations are possible to explain the minimal influence of Huari in the Moche Valley. One of the most plausible is based on chronology.

The Middle Horizon, which dates from A.D. 550 to 900, encompassed 350 years (Rowe and Menzel 1967). In this chronological scheme, the relative date for the end of Moche V is approximately A.D. 650; however, recent dates secured by Bawden are in the range of A.D. 800 (Bawden, personal communication).

Menzel (1964) divides the 350-year span of the Middle Horizon into four epochs. In this scheme the initial expansion and consolidation of the Huari state took place during Epoch 1, which would be roughly contemporaneous with Moche V. In the first part of Epoch 2, the Huari state underwent further expansion; a prestigious center was established at Pachacamac, and at the end of Epoch 2 the site of Huari was abandoned. During Epoch 3 the influence of Pachacamac waned, and Epoch 4 witnessed local derivatives of Huari style surviving on the coast.

It is difficult to mesh the events of the North Coast with the chronological sequence developed for the South Coast. However, the data presented thus far place Huari influence in the Moche Valley late in the Middle Horizon. The flexed burials occurred after the fall of Moche culture and were associated with Red, white, black pottery. This pottery, though reminiscent of Huari ceramics in filler elements and shape, was only a survival of Huari style and therefore fit well into the last epoch of the Middle Horizon. Based on this scheme, the reduction in the territory of the Moche state and the subsequent change in the seat of power from the Moche Valley to the Lambayeque Valley can be viewed as an adaptation in the face of a competitive power. Therefore, it seems that either through strength or prestige the Moche state managed to maintain its cultural integrity throughout the time of Huari expansion.

CONCLUSIONS

The traditional assumptions about Huari incursions in the Moche Valley have been weighed against current archaeological findings, and the results point to locally derived antecedents, especially in the development of urbanism.

It was noted, however, that the Moche Valley was not without outside influences from at least two spheres. Huari influence is seen in the Moche Valley in the flexed burial position and certain elements adapted into the Red, white, black ceramic style. Since the ceramics in the Moche Valley differed from those found at other Huari coastal sites, it is clear that the Moche Valley never participated in the rich religious/mythological tradition found at these sites. Based on the characteristics shown in the Red, white, black ceramic style and the provenience of the bodies buried in the flexed position, it is postulated that Huari influence in the Moche Valley came after the abandonment of the site of Huari, most probably during Epoch 4 of the Middle Horizon. The second sphere of influence was derived from Moche cultural origins on the Far North Coast. An architectural form called the audiencia, as well as mythological representations and legends, indicates strong affiliations with the northern region from Jequetepeque to Lambayeque.

Though our understanding of the Middle Horizon is not yet clear, this review has shown that the chronological hiatus once thought to separate Moche and Chimú cultures is no longer viable. It has also indicated that Huari influence on the North Coast is not as great as had been previously thought, if the Moche Valley is used as an indicator. Future work may elicit a different model for the North Coast, one which differs from the Central and South coasts during the Middle Horizon.

14

Storage and Labor Service:
A Production and Management Design
for the Andean Area

KENT C. DAY

Heritage Museum
Layton, Utah

One of the goals of the Chan Chan–Moche Valley Project and recent archaeological investigations in the Lambayeque Valley was to reconstruct the socioeconomic organization of the prehistoric inhabitants of these two valleys on the North Coast of Peru. In one case Chan Chan was the focal point for the study of the Chimú culture and in the other Pampa Grande, a large, complex Moche V site, served as the center of research. In addition, both programs were concerned with the comparison of socioeconomic models with available information on the Chimú and Inca, largely drawn from ethnohistoric sources.

The purpose of this chapter is to suggest that certain architectural structures and construction techniques at Pampa Grande and Chan Chan provide the archaeological evidence for storage facilities and labor service similar to those employed by the Inca. These two aspects of ancient Peruvian organization are essential features of a sophisticated system of production ultimately based on land tenure, demography, and reciprocity (Murra 1956, 1961). Although only the antiquity of storage and labor service is dealt with here in detail, field and irrigation systems, settlement patterns, and objects that indicate reciprocal transactions are also used in a design or model (Figure 14.1) to illustrate the fundamental structure of ancient Peruvian society. The emphasis upon structural continuity as exemplified by storage and labor service is made to demonstrate the antiquity of an adaptive system characteristic of the Andean area.

For years it has been recognized that the Inca were latecomers in Peruvian prehistory. It was also suspected that the Inca achievement must have had more ancient precedents than is immediately apparent from their sudden appearance in the archaeological record. Means (1925:411) mentions that Inca government as known at the Spanish Conquest was probably based on earlier models, but he does not specify who the precursors were. More recently Murra (1956:153), Morris (1972:400), Pease (1972:15), and Wachtel (1973:73), among others, suggest that sophisticated economic and state organizations existed in the Andean region long before the Inca. Both Rowe (1946:260;1948:45) and Rostworowski (1961:133) specify that coastal kingdoms, particularly the Chimú, probably had a profound effect upon the organization of Inca society and state. This point of view is also inherent in Bennett's (1948:6) concept of a Peruvian "Co-Tradition" in the highlands and on the coast of Peru based on the traits of corvée labor, marked class distinctions, massive construction efforts, population concentrations, and centralized political power. In addition, Menzel's (1959:140) suggestion that the Inca took advantage of existing centralized or ethnic governments when they established control over the South Coast is relevant. In this instance, the Inca adoption of coastal practices not only indicates the influence of coastal socioeconomic organization upon the Inca but—because the assimilation was very rapid—also indicates that both societies probably shared certain common structural features. Rowe (1946, 1948) also points out that the Inca may have adopted a rigid social hierarchy and probably an elaborate bureaucracy from the Chimú following the Inca conquest of the North Coast. Despite Rowe's stimulating suggestions, examination of the impact of the Chimú upon the Inca has languished until recently. Because of the need to establish a viable chronological framework for the Peruvian highlands and coast, more attention has been paid to the seriation of ceramics and compilation of trait lists than to any specific study of Chimú-Inca relationships. Furthermore, the dramatic physical and ecological differences between the coast and the highlands tend to reinforce apparent cultural differences between the two areas.

Although differences certainly exist between coastal and highland archaeological traits and environmental conditions, the structural continuity proposed here between the Chimú and Inca is an example of successful cultural adaption to a variety of conditions. If it were otherwise and the environmental conditions dictated the course of cultural development, the Inca could never have adopted anything from the Chimú and probably could not have extended their territorial holdings over as large and diverse an area as they did.

The antiquity of a common structural pattern is traced back to the Moche V occupation of Pampa Grande in the Lambayeque Valley. At one time the Early Intermediate Period was spoken of as Early Chimú and the Late Intermediate Period as Late Chimú (Kutscher 1950), an indication that cultural continuities between the two periods were strong. Even Rowe (1948:35) states that the Moche style was directly ancestral to the Chimú styles. The conventional view (Willey 1953; Rowe 1963; Schaedel 1966a, 1972; Lumbreras 1969, 1975; Morris 1972), though, holds that there was an intervention of highland peoples or "influence" upon the coast between the Early Intermediate Period and the Late Intermediate Period and that the transformed Chimú picked up the pieces and created a new, different culture that melded highland and coastal traits. Most of the critical traits (urban planning, rectangular enclosures, differential activity areas) said to have been introduced to the North Coast from the southern highlands during the Middle Horizon (Schaedel 1966a) exist in abundance at Pampa Grande and are associated with Moche V ceramics. As Mackey points out in Chapter 13, there are precedents on the North Coast for practically all the traits thought to have been introduced to the coast by highland invaders. Apparently the same suite of traits was shared by coastal and highland societies, and they might be interpreted as examples of shared behavior patterns or a common social structure.

Continuity between the Moche and Chimú is implicit in Larco Hoyle's (1938–39) study of Mochica iconography. Most features of Moche government, laws, and class structure (Larco Hoyle 1938–39; Bennett 1945) are nearly identical to those described by Rowe (1948) in his summary of Chimú ethnohistory. Although this coincidence might be fortuitous, it is reinforced circumstantially by architectural similarities at Chan Chan and Pampa Grande. These similarities, which are seen in storage facilities, controlled access patterns, U-shaped structures, rectangular enclosures, and differentiated activity

335

areas, along with adobe manufacture and construction of walls in sections, exist at both sites. In the following discussion the similarity and variation of these features are used to demonstrate the importance of storage and labor service on the coast long before they were applied by the Inca. In order to understand how storage and labor service were probably integrated into ancient Peruvian structure, the Inca are used as the first case in point.

INCA

It was shortly after the conquest of the Kingdom of Chimor that Inca Pachacuti organized a massive building program at Cuzco and imposed a sophisticated administrative system throughout his realm. When the Spaniards arrived in Peru, they found the Inca lords had the status and obligations of God kings. They attained their exalted position through heredity and acknowledged military prowess, maintaining their position as long as they met reciprocal obligations, furnished logistical support for the army, kept people employed, retained loyal agents to manage production, and avoided disasters that would alter production or adversely effect human population (Rowe 1946).

Storage was one of the major aspects of Inca socioeconomic organization. In his review of Inca storage, Morris (1967) mentions that storehouses were probably very numerous in and around imperial Cuzco and that Sacsahuaman and Coricancha were likely to have been used, in part, for storage. When the Spaniards first saw Cajamarca and Cuzco, they remarked on the number of storerooms and the vast quantities of goods, particularly textiles, that filled the storehouses in both cities. Nowadays it is difficult to find evidence of storage in or near either Cuzco or Cajamarca. Even so, these centrally located storage facilities are assumed to have held goods for the exclusive use of the Inca himself or for the military, priesthood, and nobility. Since the Inca was considered a direct descendant of the sun deity, was responsible for major military campaigns, and headed the noble class (Rowe 1946), he probably had access to all imperial stores. State or imperial goods were probably stored temporarily at rural centers while in transit to Cuzco or to supply points for the support of state projects (Morris 1967:25). Comestibles were usually stored in provincial centers, but fine goods, primarily cloth, were always sent to Cuzco (Cobo 1956 [1567]:258–59).

Storage and Labor Service

Late Horizon storehouses were built of adobe or stone (Rowe 1946; Morris 1967). Storehouses were square, rectangular, or circular in plan and were usually built in rows. The quadrangular storerooms that were built in rows had a common gable roof and were characterized by a single entrance that Morris (1967) describes as a low window or high door. Rows of storerooms were frequently isolated on steep hillsides not easily accessible to the general populace.

Inca building projects were accomplished through a labor service system administered by the state. Labor service was an obligation of able-bodied citizens and was calculated on the basis of age, sex, and census tallies. Tasks were probably reckoned on a job or man/day basis and varied according the kind of labor required and the capabilities of the workmen (Baudin 1961:66). Apparently task units were not permanently recorded in segments of walls or sections of platforms as had been done earlier on the coast. Presumably task units were accounted for on quipu by Inca administrators, a practice unknown on the coast among the Chimú and Mochica.

Labor service was an obligation for the Inca populace—probably to reciprocate for the ceremonial activities, divine intervention, and military protection provided by the state religion and nobility. The common citizen was supplied with food while working and, when married, given a plot of land in usufruct. The state was obliged, in a broad sense, to provide work so that the commoners could meet their labor obligations and hence maintain production. If population was increasing, the Inca leadership would be under pressure to provide jobs and land to young adults. In this case the economy operated on the principle of reciprocal obligations between the Inca hierarchy and the common people to the extent that both parties were required either to furnish the opportunities for the production of goods and services or to provide the labor necessary for such production.

Land tenure among the Inca consisted of royal and state fields, the produce from which supplied the nobility, priesthood, and military, as well as plots held by family or community groups. There was probably constant pressure on the limited supply of arable land because of population increase, the aforementioned reciprocal obligations, and the necessity to keep royal and state storehouses stocked with goods. Arable land could be increased through the construction of terraces on hillsides, extension of irrigation systems where necessary, and expansion or appropriation of other territory. In other words, the nobility and military had to extend the amount of arable land in order to satisfy the

Inca obligation to provide plots for farmers in return for their labor on state projects. Similarly, goods stored for the support of expansionist military expeditions and for the nobility would provide opportunities for labor service employment as the stocks were used. Whether the population increased or not, the massive ceremonial burning of cloth (Murra 1975:153–54), the use of supplies in festivals, and the exchange of cloth and other luxury items between nobles as acts of hospitality would also result in the need for labor service in order to restock the goods thus consumed. If this reciprocal cycle of intense production and consumption had ancient roots in Peru, there should be archaeological evidence for it. Since there is little forthcoming from the highlands as yet, it is necessary to turn to the coast for evidence.

CHIMÚ

Storage facilities at Chan Chan are the most numerous type of adobe structure at that great Chimú site. Most of the storerooms were located within or adjacent to ciudadelas, the large rectangular enclosures which are the most notable architectural feature at the site (see Day, Chapter 3). The monotonous rows of these structures resemble, in a way, nineteenth-century English and American working-class row houses, and this may be the reason why they have frequently been identified as dwellings. However, nothing was found in the courts or in the storerooms themselves to indicate that any sort of domestic activity took place there. Certainly the high thresholds would deter easy access to the interior of the structures and hardly be a convenient entrance to a house.

Identification of the contiguous rows of gabled structures as storerooms depends, for the time being, upon their similarity to Inca storerooms. Since there was nothing found on the floors of most of the excavated storerooms in Ciudadela Rivero, there is no proof of what the rooms contained. Quantities of mouse bones were found in a few storerooms but, because it is unlikely that the Chimú stored mice, their presence is not readily explained. In any event, it is certain that the contents of the rooms were systematically removed, suggesting that the stored goods were valuable.

The high walls of ciudadelas, tortuous corridors, and relative isolation of the storerooms also bear witness to the value placed on the stored goods. This aspect of architectural planning also illustrates the Chimú preoccupation with theft noted by Rowe (1948:49). Control over access to stored materials in ciudadelas was probably exercised by the occupants of audiencias or other U-shaped structures. Both inside and outside ciudadelas there were varieties of U-shaped structures (Andrews 1974) usually associated with storage facilities or located in strategically placed courts along corridors between major entrances and storehouses. In Ciudadela Rivero small rooms were built beside or behind audiencias, and pole-supported mat sunshades lined some walls of the courts in which the audiencias stood. On occasion shallow depressions have been found in these court floors where pots or large urns may have rested. In audiencia courts of Ciudadela Tschudi were found fire-reddened, stone-lined pits that were probably subfloor ovens. It is possible that the shallow depressions were jar stands for containers of corn beer (Francisco Iriarte, personal communication) and the subfloor ovens were pachamanca-like baking pits. The small rooms adjacent to audiencias and the sunshades indicate the audiencia courts had permanent occupants. The possible pot/urn rests and the baking pits could be construed as evidence for corn beer drinking and feasting, two of the most common expressions of Andean hospitality and reciprocity (Alberti and Mayer 1974).

In addition to the massive centralized storage at Chan Chan, there were outlying structures in the Moche Valley that were probably temporary warehousing or storage facilities under the administration of Chan Chan authorities (Keatinge 1974; Keatinge and Day 1974).

Labor service among the Chimú is not as self-evident as storage. Apparently the Chimú kept no quipu records, and there is no ethnohistoric evidence for census taking, land distribution, or other activities related to labor service. Nevertheless, millions of adobes, tons of stone, countless canes and reeds, and lakes of mortar and mud plaster were used in the construction of their capital, Chan Chan. The labor expenditure to build the city was enormous. Great walls that surround ciudadelas were uniformly about five meters wide at the base and nine meters high. Vertical and horizontal joints are visible in these walls where the mud plaster has eroded from the face. Vertical joints occur at more or less regular four- to five-meter intervals along the course of the great walls. Horizontal joints occur about the same distance above the ground and above each other in the walls. Large canes were incorporated into the walls at about the same intervals as the vertical joints.

Since adobe walls can be built without pauses for drying of the mortar, the joints did not result from necessary drying periods. Perhaps the joints were engineered so that the walls would withstand changes in temperature, or earthquakes. Although the walls expand and contract from day to night, such expansion was probably absorbed by the spaces between adobes that were not filled with mortar. When a very strong earthquake occurred in the Moche Valley in 1970, I observed that thin modern adobe walls collapsed whether or not they had joints. Meanwhile, the great thick walls of Chan Chan withstood the severe earthquake without damage. Apparently the thickness—not the joints—gives stability to the walls at Chan Chan during earthquakes.

It is also notable that adobes were never bonded in the walls at Chan Chan except where it appears to have happened by accident. There are instances where the surface of a wall has fallen away and revealed the interior or sections between joints. In some of these cases the exposed adobes are a haphazard, partially mortared jumble, evidence that the interior of certain wall sections was filled without any attention to how the job was done. Obviously, it was more important to the masons to fill the space of the sections than to concern themselves with the quality of the finished work. After all, the wall was plastered, and sloppy workmanship was hidden from sight. The jumbled interior of some of the sections shows, too, that the sections were built like caissons; that is, the perimeter walls of sections were fairly stable and were used to retain the carelessly placed interior adobes.

Neither the joints, the canes, nor the poor craftsmanship can be explained by material or structural requirements; therefore the wall sections must be accounted for in some other way. A viable explanation for the joints and sections is that they represent task units—hence, labor service—of the builders. Smaller walls of structures within ciudadelas usually do not have joints or sections, but the volume of these walls is a great deal less than the volume of the large surrounding walls. Perhaps entire small walls represent task units, equivalent to a section or sections of the larger walls.

The canes embedded in the walls are probably markers to guide the builders as the large walls were being constructed. Canes and reeds used in the construction of roofs are too fragmentary to use as evidence of task units. However, the roofs were an elaborate combination of carefully bound cane and reed crossmembers that represent considerable labor investment in their manufacture.

Only part of the Chimú land tenure system can be reconstructed at present, and that tentatively. There are remains of large, formally arranged fields on the desert north of Chan Chan. Because many of these fields were laid out along lines compatible with the plan of Chan Chan and there were few Chimú residential settlements among them, it is likely that these fields were on lands of the Chimú nobility. In a detailed study of these fields T. Topic (1971:109) points out that the Chimú state had access to a large labor pool and probably had direct control over the planning and use of a large area of arable land. This view is also upheld by Moseley and Deeds' (Chapter 2) study of the irrigation system in the Moche Valley that made this part of the valley agriculturally productive for the Chimú state. Presumed small plots that were utilized by families or communities have yet to be located, but it is possible they existed in the heavily cultivated valley floor east of Chan Chan.

PAMPA GRANDE

There is evidence for storage and task unit labor service at Pampa Grande similar to that found at Chan Chan. Pampa Grande is characterized by large rectangular and irregular enclosures, at least 18 huacas, an extensive system of intrasite corridors, and four or five "residential" areas that probably housed a permanent or transient population. There are also U-shaped structures at the site. With the exception of one or two of the "residential" areas near the western edge of the site, all these structures plus those mentioned below are associated with Moche V ceramics. The only other ceramics that were found in quantity at the site were Chimú, and these were excavated beyond the area under discussion here.

At Pampa Grande there were nine groups of contiguous rectangular structures, all built of adobe. Six of these groups were located within the confines of two large rectangular enclosures that surrounded the two major huacas at the site. One group of these structures was built on a terraced platform located in a small canyon about 700 meters from the larger of the two huaca enclosures. In this case the rectangular structures were adjacent to a small huaca but separated from it by a gully. Three groups of contiguous adobe structures were located in areas of less formal, probably "residential," buildings that were not enclosed. Most of the "residential" buildings were of stone or a combination of stone and adobe. Excavations were conducted in all of the groups of contiguous rectangular structures save one. All of the excavated chambers in huaca enclosures as well as those on the terraced platform were empty. Two of the three outlying groups of contiguous structures were partially excavated. The seven structures— three in one group and four in the other—were all burned, and there were large quantities of charred beans and corn kernels on the floors. None of the other 79 empty structures had been burned. The empty unburned chambers ranged from 3 to 4 meters wide and 3.75 to 7 meters long; the burned chambers that contained the corn and beans were 2 meters wide and 2.5 meters long in the group of three and 2 meters wide and 7 meters long in the group of four.

None of the chambers had floor-level entrances. However, one end wall of each heavily eroded chamber had a lower central section that was undoubtedly the remains of a high-threshold entrance like those in Inca and Chimú storerooms. Pieces of fallen roofing material (cane-impressed clay) were found in several chambers at Pampa Grande, but all the walls have been eroded to the point that they are too low to suggest whether or not the chambers had flat or gabled roofs. The charred comestibles in the outlying groups of chambers at Pampa Grande are convincing evidence, though, that the chambers were used for storage. The empty chambers probably also were storerooms because, except for their dimensions, their architectural attributes are nearly the same as the small storerooms and storage facilities at Inca and Chimú sites. Furthermore, the empty chambers at Pampa Grande were not associated with any remains which could indicate that they served another function. Had these empty chambers contained comestibles, it is likely that a few grains would have been preserved by chance or casts of their presence left in the fill. No such evidence exists, and it is possible, therefore, that these chambers were used to store some other kind of material. Perhaps the stored goods were bundled or packaged in such a way that they were removed without having left scattered bits or impressions on the floors and walls. Bales of textiles, cotton, or wool are the most reasonable candidates for the materials once kept in the empty storerooms at Pampa Grande.

There are 11 U-shaped structures at Pampa Grande. Very little remains other than the outlines of side walls and the thick, terraced

342

back walls of these structures. The largest of these U-shaped structures, about eight meters long and five meters wide, was constructed on the summit of the second largest huaca at the site. The other U-shaped structures occurred singly or in groups of two or three within irregular enclosures inside courts. These U-shaped structures ranged from about two by three meters to four by four and one-half meters. Except for the large U-shaped structures on the summit of the huaca and one other U-shaped structure that has yet to be examined in detail, these structures were located adjacent to a major corridor system that ran through one of the "residential" areas. All of these U-shaped structures lay outside the two major huaca enclosures at the site and were some distance away from any of the known storerooms.

Although the storerooms at Pampa Grande are similar to those at Chan Chan, the relationship between the U-shaped structures and storage facilities is different. However, the U-shaped structures at Pampa Grande all appear to be strategically located along corridor systems that probably gave access to the large enclosures where most of the storerooms were located.

Labor service at Pampa Grande is inferred from the presence of sections of the thick adobe walls that surround some of the rectangular enclosures at the site. One such wall, about 35 meters long and 4 meters thick, was examined in detail. This wall was divided into sections 3 to 4 meters long along its entire length. These sections closely butted one another but no adobes were bonded across any of the section boundaries. All of the adobes were tabular, and some had maker's marks gouged or pressed into one flat face. Sometimes a single maker's mark would predominate among the adobes used in a section; otherwise, maker's marks were mixed with one another and with unmarked adobes in a section. In other walls there were cane-marked adobes or adobes that varied somewhat in size and shape. All the thick adobe walls, whether or not they consisted of marked adobes, appear to have been built in sections. Thinner adobe walls, though, did not have regular divisions or sections.

Labor service task units may explain the wall sections at Pampa Grande for the same reasons applied to the wall sections at Chan Chan. Some of the huacas at Pampa Grande exhibited vertical wall joints like those at Chan Chan and Huaca del Sol. In addition, "retain and fill" adobe caissons were employed at Pampa Grande to construct

343

parts of the two largest huacas at the site. This construction technique also probably represented task units. The labor expenditure for the construction of adobe structures at Pampa Grande was on a massive scale (for instance, the largest huaca at the site nearly matches the estimated original volume of Huaca del Sol) and entailed the manufacture and transport of adobes to the site.

Evidence for the establishment of a land tenure system in the Lambayeque Valley contemporary with Pampa Grande is tenuous at best. The site is located at the edge of modern fields which are among the most extensive on the coast of Peru. Although there are many archaeological sites in the Lambayeque Valley, Moche V ceramics are uncommon save at Pampa Grande. Furthermore, despite the fact that there are traces of ancient fields along the edge of the valley, none of the ancient fields have been dated. Given the fact that adobes used at Pampa Grande had to be made elsewhere in the valley (the site is located on a rocky pediment) and that construction of the site demanded a great deal of labor, it is paradoxical that few Moche V sites have been found in the valley as yet. Nonetheless, there are two pieces of circumstantial evidence that can be used to suggest that the occupants of Pampa Grande had dominion over most of the Lambayeque Valley. Immediately across the valley from the site, the major water-diversion system for irrigation of the valley begins. The three major canals that still distribute water over the valley floor were in operation when the Spaniards arrived and were probably built many years before that event. The location of Pampa Grande adjacent to the point of origin of the irrigation system might indicate that the system was constructed when the site was occupied. If this were so, the entire lower valley would be dependent upon Pampa Grande for the distribution of irrigation water.

Recently a late sixteenth-century document (Susan Ramirez-Horton, personal communication) was discovered. It was written by a Spaniard who saw the Lambayeque Valley before it was converted into encomiendas and haciendas. He reported the valley was one vast cotton plantation. Even though this observation was made several hundred years after the abandonment of Pampa Grande, perhaps the valley had been planted to cotton during the Early Intermediate Period and maintained in that crop until the Spanish Conquest. If either the irrigation system or the vast cotton fields existed while Pampa Grande was occupied, it is possible to suggest economic control of the valley by an elite who resided at the site.

SUMMARY AND INTERPRETATION

Although land tenure patterns for the periods immediately preceding Inca dominance of the central Andean area are unclear, other elements of Inca socioeconomic organization occur at Chan Chan and at Pampa Grande. A rigid social hierarchy with profound class distinctions, for instance, is evident in the contrast between the crowded SIAR "residential" areas (small irregularly agglutinated rooms discussed by J. Topic, Chapter 7) and the spacious monumental enclosures at Chan Chan and Pampa Grande. Class distinctions at these sites are also symbolized by the practically insurmountable walls of enclosures, the limited number of entrances to enclosures, and, in the case of ciudadelas, complex corridor systems that appear to have determined the pattern of pedestrian traffic.

Storage also reflects socioeconomic distinctions between an ancient noble elite and commoners. Formal storage facilities nearly identical to Inca storerooms occurred in large numbers in the ciudadelas at Chan Chan. Although fewer in number, similar storage facilities also existed at Pampa Grande in the familiar context of the walled enclosures. It should be added that realistic miniature models of gable-roofed high-threshold storerooms were produced by Chimú potters. The same kind of architectural vessels were also produced in the Moche Period before the occupation of Pampa Grande or Chan Chan. These vessels show that formal storage facilities were current at Early Intermediate Period sites despite the lack of direct evidence for the existence of storage in pre-Moche V deposits at the site of Moche (T. Topic, Chapter 11). Be that as it may, formal storage at Chan Chan and Pampa Grande were associated with elite architecture and were clear precedents in the archaeological record for imperial Inca storage facilities.

Storage also implies labor in the sense that labor was necessary to produce the goods that once filled the storerooms. Inca labor by commoners was organized on an obligatory task basis as labor tax service, or mit'a, to the nobility. Labor service units that can be construed as precedents for mit'a occur archaeologically at Chan Chan as construction units in greats walls and at Pampa Grande as maker's marks on adobes and wall construction units.

Further evidence for labor service of a nonarchitectural nature is probably contained in the layout, volume, and location of storage within individual storage courts at Chan Chan and in the grouped storage units at Pampa Grande. If the stored material were known in these cases, it would be possible to suggest that variations in the number of storerooms in storage courts reflect the volume of products and, by extension, are accounts of the labor service necessary for the production of the stored goods.

Even though specific data on kinds and amounts of stored goods are lacking at Chan Chan and, except for the charred beans and corn in small storerooms, at Pampa Grande, the patterned interrelationship of U-shaped structures, corridors, and storage facilities at both sites are evidence for a socioeconomic system based on the control of production and storage of goods by an administrative bureaucracy. Just as the Inca had managers called koraka (Murra 1962:714) who oversaw production, so the nobility at Chan Chan and Pampa Grande had strategically placed managers in audiencias and other U-shaped structures. It is notable that the U-shaped structures at Pampa Grande were not as intimately placed in relationship to storerooms as the audiencias in ciudadelas at Chan Chan. Nevertheless, some of the U-shaped structures at Pampa Grande were located adjacent to enclosures where storerooms occur. The location of U-shaped structures apparently changed through time. The variation in context of these structures, then, is probably a marker in the trend toward secularization on the Peruvian coast noted by Schaedel (1966a) and Keatinge (1977). This secularization apparently consisted of the integration of an increasingly powerful bureaucracy into ancient Peruvian society.

Imperial Inca, Chimú, and Moche V storerooms would have burst had accumulation been the only purpose of bureaucratic management of labor and production. The common people were obligated to provide labor, services, and goods for the nobility. In order to maintain such production/labor obligation on a continuous basis the nobility had to consume or dispose of goods on an equivalent, sometimes grand scale. Elaborate burials in royal tombs provided singular events for the permanent disposal of products. Scheduled celebrations to honor the noble dead and the practice of split inheritance (Conrad, Chapter 5) provided other, more reliable opportunities for consumption of labor and manufactured materials. Since the nobility were no doubt unwilling to die solely for the sake of inventory turnover, other means of consumption were probably in use as standard practices by the nobility. Personal adornment, acts of hospitality to fellow nobles, support of

346

a military force, frequent fiestas, marriage contracts, and travel are possible ways used by the nobility to consume goods systematically. Perhaps, too, the huge burned area in the center of Chan Chan is the remains of ceremonial burning of products similar to the Inca sacrificial burning of textiles that was necessary to deplete stored stock.

Figure 14.1 illustrates the socioeconomic relationships in a stratified society in which one segment of the population is obligated to provide labor while a higher ranked class is obligated to provide opportunities for labor. The design is substantivist in that it relies heavily upon archaeological and ethnohistoric data from Chan Chan and the Inca as well as archaeological data from Pampa Grande. Furthermore, the principle governing the economy of these societies was the reciprocity inherent in the mutual obligations mentioned above. The disparity in status between the two classes of society was overcome by a bureaucracy that managed the reciprocal transactions that were necessary for the system to operate.

Just as the society was not egalitarian, so the reciprocal transactions between social classes were organized neither on an egalitarian basis nor for egalitarian purposes. Here, reciprocity was a matter of balancing obligations between classes, and the resultant benefit was stability and continuity. Essentially, then, production was balanced by consumption, and the balance was maintained through an elaborate bureaucracy.

Centralized control was essential to the system of managed reciprocal production and consumption in the Andean area because it afforded a locality where labor was expended in public construction, goods were stored under controlled conditions, some sort of account was made of labor expenditures, and an opportunity was provided for consumption of goods on a massive scale.

The relationships expressed in Figure 14.1 are considered linear in that they apply to the Inca, the Chimú, and at least the latter part of the Moche or Early Intermediate Period. However, this linear or traditional set of relationships is not intended to be a static system. For instance, the emphasis upon one or another part of the system could alter according to population, amount of land under cultivation, or climatic fluctuation.

The scheme of relationships proposed here was based on traditional reciprocity and was probably an adaptive response to the topographic and ecological conditions of the Andean area. Most of the Andean

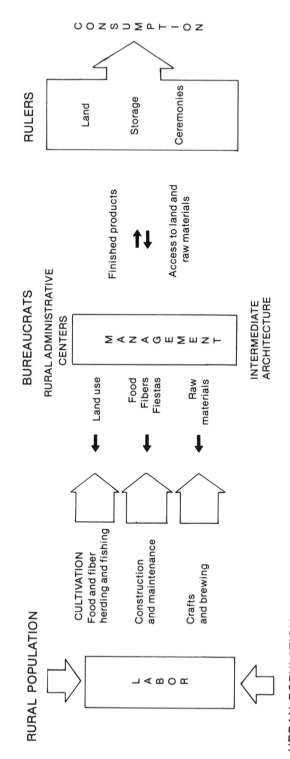

FIGURE 14.1. Design of Andean socioeconomic organization from the Early Intermediate period through the Late Horizon.

area has a benign climate and a high potential for agricultural production. The agrarian potential was tapped through the organized application of human labor to construct irrigation projects on the coast and to build terraces in the highlands. In both cases the result was increased production and population growth. Surpluses from increased production, though, were not distributed equitably but stored and consumed by those responsible for allocating organized labor assignments. In addition, as population increased, more land was necessary for distribution among commoners or for retention by the elite, who needed it not only for their own use but also to supply the opportunities for labor service to be performed.

Technological advances that would alter the capacity to work were not encouraged nor probably even envisioned under such a reciprocal system because labor-saving methods or devices would probably cause some form of unemployment or dislocation in labor/consumer obligations. In short, the alternative to technology in the Andean area was bureaucracy, a means of managing reciprocal relationships and a method of employing people and maintaining the status quo.

Centralized control and bureaucratic management of production and consumption appear in the archaeological record of the North Coast of Peru at least as early as the latter part of the Early Intermediate Period. It is likely too, that, under a somewhat different guise, these elements of statecraft have even more ancient roots on the North Coast (T. Pozorski, Chapter 10; Moseley 1975c) and were not suddenly transplanted from elsewhere. Rather, the North Coast peoples were probably one of many participating groups in a broad series of shared, pan-Andean experiments and adjustments that culminated with the Inca.

349

GLOSSARY

This short glossary contains some words that are commonly used in Peru for geographic and archaeological features, an indigenous Peruvian plant, and an animal. Other words are adaptations of Spanish or Quechua words for archaeological features.

Adobe: Sun-dried earthen brick

Ají: Chili peppers

Arcón: A **U**-shaped structure with interior bins in the walls

Audiencia: A **U**-shaped structure with six interior wall niches

Batán: A large boulder with one flat, smooth face. Used as a nether stone with a chungo

Brick: Sun-dried, unfired bricks; synonymous with adobe

Canchón: The southernmost interior section of a ciudadela; an enclosed area without standing architecture

Cercadura: A subdivided enclosure at the site of Galindo

Chungo: A stone with a convex surface used with two hands in a rocking motion to crush material against a batán

Ciudadela: A monumental, formal, rectangular enclosure at Chan Chan

Cuy: Guinea pig

Cuyero: Guinea pig pen

Florero: A ceramic vaselike vessel with a widely flaring rim

Hauquero: A person who loots archaeological sites

Huaca: An ancient elevated platform or flat-topped pyramid

Kero: A ceramic or wooden beaker

Loma: Hillock, or slope

Mitama: Forced movement of an entire population (village) from one area to another. Inca term

North Coast: The section of the Peruvian coast between the Santa Valley on the south and the Lambayeque Valley on the north

Quebrada: A ravine, dry wash, gully

Sierra: The Andean highlands of Peru and Bolivia

Tablado: A raised, daislike platform approached by a ramp

Tapia: Terre pisé, or rammed earth, usually with a high gravel content

Trocadero: A U-shaped structure with interior troughs

Wachaque: Sunken garden, also called "mahamaes"

References

ADAMS, RICHARD N.
1975   *Energy and Structure* (Austin: University of Texas Press).
ALBERTI, GIORGIO, AND ENRIQUE MAYER
1974   "Reciprocidad Andina: Ayer y Hoy," in *Reciprocidad e Intercambio en los Andes Peruanos*, ed. Giorgio Alberti and Enrique Mayer (Lima: Instituto de Estudios Peruanos).
ANDERSON, ROBERT T.
1971   "Voluntary Associations in History," *American Anthropoligist* 73:209–22.
1976   "Voluntary Associations and Power in Pre-industrial States," *American Anthropologist* 78:93–94.
ANDREWS, ANTHONY P.
1972   "A Preliminary Study of U-shaped Structures at Chan Chan and Vicinity, Peru" (B.A. thesis, Harvard University).
1974   "The U-shaped Structures at Chan Chan, Peru," *Journal of Field Archaeology* 1:241–64.
BANDELIER, ADOLPH F.
1904   "On the Relative Antiquity of Ancient Peruvian Burials," *Bulletin of the American Museum of Natural History* 20:217–26.
BAUDIN, LOUIS
1961   *A Socialist Empire: The Incas of Peru* (Princeton: D. Van Nostrand Co.).
BENNETT, WENDELL C.
1939   "Archaeology of the North Coast of Peru: An Account of the Explorations in the Viru and Lambayeque Valleys," in *Anthropological Papers of the American Museum of Natural History*, vol. 37, part 1 (New York).
1945   "Interpretations of Andean Archaeology," *Transactions of the New York Academy of Sciences* 7:95–99.
1948   "The Peruvian Co-Tradition," in *A Reappraisal of Peruvian Archaeology*, ed. Wendell C. Bennett, Memoirs of the Society for American Archaeology, no. 4.
1950   *The Gallinazo Group*, Yale University Publications in Anthropology, no. 43.
BENNETT, WENDELL C., AND JUNIUS B. BIRD
1960   *Andean Culture History*, 2d. ed. rev. (New York: American Museum of Natural History Handbook Series).
BENSON, ELIZABETH P.
1972   *The Mochica* (London: Thames and Hudson).

BENZONI, M. JERONIMO
1967   *La Historia del Mundo Nuevo*, originally published (1565) as *La Historia del Mundo Nuovo*, trans. Carlos Radicate di Primeglio (Lima: Universidad de San Marcos).
BIRD, JUNIUS B.
1948   "Preceramic Cultures in Chicama and Viru," in *A Reappraisal of Peruvian Archaeology*, ed. Wendell C. Bennett, Memoirs of the Society for American Archaeology, no. 4.
BONAVIA, DUCCIO
1961   "A Mochica Painting at Pañamarca, Peru," *American Antiquity* 27:515–19.
BRENNAN, CURTISS T.
1977   "Investigations at Cerro Arena, 1974–75: The Salinar Occupation of the Moche Valley, Peru," paper presented at the Seventeenth Annual Meeting of the Institute of Andean Studies, Berkeley.
BRUNDAGE, BURR CARTWRIGHT
1963   *Empire of the Inca* (Norman: University of Oklahoma Press).
CABELLO VALBOA, MIGUEL
1951   *Miscelánea Antártica y Origen de los Indios y de los Incas del Perú* [1586] (Lima: Instituto de Etnología, Universidad Nacional Mayor de San Marcos).
CALANCHA, (FATHER) ANTONIO DE LA
1638   Crónica moralizada del orden de San Agustín en el Perú, con sucesos egenplares en esta monarquis (Barcelona: Pedro Lacavalleria).
CARDOZO GONZÁLES, ARMANDO
1954   *Los Auquénidos* (La Paz: Editorial Centenario).
CHILDE, V. GORDON
1951   *Man Makes Himself* (London: C. A. Watts and Co.).
CIEZA DE LEÓN, PEDRO DE
1943   *Del Señorío de los Incas* [1553] (Buenos Aires: Ediciones Argentina "Solar").
1959   *The Incas of Pedro de Cieza de León* [1554], trans. Harriet de Onis, ed. Victor W. von Hagen (Norman: University of Oklahoma Press).
COBO, BERNABÉ
1956   "Historia de Nuevo Mundo" [1567], *Biblioteca de Autores Españoles*, vols. 91–92 (Madrid).
COLLIER, DONALD
1955   "Cultural Chronology and Change as Reflected in the Ceramics of the Virú Valley, Peru," *Fieldiana: Anthropology*, vol. 43 (Chicago: Field Museum of Natural History).
1962   "Archaeological Investigations in the Casma Valley, Peru," *Akten des 34 International Amerikanistenkongresses*, pp. 411–17 (Vienna).
CONRAD, GEOFFREY W.
1974   "Burial Platforms and Related Structures on the North Coast of Peru: Some Social and Political Implications" (Ph.D. diss., Harvard University).
1978   "Models of Compromise in Settlement Pattern Studies: An Example from Coastal Peru," *World Archaeology* 9:281–98.
COWGILL, GEORGE
1975   "A Selection of Samplers: Comments on Archaeo-statistics," in *Sampling in Archaeology*, ed. James W. Mueller (Tucson: University of Arizona Press).
DAY, KENT C.
1972   "Urban Planning at Chan Chan, Peru," in *Man, Settlement, and Urbanism*, ed. P. J. Ucko, R. Tringham, and G. W. Dimbleby (London: Gerald Duckworth and Co.).
1973   "Architecture of Ciudadela Rivero, Chan Chan, Peru" (Ph.D. diss., Harvard University).
1976   "Peru: The Land and Its People," in *Gold for the Gods*, a catalogue to an exhibition of pre-Inca and Inca gold and artifacts from Peru, ed. A. D. Tushingham (Toronto: Royal Ontario Museum).

References

DISSELHOFF, HANS D.
1956   *Gott Muss Peruaner Sein* (Wiesbaden: F. A. Brockhaus).
1958a   "Tumbas de San José de Moro (Provincia de Pacasmayo, Perú)," *Proceedings of the XXXII International Congress of Americanists* (Copenhagen: Munksgaard).
1958b   "Cajamarca-Keramik von der Pampa von San José de Moro (Prov. Pacasmayo)," *Baessler-Archiv, Neue Folge*, 6:181–93 (Berlin: Museum für Völkerkunde).

DONNAN, CHRISTOPHER B.
1965   "Moche Ceramic Technology," *Ñawpa Pacha* 3:115–33.
1972   "Moche-Huari Murals from Northern Peru," *Archaeology* 25:85–95.
1973   *The Moche Occupation of the Santa Valley, Peru*, University of California Publications in Anthropology, vol. 8.
1976   *Moche Art and Iconography*, UCLA Latin American Series, vol. 33.

DONNAN, CHRISTOPHER B., AND CAROL J. MACKEY
1978   *Ancient Burial Patterns of the Moche Valley, Peru* (Austin: University of Texas Press).

DONNAN, CHRISTOPHER B., AND DONNA MCCLELLAND
1979   *The Burial Theme in Moche Iconography*, Studies in Pre-Columbian Art and Archaeology, no. 21 (Washington, D.C.: Dumbarton Oaks).

DOWNING, T. E., AND M. GIBSON (EDS.)
1974   *Irrigation's Impact on Society*, Anthropological Papers of the University of Arizona, no. 25 (Tucson: University of Arizona Press).

DUMONT, LOUIS
1970   *Homo hierarchicus: An Essay on the Caste System*, trans. Mark Sainbury (Chicago: University of Chicago Press).

ENGEL, FREDERIC
1966   *Geografía Humana Prehistórica y Agricultura Precolombina de la Quebrada de Chilca*, vol. 1 (Lima: Oficina de Promoción y Desarrollo, Departamento de Publicaciones, Universidad Agraria).
1970   *Las Lomas de Iguanil y el Complejo de Haldas* (Lima: Universidad Nacional Agraria-La Molina).

ESTETE, MIGUEL DE
1872   "Report of Miguel de Astete on the Expedition to Pachacamac" [1533–1552], *Reports on the Discovery of Peru*, no. 42, ed. C. R. Markham (London: Hakluyt Society).

FANG, MADELINE W.
1975   "The Marine Theme of Chimú Friezes" (M.A. thesis, University of California, Los Angeles).

FARRINGTON, IAN
1974   "Irrigation and Settlement Pattern: Preliminary Research Results from the North Coast of Peru," in *Irrigation's Impact on Society*, ed. T. E. Downing and McG. Gibson, Anthropological Papers of the University of Arizona, no. 25 (Tucson: University of Arizona Press).

FELDMAN, ROBERT A.
1977   "Life in Ancient Peru," Field Musuem of Natural History *Bulletin* 48:6:12–17.

FORRESTER, JAY
1969   *Urban Dynamics* (Cambridge, Mass.: M.I.T. Press).

FUNG, ROSA
1969   "Las Aldas: Su Ubicación Dentro del Proceso Histórico de Perú Antiguo," *Dédalo* 5, no. 9–10 (São Paulo: Museu de Arte e Arqueologia Universidade de São Paulo, Brasil).

GARCIA ROSELL, CESAR
1942   *Los Monumentos Arquelógicos del Perú* (Lima: Sociedad Geográfica de Lima y el Instituto Sanmartiniano).

GARCILASO DE LA VEGA, "EL INCA"
1966   *Royal Commentaries of the Incas and General History of Peru*, pt. 1 [1609], trans. Harold V. Livermore (Austin: University of Texas Press).

GRIFFIS, SHELIA
1971   "Excavation and Analysis of Midden Material from Cerro la Virgen, Moche Valley, Peru" (B.A. thesis, Harvard University).

HASTINGS, CHARLES M., AND MICHAEL E. MOSELEY
1975   "The Adobes of Huaca del Sol and Huaca de la Luna," *American Antiquity* 40:196–203.

HOLSTEIN, OTTO
1927   "Chan Chan, Capital of the Great Chimu," *Geographic Review* 27:36–61.

HORKHEIMER, HANS
1965   "Identificación y Bibliografía de Importantes Sitios Prehispánicos del Perú," *Arqueológicas* 8 (Lima: Museo Nacional de Antropología y Arqueología).

HUTCHINSON, THOMAS J.
1873   *Two Years in Peru with Exploration of Its Antiquities* (London).

ISBELL, WILLIAM
1973   "Rise and Demise of Wari: A Case Study in the Cybernetics of Civilization," paper presented at the Thirty-Eighth Annual Meeting of the Society for American Archaeology, San Francisco.

ISHIDA, EIICHIRO, KOICHI AKI, TAIJI YAZAWA, SEIICHI IZUMI, HISASHI SATO, IWAO KOBORI, KAZUO TERADA, AND TARYO OBAYASHI
1960   *Andes 1: Report of the University of Tokyo Scientific Expedition to the Andes in 1958* (Tokyo: Kadokawa Publishing Co.).

JACOBSEN, THORKILD
1957   "Early Political Development in Mesopotamia," *Zeitschrift für Assyriologie und Vorderasiatüsche, Archäologie, Neue Folge* 18:91–140.

JEMENEZ DE LA ESPADA, MARCOS
1965   "Relaciónes Geográficas de Indias: Peru 1," Biblioteca de Autores Españoles, vol. 183 (Madrid).

KAUTZ, ROBERT R., AND RICHARD W. KEATINGE
1977   "Determining Site Function: A North Peruvian Coastal Example," *American Antiquity* 42:86–97.

KEATINGE, RICHARD W.
1973   "Chimu Ceramics from the Moche Valley, Peru: A Computer Application to Seriation" (Ph.D. diss., Harvard University).
1974   "Chimu Rural Administrative Centers in the Moche Valley, Peru," *World Archaeology* 6:66–82.
1975a   "From the Sacred to the Secular: First Report on a Prehistoric Architectural Transition on the North Coast of Peru," *Archaeology* 28:128–29.
1975b   "Urban Settlement Systems and Rural Sustaining Communities: An Example from Chan Chan's Hinterland," *Journal of Field Archaeology* 2:215–27.
1977   "Religious Forms and Secular Functions: The Expansion of State Bureaucracies as Reflected in Prehistoric Architecture on the Peruvian North Coast," *Annals of the New York Academy of Sciences* 293:229–45.
1978   "The Pacatnamu Textiles," *Archaeology* 31:30–41.

KEATINGE, RICHARD W., DAVID CHODOFF, DEBORAH PHILLIPS CHODOFF, MURRAY MARVIN, AND HELAINE SILVERMAN
1975   "From the Sacred to the Secular: First Report on a Prehistoric Architectural Transition on the Peruvian North Coast," *Archaeology* 28:128–29.

References

KEATINGE, RICHARD W., AND KENT C. DAY

1973   "Socio-economic Organization of the Moche Valley, Peru, During the Chimu Occu-
        pation of Chan Chan," *Journal of Anthropological Research* 29:275–95.

1974   "Chan Chan: A Study of Precolumbian Urbanism and the Management of Land and
        Water Resources in Peru," *Archaeology* 27:228–35.

KIRCHHOFF, PAUL

1949   "The Social and Political Organization of the Andean Peoples," in *Handbook of South
        American Indians*, Bureau of American Ethnology, ed. Julian Steward. *Bulletin* 143,
        vol. 5 (Washington, D.C.).

KLYMYSHYN, ALEXANDRA M. ULANA

1976   "Intermediate Architecture in Chan Chan, Peru" (Ph.D. diss., Harvard University).

KOLATA, ALAN LOUIS

1978   "Chan Chan: The Form of the City in Time" (Ph.D. diss., Harvard University).

KOSOK, PAUL

1940   "The Role of Irrigation in Ancient Peru," *Proceedings of the Eighth American Scientific
        Congress*, vol. 2, Anthropological Sciences (Washington, D.C.: U.S. Government
        Printing Office).

1958   "El Valle de Lambayeque," *Actas y Trabajos del 11 Congreso Nactional de Historia del
        Perú*, pp. 49–67 (Lima).

1965   *Life, Land and Water in Ancient Peru* (New York: Long Island University Press).

KROEBER, ALFRED L.

1925   "The Uhle Pottery Collections from Moche," *University of California Publications in
        American Archaeology and Ethnology*, vol. 21: pp. 191–234 (Berkeley).

1926   "Archaeological Explorations in Peru, Part I: Ancient Pottery from Trujillo," *Field
        Museum of Natural History Anthropology Memoirs*, vol. 2, no. 1, pp. 1–43.

1930   "Archaeological Explorations in Peru, Part II: The Northern Coast," *Field Museum of
        Natural History Anthropology Memoirs*, vol. 2, no. 2, pp. 45–116.

KUBLER, GEORGE

1948   "Towards Absolute Time: Guano Chronology," in *A Reappraisal of Peruvian Archae-
        ology*, ed. Wendell C. Bennett, Memoirs of the Society for American Archaeology, no.
        4, pp. 29–50.

1962   *The Art and Architecture of Ancient America* (Baltimore: Penguin).

KUS, JAMES S.

1972   "Selected Aspects of Irrigated Agriculture in the Chimu Heartland, Peru" (Ph.D. diss.,
        University of California, Los Angeles).

KUTSCHER, GERDT

1948   "Religion und Mythologie der Frühen Chimu (Nord Peru)," *Actes des 28 Congrès
        International des Américanistes*, pp. 621–31 (Paris).

1950   "Iconographic Studies as an Aid in the Reconstruction of Early Chimu Civilization,"
        Transactions of the New York Academy of Sciences, vol. 12, no. 6, pp. 194–203.

LANNING, EDWARD P.

1967   *Peru before the Incas* (Englewood Cliffs, N.J.: Prentice-Hall).

LARCO HOYLE, RAFAEL

1938

–39   *Los Mochicas*, 2 vols. (Lima: Casa Editora La Crónica y Variedades, S.A.).

1941   *Los Cupisniques* (Lima: Casa Editora La Crónica y Variedades, S.A.).

1942   "La Escritura Mochica sobre Pallares," *Revista Geográfica Americana* 18:93–103.

1944   *Cultura Salinar: Síntesis Monográfica* (Buenos Aires: Sociedad Geográfica Americana).

1945   *Los Mochicas* (Buenos Aires: Sociedad Geográfica Americana).

1946   "The Mochica Culture," in *Handbook of South American Indians*, Bureau of American
        Ethnology, ed. Julian Steward, *Bulletin* 143, vol. 2, pp. 161–75 (Washington, D.C.).

357

1948   *Cronología Arqueología del Norte del Perú* (Buenos Aires: Sociedad Geográfica Americana).

1965   *La Ceramica de Vicus* (Lima: Santiago Valverde).

LEACH, EDMUND R.

1960   "What Should We Mean by Caste?" in *Aspects of Caste in South India, Ceylon, and Northwest Pakistan,* ed. Edmund R. Leach (Cambridge: Cambridge University Press).

LECHTMAN, HEATHER

1976   "A Metallurgical Site Survey in the Peruvian Andes," *Journal of Field Archaeology* 3:1–42.

LUMBRERAS, LUIS G.

1969   *De los Pueblos, las Culturas y las Artes del Antiguo Perú* (Lima: Francisco Moncloa Editores).

1974   *The Peoples and Cultures of Ancient Peru* (Washington: Smithsonian Institution Press).

1975   *Las Fundaciones de Huamanca* (Lima: Editorial Nueva Educación).

MASON, J. ALDEN

1957   *The Ancient Civilizations of Peru* (Harmondsworth, Eng.: Penguin).

MCGRATH, JAMES E.

1973   "The Canchones of Chan Chan, Peru: Evidence for a Retainer Class in a Preindustrial Urban Center (B.A. thesis, Harvard University).

MEANS, PHILIP A.

1925   "A Study of Ancient Andean Social Institutions," *Transactions of the Connecticut Academy of Arts and Sciences* 27:407–69.

1931   *Ancient Civilizations of the Andes* (New York: Charles Scribner's Sons).

MEGGERS, BETTY J.

1972   *Prehistoric America* (Chicago: Aldine Publishing Company).

MENZEL, DOROTHY

1958   "Problemas en el Estudio del Horizonte Medio de la Arqueología Peruana," *Revista del Museo Regional de Ica* 9:24–57.

1959   "The Inca Occupation of the South Coast of Peru," *Southwest Journal of Anthropology* 15:125–42.

1964   "Style and Time in the Middle Horizon," *Ñawpa Pacha* 2:1–106.

MIDDENDORF, E. W.

1894   "Peru," vol. 2, *Das Kustenlan von Peru* (Berlin: Robert Oppenheim).

MORRIS, CRAIG

1967   "Storage in Tawantinsuyu" (Ph.D. diss., University of Chicago).

1972   "State Settlements in Tawantinsuyu: A Strategy of Compulsory Urbanism," in *Contemporary Archaeology,* ed. Mark P. Leone (Carbondale: Southern Illinois University Press).

1975   "Sampling in the Excavation of Urban Sites: The Case at Huanuco Pampa," in *Sampling in Archaeology,* ed. James W. Mueller (Tucson: University of Arizona Press).

MOSELEY, MICHAEL E.

1969a   "Assessing the Archaeological Significance of *Mahamaes,*" *American Antiquity* 35: 485–87.

1969b   *Prehistoric Urban-Rural Relationships on the North Peruvian Coast.* Mimeograph (Cambridge, Mass.: Peabody Museum, Harvard University).

1970   *Prehistoric Urban-Rural Relationships on the North Peruvian Coast.* Mimeograph (Cambridge, Mass.: Peabody Museum, Harvard University).

1973   *Freshman Seminar on Chan Chan.* Manuscript (Department of Anthropology, Harvard University).

References

1974   "Organizational Preadaptation to Irrigation: The Evolution of Early Water Manage-
         ment Systems in Coastal Peru," in *Irrigation's Impact on Society*, ed. T. E. Downing
         and McGuire Gibson, Anthropological Papers of the University of Arizona, no. 25
         (Tucson: University of Arizona Press).

1975a   "Chan Chan: Andean Alternative of the Preindustrial City?" *Science* 187:219–25.

1975b   *The Maritime Foundations of Andean Civilization* (Menlo Park, Calif.: Cummings
         Publishing Company).

1975c   "Prehistoric Principles of Labor Organization in the Moche Valley, Peru," *American
         Antiquity* 40:191–96.

1975d   "Secrets of Peru's Ancient Walls," *Natural History* 84:34–41.

MOSELEY, MICHAEL E., AND CAROL J. MACKEY

1972   "Peruvian Settlement Pattern Studies and Small Site Methodology," *American Antiq-
         uity* 37:67–81.

1973   "Prehistoric Urban-Rural Relationships on the North Peruvian Coast," research pro-
         posal submitted to the National Science Foundation.

1974   *Twenty-Four Architectural Plans of Chan Chan, Peru* (Cambridge, Mass.: Peabody
         Museum Press, Harvard University).

MOSELEY, MICHAEL E., AND LUIS WATANABE

1974   "The Adobe Sculpture of Huaca de los Reyes," *Archaeology* 27:154–61.

MOSELEY, MICHAEL E., AND GORDON R. WILLEY

1973   "Aspero, Peru: A Reexamination of the Site and Its Implications," *American Antiquity*
         38:452–68.

MUJICA BARREDA, ELIAS

1975   "Excavaciones arqueológicas en Cerro de Arena; un sitio del Formativo Superior en el
         Valle de Moche, Perú (B.A. thesis, Pontifica Universidad Católica del Perú).

MURRA, JOHN V.

1956   "The Economic Organization of the Inca State" (Ph.D. diss., University of Chicago).

1958   "On Inca Political Structure," in *Systems of Political Control and Bureaucracy in
         Human Societies*, ed. Vern Ray, Proceedings of the 1958 Annual Spring Meeting of the
         American Ethnological Society (Seattle: University of Washington Press).

1961   "Social Structural and Economic Themes in Andean Ethnohistory," *Anthropological
         Quarterly* 34:47–59.

1962   "Cloth and Its Function in the Inca State," *American Anthropologist* 64:710–28.

1975   *Formaciones Económicas y Políticas del Mundo Andino* (Lima: Instituto de Estudios
         Peruanos, Historia Andina 3).

MURRA, JOHN V., AND CRAIG MORRIS

1976   "Dynastic Oral Tradition, Administrative Records and Archaeology in the Andes,"
         World Archaeology 7:267–79.

ORTEGA, LUIS E.

1962   *El Valle Jequetepeque y sus Requerimientos de Riego* (Pacasmayo: Cámara de Comercio y
         Agricultura de Pacasmayo).

OSSA, PAUL P.

1973   "A Survey of the Lithic Preceramic Occupation of the Moche Valley, North Coastal
         Peru: With an Overview of Some of the Problems in the Study of the Early Human
         Occupation of West Andean South America" (Ph.D. diss., Harvard University).

OSSA, PAUL P., AND MICHAEL E. MOSELEY

1971   "La Cumbre: A Preliminary Report on Research into the Early Lithic Occupation of the
         Moche Valley, Peru," *Nawpa Pacha* 9:1–16.

359

PARSONS, JEFFREY R.
1968   "The Archaeological Significance of *Mahames* Cultivation on the Coast of Peru," *American Antiquity* 33:80–85.

PATTERSON, THOMAS C.
1971   "The Emergence of Food Production in Central Peru," in *Prehistoric Agriculture*, ed. Stewart Struever (New York: Natural History Press).
1973   *America's Part: A New World Archaeology* (Glenview, Ill.: Scott, Foresman and Company).

PATTERSON, THOMAS C., AND MICHAEL E. MOSELEY
1968   "Late Preceramic and Early Ceramic Cultures of the Central Coast of Peru," *Ñawpa Pacha* 6:115–33.

PEASE, FRANKLIN
1972   *Los Ultimos Incas del Cuzco* (Lima: P. L. Villanueva).

PEET, STEPHEN D.
1903   "Ruined Cities in Peru," *American Antiquarian* 25:151–74.

PIRENNE, HENRI
1925   *Medieval Cities* (Princeton: Princeton University Press).

PORRAS BARRENECHEA, RAUL
1959   "Cartas del Perú 1524–1543," *Colecciones de Documentos Inéditos para la Historia del Perú III* (Lima).

POZORSKI, SHELIA G.
1975   "Alto Salaverry: A Peruvian Coastal Preceramic Site," paper presented at the Seventy-Fourth Annual Meeting of the American Anthropological Association (San Francisco).
1976   "Prehistoric Subsistence Patterns and Site Economics in the Moche Valley, Peru" (Ph.D. diss., University of Texas at Austin. Also, University Microfilms, Ann Arbor).
1979   "Late Prehistoric Llama Remains from the Moche Valley, Peru," *Annals of Carnegie Museum of Natural History* 48:139–70.

POZORSKI, SHELIA, AND THOMAS POZORSKI
1977   "Alto Salaverry: Un Sitio Precerámico de la Costa Peruana," *Revista del Museo Nacional* 43:27–60 (Lima).
1979a   "Alto Salaverry: A Peruvian Coastal Preceramic Site," *Annals of Carnegie Museum of Natural History* 49:337–75.
1979b   "An Early Subsistence Exchange System in the Moche Valley, Peru," *Journal of Field Archaeology* 6:413–32.

POZORSKI, THOMAS G.
1971   "Survey and Excavations of Burial Platforms at Chan Chan, Peru" (B.A. thesis, Harvard University).
1975   *The Friezes of Huaca de los Reyes: Societal Implications.* Manuscript.
1976   "Caballo Muerto: A Complex of Early Ceramic Sites in the Moche Valley, Peru" (Ph.D. diss., University of Texas at Austin. Also, University Microfilms, Ann Arbor).
1980   "The Early Horizon Site of Huaca de los Reyes: Societal Implications," *American Antiquity* 45:100–110.

PROULX, DONALD
1968   "An Archaeological Survey of the Nepeña Valley, Peru," Research Reports of the Department of Anthropology, University of Massachusetts, no. 2 (Amherst, Mass.).
1973   "Archaeological Investigations in the Nepeña Valley, Peru," Research Reports of the Department of Anthropology, University of Massachusetts, no. 13 (Amherst, Mass.).

RICHARDSON, JAMES B., III
1973   "The Preceramic Sequence and the Pleistocene and Post-Pleistocene Climate of Northwest Peru," in *Variation in Anthropology*, ed. Donald Lathrap and J. Douglas (Urbana: Illinois Archaeological Survey).

References

RIVERO, MARIANO E., AND J. J. TSCHUDI

1853   *Peruvian Antiquities* (New York).

ROBINSON, DAVID A.

1964   *Peru in Four Dimensions* (Lima: American Studies Press).

RODRÍGUEZ SUY SUY, VÍCTOR ANTONIO

1966   "Chan Chan: Ciudad de Adobe; Oservaciones Sobre su Base Ecológica," *Actas y Memorias del 37 Congreso Internacional de Americanistas*, vol. 1, pp. 133– 52 (Buenos Aires).

1970   "Chan Chan: Observaciones sobre su Base Ecológica," paper presented at the Thirty-Ninth International Congress of Americanists (Lima).

1973   "Irrigación.prehistórica en el Valle de Moche," *Bóletin Chiquitayap*, vol. 1, año 1, no. 1, part 3.

ROSTWOROWSKI DE DIEZ CANSECO, MARIA

1961   *Curacas y Succesiones, Costa Norte* (Lima: Imprenta Minerva).

1962   "Nuevos datos sobre tenencia de tierras reales en el Incario," *Revista del Museo Nacional* 31:130– 64 (Lima).

ROWE, JOHN H.

1946   "Inca Culture at the Time of the Spanish Conquest," in *Handbook of South American Indians*, ed. Julian H. Steward. *Bulletin* 143, vol. 2 (Washington, D.C.).

1948   "The Kingdom of Chimor," *Acta Americana* 6:26– 59.

1962   "Worsaae's Law and the Use of Grave Lots for Archaeological Dating," *American Antiquity* 28:129– 37.

1963   "Urban Settlements in Ancient Peru," *Ñawpa Pacha* 1:1– 27.

1967   "What Kind of a Settlement Was Inca Cuzco?" *Ñawpa Pacha* 5:59– 76.

1969   "The Sunken Gardens of the Peruvian Coast," *American Antiquity* 34:320– 35.

1971   "The Influence of Chavin Art on Later Styles," in *Dumbarton Oaks Conference on Chavin*, ed. Elizabeth P. Benson (Washington, D.C.).

ROWE, JOHN H., DONALD COLLIER, AND G. R. WILLEY

1950   "Reconnaissance Notes on the Site of Huari, Near Ayacucho, Peru," *American Antiquity* 16:120– 37.

ROWE, JOHN H., AND DOROTHY MENZEL

1967   *Peruvian Archaeology: Selected Readings* (Palo Alto: Peek Publications).

SAHLINS, MARSHALL D.

1970   "Production, Distribution, and Power in a Primitive Society," in *Cultures of the Pacific*, ed. Thomas G. Harding and Ben J. Wallace (New York: Free Press).

SANDERS, WILLIAM T., AND BARBARA J. PRICE

1968   *Mesoamerica: The Evolution of a Civilization* (New York: Random House).

SAWYER, ALAN

1966   *Ancient Peruvian Ceramics: The Nathan Cummings Collection* (New York: Metropolitan Museum of Art).

SCHAEDEL, RICHARD P.

1951a   "Major Ceremonial and Population Centers in Northern Peru," in *The Civilizations of Ancient America, Selected Papers of 29th International Congress of Americanists*, ed. Sol Tax (Chicago: University of Chicago Press).

1951b   "Mochica Murals at Pañamarca," *Archaeology* 4:145– 54.

1966a   "Incipient Urbanization and Secularization in Tiahuanacoid Peru," *American Antiquity* 31:338– 44.

1966b   "Urban Growth and Ekistics on the Peruvian Coast," in *36th International Congress of Americanists*, vol. 1 (Lima).

1971   "The City and the Origin of the State in America," in *Actas del Congreso Internacional de Americanistas*, vol. 1 (Lima).

SCHMIDT, MAX
1929   *Kunst und Kultur von Perú* (Berlin: Propyläeon-Verlag G.M.B.H.).
SERVICE, ELMAN R.
1962   *Primitive Social Organization* (New York: Random House).
1975   *Origins of the State and Civilization: The Process of Cultural Evolution* (New York: W. W. Norton and Co., Inc.).
SHOTWELL, J. ARNOLD
1955   "An Approach to the Paleocology of Mammal Ecology," *Ecology* 36:327–37.
SJOBERG, GIDEON
1960   *The Preindustrial City, Past and Present* (Glencoe: Free Press).
SQUIER, EPHRAIM G.
1877   *Peru: Incidents of Travel and Exploration in the Land of the Incas* (New York: Harper and Brothers).
STRONG, WILLIAM D., AND JOHN M. CORBETT
1943   "A Ceramic Sequence at Pachacamac," Archaeological Studies in Peru 1941–42, *Columbia University Studies in Archaeology and Ethnography*, vol. 1 (New York).
STRONG, WILLIAM D., AND CLIFFORD EVANS
1952   "Cultural Stratigraphy in the Viru Valley, Northern Peru: The Formative and Florescent Epochs," *Columbia University Studies in Archaeology and Ethnography*, vol. 4 (New York).
TELLO, JULIO C.
1956   "Arqueología del Valle de Casma," *Publicación Antropológica del Archivo "Julio C. Tello" de la Universidad Nacional Mayor de San Marcos*, vol. 1 (Lima).
THOMPSON, DONALD E.
1961   "Architecture and Settlement Patterns in the Casma Valley, Peru" (Ph.D. diss., Harvard University).
TOPIC, JOHN R.
1970   "A Lower Class Residential Area of Chan Chan: Initial Excavations" (B.A. thesis, Harvard University).
1977   "The Lower Class at Chan Chan: A Quantitative Approach" (Ph.D. diss., Harvard University).
TOPIC, JOHN R., AND THERESA L. TOPIC
1975   "Agriculture within the Site of Chan Chan," paper presented at the Fifteenth Annual Meeting of the Institute of Andean Studies, Berkeley.
in press "La Agricultura adentro de Chan Chan," in *Chan Chan, Ciudad Prehistorica*, ed. R. Ravines (Lima: Instituto de Estudios Peruanos).
TOPIC, THERESA
1971   "Preliminary Studies of Selected Field Systems, Moche Valley, Peru (B.A. thesis, Harvard University).
1977   "Excavations at Moche" (Ph.D. diss., Harvard University).
TSCHUDI, JOHANN JACOB VON, AND MARIANO EDUARDO RIVERO
1855   *Peruvian Antiquities*, trans. F. C. Hawkes (New York: A. S. Barnes and Co.).
UBBELOHDE-DOERING, HEINRICH
1951   "Ceramic Comparisons of Two North Coast Peruvian Valleys," in *The Civilizations of Ancient America, Selected Papers of the 29th International Congress of Americanists*, ed. Sol Tax (Chicago: University of Chicago Press).
1959   "Bericht über archäologische Feldarbeiten in Perú, II," *Ethos* 24:1–32.
1960   "Bericht über archäologische Feldarbeiten in Perú, III," *Ethos* 25:153–82.
1967   *On the Royal Highways of the Inca* (New York: Praeger).
UHLE, MAX
1903   *Pachacamac* (Philadelphia: University of Pennsylvania).
1913   "Die Ruinen von Moche," *Journal de la Société des Américanistes de Paris* 10:95–117.

References

VALCÁRCEL, LUIS E.
1946   "The Andean Calendar," in *Handbook of South American Indians*, Bureau of American Ethnology, ed. Julian H. Steward. *Bulletin* 143, vol. 2 (Washington, D. C.).

VARGAS UGARTE, RUBÉN
1936   "La Fecha de la Fundación de Trujillo," *Revista Histórica* 10:229–39.

WACHTEL, NATHAN
1973   *Sociedad e Ideología* (Lima: Instituto de Estudios Peruanos, Historia Andina 1).

WALLACE, DWIGHT T.
1962   "Cerrillos, An Early Paracas Site in Ica, Peru," *American Antiquity* 27:303–14.

WEST, MICHAEL
1970   "Community Settlement Patterns at Chan Chan, Peru," *American Antiquity* 35:74–86.

WHEATLEY, PAUL
1963   "What the Greatness of a City is Said To Be," *Pacific Viewpoint* 5:163–88.

1971   *The Pivot of the Four Quarters; A Preliminary Enquiry into the Origins and Character of the Ancient Chinese City* (Chicago: Aldine).

WILLEY, GORDON R.
1953   "Prehistoric Settlement Patterns in the Viru Valley, Peru," Bureau of American Ethnology, *Bulletin* 155 (Washington, D.C.).

1971   *An Introduction to American Archaeology, vol. 2: South America* (Englewood Cliffs, N.J.: Prentice-Hall).

WILLEY GORDON R., AND JOHN CORBETT
1954   "Early Ancon and Early Supe Cultures," *Columbia University Studies in Archaeology and Ethnography*, vol. 3 (New York: Columbia University Press).

WITTFOGEL, KARL
1957   *Oriental Despotism: A Comparative Study in Total Power* (New Haven: Yale University Press).

WORSLEY, PETER
1957   "Millenarian Movements in Melanesia," *Rhodes-Livingston Institute Journal* 21:18–31.

ZÁRATE, AUGUSTÍN DE
1933   *A History of the Discovery and Conquest of Peru* [1581], trans. Thomas Micholas (London: Penguin).

ZUIDEMA, R. T.
1964   "The Ceque System of Cuzco. The Social Organization of the Capital of the Inca," *International Archives of Ethnography*, supplement to vol. 50 (Leiden: E. J. Brill).

Index

access patterns, 149– 50, 307, 337, 338– 39;
at Galindo, 295, 304, 312; of cercaduras,
297, 299– 300; of ciudadelas, 57, 59; of
elite compounds, 119, 124– 25; through
audiencias, 203– 4, 216, 282; to water,
140– 41, 155– 56, 169
Adams, Richard N., 222, 223
administration, 16– 19, 123, 155– 56;
audiencia as symbol of, 203– 4; of Moche
Phase, 276– 80, 284; rural, 17, 199– 203
adobes, 92, 100, 110, 324, 351; makers'
marks on, 272, 274, 343; types and
seriation of, 68– 72, 201. *See also* friezes
afterlife, 19, 329
agrarian collapse, 44, 47– 49
agrarian expansion, 33– 34, 51, 228
agriculture, 9, 17– 18, 198, 204; corporate,
11; preadaption to, 21– 23. *See also*
redistribution
ají *(Capsicum* sp.), 179, 184, 189, 351
Aklya-Kona, 160– 61
Alberti, Giorgio, and Enrique Mayer, 339
algarroba *(Prosopis chilensis)*, 184
Alto Salaverry site, 178– 79, 228, 251, 253
ancestor worship, 18
Ancón-Chillón-Rimac area, 228

Andean Coast, cultural overview for,
334– 36; hospitality on, 339; northern
quadrant of, 12, 215, 351; northern
periphery of, 3– 4; nuclear north of, 4– 6,
20– 24; southern periphery of, 6, 9– 12,
22
Anderson, Robert T., 146
Andrews, Anthony P., 42– 43, 60, 63, 72,
73, 77, 168, 172, 173, 200, 203, 216,
275
Anonymous History of Trujillo, 106. *See also*
The Anonymous History of 1604
arable land, as resource, 11, 15, 193, 228,
337– 38; coastal, 3, 4, 10; interior, 22– 23;
loss of, 34, 47
architecture, 25– 26, 84, 112, 114– 15;
astronomical correlations of, 235;
columnar construction in, 323– 24;
departure from traditional forms of, 302;
depicted in art, 59, 204, 216, 302;
directional orientation of, 215; domestic
features of, 268; forms of, 292– 93;
intermediate, redefined, 119– 20, 143 n.
1; repetitive patterns of, 212; temporal
sequence of, 67– 68. *See also* arcones,
audiencias, auxilios, burial platforms,

367

Kamayoq, 160–61
Kautz, Robert R., and Richard W. Keatinge, 201
Keatinge, Richard W., 11, 17, 42, 47, 72, 83, 166, 170, 188, 198, 199, 201, 202, 203, 207, 209, 221, 328, 339, 346; and Kent C. Day, 42, 83, 115, 172, 198, 199, 203, 275, 339
keros, 325, 351
Kingdom of Chimor, 102, 105, 106, 107, 111, 120, 336. *See also* Chimú polity
Kirchoff, Paul, 235
kitchens, 136, 151, 153, 154, 157, 158, 159, 163, 170, 171, 199, 310
Klymyshyn, Alexandra M. Ulana, 132, 134, 135, 173
Kolata, Alan Louis, 100, 110, 115
koraka, 346
Kosok, Paul, 5, 14, 26, 27, 48, 105, 106, 114, 204, 206–7, 209, 235, 282
Kroeber, Alfred L., 102, 105, 204, 209, 261, 265, 274, 277, 322, 325, 326
Kubler, George, 273, 323
Kus, James S., 5, 32, 198
Kutscher, Gerdt, 261, 335

labor, as resource for growth, 11–12, 21; as service or tax, 10, 14, 160, 226, 272, 274, 283, 324, 337; at Caballo Muerto, 249–50; at Pampa Grande, 343–44; Chimú, 339–41
La Cumbre canal, 5, 32, 39, 43, 48
Lambayeque Valley, 14, 26, 48, 220, 261, 273, 281, 329, 344
land reclamation, as growth strategy, 11, 15; Moche Phase, 13, 37; model for, 22–23; nonirrigational, 35
land tenure, 337–38, 341, 344
Lanning, Edward P., 9, 256, 326
Larco Hoyl, Rafael, 65, 228, 257, 261, 280, 287, 335
Leach, Edmund R., 174
league measurement, 208
Lechtman, Heather, 274
lima beans (*Phaseolus lunatus*), 179
limpets (*Fissurella* sp.), 190
littoral resources, 20
llamas (*Lama glama*), 100, 103, 151, 154, 159–60, 167, 181, 182, 186, 188, 190, 192, 194, 232, 309, 314, 316
Llapchillulli, 120, 121
lomas, 9, 251
Long-Stemmed Projectile Point, 4, 20
lower class structure, 145–46, 173–75; model for, 167–70; reconstruction for,

160–67; urban-rural comparison of, 170–73. *See also* small irregularly agglutinated rooms
lúcuma (*Lucuma obovata*), 179, 184, 185, 187, 189, 191, 192, 229
Lumbreras, Luis G., 149, 256, 335
Lurín Valley, 219

macaw (*Ars militaris*), 160, 167
Machu Picchu, 123
mahamaes, 63. *See also* sunken gardens
maichil (*Thevetia peruviana*), 185, 187
maize (*Zea mays*), 21, 180 181, 184, 185, 187, 189, 191, 192, 193, 229. *See also* corn beer
mishpingo (*Nectandra* sp.), 160, 167, 184, 187
Mason, J. Alden, 60
McGrath, James E., 61
mit'a, 10–11, 18, 65, 123, 141–42, 159, 166, 167, 202, 250. *See also* labor
mitama program, 17, 351. *See also* mit'a
Means, Philip A., 121, 122, 123, 207, 220, 334
Medanos la Joyada site, 201
Meggers, Betty J., 149
Menzel, Dorothy, 228, 324, 325, 327, 329, 330, 334
metalworking, 12, 13, 154. *See also* copper
middens. *See* refuse
Minchançaman, 106
Mocallope site, 286
Moche culture: and Chimú roots, 280–83; focal shift of, 327–28; influences on: architectural, 328, from Central Coast, 327, from Far North, 327–28, mythological, 328–29; origins of, 287; overview of, 261–62; transitional, to Chimú, 209, 211, 285, 321–22, 335. *See also* chronology; Huari culture
Moche polity, 13; as expansionist state, 270, 272–73, 287, 318; bureaucracy of, 276–80; economics of, 196, 273–75; scenario for, 14–15
Moche site, architecture at, 268–69, 270; burials at, 266–67, 269–70; description of, 262–66; occupational specialization at, 275–76; social stratification at, 266–70; subsistence at, 179–81, 182, 183–84, 194
Moche Valley, 23, 25, 198, 253, 259, 260. *See also* irrigation; Río Moche
monticulos, 212
monumental compounds: associated with elite architecture, 134–35; classification of, 117 n. 1; functional interpretation for,

371

Río Santa, 3, 6, 9, 21, 22. *See also* Santa Valley
Río Seco, 29, 226, 233
Río Virú, 34. *See also* Virú Valley
Robinson, David A., 3, 4, 204
Rodríguez Suy Suy, Victor Antonio, 31, 102, 105
Rostworowski, Maria, 14, 63, 106, 122, 123, 334
Rowe, Anne, 163
Rowe, John H., 11, 63, 65, 83, 104, 106, 107, 113, 114, 116, 123, 124, 160, 161, 165, 174, 202, 211, 216, 219, 275, 329, 334, 335, 336, 337, 339; and Dorothy Menzel, 330
Rowe, John H., Donald Collier, and G. R. Willey, 323
ruling class structure, 63; ethnohistorical evidence for, 106–7; hypothesis on, 107–8, evaluation of, 109–15, synthesis for, 115–17. *See also* ciudadelas

Sahlins, Marshall D., 115
Salinar culture, 257–59, 322
salinization, 22, 47
Sanders, William T., and Barbara J. Price, 250
San José de Moro site, 204
Santa Valley, Moche Phase, 270, 272, 279
Sapa Inca, 122, 123
satellite communities, 196, 231–32. *See also* subsistence, Chimú
Sawyer, Alan, 261
Schaedel, Richard P., 105, 204, 206, 209, 229, 230, 261, 263, 335, 246
Schmidt, Max, 221
sea lion (*Otaria byronia*), 183, 186, 190
seaweed, 184
Sechín Alto site, 12, 15, 16, 23, 24, 253
Sechura Desert, 3–4, 5, 20
secularization, 346
Service, Elman R., 115, 253
settlement growth, order in 77–82; ramifications of the order, 82–85
settlements, state-founded, defined, 17
sharks, *Mustelus* sp., 178. *See also* diet
shops, 153; discussed, 154–55
Si (Moon goddess), 122
site stratification, 250
small irregularly agglutinated rooms (SIAR): access to, 149–50, 151; administrative features of, 155–56; and craft production, 161–65; as anomalous, 149, 158–60, 165–67; as barrios, 148, 151, 153–54; as rooms-on-platforms, 148–49, 156–58,

168; as shops, 154–55; at Chan Chan, 62; chronology of, 165–67; excavations of, 150–60; residential interpretation of, 160–75; relationship to elite compounds, 120, 131, 135, 140; site context of, 148–49; surface indications of, 146–48, 150
soapberry (*Sapindus saponaria*), 191
socioeconomics. *See* economic organization
sociopolitical organization: alternative to statecraft in, 18; coastal origins of, 24; correlated to construction size, 25–26; correlated to economic unity, 49–50; cultural perspective for, 10–19; developmental perspective for, 19–24; development of: 197–98, 222–24, Jequetepeque comparisons for, 204–22, Moche Valley Early Intermediate Period, 198–204; geographical perspective for, 2–10; push-pull development of, 3; summary of changes in, 284. *See also* caste system; ciudadelas; elite class structure; lower class structure; ruling class structure
split-inheritance, 15–19, 107, 108, 116–17, 282, 284, 346
Spondylus shell, 96, 99, 103, 104, 112, 158, 203, 216, 273
squash (*Cucurbita* sp.), 178, 179, 180, 189, 191, 193, 228, 229
Squier, Ephraim G., 59, 60, 102, 105, 221
statecraft, 10, 18
stirrup-spout vessels, 13, 261, 286–87
storage, 60, 64–65, 137, 139, 283, 245–46; Chimú, 84, 338–39; Incan, 336–37; Moche, 274–75, 304–7, 341–43; urban/rural comparison of, 170–71. *See also* redistribution
street patterns, 149–50
Strong, William D.: and John M. Corbett, 219, 220; and Clifford Evans, 160, 261, 270
subsistence, 161; Chimú: at Caracoles, 185–87, at Cerro la Virgen, 187–89, at Chan Chan, 182–85, at Choroval, 189–91, comparisons of, 191–93, conclusions on, 193–95; early agricultural, 21–23; hunting as means of, 4, 9, 20; littoral, 20, 21–22; pre-Chimú, 178–81; summary, for Moche Valley, 195–96; symbiotic relationship for, 231
Sumer, 221
sunken gardens, 63, 189, 193. *See also* wachaques
Supe Valley, 228
sweet potato (*Ipomoea batatas*), 189

Index

tablados, 293, 295, 297, 299, 300, 316, 351; discussion on, 302–4
tapia, 57, 90, 92, 351
taxation, 10–12, 123. *See also* labor
Taycanamo, 106, 329
technological advances, 349
Tello, Julio C., 12, 15
terracing, 11
textile manufacturing, 163–64
The Anonymous History of 1604, 329. *See also Anonymous History of Trujillo*
thievery, 122, 339
Thompson, Donald E., 15
Titicaca Basin, 2, 3
tomato *(Solanum peruvianum)*, 187
tombs, 16. *See also* burials
Topic, John R., 63, 150 154
Topic, Theresa, 31, 47, 198, 265, 341
totora reed *(Scirpus tatora)*, 187
trading terminal, 167
Trujillo, 25, 26, 322
Tschudi, John Jacob von, and Mariano Eduardo Rivero, 102, 105
turquoise, 276

Ubbelohde-Doering, Heinrich, 204, 209, 211, 212, 219, 220–21
Uhle compound, 45. *See also* Ciudadela Uhle
Uhle, Max, 219, 220, 221, 261, 265, 267, 274, 325
University of San Marcos, 225
University of Texas, at Austin, 248

upwelling, 9, 21
urbanism, 286, 322–23, 326
U-shaped structures, 137, 304. *See also* audiencias

Vargas Ugarte, Rubén, 106
Virú Valley, 17, 50, 72, 84, 228; Gallinazo Phase, 260–61; Huari culture in, 325; Moche Phase, 270, 272, 274, 279; Salinar Phase, 257–59

wachaques, 63, 149, 159, 165, 351. *See also* sunken gardens
Wachtel, Nathan, 334
Wallace, Dwight T., 228
Watanabe, Luis, 225, 233
water management, early, 28–29. *See also* canals; irrigation
wells, 61, 124, 125, 136, 149, 155–56, 169
West, Michael, 62
Wheatley, Paul, 146, 174, 223–24
Willey, Gordon R., 5, 160, 228, 256, 257–58, 259, 261, 272, 335; and John Corbett, 160
Wittfogel, Karl, 50
woodworking, 164
work task units, 11. *See also* labor
Worsley, Peter, 223

Yana-Kona, 160–61

Zárate, Augustín de, 123
Zuidema, R. T., 160, 171, 174, 235